PIMLICO

728

FROM THE SHADOW OF *DRACULA*

Paul Murray, a graduate of Trinity College, Dublin, is a writer and diplomat who has served in London, Tokyo, Ottawa, New York and Seoul. His biography, *A Fantastic Journey: The Life and Literature of Lafcadio Hearn* (1993), won the Koizumi Yakumo Literary Prize (Japan) in 1995. He has published and lectured in Europe, the USA and Asia.

FROM THE SHADOW OF *DRACULA*

A Life of Bram Stoker

PAUL MURRAY

PIMLICO

Published by Pimlico 2005

2 4 6 8 10 9 7 5 3 1

First published in Great Britain by
Jonathan Cape 2004

Pimlico edition 2005

Pimlico
Random House, 20 Vauxhall Bridge Road,
London SW1V 2SA

Random House Australia (Pty) Limited
20 Alfred Street, Milsons Point, Sydney,
New South Wales 2061, Australia

Random House New Zealand Limited
18 Poland Road, Glenfield,
Auckland 10, New Zealand

Random House South Africa (Pty) Limited
Isle of Houghton, Corner Boundary Road & Carse O'Gowrie,
Houghton, 2198, South Africa

Random House UK Limited Reg. No. 954009

A CIP catalogue record for this book
is available from the British Library

ISBN 0-7126-7311-3

Papers used by Random House UK Limited are natural,
recyclable products made from wood grown in sustainable forests.
The manufacturing processes conform to the environmental
regulations of the country of origin

Printed and bound in Great Britain by Mackays of Chatham

In memory of Ann Stoker (1916–1998)

List of Illustrations

CONTENTS

Acknowledgements

After my biography of Lafcadio Hearn was published in 1993, I was asked by Frank Delaney, the distinguished author, broadcaster and literary commentator, what my next book would be. When I replied that I had no plans for another book, Frank suggested that I should explore Bram Stoker, who was roughly the same age as Hearn, who had grown up in a similar environment in Dublin and who was also a consummate horror writer. That conversation was the genesis of this biography and it goes without saying that Frank should head my list of acknowledgements. Since that time, Frank has consistently provided practical help and advice and I am deeply indebted to him. I am grateful also to my agents, Mike Shaw and Jonny Pegg of Curtis Brown, and to Jörg Hensgen, Dan Franklin and Will Sulkin of Jonathan Cape for consistent support and advice. Kate Worden and Rosalind Porter of Jonathan Cape and Declan Heeny of Gill Hess in Dublin have provided great practical assistance. I should also express my thanks to Neil Belton who, as the then Editorial Director of Jonathan Cape, first commissioned the book in 1995.

A chance social encounter between Noel Dobbs, Stoker's great-grandson, and Philip McDonagh, then a colleague at the Irish Embassy in London, led to my introduction to Stoker's immediate descendants, especially his redoubtable granddaughter, Ann Stoker (we agreed that she would be known by her maiden name for the purpose of this biography). Ann gave me unfettered access to her considerable collection of papers as, indeed, did her son, Noel Dobbs. To say that I am profoundly grateful to both would be an understatement. They, in turn, introduced me to Merlin Holland, Oscar Wilde's grandson, and he, too, has provided invaluable assistance.

In the late 1990s, Ann Stoker consulted me about the disposal of her collection of family papers and effects, which clearly needed safe keeping as scholarly interest in Stoker was growing exponentially. I suggested the

Library of Trinity College Dublin and was pleased that Stoker's *alma mater* (and my own) responded positively. Sadly, Ann did not live to see the transfer but her son and various other members of the family attended a ceremony to mark the event, at Trinity, in 1999. I consulted these papers prior to their transfer to the Trinity College Library and have designated them the Ann Stoker Collection and the Noel Dobbs Collection respectively for reference purposes in the notes.

Through Philip McDonagh's wife, Dr Ana Grenfell McDonagh, I was put in touch with Dr Siobhan Murphy, Consultant Physician, Department of Genito-Urinary Medicine, The Patrick Clements Clinic, Central Middlesex Hospital NHS Trust, England, who wrote a paper for me on the subject of Stoker's cause of death. She, in turn, suggested contact with J.D. Oriel, MD, formerly Consultant Physician in Genito-Urinary Medicine, University College, London, who also wrote an extensive paper for me on the subject of Stoker's health. Professor J.B. Lyons, MD, FRCPI, of the Royal College of Surgeons in Ireland, a distinguished author as well as physician, prepared a paper too and discussed the issues involved in Stoker's health at length with me in taped conversations in 1998; needless to say, I owe a great debt of gratitude to all the above for their great kindness in taking such trouble over an issue which is of crucial importance, both to Stoker's biography and to interpretations of his work.

Roy Foster, Carroll Professor of Irish History at Oxford University, has been consistently helpful, not least by reading the text in advance of publication, as has Professor Owen Dudley Edwards of Edinburgh University. Dr Ruth Dudley Edwards performed the invaluable service of providing me with material from a notebook of Stoker's discovered in London as the book was going to press which I was unable to examine myself due to my residence in Seoul. I am grateful to Professor Aidan Clarke, of Trinity College Dublin, for directing me towards the student records which have proved such a valuable source on Stoker's Trinity days; Bruce Stewart of Coleraine University who has shared his work on political aspects of Stoker with me; Christopher Frayling, a leading authority on the Gothic tradition and Rector of the Royal College of Art, London; Dr William Hughes of Bath Spa University College; and the late and much lamented Sean Ronan, a former Irish Ambassador to Greece and Japan and constant source of information and encouragement. Dr Jeanne Keyes Youngson, founder and President of the Bram Stoker Memorial Association, and Ms Jennifer O'Casey, the Association's Executive Director, have provided valuable information and assistance.

I am grateful also to the librarians and staff of all the institutions which have provided me with material; I owe an especial debt to those which I have used extensively in my research, primarily the British Library, the

National University of Ireland, the Library of Trinity College Dublin (with special thanks to Bernard Meehan, Keeper of Manuscripts), the Brotherton Library, University of Leeds, the Shakespeare Centre Library, Stratford-upon-Avon, the Royal Irish Academy, the London Library, the Chelsea Public Library, and the National Archives of Ireland (especially its Director, David Craig).

I owe a considerable debt to many other institutions, particularly those which were prepared to provide copies of material in their collections, especially the Rosenbach Museum and Library, Philadelphia, which copied for me all Stoker's notes for *Dracula*; the University of Virginia Library; the Lilly Library, Indiana University; the University of Reading; the Ellen Terry Memorial Museum; the Harry Ransom Humanities Research Center, the University of Texas at Austin; the Fales Library, Elmer Holmes Bobst Library, New York University; Harvard University Library; New York Public Library; Hallward Library, University of Nottingham; the Robinson Library, University of Newcastle; the National Library of Scotland; Miller Library, Colby College; the Folger Shakespeare Library, Washington, D.C.; the Rare Book and Manuscript Library, Columbia University; Manuscripts and Rare Books Department, Earl Gregg Swem Library, the College of William & Mary; the Huntington Library; the Pierpont Morgan Library; William Clark Memorial Library, UCLA; the Poetry/Rare Books Collection, University Library, University at Buffalo, State University of New York; Paley Library, Temple University; Richmond-upon-Thames Public Library, Surrey; and the Library of Congress.

Other institutions I wish to thank include the Garrick Club, London; the Land Registry of Ireland; the Royal Archives, England; the Bodleian Library, Oxford; the Public Record Office, Kew; Eton College Library; the Honourable Society of the Inner Temple (especially Dr C.M. Rider, Archivist); Alex Ward, Curator, Grand Lodge of A.F.&A. Masons of Ireland; Cruden Bay Library; and H. Brown, Hon. Librarian, Whitby Museum.

On a personal level, my wife, Elizabeth, and sons, Daniel and Stephen, all lovers of the Gothic, have provided not just moral and practical support but a great deal of insight. Naturally, I also owe more than I can say to my parents: perhaps it was the experience of finding an illustrated volume of Edgar Allan Poe horror tales on my late father's bookshelves at the tender age of twelve which first ignited my interest in the horror genre. Peter Haining and Peter Beresford Ellis (Peter Tremayne), authors of *The Undead: The Legend of Bram Stoker and Dracula*, have been most helpful, as has Pat Conroy of the Department of Education in Dublin. Daniel Farson, Stoker's great-nephew and biographer, lent me family letters shortly before his death. Leonard and Mrs Wheatley, the owners of 18 St Leonard's Terrace, London, where Stoker once lived, kindly showed me their home. Douglas Appleyard shared his computerised genealogical information on the Stoker family with me. Dr Denis Eustace, Consultant Psychiatrist, Highfield Hospital Group, Dublin provided valuable information on the Stoker family background. Any Stoker biographer has reason to be grateful to those who help maintain interest in his work over the years, such as Bernard Davies and Bruce Wightman who founded the Dracula Society in London in 1973. Leslie Shepherd, Albert Power and David Lass of the Bram Stoker Society in Dublin, Dennis McIntyre of the Bram Stoker Summer School, Robert Cuffe and others associated with both the Philosophical and Historical Societies of Trinity College Dublin have all assisted in various ways. Catherine Boura, formerly of the Embassy of Greece in London, deepened my understanding of the Balkan background to Stoker's fiction, as did my Romanian diplomatic colleagues, both in Seoul and elsewhere. The Reverend Ted Woods and Roger White, of the Church of Ireland, Rathfarnham, Dublin, provided valuable information on the Stoker family's religious background. I would also like to record the assistance of Elisabeth Flash, Leslie Bairstow, Edward Keeling, Dr Sally and Adrian Warwick-Haller, Trevor West, John Wyse Jackson, Mrs Hilary McCullough, Damien and Jennifer Harrington, Charlotte Downey, Edwin Wood, Billy Finn, Vere Wynne Jones, and Denis O'Brien of Trinity College Dublin. I am deeply indebted to Edmund Downey's son, Maurice Downey, for allowing me to read his copy of *A House of Tears*, a rare book, and for providing me with much useful information on his father. To all of you, I am most profoundly grateful.

INTRODUCTION

'Welcome to my house! Enter freely. Go safely, and leave something of the
happiness you bring!'

(*Dracula*, The Count to Jonathan Harker)

In the late twentieth century, as Bram Stoker emerged from obscurity and
was acclaimed as the author of *Dracula* (which had long had a popularity
independent of him) a picture close to biographical parody emerged. In his
own time, Stoker was a larger than life character, much respected for his
consummate professionalism as a theatre manager and seen by many as the
power behind the throne of his boss, the actor, Sir Henry Irving. In death,
he was interpreted as a bundle of neuroses, an abject slave, a Renfield to
Irving's imperious Dracula.

How did this negative transformation come about? Part of the answer
lies, paradoxically, with those who were largely responsible for the revival
of his reputation from the early 1970s. Stoker was rediscovered primarily
on the campuses of America by academics who found in his writings a rich
source for interpretations driven by Freudianism, Marxism and feminism.
While great credit is due to those who first insisted that there was more
than mere sensationalism in his writings, some of their conclusions, at least,
were based on insufficient biographical research. I have given a flavour of
academic commentary on Stoker, both in the text and in the notes; in this
way I have sought to reconcile the need of the general reader for a straightforward text and the demands of interpretative scholarship. Stoker himself
would, incidentally, have appreciated the justice of his cause being revived
in the United States, the country which he so admired and which had, in
his lifetime, returned that admiration.

Great credit is due to Stoker's other biographers, Harry Ludlam (who
worked in close collaboration with Stoker's son, Noel), Daniel Farson and
Barbara Belford in particular. I have attempted to develop further our understanding of Stoker, especially by using the mass of documents and contemporary books which have so much light to shed on the real man. At the
same time, it has to be admitted that, while the use of extensive contemporary material can radically alter our understanding of a complex man, he
did not leave behind much information on his interior life. He was responsible for a vast amount of correspondence but it was mostly of a factual,

businesslike nature; with some exceptions, such as his letters to Walt Whitman, there is little material extant in which Stoker bares his innermost thoughts.

The contemporary record can tell us a great deal about what Stoker did; to surmise how he felt, we have to turn to the evidence of his writings and I would contend that he was among the most autobiographical of writers, both in terms of his experience and his aspirations. As well as using a good deal of contemporary material, available for the first time, this biography also sets out to give the reader a sense of the man who lurked in his writing. Although the tendency to focus exclusively on *Dracula* is gradually being rectified, there is still insufficient appreciation of the extent to which that masterpiece grew out of Stoker's life and convictions or the fact that it can only be fully understood in the context of his entire output. As not all of Stoker's literary work has remained in print over the years (although this is rapidly changing, with new editions of some of his lesser-known works being published in recent years), I have attempted to summarise the plots and preoccupations of his various books.

The result, I hope, will show that common threads run through his fiction and that, while *Dracula* may have been his only masterpiece, it was not the product of an isolated impulse, be it a desire to eat his younger siblings, as the Freudians would have us believe, his wife's menstrual patterns, a dysfunctional relationship with Henry Irving, an identification with the fifteenth-century Walachian prince, Vlad Tepes, 'Vlad the Impaler', or any other such one-dimensional, catch-all and generally simplistic explanations.

Not only did Stoker interact with many of the outstanding literary figures of his era, but he was also a man with an important political dimension. This has led to yet more interpretations of *Dracula*, ranging from a view that the Count was negatively emblematic of the Irish landlord class, to the opposite: that he represented a fear of the mass enfranchisement of the Irish people. Yet Stoker's political views are sufficiently well documented to demonstrate the fallibility of both of these contentions.

Stoker spent almost half his life in Ireland. The sources on his Irish years (he did not leave until he was over thirty) are especially good and the imprint of his early influences is evident in *Dracula* and his other work. His deeply held and apparently sincere religious beliefs, which informed the moral landscape of his fiction, also derived from the Ireland in which he grew up. The Stokers, like some of the other middle-class Dublin Protestant families that produced literary genius in the era, the Hearns and the Synges, for example, were strongly marked by the pietism and revivalism which characterised both major religious traditions in mid to late nineteenth-century Ireland. (Patrick) Lafcadio Hearn (1850–1904), now best remembered for his writings on Japan, might seem an exotic interloper in this environment but he spent most of his childhood years in the Dublin of Stoker's youth. His exploration of the exotic was closely related to the 'Orientalism' of the nineteenth-century writers on Eastern Europe whose work provided Stoker with the background for *Dracula*. The world which produced Stoker, Synge and Joyce cannot be divorced from its religious preoccupations and yet their significance passes many commentators by. There are, indeed, attempts to substitute the secular concerns of our own time, the various 'isms', for the obvious reality of Stoker's convictions. Some will see the possibility that he was suffering from syphilis at the time of his death as Victorian hypocrisy – proof that the wholesome morality of his writing masked an unholy private life – but it may be that he failed to live up to his ideals, not that he did not hold them in the first place.

Based on the twin pillars of original research and analysis of his writings, I have attempted to illuminate a man who has been under-appreciated for too long. Now that his greatest creation has become part of the global consciousness and his vision is being increasingly reinterpreted by moviemakers and others, it is surely time to make the effort to understand Bram Stoker, the man who created and, to a large extent, *was* Dracula. The Count had a great deal in common with his author: he may have been an aristocrat but he undertook the menial duties of coachman, cook and housemaid, rather like the multi-tasked Stoker at the Lyceum. His quiet, methodical mastery of subjects like the law and his research, using maps, guides and other printed sources, was that of Stoker himself, both in his professional life and when researching the background for his fiction at the British Library. The Count mastered timetables and personally oversaw the movement of his precious boxes of earth, just as Stoker oversaw the transport of the Lyceum's vast baggage. He dealt with the estate agents and lawyers, as well as various types of workers, necessary to his nefarious enterprise, rather as his creator did for the masterful Irving. But the actor, seen by so many as the inspiration for the Count, undertook little outside the acting sphere; most things he left to his indefatigable manager who was, like his creation, a man of action, a doer. In looking for the source of *Dracula*, we have looked in many places but not the obvious one: the mind of its author.

PART ONE

Out of Ireland

ONE

Ancestral Ambition

'I myself am of an old family . . .'
(*Dracula*, The Count to Jonathan Harker)

When Bram Stoker was baptised on 30 December 1847, one of the sponsors was his maternal uncle, Thomas Blake Thornley. The Blake name was
a reminder that the blood of some of Ireland's most ancient and illustrious
families flowed in his veins. On his mother's side, he was descended from
the Blakes of Galway, one of the fourteen 'tribes' of that city, who could
trace their ancestry back to Richard Blake, Sheriff of Connaught in 1305.
From then to the surrender of Galway to Cromwell in 1654, no fewer than
thirty-seven Blakes were Sheriffs of Connaught and eighteen were Mayors
of Galway.

Stoker mined this rich seam of family history when he referred in a later
novel, *The Man* (1905), to the Sheriff of Galway who hanged his own son.
The family featured in a ballad, 'The Man for Galway', in Charles Lever's
1842 novel, *Charles O'Malley, the Irish Dragoon*, a first edition of which, almost
certainly inherited from his father, was presented to the London Library by
Stoker's son in July 1937. One stanza included a reference to the Blakes:

> Ye think the Blakes
> Are no 'great shakes;'
> They're all his blood relations,
> And the Bodkins sneeze
> At the grim Chinese,
> For they come from the *Phenaycians*;
> So fill to the brim, and here's to him
> Who'd drink in punch the Solway;
> With debts galore; but fun far more;
> Oh! that's 'the man for Galway.'[1]

Noel Stoker recalled his father reminiscing about his connection with the
novelist, Charles Lever, claiming that he had occupied the same rooms at

7

Trinity College, the University of Dublin (generally known as Trinity College Dublin) that had been previously occupied by the young Lever and that the writer had visited them as an old man when Stoker was in occupation. This is unlikely, as Stoker does not appear ever to have lived in the university, but he may have picked up the story of Lever paying a sentimental visit to his old rooms and placed himself at the centre of it. Stoker was certainly acquainted with Lever's literary output and there are some lines of influence from Lever's work to his own. Another Blake who may have an echo in Stoker's fiction is James Blake, believed to have been responsible for the poisoning in 1602 of the famous Irish chieftain, Red Hugh O'Donnell. Blake had been involved with the Spanish Armada when it lay off the west coast of Ireland and the story of the poisoning of O'Donnell was reconstructed from cipher; the plot of Stoker's novel, *The Mystery of the Sea* (1902), features both the Spanish Armada and cipher.

The Blakes were related to another ancient Galway family, the Lynchs, through the marriage of the daughter of Marcus Lynch (d. 1750), to George Blake (d. 1771). Marcus Lynch was a Roman Catholic who had become a Protestant in 1724, making his father a tenant for life under the Penal Laws then in force, designed to transfer property from Catholic to Protestant hands. His wife, Maria Blake, was the daughter of Isidore Blake of Towerhill in County Mayo. The Blakes were one of the most prominent merchant families of the city of Galway from the fourteenth century, amassing wealth as traders with France and Spain. By intermarriage and shrewd alternation of their religious allegiance, they maintained their position as an influential and wealthy family in the West of Ireland right through to the nineteenth century.

George Blake's son, Richard, married Eliza O'Donnell while his brother, Mark, married her sister, Mary, both the daughters of Colonel Manus O'Donnell of Newport, County Mayo, a landed gentleman. A descendant offered a pair of locket portraits of Richard Blake and Eliza O'Donnell to Bram's brother, Thornley Stoker, in 1890; they were actually bought by Bram for £5 and were discovered by the author in the Stoker family collection in the 1990s. The O'Donnells were believed by the Blakes to have brought with them an inheritance of 'brown eyes, reddish fair hair & long & very flippantly sarcastic tongue and ready wit with pen & tongue. *On dit* they are still in evidence. Nothing else, for there are no marriage settlements.'[2] The reddish hair and ready wit with pen and tongue were certainly in evidence in Bram Stoker.

Through the Lynchs and the Blakes, Stoker shared a common ancestry with the Irish writer, George Moore (1852–1933). In 1851, George Moore's father, George Henry Moore, married Mary Blake, a daughter of Maurice

Blake of Ballinfad, Balla, County Mayo. The position of the Blakes can be gauged from the ability of Mary Blake's father to provide a dowry of £4,000 on her marriage. Her mother, Anne Lynch Blake, was a daughter of Marcus Lynch and Maria Blake, as was Bram Stoker's great-great-grandmother.

The children of Richard and Eliza included another George Blake, one of the most colourful of Stoker's ancestors, and the events in which he was involved resonate in Stoker's fiction, from his first novel, *The Snake's Pass*, to his later work, especially *The Mystery of the Sea*. We know from family correspondence that Charlotte Stoker, Bram's mother, was familiar with the Blake family history, including that of her uncle, George Blake, and passed it on to her children. In 1793, George Blake was gazetted an officer in the 20th Regiment of Light Dragoons and was sent to Jamaica on service. He soon resigned his commission, however, and returned to Ireland; rumour had it that he had left the army after having killed a brother officer in a duel. On hearing of the arrival of French forces under General Humbert to assist the rebellion against English rule in Ireland in 1798, he set out with a servant, Patrick Nevin, to join them. In a manner worthy of the heroes of Stoker's fiction, his was an essentially quixotic gesture: he accepted the hopelessness of the venture from the start and, when some of the revolutionary United Irishmen around Garracloon and Cong in County Mayo wanted to join him, he refused their service on the basis that none of them would return.

Variously described as a French general and as being in supreme command of his countrymen, George fought from the 'Races of Castlebar', a short-lived victory for the rebels on 27 August 1798, to the Battle of Ballinamuck on 8 September a few days later, after which the French surrendered. Some sources claim that the only effective fighting at Ballinamuck was by Blake and his battalion of pikemen while others allege that most of them fled at the first shot.[3] A number of local legends were woven around Blake: that he had saved a wounded English officer and that he had fought a duel with Humbert on the eve of Ballinamuck. Yet another local tradition was that he had escaped and joined the Spanish or French armies, but this was not so.

After the battle, Blake hid in a dike but was discovered by a party of yeomanry under a Captain or Major Grant, having been betrayed by a yeoman's servant, Hugh MacDermott, who was later immortalised in ballad as a traitor. He managed, however, to pass documents to his sister, Julia, who concealed them in her petticoats, and Grant, an admirer, refused to allow his men to search her. It has been claimed that these papers would have seriously, perhaps fatally, compromised the Duke of Leinster, brother of Lord Edward Fitzgerald, a key revolutionary figure, had they come to light. Grant presided over a drumhead court-martial, following which George Blake was hanged from the shaft of a cart that was run across a demesne wall. An account of the execution was carried in a leading Irish newspaper of the time:

> Blake, the insurgent leader, who had joined the French, and was lately deservedly hanged as a traitor, begged to be shot. When that was refused, he requested to be indulged with the noose of the rope that was for his execution being soaped, that it might run free to shorten the time of dying. This, we hear, was granted, and he prepared it in that manner with his own hand.[4]

The summary justice meted out to George Blake may have inspired one of Stoker's short stories, 'The Judge's House' which features a malignant – and deadly – hanging judge. The Blake family was not, however, unequivocally revolutionary: George's brother, Manus, was an officer in the British Army while George was an insurgent commander and this gave rise to a saying in the West of Ireland: 'is cosmail le Blacaigh na Gearra-Chluana iad, ceann aca I n-arm Shasana, ceann eile I n-arm na hÉireann.' ('They are like the Blakes of Garracloon, one of them in the English army and one in the Irish army.')

A sister of George Blake, Matilda, married an army officer, Thomas Thornley, on 3 October 1817, at Ballyshannon, County Donegal, and they had three children: Stoker's mother, Charlotte Thornley (born 28 June 1818), Richard Blake Thornley (1821–34) and Thomas Blake Thornley (1822–50). Thomas Thornley joined the 43rd Regiment of the British Army in 1813 as an ensign, becoming a lieutenant in 1815. He may therefore have served under Daniel James Hearn, grandfather of the Irish–Greek writer, Lafcadio Hearn, who was Lieutenant-Colonel of the 43rd Regiment until he retired in 1815.

There was in fact a continuing connection between the Hearn and Stoker families, both of which produced great horror writers, who were only three years apart in age and who grew up in mid-nineteenth-century Dublin. The Stokers were regular visitors at 39 Rathmines Road in Dublin, the house of James Thornley (1812–83), a relative on his mother's side through the Thornleys of Ballyshannon. One source remembered their visits 'when Ellie Thornley was the petted girl, and the "Heiress of Rathmines."'[5] Ellen Thornley (1848–1908), who was James's daughter, married Charles Richard Hearn, the son of Lafcadio Hearn's first cousin, Robert Thomas Hearn, in 1875. While Lafcadio Hearn was spending a lonely childhood in Rathmines and in Leeson Street, a short distance away, under the care of a great-aunt, Thomas Thornley was enthralling Stoker with tales of his service as a subaltern in the Peninsular War, including the claim that he had marched all night *asleep*. Stoker remained close to the Thornleys of Rathmines: he gave James Thornley's name as a referee when he applied for an official position in 1871 and received a small legacy through him in the same year.

Some previous biographers have left Thomas and Matilda Thornley's youngest child out of account and confused him with his father, who was also Thomas. Lieutenant Thomas Thornley joined the Royal Irish Constabulary (RIC), the Irish police force of the era, in 1837 and was later appointed as Sub-Inspector of Constabulary at Cushendall, County Antrim, where he received severe injuries to his head, shoulders and other parts of the body while on duty on 12 December 1849 and died on 20 April 1850. The nature of his injuries might imply that they were inflicted in a politically motivated disturbance and the death of his grandfather in this manner could have influenced Stoker's lifelong emphatic support for parliamentary, as opposed to physical-force, nationalism.

In the 1820s, Thomas Thornley lived between the towns of Ballyshannon and Sligo in the north-west of Ireland. The atmosphere of piety in which Charlotte was reared in Sligo is evident in some of the contents of the Stoker collection of papers. These include a copy of *The Cottage Hymn-Book*, printed by the Religious Tract Society, London, with an inscription by her brother: 'Richard B. F. Thornley is my name. Sligo is my dwelling place and Ireland is my nation. Heaven is my expectation and Christ my salvation. When I am dead and in my grave this little book will tell my name when others are forgotten.' The book was a present from his father, given to him when he was nine years old. The Stoker collection also contains a copy of the *Parables of the Blessed Saviour* with Richard Thornley's name inscribed on it. These works are Protestant, so that even if some of Matilda's family were, like her uncle, Roman Catholic,[6] her children were brought up in an unambiguously Protestant ethos.

Sligo was a grim place when Charlotte was growing up there in Correction Street, called after the House of Correction which was, together with a treadmill and lunatic asylum, attached to the large county jail located on it. Famine, followed by fever, struck in the year prior to her birth, 1817; famine, caused by the failure of the potato and oats crops, recurred even more fiercely, in 1822, when she was four. The theme of famine is to be found occasionally in Stoker's work. It is recalled in his short story, 'The Way of Peace' (1909): 'That was the year of the potato-rot, an' throughout the counthry min an' weemin – an' worse still, the poor childhers – was dyin' be shcores.' Charlotte left behind a vivid account of the horrors of a cholera epidemic in Sligo in 1832, when she was fourteen, which is generally regarded by critics as likely to have been a key influence on the landscape of *Dracula*, one revisited by the first film of the book, *Nosferatu*, which locates vampirism in an outbreak of the plague. In Charlotte's account, as in *Dracula*, the source of contagion is in the East: Sligo was then isolated but rumours of a 'Great Plague' were heard from time to time; it was seen approaching from Germany, France and England before finally arriving in Ireland. A similar phenomenon is observed in Stoker's early story, 'The Spectre of Doom', later reprinted in his 1881 fairytale collection, *Under the Sunset*.[7]

Terrible deeds were done – a traveller was buried alive by the panic-stricken people – enough to call down God's vengeance: 'But God's hand is not to be *thus* stayed and severely like Sodom did our city pay for such crimes.' A biblical tone, that of a vengeful God exacting punishment on a sinful people, runs through Charlotte's account. The same note is struck in the title story of Stoker's *Under the Sunset* where, in the wild places, there are rumoured to be giants and a wicked wind which scatters the seeds of evil things over the whole earth, including diseases and plagues: 'Others say that Famine lives there in the marches, and that he stalks out when men are wicked – so wicked that the Spirits who guard the land are weeping so bitterly that they do not see him pass.'[8] This smacks of the contemporary evangelical view that famine was 'a providential visitation, sent to bring Ireland into a higher state of social and moral organisation through a necessary measure of pain'. To some ultra-Protestants, the toleration of Roman Catholicism (Catholic Emancipation had taken place in 1829) was a national sin now being punished by a just God.[9] Visitation, the word often used by contemporaries to describe a cholera epidemic, has a biblical, judgmental, ring to it.

One of the most horrific images in Charlotte's account of cholera in Sligo is that of the Roman Catholic priest at the fever hospital staying up night and day, armed with a horsewhip, to prevent patients being dragged out and buried before they were dead. Nevertheless, many were said to have been buried prematurely; one man found his wife alive among corpses: she lived on for many years. Others went to break the legs of a Sergeant Cullen to make him fit into a coffin, waking him up in the process (Bram Stoker later considered writing a story about a man brought to life in the dissecting room by the application of a new source of power). Not all Charlotte's neighbours were lucky enough to survive: the child of one died in her arms. When the coffin-maker came to the door and asked if any coffins were required, Charlotte threw a jug of water over him and he came no more. At this time, an old courthouse near the Thornley home was converted into a carpenters' shop and large numbers of coffins were made there to meet the emergency. Only one or two families in her street were without loss. Similar horrific images of corpses occur in 'The Spectre of Doom': 'many fell dead, and there their corpses lay'.[10]

Journeys are a key feature of *Under the Sunset* and *Dracula* but none have the sombre awfulness of that undertaken by Charlotte and her family in Sligo in 1832. Hoping to escape the plague, they set off by coach for the town of Ballyshannon, in the nearby county of Donegal, but were stopped by a mob near Bundoran and refused passage. When they got through to Donegal town, they were denied entry and a cry went up from the locals, 'howling like devils' for fire with which to burn the cholera people; they were saved by soldiers with fixed bayonets. They found, however, the rector of the parish the least merciful, with the magistrates not much better; under cover of night they went back to Ballyshannon, where they were allowed to stay, before returning to Sligo where the cholera had left over five-eighths of the population dead. Charlotte concluded on a biblical note: 'At the end of that time we abode in peace . . . and had great reason to thank God, who had spared us through such dangerous and trying times and scenes.'[11]

Tempered by these experiences, Charlotte grew up to be a determined, able woman. Certainly she was not deterred by the fact that Abraham Stoker, her future husband, was a generation older than herself when she met him in Coleraine, County Derry, where her father saw service as a police officer, although there may have been a Sligo connection between the Thornleys and Stokers: John Stoker, the County Inspector there, was the same age as Abraham Stoker and, like him, was a government official. Charlotte was twenty-five when they married in 1844 and Abraham was forty-four; she bore seven children – William Thornley (generally known as Thornley), Matilda, Abraham (Bram Stoker), Thomas, Richard, Margaret and George – in a little over nine years, between 1845 and 1854. All the births were registered in the books of the Church of Ireland parish in Clontarf, Dublin, where they lived in the early years of their marriage.

While an element of superstition may have been part of Charlotte's mental make-up – she was reputed to have heard a banshee wail before her mother died – the dominant impression is of a household ruled by a strong sense of moral righteousness. A list of 'Rules for Domestic Happiness', which survives in the family papers, relies heavily on the Bible as a recipe for happiness in life. Although nineteen years younger than her husband, Charlotte comes across as the more formidable personality, with vaulting ambition for her five sons. Her daughter-in-law, Enid, the wife of her son, Tom, stated that the family were in awe of Charlotte, if not actually afraid of her. She did not conceal her resentment when any of the children failed to come first in an examination, whatever the numbers participating. Another source recalls her as very strong-minded and notes that, while she was interested in the education of women in general, she 'did not care tuppence' for that of her own daughters.[12] Charlotte's activities were not confined to the domestic sphere: the nature of her work in the field of female advancement, especially in relation to the poor, is evident in an elaborate formal address to Queen Victoria by the Queen's Institute for the Training and Employment of Educated Women (preserved in the Stoker family papers), with which she was involved. A mixture of deference, radicalism and earnest good intentions, it could well have been written by Charlotte herself.[13]

Charlotte was also an active member of the Statistical and Social Inquiry Society of Ireland. She read a paper to it on 13 May 1863, which was published under the title, *On the Necessity of a State Provision for the Education of the Deaf and Dumb of Ireland*, later in the year. Her description of the state of being of the unfortunate deaf mute could just as easily refer to that of her son's greatest fictional creation: a being cut off from God and 'alone in the midst of his fellow-men; an outcast from society and its pleasures; a man in outward appearance, in reality reduced to the level of brute creation'.[14] Dr William Wilde, the father of Oscar Wilde, who would be a key influence on the youthful Stoker, was present at the reading of Charlotte's paper and contributed to the discussion. Dr Wilde, then forty-eight years old, was at the pinnacle of his reputation which would be severely dented by a libel case brought against him by a young woman soon after he was knighted the following year. He was not just an outstanding eye and ear specialist who had founded a Dublin hospital, but was an eminent antiquarian and author. Several illegitimate children notwithstanding, he was married to the nationalist poet, Jane Francesca Wilde. It was probably through Charlotte's involvement in social and educational issues that Bram Stoker would later have entrée to the wealthy and sophisticated world of the Wildes. Stoker later became friendly with Sir William's remarkable wife, Lady Wilde, who, writing under the pen-name Speranza, had carved out a distinctive niche in the nationalist literature associated with the *Nation*, the newspaper of the Young Ireland movement.

Charlotte showed herself to be an expert researcher, fluently quoting statistics from other European countries, and her wide reading was evident in her quotation of various authorities. Charlotte was familiar with 'works of travel in savage countries', the kind of travel works which her son would use in the construction of *Dracula*. Even more to the point, she cited Richard Burton's writing on travel in Africa; not only did the explorer become a friend of Stoker's in later years but his work and personality would influence *Dracula*.

Through her involvement with the Statistical and Social Inquiry Society of Ireland, Charlotte would have come into contact with one of its founders,

John Kells Ingram (1823–1907), the Trinity College Dublin academic and poet, now best remembered for a patriotic ballad, 'Who Fears to Speak of '98', commemorating the revolutionary events of 1798. Like Edward Dowden, another Trinity academic and close friend of Stoker's, and Cesare Lombroso, the Italian criminologist cited with approval in *Dracula*, Ingram was a follower of the French sociologist, Auguste Comte, and attempted to apply his theory to Ireland, especially in relation to operation of the Poor Law, which regulated state involvement with the poorest sections of society. Charlotte would have been attracted by Comte's vision of private morality being the domain of women in their dual roles of wives and mothers while the government and economy were administered by business interests.

Both Charlotte and Ingram addressed the society in 1864. Her paper, delivered on 20 January, was on the theme of female emigration from workhouses, and it was prepared for publication by a Dublin publisher shortly afterwards. In terms of possible influence on Stoker's later writing, *On Female Emigration from Workhouses* is probably Charlotte's most important work. She shared Ingram's critical attitude towards the operation of the workhouses under the Poor Law Amendment Act of 1834, which had standardised the system of poor relief and workhouses. As a workhouse visitor, she had first-hand experience. Charlotte's mixed attitude of moral and social concern was evident in her description of the sexual depravity into which workhouse women could sink. Charlotte's interest extended to the arrangements for the actual transfer of the workhouse girls to the colonies; assisted emigration was also her son's panacea for Irish poverty at the end of *The Snake's Pass* (1890). Her recommendations were the peculiar combination of social condescension and a desire for moral policing later evident in Stoker's work. Indeed, her statement that 'any measure calculated to encourage virtue and subdue vice must be the wisest and best policy of a nation' could just as easily have been written by her son.[15]

There was, in the second half of the nineteenth century, growing concern, reflecting fears of physical and moral contamination, with the 'great social evil' of prostitution and with female virtue generally. In Ireland, both Protestant and Roman Catholic organisations set out to reform prostitutes. Apprehension about their damaging effects on military manpower resulted in the Contagious Diseases Acts of 1864, 1866 and 1869. Under these Acts, the police could arrest prostitutes in ports and army towns and have them subjected to compulsory checks for venereal disease. If infected, they were hospitalised until they were considered cured.

Charlotte must have been aware of this official engagement with the issue. Not only was she married to a civil servant working at the heart of government in Dublin Castle, but she had mastered a wide range of primary sources of information on her subject, including official and parliamentary reports, contemporary newspapers and books. Her research covered Irish, British and colonial sources. On the theme of sexual equality, she proved to be more progressive than her son would be more than a generation later. She answered those who objected to emigration on the grounds that it was matrimonial speculation with a bluntness which must have shocked at the time: 'what is our whole system of female education but a matrimonial speculation[?]'[16] In her son's novel, *The Man*, the main object of female education for the well off is defined as maintaining well-bred ignorance. Charlotte's work among the Dublin poor also finds echoes in Stoker's later fiction. In *The Man*, Stephen, the female protagonist who has been given a male name, is much influenced by her experience amongst 'the submerged tenth' at the lower end of society when she broadens her horizons by doing social work among the poor, as does the title character in *Miss Betty*. In Stoker's early story, 'The Chain of Destiny' (May 1875), we are told that Mrs Trevor 'knew the proper way to deal with the poor'.[17]

Charlotte's moral concerns and their possible influence on Stoker have attracted critical attention in recent years. Insisting that his late novel, *The Lady of the Shroud* (1909), is 'structured by a devastating misogyny', Lisa Hopkins detects in it a 'radically ambivalent attitude towards women, and towards mothers in particular'. Examining the dynamics of Stoker's personal relations with mother-figures, Hopkins identifies a deep-seated authorial psychological unease with the woman as mother 'which may well be attributable to Stoker's own feelings of ambivalence about the devouring mother and the maternal wife'.[18] How ambivalent Stoker may have felt towards Charlotte we cannot know for sure, but his dedication of *The Watter's Mou'* to her in 1894 was affectionate and, while misogyny does surface in some of Stoker's work, overall his attitude towards women was sympathetic, if blinkered by Victorian values. Much of the day-to-day maternal role was in any case fulfilled in the Stoker household by the children's nurse, Ellen Crone. Whether Charlotte was a distant parent we do not know but she was certainly a powerful influence both on his character and his writing. At the purely material level, she had, by the time of her death in 1901, seen all her five sons make their mark. By this time, she had returned from her travels in continental Europe to live at 72 Rathgar Road, Dublin, for at least the last fifteen years of her life. She died there of cardiac arrest, brought on by influenza, on 15 March 1901, at the age of eighty-two. Only her illiterate maid, Eliza Kavanagh, was with her when she died. She was buried in Mount Jerome Cemetery in Dublin, where a gravestone commemorates her husband and herself, together with her eldest son, William Thornley, and his wife Emily.

* * *

The background to Stoker's father's family is not as well documented as that of his mother. Various claims have been made about the origins of the Stoker family in Ireland: that a great-grandfather, Richard, a quartermaster in the Old Green Horse Dragoons, arrived in Ireland around 1690 from Morpeth in Northumbria with William III of Orange; or, alternatively, that the family moved from County Down in the north of Ireland to Dublin towards the end of the eighteenth century, at which time they changed from Presbyterian to Church of Ireland. An obituary of Stoker, probably based on information provided by the family, stated that he was of Dutch extraction. It is not possible to substantiate any of these conflicting claims from the material in the Stoker family collection or public records which allow the ancestry on this side of the family to be traced back with certainty only to William Stoker, Stoker's paternal grandfather.

The family did, however, take pride in its heredity: in 1874, when he was travelling in Switzerland, Stoker's father wrote that the previous day he had come upon a 'Pension Stoker' but the owner told him that it was quite a common Swiss name. Stoker's brother, Thornley, commissioned genealogical research into the family history in 1907, which stated that the earliest records locate the name Stoker in Ireland at the time of Charles II, in the seventeenth century.[19] This was inaccurate as the Stoker family was established in Ireland from Elizabethan times and branches were to be found in Cork city, Bandon, County Cork and Newport, County Tipperary. In the eighteenth century, the Stokers were distributed in Counties Limerick, Tipperary, Waterford, Wexford and Cork, as well as in Dublin, although Stoker is not generally included in Irish reference works on surnames. The origin of the name is variously given by other authorities as English, Flemish, Dutch and Scottish.

In a publication after Sir Thornley Stoker was knighted in the 1890s, his lineage is traced back only to his grandfather, William Stoker (1759–1825), whose place of employment is given as 'the Ordnance Office, Dublin'; no mention is made of his trade as a stay-maker. This may have been a discreet element of retrospective social elevation, befitting Sir Thornley's new-found status.[20] The art historian, W. G. Strickland, made some attempt at scientific research into the Stoker family origins early in the twentieth century and his findings probably constitute the best source of information on William Stoker. He discovered an entry in the books of the Corporation of Taylors, the Guild of St John, under the date 9 November 1780, revealing that William Stoker, a stay-maker, was admitted a freeman of the Tailors' Corporation, by service to Robert Whitstone. Strickland commented:

This Robert Whitstone was for many years a staymaker at 23 St Andrew St. He is last mentioned in 1803. William Stoker was, as appears from the above entry, apprenticed to him; – but the records of apprenticeships of the Guild are lost. If they existed, we should find who his father was. His name does not appear in directories, so that it would seem that he did not trade on his own account, but was probably partner or assistant with Whitstone. He was at one time representative of the Tailors' Guild in the Common Council of Dublin.[21]

A document in the Stoker collection contains much the same information but adds that, 'by tradition', William Stoker was also in the Ordnance Office. This, however, may be a confusion with another William Stoker who is recorded in the census of 1821 as being a clerk in the Ordnance Office and was aged fifty-six, while Stoker's grandfather was then sixty-two.[22] William Stoker, presumably Bram Stoker's grandfather, married Frances Smyth in Dublin in 1780.[23]

We do know for certain that Abraham Stoker, Stoker's father, was born on 12 March 1799 and was married in Coleraine Parish Church on 16 January 1844 by the Reverend Knox Homan, with J. D. Thornley and John Batchelor as witnesses. He died on 12 October 1876 at Cava de' Terreni, Naples. Most of Abraham Stoker's seventy-seven years were spent in honest toil in the government service in Ireland. He entered the Civil Service as a clerk in the Chief Secretary of Ireland's Office in June 1815 at just over sixteen years of age. From 1833, he was in charge of parliamentary business, a position he regarded as entailing a fair degree of responsibility. He survived in family legend as fine-looking, a gentle and good man, fond of his family, who offered prayers every night thanking God for his mercies. His family, in turn, were fond of him: a lock of his hair is preserved in the Stoker archive. His daughter-in-law, Susan Stoker, remembered him as 'so gentle & quiet . . . I knew him very well [.] I spent 6 weeks with him in Paris & he & I used to go to the Tuilleries Gardens by ourselves & he loved me[;] indeed they were all most loving to me.'[24]

One modern critic has described the world in which Stoker grew up as 'rigidly middle class, monogamous, and male dominated – under an all-seeing God'.[25] Abraham Stoker certainly appears to have been a righteous man who was still counselling his children on morality when they were adults, as a letter written to Bram from France in 1872 demonstrates: 'Honesty is the same in every relation of life, and anything obtained by a different course cannot be right. Ever since I have had a family, a part of my nightly prayer has been that I might be able to rear them in honesty and uprightness . . .' He was active in the Sunday School Society for Ireland

and may also have been a member of the Orange Order, a bulwark of Protestant influence in Ireland. He did not share his son's later liberal attitudes on the intertwined issues of religion and politics in Ireland. In a letter written from abroad to his son in 1874 he referred to a row at the National Board of Education and asked: 'is the "Roman Beast" [the Roman Catholic Church] getting rampant [?]'[26] Writing to Walt Whitman in 1872, Stoker described himself as having been 'reared a conservative in a conservative country', in a manner which implied that by his mid-twenties he had shaken off his father's conservative influence.[27] Abraham was, however, reticent about his political views, probably because of his position as a civil servant. He began to feature in some of the electoral lists of the 1850s, which generally recorded the party for which individual electors had voted, but they do not show how he voted or, indeed, if he voted at all.

To understand Stoker's fiction, it is important to locate his family background correctly in the social spectrum. Abraham's relatively lowly status in the Civil Service is evident from the directories of the time. As late as 1836, after more than twenty years in the Civil Service, he was still listed as a junior clerk, below the Chief Clerk, senior clerks and assistant clerks in the office of the Chief Secretary at Dublin Castle. He did, however, have 'Esq.' after his name, entitling him to the rank of a gentleman, unlike those immediately below him, such as messengers, and thus he had achieved a social advance over his father's position as an artisan. It represented a precarious respectability and Stoker's fiction would show an acute awareness of social distinction. By 1837, Abraham had made it to the bottom of the list of assistant clerks. Yet he was not included in the lists of Dublin freeholders and leaseholders in the 1830s.

In 1853, after almost forty years in the service, Abraham applied for the post of Senior Clerk. An old friend of his, Alex Mcdonnell, wrote to Sir John Young at the Education Office in Marlborough Street, Dublin, in support of his candidature. Mcdonnell stated that as Chief Clerk in the Castle for four years he had had the opportunity of becoming acquainted with Abraham's character and talent: he had never known a better public servant: 'I consider him a *model* man in all the great points required in one who is to fill such an office as that which he is for – thorough integrity – good temper – judgement – close application and devotion to his duty and thorough knowledge of the business of the department.' He would not be acting justly by the government or 'by this most meritorious & modest man' if he did not give testimony in his favour.[28] Abraham was successful but did not remain long in this position; he resigned from the post of Senior Clerk in October 1865, citing advanced age and recent attacks of illness as reasons why he could no longer meet the demands of the job. In December 1865 he was granted a 'retired allowance' of £650 a year, equal to his full salary. It has been assumed that, armed with this pension, Abraham went on a prolonged continental tour which lasted until his death, leaving all his business affairs in Bram's hands. This did not happen, however, for some years after his retirement: he was living in Dublin, at 5 Orwell Park, Rathgar until 1869 and at 43 Harcourt Street, until 1872, with his sons, Thornley and Bram. The lists of *pensions*, means of transport and costs of journeys extant in Charlotte Stoker's address book are evidence of the thoroughness with which the eventual tour of continental Europe (including France, Switzerland and Italy) was prepared.

When Abraham Stoker died in Italy, Bram went to Italy to arrange support for his mother and two sisters who had decided to stay on. Stoker handled the business end of things. His mother appointed him to act for her and the Court of Probate granted letters of administration to him on 15 December 1876. It is noteworthy that it was Bram, not his eldest brother, Thornley, who shouldered this responsibility. Bram arranged for his father to be buried at Cava de' Terreni where he had died in Italy after he had kissed his father's forehead for the last time in the vault of the church there. He arranged for the erection of a gravestone that noted Abraham's vital dates and, later, for a brass memorial plate to be placed on the wall of Rathfarnham Church of Ireland Parish Church in Dublin, where it remains. The choice of Rathfarnham, rather than the more evangelical Zion Church, which was closer both to the Orwell Park address at which the family had lived in the 1860s and the Rathgar Road house where Charlotte lived after her return to Ireland as a widow, may be indicative of Bram's preference for the more mainstream, rather than the evangelical, strand in the Church of Ireland. There may also have been an element of snobbery involved, with the more High Church Rathfarnham seen as having a greater social cachet.

Other than his salary, Abraham Stoker's financial dealings when his children were young centred on a life assurance policy on his own life for £1,000, taken out in 1854. He seems to have used it as a source of income for his children's education in the 1860s and it loomed large in his will, in which he left everything to his wife, Charlotte. The critic, Carol A. Senf, has commented on the importance of money to all the characters in *Dracula* and on the differentiation of the values of the middle and working classes in its characters.[29] This surely has its roots in the slow, painful ascent of Abraham Stoker towards middle-class respectability. It is curious, therefore, that his son Bram has been referred to as having derived from 'Anglo-Irish' and 'Protestant Ascendancy' stock in contemporary critical discourse, terms whose aristocratic connotations are at odds with the relative humility of his background. Roy Foster, Carroll Professor of Irish History at Hertford

College, Oxford, admonished a previous biographer on this score: 'Bram Stoker was a middle-class Irish Protestant from the professional classes – not, as [Barbara] Belford repeatedly states, Anglo-Irish.' Much the same point is made by other modern critics: Chris Morash points out that 'Stoker's family were middle-class civil servants, not landowners' and David Glover, author of a 1996 book on Stoker, sees Stoker's middle-class Irish Protestant origins as having provided him with models of respectability and penury that remained with him all his life.[30]

TWO

The Wondrous Child

Perhaps it is because I am weak at present . . . that their devotion was manifested.

(*Dracula*, Dr Seward's Diary)

Clontarf, where Abraham and Charlotte Stoker had settled in the early days of their marriage, had formerly been a fishing village of some importance. Three miles from the centre of Dublin, it had a population of a few thousand inhabitants but at the time when Bram lived there it was being absorbed by the city of Dublin. It was much frequented by sea-bathers from the north of Dublin attracted by the scenery and the hot and cold sea baths at the old Charter School. The Drogheda, or Northern Trunk, Railway skirted the village near the Stoker home at Marino Crescent, where there was a station, thus opening the village up to the kind of commuter travel being undertaken by Abraham Stoker to his Civil Service job in the centre. Near Dollymount, at the eastern end of Clontarf strand, was an extensive causeway or break-water, called the 'Bull Wall', erected by the Ballast Board earlier in the century to deepen the channel and allow the passage of large vessels which Stoker would have seen from the shore as a child. A Victorian contemporary of Stoker's portrayed Clontarf as 'drowsy': 'Your lanes are of the greenest of green leafydom, before which the lanes of Surrey or Devonshire pale; your rows of little cottages with steep steps . . . are unchanged; so too . . . the more ambitious Crescent, where the houses are mostly to let; your strag-gling seaboard, where the tide is nearly always out . . .'[1] In the past Clontarf had been fashionable among titled people, when the architecturally outstanding Marino was the home of the Earl of Charlemont. The mansion of the Guinness brewing family, St Anne's, was also nearby.

Historically, Clontarf was – and remains – indelibly associated with the major Battle of Clontarf in 1014, in which the Irish High King, Brian Boru, defeated a Viking alliance. 'The Fatal Sisters', a Norse song about the battle, featured in the 1801 collection, *Tales of Wonder*, edited by the great Gothic horror writer, Matthew Lewis (a book which gave Stoker's contemporary, Lafcadio Hearn, nightmares when he was growing up in Dublin at that time). It includes the lines:

Horror covers all the heath,
Clouds of carnage blot the sun.
Sisters [Valkyries], weave the web of death. –
Sisters, cease: the work is done.[2]

Contemporaries would have been more conscious of Clontarf as the place where Daniel O'Connell, the Irish nationalist leader, was to have held a 'monster meeting' for repeal of the Act of Union in 1843, just four years before Stoker's birth. The government prohibited the meeting and O'Connell backed down lest blood be shed, with adverse consequences for his political authority and subsequent reputation.

At the time of her death, it would have seemed to Charlotte that none of her children had equalled the achievements of her eldest son, Thornley Stoker. More than any other member of a successful family, he epitomised ability and drive, rising from a relatively modest background to the pinnacle of social success in Dublin. An obituary in a medical journal caught well the nature of his achievement: 'Starting in life without resources other than intellect and energy, he arrived at a professional position given to few, and at a social position in his native land second to none.'[3]

Born on 6 March 1845, William Thornley was cared for in his early years by a nurse, Ellen Crone, to whom he remained deeply attached: he kept a photograph of her in an envelope with a lock of her hair throughout his life. He also kept a photograph of her gravestone. Ellen Crone also acted as nurse to the younger children, including Bram, who remembered one of her stock sayings, that they would do little for God's sake if the Devil were dead. Indeed, her role in caring for the Stoker children may help explain the recurrence of surrogacy throughout Stoker's fiction. Charlotte's second child, Matilda, was born on 9 June 1846, just fifteen months after the birth of her first. She was named after a Blake ancestor. The third child, called after his father but known to the world for most of his life as Bram, came after a similarly short interval, on 8 November 1847.

Some time around the end of the decade, the Stokers moved a short distance to the neighbouring village of Artane, where they occupied Artane Lodge. Artane, now, like Clontarf, swallowed up by the expansion of Dublin, was then a village and parish in Coolock, County Dublin, three miles north from the centre of the city, and had a population of just a few hundred. The scanty neighbours listed for the Stokers included builders, farmers, a blacksmith, a solicitor, a vintner, and a postmistress. Artane may not have been able to match Clontarf's historical prominence but its past was not lacking in drama: Artane Castle was the scene of the death of John Alen or Alan, a sixteenth-century Archbishop of Dublin, who became embroiled in the turbulent politics of the era and was slain in the great hall of the castle on 28 July 1534.

It was in this environment that Stoker matured and he remained there until the late 1850s when the family moved to 17 Buckingham Street Upper, Summerhill, on the north side of the city of Dublin. During this period, Stoker tells us in his *Personal Reminiscences of Henry Irving* (1906), he was often on the point of death and was unable to stand upright until he was about seven years of age. He hints strongly that the experience was a valuable one from the perspective of his later writing: 'I was naturally thoughtful and the leisure of long illness gave opportunity for many thoughts which were fruitful according to their kind in later years.' There was no element of self-pity in Stoker's declaration of his childhood weakness: he was contrasting it with his later metamorphosis into 'a very strong man', the biggest member of his family, who became 'Athletic Champion of Dublin University' at the age of twenty.[4] He may, however, have felt differently about it in his youth: in his twenties, he confided to his notebook that as if he were his own child, he felt an infinite pity for himself, a poor little lonely child – which he almost certainly was during his years of illness.

In the published version of his *Personal Reminiscences of Henry Irving*, Stoker excised details that he had included in the manuscript, of his mother thinking he was dying on occasion and of his being taken in people's arms and laid on a bed or sofa. In neither version does Stoker tell us of the nature of his illness and it has prompted much speculation on its causes and its likely psychological effects. Stoker revisited this experience of childhood illness in his fiction. In 'The Chain of Destiny' Frank Stanford, the narrator, wakes in bed after crashing through a window to save the heroine:

> I became gradually conscious of something cool on my forehead. I wondered what it was. All sort of things I conjectured, but could not fix my mind on any of them. I lay thus for some time, and at length opened my eyes and saw my mother bending over me – it was her hand which was so deliciously cool on my brow. I felt amazed somehow. I expected to see her; and yet I was surprised, for I had not seen her for a long time – a long, long time.[5]

In *The Mystery of the Sea*, Stoker reveals the origin of a lifelong interest in codes and secret writing: 'I knew something of secret writing, for this had in my boyhood been a favourite amusement with me. *At one time I had been an invalid for a considerable period* [emphasis added] and had taken from my father's library a book by Bishop Wilkins, the brother-in-law of Oliver

Cromwell, called "Mercury: or the Secret and Swift Messenger" . . . This experience has set my mind somewhat on secret writing.[6] In 'The Chain of Destiny', Stoker also gave a sense of the experience of recovering from illness:

> It was a good sign of returning health, for it was like the waking from a dream to a world of fact, with all its troubles and cares. There was a sense of coldness and loneliness in the world, and I felt I had lost something without gaining anything in return – I had, in fact, lost somewhat of my sense of dependence, which is a consequence of prostration, but had not yet regained my strength . . . As I sat I could not help thinking of what my future would be. I felt that I was getting strong, and the possibilities of my life seemed very real to me . . .

The exact nature of this long illness has never been clear. It has been suggested that Stoker left a clue in *The Man* by having Harold, his *alter ego*, suffer a recurrence of rheumatic fever after swimming to save a child's life.[7] However, the most serious sequel of rheumatic fever is valvular heart disease, such as mitral stenosis, and there is no evidence that Stoker ever had heart disease. At the same time, a Victorian doctor might have misdiagnosed a heart problem and prescribed confinement to bed as a remedy. It has also been suggested that the disease was a romantic fantasy, but Stoker is unlikely to have fabricated such a claim when his siblings, three of them doctors, were still alive at the time of the publication of *Personal Reminiscences of Henry Irving* and would have known the truth.

Freudians have sought to locate the origins of *Dracula* in Stoker's early illness. It is speculated that his mother may have taken him, struggling, to hospital and then abandoned him there to suffer traumatic treatment alone. Stoker is, however, very unlikely to have been taken to hospital in an era when they were the preserve of the poor and even operations were performed at home. The Freudians are on safer ground when they propose that Stoker might have suffered surgically induced trauma by bloodletting, still in use by doctors at that time. Two early stories, 'How 7 Went Mad' and 'The Wondrous Child' are seen as tales of sibling rivalry and dreams, a result of the bedridden Stoker being unable to dissipate his aggression through healthy outlets but instead expressing it orally as a wish to kill his brothers and eat them.[8] If this is true, Stoker managed to overcome such feelings as an adult when he had close and loving relations with these same brothers.

Stoker's illness raises the tantalising question of the identity of the doctor, William Stoker, who has become a confusing figure in recent Stoker biography. According to one biographer, he was an uncle who cared for the invalid young Stoker; according to another he was Stoker's grandfather. A physician, William Stoker (1773–1848), certainly existed and is, indeed, well documented as he was employed at the Cork Street Fever Hospital in Dublin. The fact that he died when Bram was only one year old means that he could not have tended him during his later childhood. He does, however, appear to have been related to Bram Stoker's family. Material in the Stoker family collection indicates that William Stoker, the doctor and William Stoker, Bram Stoker's grandfather, may have been cousins. There was also a belief in the existence of a relationship within the two Stoker families: when Marie Letitia Stoker (1877–1946), a direct descendant of William Stoker the physician, decided to become a nurse, her family approached 'cousin Thornley' Stoker, Bram Stoker's brother, and he arranged a job for her in the Richmond Hospital.[9]

The future author of *Dracula* may have read Dr William Stoker's prolific medical writings on the linked issues of blood and contagion in his youth. His clinical descriptions of the horrible deaths and the post-mortem dissection of the bodies of his patients might have affected his often morbid imagination. William Stoker bled his patients as a matter of course and one of his case histories describes a doctor who became infected while performing a dissection and died having been reduced to a 'skeleton'; it includes a horribly graphic account of his terrible symptoms.[10]

In a chapter in his one of his books on 'Topical Bleedings', William Stoker deals with the application of leeches to the patient's head.[11] Stoker used the leech as an image of repulsiveness in *Dracula* when Jonathan Harker, surveying the sleeping Count in his coffin, says: 'There he lay like a filthy leech, exhausted with his repletion.'

William Stoker was professionally involved with a Dr William Stokes,[12] another doctor who was a scion of a distinguished Irish family. In 1849–50, Stokes read a paper on mesmerism to the College of Physicians in Dublin in which he highlighted the similarity of certain features of mesmerism to the epidemics of nervous diseases prevalent in Europe in the Middle Ages; these were attributed to heavenly inspiration or the control of Satan and his demons at a time when belief in witchcraft was universal. Dracula personified the point where mesmerism and the demonic intertwined and Stoker would also explore the phenomenon of mesmerism in a more sober fashion in *Famous Impostors* as well as alluding to it in his last novel, *The Lair of the White Worm* (1911).

Some of the themes of his later writing, including a pantheistic exultation in nature, may have been influenced by Stoker's long period of childhood illness. This is especially obvious in the character of Esse in *The Shoulder of Shasta* (1895) who, like Stoker himself, is possessed of 'restless imagination, at once stimulated and cramped by imperfect health' and dips into 'eccentric forms of religious thought', including Swedenborgianism (an eighteenth-century religion which permeates the work of the Irish horror writer, Joseph Sheridan Le Fanu (1814–73), a well-known figure in the Dublin of Stoker's youth) and the pantheism of the poets of the Lake School, which leads to a state of 'semi-religious, semi-emotional exaltation'.[13] The Swedish philosopher and theologian, Emanuel Swedenborg (1688–1772), posited that God is the life within all creation. The divine trinity corresponds in humans to the trinity of soul, body and mind. There is an absolute unity of God in both essence (*essentia*) and being (*esse*). Stoker's use of Esse as the name for his Swedenborgian character can be seen as a conscious echo of this philosophical strand of the novel.

While youthful pantheism is most evident in *Shasta*, it is a strand running throughout Stoker's work: Arthur Severn in *The Snake's Pass*, who has 'stepped but lately from boyhood', has a sense, in the midst of the natural beauty of Ireland, that he had 'passed into a new and more real life'. In *The Mystery of the Sea*, the narrator, who is 'abnormally susceptible to the moods of nature', begins 'to understand the grand guesses of the Pantheists' and undergoes a spiritual transformation:

> The spirits of the earth and sea and air seemed to take shape to me, and all the myriad sounds of the night to have a sentient cause of utterance . . . I was becoming wrapped in the realisation of the mightier forces around me . . . my own heart seemed to stand still, to be a part of the grim silence of the waiting forces of the world.[14]

The imprint of his parents' more orthodox religion is also evident throughout Stoker's fiction. In 'Dracula's Guest', published separately from the novel in short story form, Jonathan Harker relies on it to retain some composure: 'It took . . . all the religion I had been taught . . . not to collapse in a paroxysm of fright.' Similarly, the narrator in 'The Judge's House' refers to the bible given to him by his mother, which may recall the bible Stoker was given on his ninth birthday, in November 1858. It is still extant and the underlining shows that he read it with great care.[15] The Protestant Irish world in which he grew up was in the throes of an evangelical revival that had developed in the decades immediately before his birth. Stoker's contemporary at Trinity College Dublin, Standish O'Grady, later a founder of the Irish literary renaissance, recalled growing up in Ireland at that time: 'To my father and mother . . . the world was filled with spirits good and bad, ministers of God or of His enemy. Neither of them would have been greatly surprised had they seen angels, or if the arch-enemy himself has taken shape before them.'[16] This intensely religious upbringing was a conditioning which Stoker would later share with his employer, the actor, Henry Irving, whose earliest memory was of his mother reading to him from the Bible. Its imprint is clear in Stoker's fiction. So is an ambiguous fascination with the symbols of Roman Catholicism, objects of horror for devout Protestants but imbued with strange, if unorthodox, power in *Dracula*. Henry Irving embodied a similar ambiguity, having a large crucifix hanging over his bed and another on a bedside table, his strict Methodist background notwithstanding.

The impact of the sea beside which he had grown up is also evident in Stoker's writing. The anonymous author of a profile of Stoker in the *Literary World* in 1905 divided his fiction into two categories, the supernatural and the marine, with *The Watter's Mou'* (1895), *The Mystery of the Sea* and *The Man* specimens of the latter, 'for they all possess a paramount attraction in their sea-scapes and sea-scenes'.[17] In fact, fables, legends and superstitions of the sea were a significant theme of the books which we know Stoker used when he was researching *Dracula*. The Dublin seaside of his youth was the location of an early story, 'Buried Treasures', published in 1875.[18] 'Buried Treasures' contains descriptions of the north Dublin coast which Stoker explored as a child: landmarks such as Dollymount, Crab Lake, the Bailey lighthouse and the North Bull; and some of the experience is clearly autobiographical: 'All the way back from town they could see the great [mud] flats opposite Clontarf lying black in the moonlight . . .' The plot revolves around Ellen Stedman's father rejecting the suit of Robert Hamilton for her hand on grounds of insufficient wealth. Hamilton remembers that his father had disappeared while returning from the Gold Coast with his savings. Robert dreams of finding treasure on a sunken ship and, with his friend, Tom Harrison, investigates a wrecked ship on Dublin's North Bull, near Clontarf. After some unsuccessful efforts together, Robert raises the treasure alone on Christmas Day, a kind of profane paralleling of the spiritual transformation wrought by the birth of Christ with the material rebirth of Robert through treasure. Other elements of the story, such as the careful study of the almanac to divine the weather, would later carry over into *Dracula*. An echo of these childhood experiences is to be found in another early story, 'The Crystal Cup': 'In my ears I heard again the old song we used to sing together when, as children, we wandered on the beach.'[19]

As he was approaching manhood, Stoker must have missed the sea when he moved with his parents to 17 Upper Buckingham Street in Dublin's north inner city where they stayed until the mid-1860s. The Stokers then followed the prevailing social trend by moving to the expanding southern suburbs of Dublin, in their case Rathgar. By this time Stoker was already 'a bit of a scribbler', his chief companions being his sister, Matilda, and his younger brother, Tom. He continued, however, to attend a school, run by the Reverend William Woods at 15 Rutland Square East, on the north side of Dublin. That he was a pupil at a school run by Woods is supported by the Trinity College entrance records – although the Trinity rugby club records state that he was educated at 'Mr. Moors School' – and a biographical note which Stoker gave to his friend, the Irish writer and politician, Justin McCarthy, for his *Irish Literature* in 1904.[20] Some confusion has been caused by the fact that the actual name of the school was Bective House College, in which Woods was a teacher before becoming the owner in 1869. In 'The Seer', a story Stoker published in 1901, he says of his education: 'Hitherto my life had been an uneventful one. At school I was, though secretly ambitious, dull as to results. At College I was better off, for my big body and athletic powers gave me a certain position in which I had to overcome my natural shyness.' The phrase carried over into his novel, *The Mystery of the Sea* (1902), underlining its autobiographical authenticity.[21]

THREE

Master of Arts

> For reply he reached over and took my ear in his hand and pulled it playfully,
> as he used long ago to do at lectures, and said . . . 'You were always a careful
> student, and your case book was ever more full than the rest.'
>
> (*Dracula*, Van Helsing to Dr Seward)

In *The Man*, Stoker drew on his recollections of his first days at Trinity College Dublin, to provide the main character, Stephen, with her reaction to Cambridge University:

> There was something in the stir and movement, the endless shifting of the pieces which made up the kaleidoscope of life, ever bringing up new thoughts, new emotions, new experiences; new combinations of thought and emotion and experience in endless variety, till the brain reeled. It was like trying to understand and formulate into memory a glimpse of a new and strange world . . . The self-content, the sex-content in the endless tide of young men that thronged the streets and quads and parks; the all-sufficing nature of sport or study to whichever their inclinations tended. The small part which womankind seemed to have in their lives . . . The half confidences of scandals, borne on whispered breaths. The whole confidences of dormitory and study . . . All were parts of the new and strange world.[1]

Like Stephen, Stoker was around sixteen when he went up to Trinity in early November 1864, in his case just a few weeks short of his seventeenth birthday.

A contemporary novel gave a good description of the scene Stoker would have faced when sitting his entrance exam:

> On a fine October morning . . . in the theatre of Trinity College, Dublin. About twenty other students were seated at the low wooden tables; some engaged in *viva voce* examinations by the Fellows, while others were busy translating and writing answers to the questions on the printed papers. Those present had, on the previous day,

matriculated with a crowd of others, and for their superior attainments had been selected for a second examination, in order to be placed according to their respective merits.[2]

When Stoker confessed that he had not been bright at school, he was not being excessively modest. His entrance grades at Trinity were unimpressive: he was placed fortieth out of fifty-one. His fellow students were the children of physicians, clergymen, merchants, bankers, private gentlemen, schoolteachers, farmers, lawyers and manufacturers; in other words, they were predominantly middle class. Those who started out as junior freshmen with Stoker in November 1864 included the future writers, Standish O'Grady and Alfred Perceval Graves. O'Grady, a year older than Stoker, was the son of a Church of Ireland rector in County Cork who became absorbed in Irish myth and legend in the 1870s and published a number of books whose concept of a heroic past is widely acknowledged as an important influence on the writers of the Irish literary revival, especially William Butler Yeats. Alfred Perceval Graves, born the same year as O'Grady, was also the son of a Church of Ireland clergyman. After graduating from Trinity College Dublin, he became a school inspector in England. A prolific poet, he attempted to embody the essence of Gaelic literature in English. He was the father of the poet, Robert Graves.

If Stoker was impressed by the buildings of Trinity, he was not alone among his contemporaries. Alfred Graves recalled:

No stranger to Dublin could fail to be attracted by the massive front of Trinity College in the greatest thoroughfare of our faded capital. Noble statues of Burke and Goldsmith stand before the gate. Ussher and Berkeley and Grattan are in the hall. The buildings, too, are of the type that was common when Dublin was the seat of Government and the home of the nobility. The library has not its equal among library buildings in England; and the Provost's house looks like the town residence of an English nobleman.[3]

Not everyone shared this view, however. Charles Barrington, an outstanding athlete who played on the college rugby team with Stoker, was anything but impressed: 'I came from Rugby to Trinity College in 1867 & found that there was nothing much to do during the winter term. There were no cycles, no golf, no hockey, no anything. Cards, billiards & whiskey & the more social dressed smartly, & paraded down Grafton St every afternoon & were known as the "Grafton St Hussars." A poor time indeed.' John Butler Yeats, painter and father of the poet, William Butler Yeats, entered the university in 1857 and found 'the Trinity College intellects, noisy and monotonous, without ideas or curiosity about ideas, and without sense of mystery, everything was sacrificed to mental efficiency . . . Trinity College is intellectually a sort of little Prussia.' Stoker agreed; addressing the university's Historical Society as Auditor in 1872, he lamented that history, oratory and literature were sadly neglected at Trinity. On a less serious note, the students played a variety of pranks on the generally unreceptive Dubliners, 'blowing doors open with gunpowder, wrenching off city knockers, and drawing caricatures of obnoxious individuals on the walls or doors of their chambers'. It is not surprising that there were occasional 'town and gown' rows between the ordinary people of Dublin and the student body in their midst.[4]

In a pamphlet written in mocking, ironic style, a contemporary writer wrote disparagingly about the lofty notions of young undergraduates at the College:

> The student, when first he enters College, forms an exaggerated idea of his own dignity, and invariably signs his name with a large T.C.D. and a flourish in his books. He takes, with unconcealed satisfaction, the cards which are thrust into his hands by Hawkins and the other porters who sell caps and gowns, and shows them to all his friends, or puts them up over his chimney-piece; and has the innocence to believe it, when trying on his cap and gown, Mrs. Hawkins tells him he looks very handsome, little thinking that she has said the same to every person who has ever bought one, and that a heavy discount is charged for such compliments . . . He patronises the theatre on command nights, and goes to the front row of the dress circle, in a very stiff white cravat, white waistcoat, and three and sixpenny gloves . . . He is a constant attendant at flower and cattle shows; and he is always to be seen in Merrion-square on Sundays, escorting the same set of young ladies, by whom he is considered a *very nice young man*.[5]

Stoker was a 'pensioner', which meant that his parents were of moderate income, ranking him above sizars, the children of poorer parents, and below fellow commoners, whose parents were wealthy. The social distinctions involved are well caught in the characters of O'Neill and Butler in Thomas Mason Jones's contemporary novel, *Old Trinity*: 'O'Neill had been entered on the College books as a fellow-commoner, a privilege which entitled him to pay a double price for his tuition, rooms, and dinner, to sit at the Fellows' table and to wear a silk gown. He at once obtained chambers and commenced residence. Butler was only a pensioner. He resided principally in the country, and only came up to College three times a year to pass his term examinations.'[6]

The tutor assigned to Stoker, Dr George Ferdinand Shaw, a Fellow of the College, would prove to have a lifelong influence on him. Conversations with Shaw recorded in Stoker's notebook in the 1870s reveal an easy intimacy and they kept in touch after Stoker's move to London, where the Trinity academic frequented the Lyceum Theatre. Stoker remained a student at Trinity until 1870, when he finally graduated. His attendance at college was fitful, a result no doubt of the fact that he took up a full-time position in the Civil Service in 1866. While he completed a number of terms in his junior and senior freshman years in 1864–5 and 1865–6, in what should have been his junior sophister (1866–7) and senior sophister (1867–8) years his attendance declined further and, on 12 September 1867, he was 'degraded' by his tutor's order. The student residence records confirm the impression of Stoker's erratic university career: he is unlisted from the Michaelmas term of 1866. He does not feature at all in the records for 1868; in 1869 and 1870, he is not listed in the examination records, although he finally graduated as a Bachelor of Arts in the spring of 1870. As a graduate, he was entitled to buy a Master's degree and this he duly did five years later, in 1875. It is difficult to square Stoker's tortuous progress towards finalising a four-year BA course in almost six years with his claim that he had graduated with 'Honours in Pure Mathematics'. Two students did graduate with honours in mathematics in the spring of 1870 but Stoker was not one of them.[7] By contrast, his younger brother, Tom, came up to Trinity College in 1868 and won the term Composition Prize in English Literature awarded by Professor Edward Dowden. Standish O'Grady, now a senior sophister and a Trinity Scholar (an outstanding undergraduate achievement), was a previous winner. Alfred Perceval Graves was another of Stoker's contemporaries to become a Scholar.

If Stoker did not distinguish himself academically at Trinity, he certainly did so in the College Historical Society and the Philosophical Society, the pre-eminent fora for student debating and literary activities. Stoker managed the rare feat of becoming both Auditor of the Hist and President of the Phil, the highest offices in both societies.

The College Philosophical Society was more a place for reading and discussing papers than a debating society like the Hist. Founded in 1845, its honorary members in the 1870s included, in addition to Stoker himself, Charles Graves, Bishop of Limerick, father of Alfred Perceval; George F. Shaw, Stoker's former tutor; the Reverend J.P. Mahaffy; Professor Edward Dowden; John Butler Yeats; and John Todhunter, the poet and playwright.

Todhunter, Standish O'Grady and William Wilde, Oscar Wilde's brother, formed the backbone of the prizemen and medallists in the Phil around Stoker's time at college. Presidents of the Phil included Mahaffy (1858–9) and Dowden (1862–3), as well as Stoker (1869–70). Through close contact with men such as these, Stoker was exposed to a wide variety of influences, both political and literary. Politically, they ranged from those who would later be dedicated Unionists, such as Dowden and Edward Carson, to Home Rulers like Isaac Butt; in the literary field, he was involved with writers such as O'Grady, Graves and Todhunter. Stoker's interaction with these figures is clear in the minute books of the Phil for the 1860s and 1870s. An interest in the supernatural in literature is also evident: on 7 May 1868, Stoker read a paper on 'Sensationalism in Fiction and Society'. At a meeting a few weeks later, which Stoker addressed, a paper was read on 'The Supernatural as introduced by the English Poets' and he was present when papers were read on 'The Demonology of Milton' and 'The Byronic School and its Mission' in late 1868/early 1869. In June 1869, he read a paper on the poet, Percy Bysshe Shelley. The Faust legend, which would later form part of the literary backdrop to *Dracula*, recurred repeatedly as a subject for papers delivered to the Phil in these years.

Stoker was busy at these meetings, introducing motions, proposing and seconding votes of thanks and proposing undergraduates for membership. In June 1869 he decided to provide the funding for a silver prize for aesthetics when it became clear that the society's own funds were inadequate. Both Stoker and Alfred Perceval Graves were elected to the council of the Phil at the meeting of 4 June 1868. Graves was an ally in the politicking endemic in a student society like the Phil and it is clear that Stoker must have co-ordinated many of his tactical manoeuvres with him in advance. They became rivals, however, when the President of the Phil resigned in April 1869 and both Stoker and Graves were proposed for the office of secretary (the incumbent became President). Stoker was elected by eleven votes to nine. In May he was proposed for the office of President but was defeated. He was, however, elected President on 8 May 1870, following the resignation of the incumbent.[8] His term of office was short; it lasted only until the final meeting of the 1869–70 session on 23 June 1870, when he read a paper on 'The Means of Improvement in Composition'. Reflecting perhaps Stoker's flair for publicity, his reading of the paper was widely reported in the Dublin newspapers.[9] Stoker continued to be active in the Phil, not only in procedural matters, in which he clearly revelled, but also in producing papers. In December 1870, he read essays on 'Style' and on 'D.G. Rossetti's Poems' (he would later be friendly with the writer, Hall Caine, who acted as Rossetti's assistant in 1881–2). Early in 1873 Stoker was made an honorary member of the society. He continued to participate in it until 1877, the year before he left for London.

Stoker had a high opinion of the College Historical Society, describing it as no ornamental appendage to Trinity College but its 'supplementary school'.[10] Its origins date back to the mid-eighteenth century when the young Edmund Burke, then a Scholar of Trinity, felt the need for a club to facilitate discussion of historical and philosophical issues. Since then, it has attracted the participation of many Trinity students who have gone on to make a mark in the world, including key figures in the history of Irish nationalism, such as Theobald Wolfe Tone and Robert Emmet, as well as Stoker's contemporary, Edward Carson, on the Unionist side.

Stoker was first among the principal speakers of the 1868 session and was elected to the general committee of the Hist in May 1869. He was actively involved in the society, as he was with other facets of college life, throwing himself with gusto into debates and the politics of the Hist, especially its committee work. In later life, he was clearly proud of his achievements in this arena, generally the breeding ground of politicians and lawyers; in his *Personal Reminiscences of Henry Irving* he recalled: 'In my University days I had been something of a law-maker in a small way, as I had revised and carried out a revision of the laws of order of the College Historical Society, Dublin University – our great debating society founded by Edmund Burke.' There is no evidence that Stoker was responsible for any general revision of the laws of the society; indeed, in his auditorial address in 1872, he stated that he did not advocate any change in either the constitution or the workings of the Society, for no reform was needed. Despite this, three motions of his for amendment to the laws of the society were carried by large majorities at one meeting in 1870, although another was thrown out by a large majority around the same time.[11] In the 1869–70 session of the Hist Stoker was elected to the office of librarian. Among those seated on the platform for the opening meeting of that session were Sir William Wilde and the Reverend J.P. Mahaffy, later Provost of Trinity and a powerful influence on the young Oscar Wilde. Stoker was awarded the fifth certificate for oratory. Early in 1870 he was elected to the committee that was to prepare for the Hist's centenary celebrations the following March, together with Sir Arthur Guinness. In June 1870, Stoker was elected record secretary. In the 1870–1 session, he repeated his previous achievement by winning a certificate for oratory, the Silver Medal in History and a special medal for English composition. At the end of May 1871, Stoker was one of three candidates for the post of Auditor, but was beaten into second place, losing narrowly by twenty-two votes to nineteen. He showed magnanimity by vigorously opposing attempts to disqualify the successful candidate on a technicality. The following year he stood again and, on 14 June 1872, was elected Auditor by a single vote in a two-horse race.

Stoker was an active participant in many Hist debates in the decade prior to his departure for London. While his stance on various issues can give some insight into his early values and development, it is important to realise that as a debater he was sharpening his skills rather than necessarily setting out his fundamental values. For example, in May 1869 he spoke in favour of the motion, 'That the dramatic taste of the present day exhibits marked symptoms of degeneracy'. This is of particular interest in view of the influence which Max Nordau's 1892 book, *Degeneration*, a scathing attack on much of the more radical culture of the nineteenth century, would have on Stoker when he was writing *Dracula*, and his later strong support for censorship. However, he spoke against similar motions over the following two years and did not intervene in a debate on abolition of the censorship of drama: this did not then apply in Dublin, unlike London. On the other hand, when he opposed the motion 'That the social and political disabilities of women should be abolished', which was supported by Standish O'Grady, we may assume that his later views on the subject had been formed early in life. The debates of Stoker's year as Auditor were unexceptional, following well-worn topics. A motion of impeachment of Stoker as Auditor for having ruled that a member in possession of the House could speak on any subject he liked was lost twenty-five to three in June 1873.

Stoker's auditorial address at the opening meeting of the 1872–3 session on 13 November 1872, 'The Necessity for Political Honesty', was the high point of his Hist career. The platform contained far more dignitaries than usual, reflecting Stoker's organisational abilities; VIPs included Professor Edward Dowden, Sir William Wilde, Dr George F. Shaw, and the Lord Mayor of Dublin. Stoker's status as an outstanding Trinity and, indeed, Dublin, personality was reflected in the larger than usual attendance; the college Dining Hall where it was held 'was thronged in every part by visitors and students'. There was some good-humoured noise but the audience obeyed an injunction against party demonstrations.

While the positions adopted by Stoker in debates may not have reflected his deeply rooted convictions, his address as Auditor was a major statement of his beliefs and is of importance in understanding the landscape of his later development, especially the political outlook which underlay his fiction, *Dracula* and *The Lady of the Shroud* in particular. One basic element – that reform, in the Irish context especially, obviated the need for violent or revolutionary change – was evident from the outset; his views on international relations were also well formed: he saw the rise of new powers, such as Germany, as creating instability, while Russia was threatening the future peace of Europe 'and stretches already a greedy arm towards British India'. A specific concern with protecting British interests in the East would surface decades later in *The Lady of the Shroud*. Stoker's concern about the perceived degenerative tendencies of advanced Western culture and its possible decline, an element in his later fiction, often labelled *fin de siècle* by critics and attributed to the intellectual currents of the later nineteenth century, is in fact evident in this address. Critical of 'the hollowness and artificialness of society within, and its wastefulness and extravagance without', he proclaimed that society was rapidly becoming effete and that its regeneration depends on 'that personal purity which still exists with individuals'. This was especially true of America, where the Anglo–Saxon race was supposed to be dwindling and could never be restored to its former vigour by the new immigration from the East; the Irish were 'to serve to counterbalance effeteness in the American, and want of principle in the Mongolian . . . this leavening race of future America . . . may become in time the leading element of Western civilization'.[12] This notion of the Irish regenerating the United States may well have come from Stoker's friends, Sir William and Lady Wilde; and his contemporary and later friend, William O'Brien MP, held similar beliefs. A key figure in Irish nationalist politics in Stoker's era, he presented Irish-Americans as models for the future, reconciling enterprise and democracy with national and religious sentiment.[13] Similar ideas carried through to *Dracula*; indeed one modern critic sees fear of English decline as the situation upon which the novel was predicated, with nineteenth-century thinkers such as Oswald Spengler, Max Nordau and Cesare Lombroso believing that the decline of the West must be halted by an infusion of fresh energy such as that to be provided by the Irish in America. When Dracula arrives in England in the *Demeter*, 'he returns from the underworld bringing new growth to a dead land, fresh blood to an enervated race'.[14]

At the outset of his auditorial address, Stoker struck a chord which would resonate in *Dracula*: the intrusion of the past into the present, of how the dead and the living are linked, in this case by Trinity College's old traditions. Overall, it is a stirring expression of a young man's rhetoric, a clarion call for political honesty, justice and internationalism. Identifying with a tradition of 'British valour' which stretched from the early victory against the French at Agincourt in the fifteenth century to the later one at Waterloo, he celebrated the imperial gallantry of the British garrison which held out at Lucknow, India, during the mutiny in 1857. He also celebrated a Protestant and Puritan tradition, invoking Bernard Palissy, a sixteenth-century French Protestant oppressed for his views, as well as Galileo and the victory of Cromwell's New Model Army over the Royalists at Naseby in the English Civil War in 1645. Simultaneously, Stoker invoked the Irish nationalist tradition of suffering and strife but with a positive spin: the qualities which had tempered the Irish would prove valuable for the economic development which he saw as imminent. He regretted contemporary political problems in Ireland, the 'renewal of the old strife and old disaffection', and called for tolerance and liberalism in the place of bigotry, prejudice and cynicism. He also regretted ideological differences, the strife of capital and labour, 'so ruinous to a commercial country'. Declaring that the Irish race had within it all the elements of greatness, he predicted that 'the Ireland of the future is a subject for ambitious dreams'. The rider was that the new order in Ireland must transcend sectarian feuds, old animosities must be forgotten and the dead left to rest in peace: 'We must choose whether we shall live for the future or the past; and it needs little effort to see the nobler choice.'

Dr Shaw moved a motion that the Auditor's address be printed at the expense of the society, the usual procedure, and Stoker was again awarded a certificate for oratory. His address was extensively reported in the Irish newspapers and prompted some editorial comment, mostly favourable. One of the other speakers, the Reverend George A. Chadwick, who seconded the vote of thanks to Stoker after his address and so must have been a friend of his, used the occasion to attack Cardinal Cullen, the Roman Catholic Archbishop of Dublin, and the educational policies of his Church. This generated controversy, with the Dublin *Daily Express*, managed by the family of one of Stoker's closest friends, John Joseph Robinson, weighing in to support Chadwick, while the *Freeman's Journal*, representative of the views of the Roman Catholic majority, carried an editorial critical of Chadwick.[15]

In the following session of 1873–4, Oscar Wilde was proposed for membership by his brother, Willie, and the correspondence secretary, Charles Arundell; contrary to what some have believed, Stoker was not involved, unless it was behind the scenes. (Neither, incidentally, did he propose Wilde for membership of the Philosophical Society, in November 1871: Oscar was proposed by Charles Arundell, now the President of the Phil, and seconded by its secretary, Kendal Franks. The fact that Arundell was involved in both memberships makes it likely that he, rather than Stoker, was the one Oscar Wilde relied on for assistance.) Two weeks later, a certain Edward H. Carson of 25 Harcourt Street, the future leader of Unionism whose brilliantly destructive cross-examination of Oscar Wilde at his trial for homosexuality in 1895 would be largely responsible for his conviction, was also proposed for membership of the Historical Society. The following month, Stoker was elected an honorary member of the Hist and he continued his involvement in it. He was on the platform as a VIP for the 1874–5 opening session and continued to chair meetings until late 1875. If Stoker's activities in the Hist impressed contemporaries, he has been less fortunate with posterity. In a survey of 'Personalities in the Hist' by a Trinity College historian, R.B. McDowell, in an address in 1970, Stoker featured in a bizarre fashion: 'it would be a mistake to think of Stoker as a typical product of our Society in the nineteenth century,' he said. 'It was a serious century and I suppose the greatest crop of our members were the Lawyers.'[16] Even making due allowance for an attempt at humour, it is curious that Stoker has been typecast as unserious and untypical of Hist personalities of the period, especially as he would later qualify as a lawyer, although he did not practise.

Despite his involvement with the Hist and the Phil, not to mention his Civil Service job, Stoker found time to make a serious commitment to sport at Trinity. The critic, Maurice Richardson, has described *Dracula* as 'plainly an athlete's phantasy'. In Athena Vrettos's view, 'Dracula's physical strength, health, and longevity directly correspond to scientific and cultural anxieties about the racially superior body', while H. L. Malchow sees Stoker's athleticism as revealing anxiety about the intensity of his 'homosocial' relationships (presumably a reference to the concept, developed in modern gay and lesbian studies, of erotically tinged bonds that connect men in a socially empowering manner).[17] Whatever its psychological motivation, Stoker's memory of his youthful athletic prowess permeated, not just *Dracula*, but also much of his entire fictional output. In his late novel, *Lady Athlyne* (1908) he makes clear his contempt for flabby types, 'half-pulselessboys [*sic*], flabby of flesh and pallid with enervating dissipation . . .' In *The Mystery of the Sea*, the narrator is credited with vast strength which the athletic training of his youth had developed. It is, however, in the character of Harold An Wolf in *The Man* that Stoker comes closest to self-portrait: 'He was of fine stature, more than six feet two in height, deep-chested, broad-shouldered, lean-flanked, long-armed . . . Altogether he had that appearance of strength, with well-poised alert neck and forward set of the head, which marks the successful athlete.' It is not surprising to find Stoker opposing a motion in the Hist in 1871, 'That too much attention is bestowed on the cultivation of athletics in our public schools and universities'.[18]

Stoker was also active both as an organiser and participant in the annual Civil Service sports competition. The *Irish Times* of 2 September 1867 featured a report of Stoker throwing a cricket ball further than the actual winner in one competition which he had not entered, and winning the strangers' race 'in admirable style'. The *Daily Express* also noted the same incident, reporting that Stoker had picked the ball up and thrown it 105 yards (the winner threw it a mere 60 yards!). In addition to winning the strangers' race, he also won the three-mile walking race though both results were disputed. An editorial commented on the attempt by the Civil Service sports to rival those of Trinity, noting that the 'muscular Christians of Trinity College have hitherto enjoyed undisputed public favour'. Stoker had been a member of a four-man executive committee which was commended for the excellence of arrangements, 'conceived and carried out with such fore-thought and wisdom that failure was almost impossible'.[19] The following year, the newspapers again gave prominence to Stoker's performance at the Civil Service sports. According to the *Daily Telegraph*, Stoker won the five-mile walking race in the athletic sports at Beaufort House Grounds in June 1868 but was disqualified because he broke into a run at the end. Another account in an English journal stated that Stoker's disqualification was to be regretted, as the 'Hibernian friend . . . only requires proper tuition to be a star'. It further claimed that the officials were so satisfied with Stoker's performance that he would be presented with a prize in any event and this indeed was the case. Yet another English account of the story described Stoker as 'the gallant son of Erin'.[20]

Stoker developed into an outstanding athlete in his early twenties. In addition to his exploits at rugby – he was one of a group which played a leading role in the establishment of the sport in Ireland – he was a multiple champion in walking races, the premier events of the Trinity (College) Races, then the major sporting event in Ireland. A younger contemporary, Newport John Davis White, recalled the scene vividly:

> For two days the [College] Park was filled with a very great concourse, sometimes as many as 30,000 people. There were two rows of seats, and in some places three rows, all around the field. The crowd was so great that schoolboys had no difficulty in squeezing through the entrance gates undetected by those who were taking the tickets . . . The walking races of seven miles and four miles were a leading feature in the old sports as I remember them. I have a distinct recollection of one champion walker, Bram Stoker, who afterwards became Henry Irving's business manager and the author, in 1897, of a weird and blood-curdling romance, *Dracula*. Bram Stoker's family and mine were on intimate terms. He was the special friend of my eldest brother. He was an exceptionally tall man, and when he came to our house he often hoisted me on his shoulder.[21]

The cups in the possession of Stoker's descendants bear testimony to his athletic achievements. These include silver cups for two-, five- and seven-mile walking races from 1868 to 1870, as well as the 'Dublin University Gymnasium First Weights Won by Abraham Stoker 1870'. The prize of which he was most proud was that for being the overall 'Champion' in the May 1867 sports. It was clearly a year of outstanding athletic achievement for Stoker. At the May Trinity Races, he came from behind in the seven-mile walking race, to win dramatically from a field of thirteen, after which he 'was immediately raised by his fellow students and borne on their shoulders, amidst the most deafening applause around the ring'.[22]

The Civil Service event which had followed hard on the heels of the Trinity Races in early May 1868 had drawn an 'immense and fashionable assemblage'. Stoker won first prize in the two-mile walking race, finishing fully 100 yards in front; he also competed in the 600-yard hurdle. Stoker's popularity was evident in a newspaper account of yet another victory: 'Out of 12 entries for the great event of the day – the walking race of seven miles – 8 men started. Mr. Craig took a bold and prominent lead, which he maintained till the end of the second mile, when Mr. Stoker drew forward, and Mr. Craig fell behind Mr. Simpson and Mr. Hart. Mr. Stoker kept his position, and won with ease, amidst tremendous cheers, Mr. Simpson coming in second, and Mr. Hart third.' There is an echo of this achievement in *Dracula* when we are told that the correspondent of the *Dailygraph* was a fairly good runner.[23]

Stoker's versatility was also impressive. In June 1870, he enjoyed a string of successes at a gymnastics event organised by the votaries of 'muscular Christianity' in Trinity. He came first in putting the 42 lb weight, the 16 lb shot, slinging the 56 lb and the 42 lb weights. He also came joint first in vaulting, the high jump, and the long jump with trapeze. When the event was repeated in March the following year, Stoker's exploits were even more colourful. He performed in front of a large and fashionable assembly at the Gymnasium Club at Trinity:

> Mr. A. Stoker – who is the foremost . . . [amongst] his confreres in the gymnasium, in the class room, and in the various college literary societies – possessing great physical power, successfully attempted a feat on the trapeze, which even few professionals have achieved, and which it would be foolhardy for the majority of those matched against him on this occasion to essay. Suspended by the feet from the high stationary trapeze he attached second 'ropes and bar' to his wrists, and these being depended, two members – Messrs. S. Abraham and W. Gabbett – performed a number of difficult evolutions thereon, Mr.

Stoker meanwhile drawing them towards him apparently with perfect ease and certainly with very commendable self-confidence.

Another Dublin daily commented: 'On the rings and trapeze . . . Mr. A. Stoker was a powerful and daring performer.' Stoker was loudly applauded, though the journalist who covered the story speculates on the possible negative long-term physical effects on Stoker's constitution. Stoker also won at vaulting, clearing 6 feet 11 inches and competed in a climbing event.[24] A few years later, in March 1873, when Stoker dropped in to the university gymnasium and saw a student called Thornhill performing on the trapeze, he took him to task for neglecting his studies in favour of athletics. Stoker said he had heard that Thornhill never did any work except on the trapeze, to which the student replied, seriously, that this was not true: he also did a great deal on the horizontal bar!

Given his size and athletic prowess, it is only to be expected that Stoker should have left his mark – sometimes quite literally – on the brawny sport of rugby. Stoker's experience as a rugby player also left an imprint on his work. In *The Snake's Pass*, Arthur uses an old rugby football trick when felling the villain, Black Murdock. In *Personal Reminiscences of Henry Irving*, Stoker recalls the sensation of playing rugby at Trinity: 'It was like looking at a game of Rugby football when one is running with the ball for a touchdown behind goal with all the on-side men of his team close behind him. *He could* not fall or fail if he wanted to. They backed him up in every possible way.'[25]

The Trinity College rugby club had been founded in 1854 and the dominant figure in its early development was Charles Burton Barrington who was captain from 1867–8 for three years. His arrival coincided with a general expansion and reorganisation of the club and he was instrumental in drawing up a set of laws which were an important step forward in the evolution of the game in Ireland. The Trinity team was then so strong that it stipulated that any team wishing to play the first XV must first beat their second string. Trinity provided eight of the twenty chosen for the first Irish international team to play England in 1875; the selection committee met at the college and picked themselves *en masse*; if one could not be accommodated as a back, he was picked as a forward! Barrington later drove his own ambulance in the First World War, rather as the characters de Escoban and Marjory Anita Drake in *The Mystery of the Sea* equip ships for their respective navies at their own cost. Sixty years later, Barrington remembered Stoker vividly, as an oarsman as well as a rugby player: 'Stoker. A big strong awkward chap, rowing in the four at No 3. His mother keeping up along the wall on a car called out: "They'll be beaten [as] none of them are keeping stroke with *Abraham*."'[26] Another team-mate had good reason to remember Stoker as a rugby player: 'I have still the scar over my left eye where "Stoker" threw an opponent against me!'[27]

Stoker played for the Trinity second XV in the 1867–8 and the 1868–9 seasons and managed to make an immediate impression, as a contemporary account of a match between the 'Externals' and 'Internals' reported: 'The tables were then turned and the Externals by judiciously backing up their forward players kept the ball close to their opponents' goal & Messrs. Stoker and Kennedy each getting a touch down.'[28] Ever the keen committee man, Stoker served on the Trinity Football (Rugby) Club committee for the 1868–70 seasons. In November 1868, Stoker was among those chosen to play for the first XV for the 1868–9 season during which it won all twenty-seven matches played. He then played for the first XV for a further two years, 1869–70 and 1870–1. When Barrington and a collaborator drew up the rugby rules in January 1868, they decided to award five 'colour Caps' to members of the 1866–7 team: 'The caps were of red and black velvet in quarters, separated by gold braid, with a large gold shamrock in front and a gold tassel.' Stoker was awarded caps for the 1869–70 and the 1870–1 seasons 'for superior play'. He was not the only literary figure to play rugby for Trinity at that time. When he was chosen to play for the second XV in 1867, Standish O'Grady was among the substitutes. Alfred Perceval Graves was on the first XV in 1865–6 and 1866–7. Stoker proposed the adoption of the report and was elected with seven others to be an officer of the committee for the new season at the AGM in October 1869. He seems to have retired from playing at the end of the 1870–1 season.

FOUR

Petty Clerk

Let me begin with facts, bare, meagre facts, verified by books and figures,
and of which there can be no doubt.

(*Dracula*, Jonathan Harker's Journal)

As noted earlier, while Stoker was active in various aspects of Trinity life, he was making a career for himself in the Civil Service. In *Miss Betty*, Stoker expresses his belief in the value of hard work and, concomitantly, his contempt for idle young gallants. Alderman Fenton, Betty's cousin, is critical of the gentlemanly upbringing of Rafe and emphasises the virtues of having had to work in one's youth: 'It somehow makes us think more of our work and less of ourselves, than the breeding of those young gallants teaches them.'[1] Stoker's perspective was based on solid personal experience: he had joined the Civil Service in Dublin at the age of eighteen and had to work hard throughout his adult life. It is a subject about which there has been a great deal of misapprehension in Stoker biography, notwithstanding the clarity both of the record and Stoker's own testimony. In *Personal Reminiscences of Henry Irving*, he states that when he took up employment with Henry Irving in 1878 he had spent thirteen years in the Civil Service. This was a slight exaggeration: he joined in 1866 and resigned in 1878. Having joined the Civil Service as a teenager, he did not enjoy the leisurely student life so fondly imagined by modern commentators.

Stoker may have joined in a temporary or unestablished capacity, as the Civil Service Commission did not examine him until 19 March 1867 for a clerkship. Quite why Stoker decided to join the Civil Service while he was not yet halfway through his degree course at Trinity College Dublin is not clear: his father had just retired, in December 1865, and perhaps Abraham Stoker was able to reach an informal understanding with his superiors that his son would get a job at Dublin Castle after he stepped down. When Bram Stoker wrote to Walt Whitman in 1872, he described himself as 'a clerk in the service of the Crown on a small salary'.[2] This was indeed the case: for most of his career Stoker was a 'Clerk, Second Class' in the Department of Registrar of Petty Sessions Clerks, which came under the Chief Secretary's Office in Dublin Castle. Stoker's life was tightly controlled by

44

regulations which ordained that clerks had to attend from 10 a.m. to 4 p.m. every day except Saturday, when they worked from 10 a.m. to 1 p.m. They could not be absent for more than half an hour except at the discretion of the Senior Clerk. A strict hierarchy was in operation, which laid down, for example, that only the Senior Clerk could conduct business of a financial nature: this was a forerunner of the system that Stoker later installed at the Lyceum, which centralised the finances of the theatre in the hands of Henry Irving and himself.

The Petty Sessions court service had been established in 1827 to deal with minor offences, as part of the nineteenth-century systematisation and reform of government in Ireland. Its sessions were described by Stoker in *The Man* (1905) as 'low people speaking of low crimes'. While not underestimating the drudgery of the clerking which constituted Stoker's working life, it is also necessary to bear in mind that the Civil Service was undergoing major modernisation reforms before and during his period of service. In 1855 the Civil Service Commission was appointed to replace patronage with objective qualifying tests for admission to the service, and in 1871 competitive examination was established as the normal means of recruitment. Under the latter, those entering under the higher grade of clerk were 'expected to be drawn from the best class of university men and were intended to join the superior class in those offices which need high social and educational requirements'.[3] The general effect of these reforms was to substitute middle-class meritocracy for aristocratic patronage and nobody reading *Dracula* can fail to spot the middle-class, meritocractic values which underlie it. Stoker's joining the Petty Sessions service was part of this process of innovation. In 1867, a staff consisting of a registrar, two senior and six junior clerks was sanctioned by the government and the office was divided into two sections, administrative and financial. By 1876, when a report on the service was published, the number of junior clerks had increased to eight and Stoker was top of the list. His salary was then £180, on a scale from £90 to £280, with annual increments of £10.

While much of the work may have been boring, the stories of the activities of the clerks left behind by Stoker give the impression that they knew how to have a good time. One recounted the riotous exploits of a six-person delegation sent by the Irish Petty Sessions clerks' association to London to lobby for passing of favourable legislation in 1874: they managed to spend the then enormous sum of £600 in a fortnight. Clearly there was a good deal of wild drinking and attention paid to the ladies. Two of the clerks did not even stay in London but went off to spend a week on a 'bend' in Paris. In London, one of the delegation wanted to take the whole female staff of the Westminster telegraph office for a picnic in Richmond. Some members got involved in a fight and a number of them came back with black eyes and cut faces. On the day of their interview with the Chief Secretary, their spokesman was so drunk that they first had to put him under a pump in an attempt to sober him up, after which his head was, in Stoker's phrase, steaming like a wet furnace. They left a package of tobacco and a case of whiskey at the Carlton Club for a London-based Irish official lest he should be lonely following their departure. On another occasion, Stoker went with two colleagues to a ball in Dublin. Late in the evening, when many were drunk, one man threw up in the centre of the hall and others started to use the vomit as a slide, bringing a drunk from the bar to replenish the slide at one point!

The 1876 report noted that four clerks, including Stoker, under one of the senior clerks, were employed in auditing accounts from the courts. Stoker was responsible for most of the detailed work of the division. As usual, he was the willing horse but he was also climbing the hierarchical ladder: one of the junior clerks below him had more service. The report proposed a new system, with the creation of a new post of Chief Clerk, to which the serving Senior Clerk was to be appointed, and a new post of Inspector, to be filled by the dynamic Mr Stoker:

> The necessity for appointing a competent person to visit the different petty sessions districts, and to inspect the clerk's books and accounts, has been very clearly proved to us . . . We propose that the clerk of inspection should rank next to the senior clerk, and that Mr. Stoker, who is now head of the junior clerks, should be offered the appointment.

The Clerk of Inspection was to get £250 per annum, rising by annual increments of £12 to a maximum of £400, with a personal allowance of 12 shillings a night when absent from home on duty, and his actual travelling expenses. When the inspector post was created in March 1876, Stoker was duly appointed.[4] In 1882, a few years after Stoker had left, the Petty Sessions clerks were described as a semi-independent body, much of whose discipline depended upon the work of the Inspector of Petty Sessions. The service expanded rapidly: by 1895 there were 406 clerks of Petty Sessions and 606 sets of books to be examined by the Inspector. In resigning and joining Henry Irving, Stoker was not giving up an obscure clerking job but a well-paid and powerful position. He had clearly made his mark within the Civil Service and could have expected to rise higher.

Quite how Stoker saw things is another matter. It is a moot point whether he shared the perspective of the character in 'The Castle of the King' (1876) who felt that all the sunshine of his life seemed to be passing away. Despite his relative success in climbing the Civil Service ladder, he may have found its atmosphere stifling: in *The Snake's Pass*, he unleashed deadly sarcasm on the bureaucracy endemic in the Irish administration, when the purchase of an estate at Knockcalltecrore is completed: 'with the endless official formalities and eccentricities habitual to a country whose administration has traditionally adopted and adapted every possible development of all belonging to red-tape'. Similarly, in 'The Burial of the Rats', he sees Paris as resembling a devil fish, the product of absurd centralisation.[5] Stoker may also have been influenced by the views of his friend, Lady Wilde, which were generally hostile to Dublin Castle and its role in Irish history. Indeed, she explicitly connected Dublin Castle both with the bloody history of Irish rebellion and the Gothic literary tradition: 'Strange scenes, dark, secret, and cruel, have been enacted in that gloomy pile. No one has told the full story yet. It will be a Ratcliffe [*sic*] romance of dungeons and treacheries, of swift death or slow murder.' The reference here is to the work of Ann Radcliffe, the English Gothic novelist whose outstanding work was published in the 1790s. Another friend of Stoker's, Lady Aberdeen, the wife of a Viceroy, described Dublin Castle as 'that name of evil omen'. Bearing in mind that Stoker was employed in the system of justice, it is noteworthy that modern criticism sees in his work deeply negative attitudes towards justice and those involved in its administration.[6]

It was ironic therefore that Stoker should have chosen to write a manual for the Clerks of Petty Sessions at the time he was preparing to give up his post. He was still deep in the research for his *Duties of Clerks of Petty Sessions* when Henry Irving came back to Dublin in 1877. He finished the volume in the interval between resigning his post and joining Irving. In *The Nineteen Hundreds* (1922), Horace Wyndham, writing under the pseudonym, Reginald Auberon, made the somewhat unlikely claim that, of all Stoker's writings, the volume of which he was most proud was a 'slim and severely technical little brochure' dealing with the 'Duties of Clerks of Petty Sessions'. Stoker himself described the book as 'dry-as-dust' and recommended it ironically to his son, Noel, at school in Winchester: 'you will find it interesting and amusing and . . . the continuous nature of the narrative is instructive'.[7] In his introduction to the book, dated 31 December 1878, Stoker was more serious in setting out his approach and methodology. He had compiled it from all the sources of information at his disposal: statutes, files, registry books, etc., as well as basing it on the practical fruits of his own experience as an auditor and inspector. He argued that a certain uniformity of method was necessary and looked forward to 'the founding and development of a great and effective system of procedure which must sooner or later be adopted for the whole British Empire'. Official sanction for the publication of *Duties* was signed by Stoker's superior, Richard Wingfield, the Registrar, who strongly recommended it to clerks of Petty Session. Whether Stoker was asked by Wingfield to undertake the writing of the book or whether it was a product of Stoker's natural enthusiasm and energy is not known but its publication would have done his Civil Service career no harm had he decided to remain on. The book's layout is very clear, with summaries of paragraphs on the right-hand side. The manner of quoting from the various sources is very similar to the style of *Dracula* and this has generated some critical comment in recent years. Like a good civil servant, Mina Harker draws up a detailed memorandum on strategy for dealing with the Count.

The Duties of Clerks of Petty Sessions has been seen as part of what Thomas Richards calls the 'imperial archive' – 'a fantasy of knowledge collected and united in the service of state and Empire' which, in Stoker's novel, is responsible for the defeat of Dracula. In this view, Dracula is a feudal lord who represents the recrudescence of an obsolete form that must be overcome by an emphasis on the positive form of knowledge if the imperial project is to retain its coherence. Yet Dracula himself owes much of his power to the then modern informational order, and uses books, directories, almanacs, the Army and Navy Lists, the Law List, etc.[8] Both the Count and his pursuers use the methodology unveiled by Stoker in the *Duties of Clerks of Petty Sessions*, creating an identification of Stoker with his most famous creation. It is the superior use of this information technology by the Count's enemies, primarily Mina Harker, which tips the balance against him. Stoker's approach may have been influenced by his mentor, Edward Dowden, who identified 'the modern spirit' with a belief in the virtue of knowledge gained by methods of interrogation and research.[9]

One of the effects of his two years as Inspector of Petty Sessions was that Stoker was able to travel around Ireland and observe the life of the country-side. His notebook for the 1870s records travels the length and breadth of the country. That he tried to work, probably on his fiction, is clear from one entry, ironically headed 'Authorship in a Country Inn', in which he details the irritating distractions of his fellow guests – one man sniffing, another snoring, another arguing with a waiter – that prevented him from getting on with his work. The impact of the countryside on his writing is evident, both on his first novel, *The Snake's Pass*, and on some of his short stories, such as 'The Way of Peace', in which he paints an idyllic view of rural life. In his short story, 'The Burial of the Rats', he compares a squalid area of Paris with rural Ireland: 'Presently I got into what seemed a small city or community of chiffoniers. There were a number of shanties or huts, such as may be met with in the remote parts of the Bog of Allan [*sic*] – rude places with wattled walls, plastered with mud and roofs of rude thatch made from stable refuse

– such places as one would not like to enter for any consideration . . .' The story which owes most to these travels is 'The Man from Shorrox'', a lively, humorous, Trollopian account of goings-on in the type of commercial traveller establishment that Stoker would have stayed in at that time. 'A New Departure in Art', one of the stories in *Snowbound* (1908), may also have biographical roots in this period. It features a low comedian who tells of playing the part of Con in Boucicault's *The Shaughraun*, as part of a wretched travelling theatre company in the little town of Fenagh, on the west side of the Bog of Allen, which is in the centre of Ireland (a town of that name does exist in County Leitrim, in the West of Ireland). The company was taken to a wake to cheer up the widow and the others present.

During his years in the Civil Service, Stoker lived in various locations around Dublin. He was at 43 Harcourt Street until 1872, which he seems to have vacated around the time his parents left for the Continent, leaving Thornley in sole occupation. He moved to 11 Lower Leeson Street, which he shared with a Herbert Wilson and William Delany, an artist – Abraham Stoker warned his son against the doubtful influence of an artist around this time; he may have had Delany in mind. The Leeson Street address may have been the one to which Stoker refers in *Personal Reminiscences of Henry Irving*: 'I was a bachelor, living in the top rooms of a house, which I furnished myself.'[10] After two years he moved back in with Thornley at a new address, 16 Harcourt Street, in 1874 which, as part of 'Clonmell House', had been home in the late eighteenth century to a famously severe judge. Stoker could therefore claim to have lived in 'The Judge's House', the title of one of his most celebrated short stories in which a house retains the malign influence of its former judicial occupant. He remained there until 1877, when he moved to 7 St Stephen's Green North, where Robert and Victor Smyth, grocers and wine merchants, had a business which remained a Dublin landmark until a generation ago. There Stoker remained until he left for London. Judging from his correspondence, he seems also to have occupied some other addresses in these years. In 1874, his father wrote to him at 47 Kildare Street. In one letter, dated 7 November 1874, Abraham expressed the hope that his son would be comfortable in Harcourt Street, so Stoker must have moved in around that time. Although the directories give 16 Harcourt Street as his address up to 1878, letters were written to him in 1876 and 1877 at 119 Lower Baggot Street, Dublin, by correspondents as diverse as Walt Whitman, the actress, Geneviève Ward, and the London Assurance Corporation. Stoker is never listed as having lived there but his future brother-in-law, William Thomson, was an occupant in these years. A plaque has been erected to Stoker at 30 Kildare Street, then the site of Cunningham's Lodging House, although there is no record of him having stayed in it.

* * *

Stoker was at this time involved in his father's convoluted finances. In August 1867 he was party to an agreement, with his father and brother, with the West of England Fire and Life Insurance Company 'in the penal sum of one hundred and fifty pounds sterling' to be paid to the company, which was insuring the life of Abraham Stoker for £500 and had given him a loan on the basis of this. He paid off the loan in instalments between February 1868 and August 1870. Quite what the purpose of this loan was is unknown. Stoker was employed in the Civil Service and his father was enjoying a pension which should have made him comfortably off by the standards of the time. Yet loans against insurance policies were a feature of Abraham Stoker's life. In 1872 he took out a loan of £300 against his life assurance policy of £1,000 dating from 1854. This loan may well have been to fund the move abroad which Abraham was undertaking with his wife and some of his children. The whole affair of Abraham's finances remains puzzling in the extreme: for example, in 1871 he lodged £800 with a Miss Julia Frances Rochfort, of Salt Hill, Galway, to be invested in 3 per cent stock in their joint names. Who Miss Rochfort was – her Galway address may point to a Blake connection – and how Abraham was involved in the investment of such a large sum of money remains a mystery. At the same time, the Stokers were recording household expenditure and moneys owed to tradesmen in meticulous detail in a way that does not create the impression of a comfortable financial situation.

While Stoker was shouldering the burden of his father's financial affairs he was reacting against his conservatism, and it is clear that his lifelong attachment to Liberalism was formed as a young man in Dublin. In his *Personal Reminiscences of Henry Irving*, Stoker recalled the marvellous effect of hearing the oratory of Lord Brougham and of John Bright in Dublin. He also recalled a sermon on the Italian statesman, Garibaldi, as an early political influence. Stoker is quite definite about the experience of hearing Brougham: 'I had heard Lord Brougham speak amid a tempest of cheers in the great Round Room of the Dublin Mansion House.'[11] Quite when this was he does not say: the great Whig statesman died in 1868, aged ninety, and his biography contains no reference to visiting Ireland when Stoker was young. Brougham certainly was active on Irish issues: he was a proponent of lightening the burden of Church of Ireland tithes on the Irish Roman Catholic population and prepared his own draft of a bill, but this was in 1833, years before Stoker was born. In addition, his powers were seen to have failed in his later years, when he spent much of his time in Cannes, so the mystery remains of how Stoker could have experienced the oratory of a man evidently at the height of his powers.

The case of John Bright was more straightforward. Stoker recalled the experience of his oratory in lyrical detail. From 1857 to 1870, Bright had pressed for reform in Ireland. At the request of twenty-three Irish Liberal MPs, he came to Dublin in 1866 to attend a banquet in his honour, where he proposed a plan of land purchase for tenants. Interestingly enough, the most ardent supporters of Bright's plan came from the middle-class commercial interests of Dublin, rather than from the tenants themselves. Bright's aim, which Stoker shared, was to reform the landed interest in Ireland, to create 'contentment and tranquility' and thereby to underpin the union of Ireland and Britain. His visit to Ireland in 1866 reinforced the belief of the reform-minded, but not revolutionary, Irish that they could look to the Westminster Parliament for support. At the same time, Bright detested the Fenians – fear of whose activities reached a high point in England in 1866 – and their aim of achieving Irish independence by violent means. In his politics, evident in his fiction, Stoker shared Bright's advocacy of ameliorative reform, combined with detestation of Fenianism, expressed through the character of Mrs. O'Brien in *Lady Athlyne*. Stoker did, however, remain loyal to Home Rule when Bright rejected it although he continued to take an interest in Bright's career until his death in 1889, when he made notes of the resultant by-election.

Bram Stoker was active in many directions in these years, as if he was trying to emulate his hero in an early story, who 'had striven with the single idea of winning such a place in the history of his time', so that he could say: 'I am worthy, for I too have become great.'[12] *The Green Room Book* of 1908, presumably on the basis of information provided by Stoker himself, stated that he had 'acted as dramatic, art and literary critic for several journals in both England and Ireland' in addition to his Civil Service job and Trinity College activities; he was also teaching grinds.[13] He even found time to crusade for the arts. In 1872 he tried, unsuccessfully, to persuade Sir Richard Wallace, whose bequest later formed the Wallace Collection in London and who was a director of the National Gallery of Ireland, to bring his collection to Dublin. On a personal level, he applied for the post of Dublin city treasurer; Lady Wilde had high hopes of his success: she wrote to Oscar about the absconding of Nugent Burke, treasurer of Dublin Corporation, with large debts and reported that Stoker was expected to get the vacancy: 'He never gets into debt, and his character is excellent.' Abraham Stoker, however, had no such illusions: he advised his son that only an advanced Liberal or Roman Catholic would get the post and Stoker was indeed unsuccessful.[14]

A visit that Stoker made to Dublin, after he had become Irving's acting manager, precipitated reminiscences of Stoker as he had appeared to his Dublin contemporaries in these years:

> We are all intensely delighted at the thought of having Bram Stoker amongst us again, even for a few days. We have missed him dreadfully since Henry beguiled him from Dublin. He was never a beauty by any means, but we all loved him. He was an excellent 'party' young man, and of course, had always heaps of invitations. He talked to the old ladies – got supper for half-a-dozen fair ones together, by diving his tall form hither and thither amongst the crowds about the tables – and, when he stood up to dance, had a way of making a charge, which effectually cleared a passage through the most thronged ball-rooms. Everybody made way for Stoker – his coming was like a charge of cavalry, or a rush of fixed bayonets – nobody dreamed of not giving way before him, and so he and his partner had it all their own way. How my heart used to jump in my dancing days when Stoker asked me for a waltz! I knew that it meant triumph, twirling, ecstasy, elysium, ices, and flirtation![15]

Years after his death, a Dublin columnist also recalled the impression which Stoker had made in this era:

> There are still many Dubliners who knew Bram Stoker well; for he played no small part in the life of Dublin . . . Bram Stoker was one of Dublin's personalities – or, as we prefer to call them, 'characters' – and was as famed in his work as a dramatic critic and man of letters as his brother, Sir Thornley Stoker, was in his profession of surgeon . . . For twenty-seven years he remained [in London] as private secretary to Irving – but he never lost his Dublin accent![16]

Trinity College was the basis of Stoker's circle of friends. He was not exaggerating when he wrote to Walt Whitman in 1872 that he had a large number of acquaintants and five or six friends who cared much for him.[17] These might have included Marie and Ina Godkins whom he saw off on the Liverpool steamer from the North Wall in Dublin in October 1871. And Stoker would surely have included John Joseph Robinson as one of his close friends. Robinson was younger than Stoker, having entered Trinity College Dublin in 1869, from Blackheath School. He shared Stoker's literary, debating and sporting interests at Trinity, before becoming a clergyman on graduation. Letters he wrote after Stoker had moved to London reveal a deep and emotional relationship. On New Year's Day 1880 Robinson wrote to Stoker, just after the birth of his son, Noel, addressing him as 'Very dear old Boy', sending hearty congratulations on the birth of a son and waxing lyrical about the new feelings of fatherhood in Stoker and of maternity in Florence. Stoker, however, does not appear to have been as committed to the friendship after he settled in London and a clearly worried Robinson wondered if he had upset him in any way.[18] Hints of another friendship and echoes of an active social life in Dublin are contained in a letter written to Stoker from Yokohama in 1903 by R.F. Walsh, recalling happy evenings in the Queen's Theatre and memories of 'old Rathgar times'.[19]

FIVE

Emerging Writer

I shall get my typewriter this very hour and begin transcribing.

(*Dracula*, Mina Harker's Journal)

Even as he came to the end of his rugby career, Stoker was trying his hand as an actor in the Trinity College Boat Club Dramatic Society at its clubhouse in Ringsend. In February 1870 he 'elicited frequent rounds of applause' as David in Richard Brinsley Sheridan's comic masterpiece, *The Rivals* (1775); in March and June 1870, he received positive notices in the Dublin newspapers for his role in *The School for Scandal*. Traces of Sheridan's influence might be glimpsed in the malapropisms used by Andy, the driver in *The Snake's Pass*. Stoker continued his career with the Trinity Dramatic Society: in 1871 he featured in Samuel Lover's one-act extravaganza, *The Happy Man* (1839), in which he was held to have 'showed great knowledge of the principles of burlesque', playing the major character of Ram-Rusti.[1] Lover was, like Stoker, a Dubliner who had found success as a writer in London. The celebrations which followed these performances would continue to a late hour and were fairly boisterous. In April 1874, for example, at the impromptu dance after a performance in Ringsend, a lady and gentleman fell down and while most of the men present rushed to help the lady up, one horsy individual sweeping around in the dance called out: 'sit on her head!'

Stoker's work is replete with allusions to the theatre. When he wrote of the infatuation of the character of Esse in *The Shoulder of Shasta* with the theatre, he was writing from the heart:

to Esse a theatre was a veritable wonderland. Like all persons of pure imagination, the theatre itself was but a means to an end. She did not think of a play as a play, but as a reality, and so her higher education – the education of the heart, the brain, and the soul – was pursued; and by the sequence of her own emotion and her memory of them, she became [*sic*], each time she saw a play, to know herself a little better, and so to better know the world and its dwellers.[2]

Even earlier, in 'The Primrose Path', Stoker had expressed his ambiguous fascination with the stage through the character of Jerry and his feeling that he needed to move to London to develop as a writer:

> He had . . . a strange longing to share in the unknown life of the dramatic world. Moth-like he had buzzed around the footlights when a boy, and had never lost the slight romantic feeling which such buzzing ever inspires. Once or twice his professional work had brought him within the magic precincts where the stage-manager is king, and there the weirdness of the place, with its myriad cords and chains, and traps, and scenes, and flies, had more than ever enchanted him.

He was also aware that theatrical life, 'save on occasions, begins late, even for subordinates', and: 'It is the misery of all those whose work is connected with the arts that there is a spice of uncertainty in everything.' Stoker would live much of his subsequent working life under the shadow of the first prophecy and the remainder of his days after Irving's death with ample time for reflection on the second. Nevertheless, Stoker's larger ambition won the day: while a character called Parnell makes the case for staying in Ireland, Jerry's desire to go to England is compared with the ambition of Alexander the Great, the need to expand horizons. Another character muses that London is the place 'where Progress speaks with no puny voice and works with no lazy hand' but with the rider that 'the greatness, and wealth, and strength, have their counterfoils in crime, and poverty, and disease'.

In 1890 he would mock provincial theatre critics, stating that provincialism implied 'a narrowness of vision or an intolerance of spirit tacitly taken to arise from inadequate experience . . . [Provincialism applies to] those who, though enjoying the opportunities of larger culture, find themselves . . . eternally limited by their provincial littleness.' He was not going to be caught in that trap. The chance now offered of employment was indeed a temptation. If he could adopt the new life he would have an opportunity to combine his romantic taste and his trade experience, and would be moreover in that wider field for exertion to which he had long looked forward.[3]

Stoker's love affair with the theatre had begun early: he admired the actor, John Lawrence Toole, the lifelong friend of Henry Irving, from the age of twelve. As a youth he saw him from the pit of the theatre and once or twice in the street. He used to look at the house near the gasworks in Ringsend where Toole had lodgings; there was a belief among the Dublin boys that if you were lucky enough to catch him when he looked out occasionally and made faces, you were sure to lose some of your buttons laughing. He knew Toole to speak to from about 1872.[4] Stoker first saw the touring English actor, Henry Irving, at the Theatre Royal in Dublin on 28 August 1867 as Captain Absolute in Sheridan's *The Rivals*, and then saw him again in May 1871 as Digby Grant, the role in which Irving had had his first major London success the previous year, in James Albery's *Two Roses*.

Disgusted that no review appeared in the Dublin newspapers, Stoker approached Dr Henry Maunsell, proprietor of the *Dublin Evening Mail*, asking that he be allowed to do such reviews. Maunsell was a striking figure of military appearance, tall and slight, and sporting a moustache. Qualified as a medical doctor and a graduate of Trinity College Dublin, he had literary interests and was a close friend of the writers, Charles Lever, also a doctor, and Samuel Lover, both of whom wrote for the *Mail*. Maunsell, the paper's first proprietor, was later joined by Joseph Sheridan Le Fanu, and control of the *Mail* was divided between Maunsell, Le Fanu and Mr J.A. Scott, later editor of the *Irish Times*. Stoker accepted Maunsell's condition that the work be unpaid and began his career as a drama critic in November 1871.

In typically energetic fashion, Stoker revolutionised theatre reviewing in the Dublin newspapers by working out a system under which the reviews could appear the day following a performance, rather than after a day's interval, as had been the case. Established in 1823, the *Dublin Evening Mail* had the reputation of being a Unionist paper from the start. Thomas Sheehan, one of its early literary staff, wrote virulent leaders against the nationalist leader, Daniel O'Connell, and was sentenced to three months' imprisonment for actually assaulting O'Connell. While Stoker evidently had no difficulty writing for a newspaper with this editorial line, it would be a mistake to identify him completely with it, especially as he was a theatre critic rather than a journalist *per se*. The *Mail* was, for example, solidly anti-Gladstone while Stoker was a great admirer of the Liberal statesman. Other, more diverse, influences may have come from the news which Stoker would have imbibed from this paper: its extensive coverage of the 'Eastern War' in 1877 included accounts of the campaign in Montenegro in which the Ottoman forces defeated the Montenegrins: Stoker would later situate the action of *The Lady of the Shroud* in Montenegro, as the Land of the Blue Mountains, with the gallant mountaineers taking on the might of the Turkish forces.

Dublin's Theatre Royal was central to Stoker's life as a theatre critic. It had been founded by Henry Harris of Covent Garden, George IV had visited it in 1821 and stars appearing there in the 1820s and 1830s included Macready, Edmund Kean and the Kembles. Fanny Kemble wrote of being escorted back to her hotel by a bodyguard of 200 men 'shouting and hurrahing like mad'. John Harris, who became a friend of Stoker's, took over the Theatre Royal in 1851 and refurbished it. Stoker remembered it as a huge theatre, which indeed it was. This was not the only Dublin theatre which he visited as a drama critic: he covered the opening night of Oliver Goldsmith's *She Stoops to Conquer* at the new Gaiety Theatre and also reviewed plays at the Queen's Theatre and the Exhibition Palace. Stoker's easy intimacy with the theatre and actors was illustrated by the fact that he was on stage at the Theatre Royal in August 1872 chatting with the cast during their performance of Sheridan's *The School for Scandal* by the visiting Haymarket Company. The animation of the conversation was such that Stoker feared the audience would hear them.

It was only natural that Stoker should have mixed freely with the theatrical profession. He was friendly with luminaries such as Dion Boucicault, the nineteenth-century Irish-born actor and playwright who influenced the evolution of drama on both sides of the Atlantic. In April 1872, Boucicault remarked in conversation with Stoker that one reason why national theatres were failures was that an audience should never come to the theatre with their sentiments in their pockets, and Stoker remained a lifelong opponent of a national theatre in Britain. Stoker provided encouragement to actors and actresses and corresponded with some of them at length. The actress, Helen Barry, unburdened herself to him, hinting darkly at an unsuitable 'past' as well as asking his opinion on her play, to which he replied with a fourteen-page letter of advice. The world of the theatre even permeated Stoker's dreams: in October 1871 he dreamed of a mad female theatre critic who got into a butter cask to shoot pirates through the bung-hole with a crossbow!

Within his family, the situation was ambiguous: his father was a keen theatregoer who had introduced him to its delights from an early age but frowned on it as a profession. Late in life, Stoker noted that there was not in the United States the same violent opposition to the choice of the stage as a profession 'that holds more or less in all the European nations. Of course, the situation is always looked in the face by parents and guardians, and the pros and cons summed up and weighed.'[5] Abraham Stoker's opposition to the theatre as a way of life may have been grounded in direct family experience. The Stoker family papers contain a letter dated 1882 from an Eliza Sarah Stoker to a Mr Billington – a name that would feature in *Dracula* – setting out the circumstances of her life as an actress. She had played on the London stage before a broken leg made her unfit for the profession and reduced her to straitened circumstances. The nature of her connection to Stoker's family is not clear but the fact that the letter was in its possession would point to a fairly close link.[6]

Abraham Stoker may have been concerned about the nature of his son's relationship with one of the most remarkable actresses of her generation.

When Stoker dedicated *The Lady of the Shroud* 'To my Dear Old Friend The Comtesse De Guerbel (Geneviève Ward)' towards the end of his life, he was publicly acknowledging a deep friendship which went back to November 1873, when he had strolled into the Theatre Royal, Dublin, to see what was on. The play being performed was Legouve's *Adrienne Lecouvreur* and he was captivated by Geneviève Ward: 'The lady who played Adrienne interested me at once; she was like a triton amongst minnows. She was very handsome; of a rich dark beauty, with clear-cut classical features, black hair, and great eyes that now and again flashed fire. I sat in growing admiration of her powers . . . she was so masterful, so dominating . . . that I could not understand it.' He asked John Harris, the theatre manager, to arrange an introduction. Four days later, Stoker was introduced a second time to Ward, by Wilson King of Pittsburgh, the United States Consul and a great friend of Stoker's: 'And there and then began a close friendship [with Ward] which has never faltered, which has been one of the delights of my life and which will I trust remain as warm as it is now till the death of either of us shall cut it short'.[7]

Stoker first wrote about Ward in the *Dublin Evening Mail* of 17 November 1873 when he announced that 'the celebrated tragedienne' was to appear at the Theatre Royal. He reviewed her in the role of Lucrezia Borgia in the *Mail* of 18 November, and in *Adrienne Lecouvreur* three days later, when he termed her performance 'a decided success'. Her movements were graceful, he told his readers, 'she walks across the stage rhythmically, as it were music'. He was more critical of her performance in *Medea* on the 25th when he mixed a generally positive review with the advice that she should pace better her 'magnificent tragic powers'.[8] Their correspondence shows that they socialised together in intellectual circles in Dublin, which included figures such as Edward Dowden and Sir William and Lady Wilde. Stoker's friendship with Ward was such that he stayed with her and her mother, Lucy, when he passed through Paris in 1875 on his return from visiting his parents in Switzerland. Among the sights he saw was the Paris Bourse, where his first impression on entering was of ten thousand cocks crowing at once. He told his parents that he had met in Paris a 'Miss Henry' and decided to write a play for her. His father was less than impressed, telling Stoker in 1876 that in his own early life he had known actors and actresses and their society, while agreeable, was not desirable. Abraham was presumably alluding to the perception of loose morality in the theatrical profession. 'Miss Henry' may have been the girl in Stoker's excellent short story, 'The Burial of the Rats', which is set in Paris; the central character is in love with her but they are forbidden by her parents to communicate for a year. She was almost certainly Geneviève

Ward, although in real life the disapproval was more on his parents' side than hers.

Ward's social position at this time was certainly difficult: the daughter of a well-to-do American family, she had, in 1855 as a young girl, fallen in love with and married the Russian Count de Gerbel of Nicolaeiff in a civil ceremony in Nice. He attempted to use legal trickery to declare the marriage invalid but, through the medium of the Tsar was forced to marry her in a religious ceremony at Warsaw, her father packing a firearm in case he again had second thoughts. At the church door she bowed to him before parting; they were never to see each other again. She retained therefore a title but not a husband and developed a career, first as a singer and then as an actress.

The surviving correspondence between Stoker and Geneviève from the mid-1870s underlines the affectionate nature of their relationship although it is uncertain if they were actually lovers. In one letter, she expressed approval that he was drawing inspiration for a play he was then writing from Madame Roland (1754–93), a conspicuous intellectual figure during the French Revolution who was executed when power shifted from her husband's Girondist party to more radical revolutionary elements. She was clearly to be the subject of his play which does not seem to have come to fruition. Ward suggested that a visit to Paris, where she lived with her mother, might be the way to develop his research and offered to assist. Another letter, written to Stoker from Paris in 1875, is also very warm and affectionate. Ward was, she said, in an apartment overlooking the spot where the guillotine had stood during the French Revolution (where Madame Roland would have been executed). She was anxious to hear how Stoker was progressing with the plot for his play. Her own research into Madame Roland did not quite agree with Stoker's approach and again she suggested that if Stoker came to Paris they could do research together in the Bibliothèque Nationale.

Lucy Ward struck a similar note when she wrote to Stoker from Leicester in September 1875. Her daughter had had two nights of great success as Lucrezia Borgia and she almost fancied that it was before 'our dear Dublin audience'. Lucy wondered why they had not heard from Stoker in such a long time. She asked how his play was coming along and if he would visit Paris again soon: he knew their 'den' and a plate, knife and fork were always marked for him. Stoker must have given illness as an excuse for his silence, as Lucy Ward expressed her sympathy in a letter of December 1875 and renewed her invitation for him to come and stay. Stoker travelled in France and Italy again the following year, in October, but it is not clear if he went to Paris this time. While Lucy Ward wrote to Stoker as 'My dear young Friend', her daughter preserved a more correct form, addressing him as

'Dear Mr. Stoker' in her letters. She repeated her mother's invitation to him when she wrote from London in September 1876. She mentioned casually that she was conversing with Victor Hugo.[9]

Stoker added to his extraordinary range of activities by acting as editor of a new Dublin evening paper, the *Irish Echo*, published from 6 November 1873 until 24 December 1875. Stoker seems to have stepped down as editor in the spring of 1874. In May 1874 his father wrote him a letter expressing the hope that he would resume his post as editor when the *Echo* was in a more flourishing position, which suggests that Stoker's departure had a financial basis. Abraham Stoker followed up with a letter in June which represented a considerable change of tack from his previous attitude: now he was glad that Stoker had given up the *Echo*: he was sure that the pay would never equal the amount of trouble it entailed and, also, the government did not like its officers being connected with a newspaper, even if it was not a political one. In December, he told Stoker not to worry himself with journalism, as he had not been properly paid for all the trouble he had had with the *Echo*. Abraham's letters show that Stoker continued his efforts to be published elsewhere. In March 1874 he asked if the Dublin periodical, the *Warder*, had returned the story that he had spoken of some time previously.[10] Stoker may have had an entrée to the *Warder* through his Trinity friend, John Robinson, whose family controlled the *Dublin Daily Express* which had been started in 1851 on the premises of the *Warder*.

Some idea of Stoker's earliest creative writing can be gained from an adolescent poem expressing a longing for peace when passionate youth is past.[11] Given his early interest in writing, it seems anomalous that, at Trinity, Stoker was not part of the literary set that published in the various college journals. *Kottabos*, a college miscellany, was started by Robert Yelverton Tyrrell shortly after his election as a Fellow of Trinity in 1868. Just three years older than Stoker, Tyrrell would later hold the positions of Professor of Latin, Greek and Ancient History at the university where he was, like Stoker, an advocate of Walt Whitman's in the 1870s. He remained friendly with Stoker and frequented the Lyceum Theatre when Stoker was acting manager there. *Kottabos* published translations from the classics and original work. Its list of contributors included many of Stoker's friends and contemporaries: Tyrrell himself, Edward Dowden, Standish O'Grady, Oscar Wilde and William Gorman Wills, the writer and painter who would later be a major creative force as a playwright at the Lyceum. Although Stoker was not a contributor, he would have read *Kottabos* and it is interesting that W.G. Wills's 'Ballad of Graf Brom', published there, featured a ghostly procession of dead women undone by a rake who had come to gloat over his death, rather like the procession of the dead in Stoker's later novel, *The Mystery of the Sea*. An older contemporary of Stoker's, Robert Henry Martley, was the author of a poem, 'The Vampire', which featured in the journal in 1875. Thomas W.H. Rolleston's poem, 'On Walt Whitman's "Leaves of Grass"', also published in *Kottabos*, is indicative of the worship of Whitman by Stoker's Trinity contemporaries, in which he fully shared. Rolleston was ten years younger than Stoker and was educated at Trinity in the 1870s; in 1885 he founded the *Dublin University Review*, which published early works of the Irish literary revival. He was secretary to the Irish Literary Society in London in the early 1890s. Nor is there any indication that Stoker contributed to another contemporary review, *Hermathena* or to the *Dublin University Magazine*, which Joseph Sheridan Le Fanu edited following his purchase of it in 1861, although many of its articles were unsigned.

The possibility of a direct connection between Stoker and Le Fanu is fascinating. The influence of Le Fanu's 'Carmilla' (1872) on Stoker's story, 'Dracula's Guest' and on *Dracula* is generally, if not universally, accepted; indeed, some critics see Le Fanu as exercising a pervasive influence on Stoker's general fictional output. From a biographical perspective, the question is whether he exerted a direct personal influence on Stoker in his formative years. Certainly, Le Fanu was an influential figure in the Dublin of Stoker's youth, especially in the Trinity College circles that Stoker inhabited. As a young man with literary ambition, he could hardly have been unaware of Le Fanu's extraordinary output of a dozen novels published between his return to novel-writing in 1863 and his death a decade later, especially as much of this output was published in the *Dublin University Magazine*. Le Fanu's *The Watcher and other Weird Stories* (1894) was in Stoker's library. Given Le Fanu's eccentric personal habits, he might certainly be added to the long list of potential influences on the shaping of the character of Dracula. According to Percy FitzGerald, a London-based Irish man of letters who would be connected with Stoker at the Lyceum Theatre, Le Fanu lived in a gloomy mansion in Merrion Square, where he was a neighbour of the Wildes; indeed, Oscar played with the Le Fanu children as a boy. Alfred Perceval Graves recorded how Le Fanu withdrew from society after the death of his wife and was dubbed 'The Invisible Prince' by Dubliners: 'and indeed he was for long almost invisible, except to his family and most familiar friends, unless at odd hours of the evening, when he might be seen stealing, like the ghost of his former self, between his newspaper office and his home in Merrion Square.'[12] The father in Le Fanu's *Uncle Silas* behaves in similar fashion after the death of his wife.

Le Fanu took an interest in Graves after he came second in a Shakespeare prize ode competition in 1864, offering to publish the ode in the *Dublin University Magazine* and to arrange favourable mention of it in the *Dublin Evening Mail*, both of which he edited at that time. It was to be the foundation of a long friendship. It is indicative of how Le Fanu kept in touch with intellectual developments at Trinity and, given the common circles in which they moved, that Stoker and Le Fanu must have been aware of each other. Another possible link was Thomas Le Fanu, a nephew of the writer, who was a first-class clerk in the Chief Secretary's Office when Stoker served there.

Whether or not he knew Le Fanu, few influences on Stoker's development were more profound than that of Edward Dowden, the Corkman who was Professor of English at Trinity College. A few years older than Stoker, he outlived him by a year. Though he has now fallen into critical disfavour, he had an international reputation in his lifetime as a critic, for his work on Shakespeare and Shelley especially. Inclined to be dismissed nowadays as a stodgy Victorian, his early espousal of Walt Whitman was radical by contemporary standards. The son of a Presbyterian mother and Church of Ireland father, his upbringing, like Stoker's, was devoutly Christian with a strong evangelical puritan streak. Dowden shared with Stoker too the political complexity of background common to so many of the families of Irish Protestant writers in the nineteenth century. While his uncle Richard, who was Lord Mayor of Cork in 1845, was an active supporter of nationalist causes, Dowden was passionately committed to maintaining the political union of Great Britain and Ireland and spent much of his energy later in life promoting this cause.

Dowden entered Trinity College Dublin at sixteen and shared rooms with his brother, John, later Bishop of Edinburgh and a source of information for Stoker's novel, *Lady Athlyne*. Like Stoker, he was active in the Phil. Indeed, there was a nice symmetry in the coincidence of Dowden being presented with a key to the society's rooms and Stoker being made an honorary member at the same time. In 1867 he filled the newly created Chair of English Literature at Trinity College Dublin which he occupied until his death. His friends included major contemporary writers such as the poet Robert Browning, the novelist George Eliot and, most notably, Walt Whitman, which scandalised his more conservative Trinity contemporaries. John Butler Yeats later held Edward Dowden up to his poet son as a perpetual warning of what happens to gifted men who refuse to trust their own nature and so cannot become themselves and instead lapse into provincialism. When James Joyce called on Dowden for support in seeking a position at the National Library of Ireland, Dowden dismissed him as unsuitable. He also refused to join W.B. Yeats and others in supporting Oscar Wilde in his hour of need. Stoker's friend, John Todhunter, was among those who tried, unsuccessfully, to bring Dowden around to a more positive view of Irish nationalism and bitter words passed between Dowden on the one hand and Yeats and Standish O'Grady on the other as the 'leaders of nationalist literature'.[13]

It was Dowden's championing of Walt Whitman that exercised the most direct influence on Stoker in the 1870s. The initial spark had been the hostile response of some British critics to Michael Rossetti's 1868 selection of Whitman's poems that created a stir at Trinity College Dublin where conservatives rejected its sexual content (included in its titles was 'To a Common Prostitute'). Stoker gave two somewhat different accounts of how he first came into contact with Whitman's work. He wrote to Whitman himself in 1872 saying that he had heard two men in college discussing his work. One of them was reading aloud passages at which both of them laughed: 'They chose only those passages which are most foreign to British ears and made fun of them. Something struck me that I had judged you hastily. I took home the volume and read it far into the night.' In his *Personal Reminiscences of Henry Irving* he said that he had asked a man in possession of the poems in the college if he could have a look at his copy; the man gave it to him:

'Take the damned thing,' he said; 'I've had enough of it!'
I took the book with me into the Park and in the shade of an elm tree began to read it. Very shortly my own opinion began to form; it was diametrically opposed to that which I had been hearing. From that hour I became a lover of Walt Whitman.

He found others of the same view and they began propagating the gospel of Walt Whitman in the teeth of conservative opposition, with resultant feelings of intellectual superiority sufficient to overcome the pain of ridicule. Edward Dowden was one of the few who took a more liberal view of *Leaves of Grass* and his opinion carried great weight.[14] Stoker and Dowden were young men reacting enthusiastically to a radical new literary star. Stoker may have felt a particular attraction to the 'Old Ireland' poem in *Leaves of Grass* with its image of Ireland as a fallen queen whose son is reborn in a new country, similar to the belief in an Irish rebirth in the United States expressed in his address to the Historical Society as Auditor in 1872.

Edward Dowden was in touch with Whitman from 1871, when he wrote to him: 'You have many readers in Ireland, and those who do not feel a qualified delight in your poems – do not love them by degree, but with an absolute, a personal love. We none of us question that yours is the clearest, and sweetest, and fullest American voice. We grant as true that all you claim for yourself [*sic*]. And you gain steadily among us new readers and admirers.'

Dowden mentioned that R.Y. Tyrrell, a Fellow of Trinity College Dublin, had recently given a good public lecture on Whitman's poems.[15] Robert Atkinson, Professor of Sanskrit at Trinity and another of the Whitman enthusiasts in the Dublin of that era, was also a friend of Stoker's.

In 1876 Dowden wrote to Whitman in the wake of a vicious attack on him by Peter Bayne in the *Contemporary Review*, drawing attention to a refutation by Standish O'Grady. Whitman referred to O'Grady as 'a young man of great spirit – talent: of high and masterful ambition'. O'Grady was one of the circle of Whitman's admirers clustered around Dowden and was impressed especially with Whitman's engagement with the supernatural, as well as the passion which permeated his concept of male friendship. Dowden also told of reading a paper on Whitman to the Fortnightly Club and getting a positive response from his students at Trinity when he read his poems aloud. Stoker attended that meeting of the Fortnightly Club, an informal occasional gathering of Dublin men for free discussions, on 14 February 1876, at which Whitman's poetry was attacked by a speaker 'challenging . . . the whole collection of poems for mention of one decent woman'. Both Dowden, in 'an impassioned speech', and Stoker argued for the merit of Whitman's work and, in Stoker's opinion, they carried the issue. Stoker wrote a self-styled egoistical entry in his diary: 'Spoke – I think well.'[16] So excited was he that he stayed up that night writing a long letter to Whitman; Stoker stated that he had written to him before 'but never so freely'. He had indeed drafted a letter to Whitman, four years previously, in 1872, but shrank from mailing it. He now enclosed it with his covering letter, explaining that he had become even more devoted to the poet in the meantime and how he waged 'a perpetual war with many friends' on Whitman's behalf.

The 1872 letter was written in a tone of defiant self-revelation. Stoker described himself as a man living in an atmosphere 'prejudiced to the truths you sing and your manner of singing them'. He spoke of wanting to call Whitman 'Comrade' and to talk to him 'as men who are not poets do not often talk . . . You are a true man, and I would like to be one myself, and so I would be towards you as a brother and as a pupil to his master.' Stoker went on to give an extraordinary self-portrait, describing himself as 6 feet 2 inches tall and weighing 12 stone: 'I am ugly but strong and determined and have a large bump over my eyebrows . . . I am equal in temper and cool in disposition and have a large amount of self-control and am naturally secretive to the world.' He went on: 'How sweet a thing it is for a strong healthy man with a woman's eyes and a child's wishes to feel that he can speak so to a man who can be if he wishes father, and brother and wife to his soul. I don't think you will laugh, Walt Whitman, nor despise me, but at all events I thank you for all the love and sympathy you have given me in common with my kind.' Whitman wondered if Stoker's apparent spontaneity was in fact studied but was inclined to accept it at face value. He drafted a reply, dated 6 March 1876:

> My dear young man,
> Your letters have been most welcome to me – welcome to me as Person and as Author – I don't know which most – You did well to write me so unconventionally, so fresh, so manly, and so affectionately, too. I too hope (though it is not probable) that we shall one day meet each other. Meantime I send you my friendship and thanks.
> . . . Write to me again.[17]

A good deal could be read into Stoker's letter to Whitman. There is an element of hero worship and, at the very least, a need to elicit understanding from an older man whose poetic sensibility would have equipped him to empathise with the younger man's deepest feelings. These feelings included a lack of confidence in his appearance: when a child called him ugly in 1871, he felt that the accusation was true. He was also describing himself as a strong man with a woman's heart and the wishes of a lonely child in his notebook in 1871, the year before he drafted the letter to Whitman. Whether the belief that he had a woman's heart and eyes reveals insecurity about his sexual identity or even homosexual tendencies is a moot point. A poem written in March 1870, 'Acrostic', could be to a man: intertwining the pursuit of love and glory, it ends with a reference to entombing love within the sepulchre of a friend. An 1874 poem, 'Too Lightly Won', is written from the perspective of a jilted woman. Equally, however, there are many references in Stoker's private notebook to pretty women whom he admired and discussed with friends.

At this time, Stoker was also very closely connected with the Wilde family. When, in *The Snake's Pass*, Stoker has the character of Andy, the 'Irish coachman', exclaim, 'Musha, but Docther Wilde himself, Rest his sowl! Couldn't have put is aisier to grip',[18] he was paying tribute to the memory of his old friend, Sir William Wilde and his ability as a scientist and antiquarian. Stoker's intimacy with the Wildes is evident from a letter written by Abraham Stoker to his son in December 1874 when he says: 'I suppose you dined with Lady Wilde as usual.'[19] At the time Stoker knew them, Sir William and Lady Wilde lived in great style in a large Georgian house at 1 Merrion Square in the centre of Dublin. Sir William's position may have been blighted by a libel case brought by a young woman soon after he was knighted in 1864 but he and his wife continued to be a social and intellectual force in Dublin up to the time of Sir William's death in 1876. According to W.B. Yeats, the Wilde family was 'dirty, untidy, daring'; the Dublin-born playwright, George Bernard Shaw, had similar memories, adding that Sir William Wilde was reported to have had a family in every farmhouse, the wonder being that Lady Wilde did not mind. The contrast for Stoker, who stayed with the Wildes over Christmas 1875, with his own background of biblical respectability, could hardly have been greater and he must have found the intellectual daring of the Wildes exhilarating. Through them, he would have come into contact with the leading intellectual figures in the Dublin of the day.

Stoker's first major published piece had been in an English journal: 'The Crystal Cup' appeared in the *London Society*, a popular monthly, in September 1872 and attracted a very positive newspaper reference. It has been described by a modern critic as 'the first flowering of Stoker's talent at the age of twenty-five, as well as the first faint shade of the vampire masterpiece to come'.[20] Divided into three sections, 'The Dream-birth', 'The Feast of Beauty' and 'The Story of the Moonbeam', the key to the story is the dream of the narrator, Frank, to create a vase of outstanding beauty which will earn the freedom of his new bride, Aurora (whose name Stoker had, of course, borrowed from the Greek mythological goddess of the dawn). Both are prisoners of a king who is a lover of beauty. Called upon to sing, Aurora performs a song to Freedom which holds the King spellbound; at the song's climax, its power causes the crystal cup to shatter, leaving the King dead and Aurora free.

Stoker maintained his efforts to be published in London. In 1874 he wrote to the editor of *Blackwood's Magazine*, enclosing a manuscript entitled 'Jack Hammon's Vote', which had already been refused by the journals, *Cornhill*, *McMillan* and *Temple Bar*, with prophetic pessimism: 'I am anxious to see if you will add to the number.' He even took the precaution of folding it into a stamped wrapper in case they did not read it; he asked not to be thought impertinent, pointing out that it would take only fifteen or twenty minutes to read. Stoker's defeatist approach was tactically maladroit, virtually inviting refusal. *Blackwood's* duly obliged by neither reading the story nor reaching a decision speedily: Stoker again wrote to the editor in August 1875, this time in a more conciliatory mood, asking that his manuscript be returned if it was not going to be published but suggesting that the editor hold on to it if there was a prospect of publishing it in the future.[21] While Stoker may have lacked confidence in this instance, his overall determination to succeed as a writer in these early days underlines the point that his creative impulses were not simply the response to Henry Irving with which some critics explain away the writing of *Dracula* twenty years later.

He began writing for the *Shamrock*, a Dublin weekly journal which provided an outlet for popular fiction, some time in the early 1870s. A letter from his father in 1874 enquired: 'Have you been writing anything new lately? Some of what you had in the "Shamrock" I liked very much.'[22] His breakthrough came in 1875 when, within four months of each other, the *Shamrock* published three of his multi-episode stories. The first of these, 'The Primrose Path', appeared from 6 February to 3 March 1875. It is the story of an Irish carpenter, Jerry, who is ruined by taking his family from Dublin to a job in a London theatre. A series of misfortunes lead him down the path of drunkenness, culminating in the murder of his wife and his own suicide. Its setting in a working-class world contrasts with the snobbery and effortlessly upper-class attainments of Stoker's later fictional characters. In this story, the rich, in the personages of Mr Muldoon and his wife, are portrayed negatively; it also has a strong anti-drink moral, embodied in the teetotaller, Mr Parnell, whose name may have been borrowed from Charles Stewart Parnell, the Irish nationalist leader who entered Parliament the year the story was published and was tall, like Stoker's character, as well as possessing obvious political gifts: 'He was a great man at meetings, and liked to talk, for he knew that he talked well.'

'The Primrose Path' is also notable for its mention of Faust when the central character, Jerry, watches a dress rehearsal at the theatre: 'The play was a version of Faust, and the dresses were the same as those used in Gounod's opera . . . Amongst the actors was a tall individual who was performing the part of "Mephistopheles".' Prophetically perhaps, Henry Irving, also a tall individual, who later played this role, has been seen as influencing Stoker's creation of Count Dracula, yet Stoker had not yet seen him perform the role when he wrote this story. His interest in Faust is also shown by a reference to Thomas Carlyle, the Scottish historian and essayist who was an admirer and translator of Goethe. Stoker's mention of Gounod's opera is an early indication of his awareness of the musical tradition connected with Faust. Later, in *Dracula*, he would have Mina Harker write in her journal of hearing good music by Spohr and MacKenzie; Louis Spohr (1794–1859), an avid Wagnerian, composed a Faust opera in 1813.

Stoker's concern with the struggle between good and evil, central to *Dracula*, is evident when Parnell draws for the central character, Jerry, an allegorical picture of the evils of drink: the scene is a bleak moor with blasted trees, reminiscent of the opening of *Macbeth*, with two travellers on a sorry nag, one of whom has but a skull under his slouched hat. Another recurrent theme in Stoker's later work is the conflict inherent in the natures of the two sexes; Jerry's desire to go to England and his wife's equally strong desire to stay in Dublin represent 'the masculine resolution . . . asserting itself over the feminine'. Katey has 'womanly delicacy' and the story is told from her perspective. Sensuality is suspect: the sensual nature is seen as having two evil qualities: obstinacy and cruelty, which are found in Jerry's character. Stoker's ideal relationship between the sexes is evident in the advice which Parnell gives to Katey: there must never be a shadow of suspicion between husband and wife otherwise there would be over their lives 'the shadow of a dark future'.

Certain features of this story anticipate elements of Stoker's later fiction, including the use of dialect. Perhaps the most important prototype which Stoker created in this story is that of the evildoer, a mixture of human and supernatural, living and dead. The barkeeper, Grinnell, has the most repulsive face that Jerry had ever seen: 'a face so drawn and twisted, with nose and lips so eaten away with some strange canker, that it resembled more the ghastly front of a skull than the face of a living man'. Elements of Grinnell would be recreated in Stoker's later fictional monsters, such as Black Murdock in *The Snake's Pass* and Count Dracula. Jerry too has hints of the demonic in his character; just before he murders Katey, he laughs 'the hard, cold laugh of a demon'. The heading of the final instalment, which appeared on 6 March 1875, 'The Trail of the Serpent', anticipated both the title and some of the key features of *The Snake's Pass*, especially the terrible dreams which Katey suffers as doom approaches; these are also similar to the dream world of *Dracula*, which in turn bore more than a passing resemblance to the disturbing dreams which were a leitmotif of Le Fanu's *Carmilla*.

Serialisation of another story, 'Buried Treasures', began in the *Shamrock* the week after 'The Primrose Path' concluded. It too featured themes which would recur in Stoker's later fiction: surrogacy, male bonding, *deus ex machina* means of achieving wealth (Count Dracula was only one of Stoker's fictional characters who does not have to earn money by conventional means), and dreams which are linked with horror and death.

The third of Stoker's stories to appear in the *Shamrock*, 'The Chain of Destiny', was published in May 1875. It opens with the central character, Frank Stanford, having just arrived at Scarp, an old baronial house owned by an elderly couple, the Trevors, which is capable of being 'grim and gigantic in the gloom' in the fashion of Ann Radcliffe. In mentioning that the fireplaces, carved with biblical scenes, would have delighted Washington Irving or Nathaniel Hawthorne, Stoker was paying homage to some of his sources of inspiration. It is easy to see how Irving's tales, Americanised versions of German folk originals, would have appealed to him. Hawthorne's allegorical tales, with their imprint of ancestral guilt derived from his Salem, witch-hunting, judge ancestor, is evident in Stoker's 'The Judge's House' especially, while the Transcendentalism of his associates in Concord, Massachusetts finds an echo in *Dracula*, where it is mentioned as 'a beacon to the angels'. Hawthorne's puritan moral earnestness, his concern with original sin and guilt, reveal preoccupations very similar to Stoker's own. One might see the public marking of sin, the wearing of the letter A for adulterer in *The Scarlet Letter*, as paralleled in the mark on Mina's forehead in *Dracula*.

Mrs. Trevor functions as a surrogate mother figure in 'The Chain of Destiny'. The bond which forms between her and Frank Stanford is a deep one and the relationship which ensues may have reflected that between Stoker himself and Lady Wilde. Mrs. Trevor has a Miss Diana Fothering come to stay with the intention that Frank will fall in love with her, which he duly does. Diana has 'more the independence of a man than the timorousness of a woman', like the later female characters of Stephen in *The Man* and Mina Harker in *Dracula*. Another anticipation of *Dracula* is Frank's difficulty in reconciling apparently supernatural events with the realities of 'this practical nineteenth century'. Illness heightens Diana's natural beauty, just as the beauty of the vampire women in *Dracula* is enhanced by their ghoulish condition. Following a complicated plot, which features visions, demonic transformations, ancient family quarrels and sinister portraits, Frank wins Diana's hand by rescuing her. The rescue theme, common in Stoker's later work, predates his attempted rescue in London some years later of a drowning man.

Similar themes are found in the story, 'Greater Love', published in the *London Magazine*, in 1914, after Stoker's death. This may have been an early story from this period which remained unpublished in Stoker's papers until his widow sifted through them and decided on publication. It is the tale of two men, the best of friends, who love the same girl, Mary. They decide that the narrator, Joe, will first approach her with an offer of marriage. If she rejects him, his friend, Bill, can then try his hand. She accepts Joe and they get married. At the wedding feast Mary falls into the sea and is rescued by Bill, who is drowned in the process. The location of 'Greater Love' beside the sea might point to a location near Clontarf while its ability to deal sympathetically with working-class characters is indicative of early, rather than late, provenance. The plot may draw on an early memorandum for a story which Stoker planned to write of two sailors in love with the same girl. She marries one, but when her husband returns from a sea voyage he sees his young wife crucified on a great cross which stands at the end of the pier, presumably a horrific act of vengeance by the thwarted suitor.

SIX

London in View!

I long to go through the crowded streets of your mighty London, to be in the
midst of the whirl and rush of humanity, to share its life, its change, its death,
and all that makes it what it is.

(*Dracula*, The Count to Jonathan Harker)

Stoker's continuing connection with Trinity College in the 1870s, as well
as his work as a theatre critic, was central to the most momentous meeting
of his life. When Henry Irving gave a 'University Night' during a visit to
Dublin late in 1876, a group of Trinity academics, including the Fellows,
Professor R.Y. Tyrrell and Stoker's former tutor, G.F. Shaw, gathered an
informal 'committee' to write an address of thanks to Irving. This was given
on 11 December 1876; Stoker was asked to do the drafting. In the address,
Stoker laid heavy emphasis on the theatre as an instrument for the improvement of both intellectual and moral culture and paid tribute to Irving for
commending it to a section of society which usually held itself aloof from
it, a theme taken up by Irving in his response. The University Night ended
with tumultuous scenes and Irving's carriage was pulled back to his hotel
from the theatre by wildly enthusiastic Trinity students.

Stoker's contact with Henry Irving on this occasion was to be the start
of a relationship which would dominate the rest of his life.[1] Born John Henry
Brodribb in 1838, Irving derived his stage name from the writer Washington
Irving (who was, as we have seen, an influence on the writing of the young
Stoker) and the evangelical Scottish preacher, Edward Irving. Irving's childhood was spent mostly in Cornwall with his staunchly Methodist maternal
aunt, Sarah Penberthy, and her husband, Isaac, captain of a Cornish tin
mine. Reunited with his parents, now in London, at the age of ten, he
became a clerk after leaving school but was able to enter the world of the
theatre by virtue of a legacy of £100 from a Brodribb uncle. Joining a stock,
or travelling, theatre company in the North of England, he played over 400
roles in more than 300 plays over a period of ten years, until he enjoyed his
first success in London in 1866. On a theatrical tour in Dublin the following
year he met Florence O'Callaghan, daughter of a surgeon-general, and they
married in July 1869. Two children were born in quick succession but

tensions between the couple finally came to a head in 1871 when, following Irving's success on the opening night of *The Bells*, Florence asked him in the carriage on the way home: 'Are you going on making a fool of yourself like this all your life?' Irving got out of the carriage and never returned to their home. He never spoke to Florence again. *The Bells* was staged at the Lyceum in London by the American impresario, H.L. Bateman and catapulted Irving to the front rank of his profession. He was the star of Bateman's company from this point until the American's death in 1875, and for a further two years under the management of his widow.

When Irving came to Dublin with Bateman's company in 1876, Stoker was initially apprehensive that he would 'overthrow [as his theatrical idol] my friend and countryman', the Irish actor, Barry Sullivan, then a great favourite with the Dublin public, but was completely won over by Irving's acting, especially his Hamlet. His enthusiasm is clear from his reviews in the *Dublin Evening Mail*. On the evening of Saturday, 9 December 1876, when Irving gave the 'University Night', Stoker waxed lyrical:

Mr. Irving's performance was magnificent. It seemed as though he were put on his mettle by the University distinction of the day to do justice to the stateliness of his mighty theme and, at the same time, was fired to the utmost enthusiasm . . . at the warmth of his reception. Not Mr. Irving alone, but the whole of the profession should be proud of such a tribute to histrionic genius . . . it marks an era in the history of the stage.[2]

Irving was sufficiently impressed by Stoker's insights into his playing of Hamlet as a mystic that he asked John Harris to introduce him to the author of the review. This was arranged and they had supper together, with three of Irving's friends, at his hotel. The following Sunday they met again for dinner, also in the company of a few of Irving's friends. Stoker identified this point as the start of a loving friendship which he described in distinctly undead terms: 'then began the close friendship between us which only terminated with his life – if indeed friendship, like any other form of love, can ever terminate'.[3] Irving reciprocated Stoker's feelings and recited Thomas Hood's dramatic poem, 'The Dream of Eugene Aram' for his new friend's benefit. Based on the true-life story of an eighteenth-century English scholar who murdered his close friend, Daniel Clark, in a fit of jealousy following the discovery of an affair between Clark and his wife (changed to a mercenary motive by Hood), the poem explored the psychology of a conscience-stricken murder and featured stanzas such as:

And how the sprites of injured men
Shriek upward from the sod;
Ay, how the ghostly hand will point
To show the burial clod;
And unknown facts of guilty acts
Are seen in dreams from God!

The poem ends with stern-faced officers of the law bringing Aram to face justice.

Stoker's description of the effect which Irving's masterful performance had on him has been a key element in psychological analyses of their subsequent relationship. Stoker was 'spellbound' by 'Irving's commanding force', by 'the magnetism of his genius'. After the melodramatic climax of his reading, Irving 'collapsed half fainting'. This, however, was nothing compared to the effect that his reading had on Stoker, who 'burst out into something like a violent fit of hysterics'. Irving went into his room and returned with a signed photograph of himself, dedicated to his 'dear friend Stoker'. In retrospect, Stoker attributed this gesture to Irving's realisation that Stoker's 'capacity for receptive emotion was something akin in forcefulness to his power of creating it . . . In those moments of our mutual emotion he too had found a friend and knew it. Soul had looked into soul! From that hour began a friendship as profound, as close, as lasting as can be between two men.' The emotion remained with Stoker all his life and came flooding back as he wrote his reminiscences of Irving after his friend's death with such strength that he was 'unmanned'.[4]

What Stoker does not say in his *Personal Reminiscences of Henry Irving* is that 'Eugene Aram' was very much part of Irving's repertoire and that he must have been conscious of the effect it had on people. In other words, in performing it for Stoker in a confined situation, he set out to create precisely the effect achieved. Ellen Terry, who noted that Irving was always ready to recite it, got him to tone down the intensity of his recital in ordinary rooms as the effect was overpowering. The critic, Austin Brereton, author of a brief biography of Irving, recounted how the actor would be bathed in sweat after a performance of 'Eugene Aram', such was the intensity of effort he put into it. Percy FitzGerald, a theatrical friend of both Stoker and Irving, wrote of the piece's power while Irving was still alive: 'The audience sat spellbound . . . I have seen all kinds of audiences in both hemispheres, and under all sorts of circumstances, and never saw a theatre full of people more under the control of a story.' Clement Scott (1841–1904), author and principal dramatic critic of the *Daily Telegraph*, recalled how Irving 'electrified the audience' with the piece. Irving's grandson, Laurence

Irving, has suggested that Irving may have had some ulterior motive in offering to read 'Eugene Aram' to Stoker; while he was not specific about this, it can be assumed he meant to suggest that Irving calculated, successfully, that Stoker would fall under his spell.[5] If ever there was a point in their lives when they enacted the roles of Count Dracula and his hypnotised victims, this was surely it.

The techniques used by Irving in 'Eugene Aram' were also part of his stock in trade. For example, at the end of playing Richelieu, 'he collapsed, almost sinking into a swoon'. Similarly, after playing all the roles in *Hamlet*: 'When he ceased, almost fainting with the prolonged effort and excess of emotion, the pent-up enthusiasm burst forth like a storm.' It is important to remember though that Stoker did not equate a man breaking down with weakness: on the contrary, in *Personal Reminiscences of Henry Irving*, he emphasises his own strength at this time and, in *The Watter's Mou'*, Stoker has Willy breaking down crying with the abandon which marks strong men when spiritual pain breaks down the barriers of their pride. Stoker was using the term 'hysterics' in its contemporary context, not that of more than a century later. The great nineteenth-century authority on the subject, Jean-Martin Charcot, of whom Stoker was well aware by the time he wrote *Personal Reminiscences*, saw hysteria as a disorder suffered by women or very impressionable men who were 'well-developed, not enervated by an indolent or too studious mode of life'.[6]

Irving returned to Dublin the next year to give a reading at Trinity College which Stoker wrote up in breathless terms for the *Dublin Evening Mail*. He reported that the examination hall of the College had been full to overflowing the previous afternoon, when Irving was greeted by a hearty welcome. He gave the third act of *Othello* 'triumphantly', performing the characters of Othello, Iago and Cassio himself, without props. He also did excerpts from *Richard III* and 'Eugene Aram', which moved Stoker to write:

> Mr Irving is a great tragedian . . . He is a great melodramatic actor . . . but in nothing does he sustain his terrible force so well as when reciting Hood's poem . . . The onlooker feels his blood turning cold to look at the actor's face and to listen to the broken tones of his voice. And surely the rapt attention of the audience, the thrill of fear and terror, the pause at the end, followed by the wild burst of applause, will live as memories of success in the mind of the actor as truly as his marvellous performances will live in the hearts of his audience.[7]

Irving was accompanied on this occasion by Harry J. Loveday, a former musician whom he engaged as stage manager at the Lyceum towards the end of the Bateman era. Loveday was steeped in theatrical history, his father having been musical director at Drury Lane when the great early nineteenth-century actor, Edmund Kean, reigned supreme there. Irving was gathering around him members of the management team which would sustain his long reign at the Lyceum after he took over the management in 1878. Also with Irving on this occasion was Frank Marshall, who later wrote a play about the executed Irish patriot and Trinity College Dublin graduate, Robert Emmet (to whom Irving was seen by Irish people as bearing a close resemblance) and afterwards collaborated with Irving in producing Shakespeare editions. Following an early dinner in Trinity dining hall, Stoker and a young journalist friend, Edward Lefroy, saw Irving's party off from Kingstown, now Dun Laoghaire.

Irving was back in Dublin in the autumn of 1877, opening in *Hamlet* on 19 November, when Stoker's notice again repeated the notion of Hamlet as a mystic. After the evening performance, Irving would arrange for a small party, which always included Stoker, to dine in various restaurants, especially Corless', then famous for its hot lobster. It would later feature as the setting for James Joyce's short story, 'A Little Cloud', published in *Dubliners*, the grand restaurant where the returning emigrant, Ignatius Gallagher, takes the stay-at-home Little Chandler to impress him. Irving was no doubt working a similar magic on Stoker when he spoke to him of his plans for the future when he would have his own theatre and about the possibility that Stoker might give up his Civil Service post to join him, something he had hinted at shortly after their first meeting: 'The hope grew in me that a time might yet come when he and I might work together to one end that we both believed in and held previous in the secret chamber of our hearts. In my diary that night, November 22, 1877, I wrote: "London in view!"'

According to his grandson, an attack on Irving by a pamphleteer in Edinburgh made him realise that he would need a publicist – 'a henchman who, skilled in the arts of publicity, could handle these matters for him . . . There was something about Bram Stoker which reminded him of the Colonel [Bateman] who had previously controlled the Lyceum.'[8]

In *Dracula*, Van Helsing asks in relation to the Count's arrival in London: 'What more may he not do when the greater world of thought is open to him.' We sense Stoker's own love affair with London in *Dracula* when the Count tells Jonathan Harker that he longs to visit London and savour its greatness. In this, Stoker was echoing the conclusion of his Dublin contemporary, George Bernard Shaw, who stated that: 'Every Irishman who has felt that his business in life was on the higher plane of the cultural professions felt that he must have a metropolitan domicile and an international culture: that is, he felt that his first business was to get out of Ireland. I had the same feeling. For London as London, or England as England, I cared nothing . . . but as the English language was my weapon, there was nothing for it but London.' Shaw moved from Dublin to London in 1876, two years before Stoker, at the much earlier age of twenty. While Stoker's dilemma may have been acute in the mid-1870s, he did not regret his decision to move to London. At the time of the publication of *Dracula*, he told an interviewer he believed London was the best possible place for a literary man: 'A writer will find a chance here if he is good for anything; and recognition is only a matter of time.'[9]

On 7 June 1878, Stoker arrived in London, the day before Irving's production of Wills's version of the Flying Dutchman legend, *Vanderdecken*, opened at the Lyceum. Wagner's opera, *The Flying Dutchman*, had been produced in London in 1876 and Bateman felt that a play on the subject should be mounted at the Lyceum, with Irving well suited to the role of the phantom sea captain condemned to eternal travel. He commissioned Percy FitzGerald to write the play and then engaged W. G. Wills to polish it up. It made a deep impression on Stoker:

> Irving was fine in it, and gave one a wonderful impression of a dead man fictitiously alive. I think his first appearance was the most striking and startling thing I ever saw on the stage . . . It was marvellous that any living man should show such eyes. They really seemed to shine like cinders of glowing red out of the marble face . . . In my criticism I wrote: 'Herein lies the terror . . . of the play. The chief actor is not quick but dead . . . he answers Thekla's question: "Where are we?": "Between the living and the dead!"'[10]

Here, surely, lay part of the genesis of *Dracula*, a terrifying tale of an undead man suspended between life and death. Stoker was no passive spectator: he helped Irving edit the text of *Vanderdecken* and modestly thought that the play was greatly improved in the process. Afterwards, Stoker dined with Irving at the Devonshire Club and then stayed up with him in his rooms until 5 a.m., no doubt discussing the horrific play. It was the start of a nocturnal existence which would be a feature of Stoker's life at the Lyceum and which suggests obvious parallels with the habits of Count Dracula.

When Stoker returned to Dublin, he acted as a witness at the marriage on 27 June 1878 of his sister, Margaret Dalrymple Stoker, to William Thomson. Margaret, who was born on 20 March 1853, was the second-youngest of Abraham and Charlotte's children. She had travelled in Europe with her parents as a girl and became engaged for the first time in about 1875 to the son of a British banker at Naples. The bank failed, however, and the engagement was called off. Margaret almost certainly met William Thomson through her brother, Thornley. Both men had the same medical qualifications and had attended the same university, Queen's College, Galway, where Thomson went after he had abandoned journalism in his mid-twenties to study medicine. He duly qualified and, in the 1870s, was surgeon to the same Dublin hospitals as Thornley: the Richmond, Whitworth and Hardwicke. Like Thornley, he rose in time to one of the foremost positions in the medical profession, becoming President of the Royal College of Surgeons in Ireland and receiving a knighthood. After their marriage, William and Margaret took up residence near to Thornley in Harcourt Street and they remained neighbours until about 1890.

Stoker was back in London the following month. On the morning of 12 July 1878, as Irving had arranged, he met James Knowles, editor and owner of the *Nineteenth Century* magazine, who attempted to dissuade him from fulfilling his ambition of coming to London, arguing that he could write for his journal from Dublin. Stoker's response was that he could write well enough but knew 'the joy of the waste-paper basket and the manuscript returned – unread'. When he pointed out to Knowles that he himself, as a Scotsman, had made precisely such a transition, the editor accepted Stoker's logic. In *Personal Reminiscences of Henry Irving*, Stoker tells us that, despite having his 'full share of ambition', he had given it up to work for Irving, who knew of his wish to move to London where he would have greater scope as a writer. In other words, Stoker's initial impulse to go to London was a result of his desire to develop as a writer, and it predated the notion of working for Irving. The latter, indeed, acted – or appeared to act – as an ally in furthering these ambitions, before making his own offer for Stoker's services.

On 12 August 1878, Irving came again to Ireland, when he was met by Stoker at Kingstown. He stayed with Thornley and spent three days touring the outskirts of Dublin. Stoker and Loveday then went to Belfast to prepare for Irving's visit, which would be a huge success, with an audience of 3,000 crowding into the Ulster Hall: 'There were of course lots of speeches. Belfast is the very home of fiery and flamboyant oratory and all our local friends were red-hot Orangemen. On this occasion, however, we were spared any contentious matter . . .' They again kept late hours, staying up until 7 a.m. Stoker understood that Irving did not want to sleep after 'a hard and exciting day or night – or both. He feels that sleep is at arm's length till it is summoned.' There was a hint of reluctance on Stoker's part when he says: 'I did not like to thwart him.'[11]

Irving returned to Dublin the following month for a two-week engagement, beginning on 23 September. They dined almost every day with

Thornley and his wife: Irving was 'great friends' with them and it was 'a sort of gala time to us all'. Stoker and the actor had now been close friends for over two years: 'We understood each other's nature, needs and ambitions, and had a mutual confidence, each towards the other in his own way, rare amongst men.' Six weeks later, Stoker got a telegram from Irving in Glasgow asking to see him on urgent business: Stoker was with him the next evening. Irving was taking over as manager and lessee of the Lyceum Theatre and was establishing his own company. He asked Stoker to give up the Civil Service and join him as acting manager at the Lyceum and Stoker decided to throw in his lot with him, starting on 14 December 1878; Irving's first production under his own management of the Lyceum was to open on 31 December and there was precious little time to get the necessary arrangements in order. Stoker actually joined Irving at Birmingham on 9 December, having completed his *Duties of Clerks of Petty Sessions* and married five days previously, a year earlier than planned: Irving 'was mightily surprised when he found that I had a wife – *the* wife – with me'. Whether this reflected personal jealousy on Irving's part or was simply concern that his new acting manager might be distracted from his professional duties is a moot point. Stoker's mother reacted with distaste to her son's linking his fortunes to Irving, always referring to him as a 'strolling player'.[12]

In marrying Florence Balcombe, Stoker united himself with a family whose social dynamism was even more remarkable than his own. Her grandfather, Bernard (or Burnet) Balcombe, was an English labourer who enlisted in the army as a private at Maidstone in 1811 at the age of sixteen; he was promoted to corporal in 1820 and sergeant in 1824. He resigned in 1829 and died in 1837. He married Mary Ronan in Waterford in 1819 and together they had five children, the eldest of whom was James, born in 1820 in Kilkenny. He followed his father into the army, joining as a private in the 57th Foot in 1835 and rose through the ranks to become captain in 1857. He served successively in the East Indies, the Crimea, the Ionian Isles, Malta and again in the East Indies and was awarded the Crimea Medal and clasps for the battles of Balaclava, Inkerman and Sebastopol. He married Phillipa Anne Marshall of Dover in 1847 and the series of lengthy letters he sent to his wife from the Crimea in 1855 give an interesting insight into conditions in that campaign. He joined the Royal South Down Militia in 1860 as adjutant, rising to major in 1875 and lieutenant-colonel in 1876. The large silver inkwell, together with a salver and pair of candlesticks, given to him by his brother officers on his retirement from the adjutancy of the South Down Militia, after sixteen years of service at Downpatrick, in October 1875, is still in the Stoker family. James and Phillipa Anne had eight children, including Florence Ann Lemon Balcombe, who was born on 17 July 1858 at Falmouth, in Cornwall. The Marshall and Lemon families had inter-married in the English West Country in the eighteenth century, hence this rather unusual middle name given to Florence. Around the time of James's retirement from the South Down Militia in 1876, his son, also James, assumed the post of secretary to the Commissioners of Clontarf Township Office and took up residence at 1 Marino Crescent, Dublin.

Also about this time, Florence began her two-year romance with Oscar Wilde. The painful break-up with Oscar was precipitated by her engagement to Stoker in mid-1878. Quite how they met is not clear, as the Stokers had moved out of Marino Crescent many years previously. It may have been through her brother, James, whom Stoker would have known in the small world of Dublin officialdom or through Stoker's friendship with the Wilde family, which would naturally have heightened Oscar's sense of grievance as the jilted suitor, although he does not refer to it in his letters to Florence. Oscar was very much in love with Florence but his biography may have exaggerated the length of their relationship, starting it in 1875 rather than 1876, the more likely date. Merlin Holland, Oscar's grandson, points, convincingly, to the likelihood that they had just met when he wrote excitedly to Reginald Harding in 1876: 'I am just going out to bring an *exquisitely pretty girl* to afternoon service in the Cathedral. She is just seventeen with the *most perfectly beautiful face I ever saw and not a sixpence of money*. I will show you her photograph when I see you next.' When Florence announced that she was marrying Stoker, Oscar, with characteristic theatricality, asked her to return a small gold cross he had given her on a Christmas morning: it would serve as a reminder of 'two sweet years – the sweetest years of my youth – and I should like to have it always with me'.[13]

Why Florence chose Stoker over Oscar is unknown. She was hardly opting for stability, as her fiancé was giving up a secure Civil Service position for the more hazardous, if better paid, adventure with Irving. It was a whirl-wind romance and Stoker would reprise this passionate experience in his later fiction such as *The Snake's Pass* when Arthur kisses Norah the day after their engagement: 'Our happiness was complete. Anyone who has met the girl he loved the day after his engagement to her, can explain why or how – if any explanation be required.' Stoker was similarly romantic about weddings and that in *The Mystery of the Sea* probably recalled his own: 'She looked oh! So sweet in her plain white frock; and her manner was gentle and solemn. It all seemed to me like a dream of infinite happiness; from which every instant I feared I should wake, and find in its stead some grim reality of pain, or terror, or unutterable commonplace.'[14] The congruence of horror with supreme happiness may have had some autobiographical basis. There was at least a hint of familial disapproval and social impropriety about Florence's suggestion of meeting Oscar at Thornley Stoker's rather than her parents' house to tie up the loose ends of their failed relationship. Florence's father was perturbed by Stoker's unusual friendships and unusual prospects. Indeed, Stoker telegraphed Florence and her father as soon as he had accepted Irving's offer to take up his post at the Lyceum. The marriage was brought forward to enable them to go to England as a married couple and there was no time even for a honeymoon. Their hurried wedding arrangements would later have their fictional counterpart in *Dracula*, where Jonathan Harker and Mina Murray marry in haste in Budapest, as he recovers from the trauma of his visit to the Count.

If this turn of events left Lieutenant-Colonel Balcombe less than delighted, this might explain why Florence did not give her parents' home as her address on the marriage certificate, using instead Thornley Stoker's at 16 Harcourt Street. Stoker then lived at 7 St Stephen's Green North, a short distance away. It is also somewhat curious that Stoker's witness was a friend and work colleague, Thomas W. Martelli, rather than a member of his own family, when he married Florence in St Ann's Church in Dawson Street, Dublin, on 4 December 1878. Whatever the reason for Florence's decision not to use her parents' address, there was clearly no long-term difficulty between Stoker and his parents-in-law, as he was made executor of his mother-in-law's will. When probate was granted in 1895, the gross value of her estate was £535 and Florence inherited £100, together with a silver salver.[15]

Little is known about the intimate marital relationship between Stoker and Florence, other than the fact that they produced one child together. Yet speculation premised upon it has become central to critical theory purporting to explain Stoker's fiction. In recent times it has been alleged, without supporting evidence, that Florence, allegedly as 'frigid as a statue', was likely, because of her 'unsatisfactory sex life', to have had very bad menstrual disturbances: 'Was it some image of these that gave Stoker's subliminal mind the hint that formulated a myth of formidable power, out of the ferocity of a frustrated bleeding woman, crackling with energy and unacknowledged sexuality? It is certainly possible.' The writer, Fay Weldon, carries this speculation a step further, seeing Florence's frigidity as attributable to the fact that sex with Stoker, a closet gay, was not much fun.[16] This line of thinking has its roots in the claim of Daniel Farson, Stoker's great-nephew and biographer, that Florence was a cold, frigid woman who refused to have sex with Stoker after the birth of their only child in 1879. He cited the evidence of Stoker's granddaughter, Ann Stoker, for this and indeed, dedicated his biography of Stoker to her under her married name of Ann MacCaw. Ann Stoker, however, denied categorically that she was the source of Farson's claims on the subject and expressed considerable indignation on this score.[17] As both are now dead, little further light is likely to be cast on the subject. In conversation with the author before her death, Ann Stoker emphasised the fierce devotion to Stoker of Florence, who she knew well in her youth. Few clues exist as to their actual relationship, but in a letter to her mother in 1891 Florence describes her 'harmony' lessons as her only amusement as she had so much to do now for Stoker.[18] The impression is of a woman who saw herself in partnership with her husband, not crackling with sexual dissatisfaction. Florence was remembered by the noted Celtic scholar, Eleanor Knott, daughter of Florence's brother-in-law, John Freeman Knott, as 'a wonderful letter-writer . . . always crisp & gay – often sardonic; never dull'.[19]

Yet one cannot be sure that Stoker and Florence did not encounter difficulties in their sex life. Whether or not Stoker was suffering from syphilis when he died is a major biographical issue and will be examined in detail later in this book. If he was syphilitic, it is possible that the infection dated as far back as the early 1880s, thereby fitting Dan Farson's allegation that Florence had suspended sexual relations after the birth of their son in 1879. It is also possible that Florence was afflicted by the condition known as Simmonds' disease which affects women whose pituitary gland is damaged by severe bleeding when giving birth, and can give rise to frigidity. However, it also causes languor, and Florence seems to have had a lively personality. If, of course, Stoker had already contracted syphilis at this early stage of their marriage, which is not inconceivable, then any reluctance on Florence's part to have sex with him would have been entirely logical. She might have echoed Mina Harker in *Dracula*: 'Unclean, unclean! I must touch him or kiss him no more.'

Homosexuality on Stoker's part could have been another reason for discontinuation of heterosexual relations with Florence. Hall Caine, who may have flirted with homosexuality in his youth, moved to an address near Stoker's in 1881 and the two formed a close and lifelong friendship. Caine wrote late in life that the affection between two men could be as tender and strong as the love between women and men. The nature of Stoker's early relationship with Irving has given rise to speculation about its nature, as has the tenor of Stoker's letters to Whitman (among the few significant personal letters of his to survive). Even the athletic masculine prowess of Stoker's youth is sometimes seen as over-compensatory. There is, however, no evidence that Stoker was ever actively homosexual.

Another line of thinking is that Florence was reluctant to have further children in order to keep her figure. That she was beautiful was beyond dispute: the contemporary caricaturist and writer, George du Maurier, who was part of the Stokers' social circle, regarded Florence as one of the three most beautiful women he had ever seen. Contemporaries certainly agreed: a report on a ball at Dublin Castle in 1897 stated that she 'was one of the most brilliant constellations at the first Drawing-room of the Dublin season . . . Mrs Bram Stoker was considered the most lovely lady present, and was beautifully and artistically dressed.'[20] Mary Gladstone referred to her in the 1880s as '*the* beauty'.[21] Her beauty was evident in Walter Osborne's portrait of her, exhibited at the Royal Academy's Summer Exhibition in 1895. At the Lyceum, men would stand on seats to get a better view of her.

For an inkling of how Stoker felt about Florence, we have to comb his fiction for clues. 'A Yellow Duster', published in *Lloyd's Weekly Newspaper* in May 1899, is the story of a duster kept as a treasure by a husband, Frank Stanhope, after it helped resolve doubts about his wife's love for him. As usual with Stoker's main characters, Stanhope inherits a huge fortune late in life from a great-uncle. He marries a wife who is some years younger than him 'just about . . . that time of life when a man begins to distrust himself as important in the eyes of a beautiful young woman'. He comes to have doubts about his wife because she seems so willing to yield her wishes to his, while he is also worried about his work. They are about to have a child and a spirit of distrust grows 'like the genius in the *Arabian Nights* until it fills the universe'. This story may fit the circumstances of Stoker and Florence's early married life but whether or not it was autobiographical must remain speculative. Equally speculative perhaps as a pointer to their early sex life is the fact that Archibald Hunter in *The Mystery of the Sea* felt that 'restraint' – non-consummation – in his married life was a formative influence for good. In his fiction, if not in his life, Stoker seems to have valued friendship, especially between the sexes, over love. In *Dracula*, Quincy Morris, coping with his rejection by Lucy Westenra, tells her: 'Little girl, your honesty and pluck have made me a friend, and that's rarer than a lover; it's more unselfish anyhow.'

A much grimmer light is cast on marital relations in Stoker's brutally misogynistic late short story, 'The Way of Peace', featuring Michael Hennessy and his wife, Katty, who are about to celebrate their golden wedding anniversary. Katty narrates a story of how, fifty years previously, on the day after their marriage, Michael asks her to fetch the rack-comb before setting off for the fair. She refuses, to prevent him from going. He kisses her on the mouth, before slapping her on the side of her head: 'that made me think that the house was full iv bells all clattherin' away at wanst

. . .' She then obeys, bringing him the rack–comb and they have never had a cross word since; she professes to be the happiest woman in Ireland. Katty comments: 'that's the way to thrate a woman; an' that's the way a woman ought to be thrated. Sure, afther all, they're but childher iv a bigger kind . . . They want to get the hard hand now and again . . . that's the aisiest punishment they iver gets.'

Perhaps both Stoker and Florence needed the constant company of other people when they were together. The narrator in Stoker's short story, 'The Squaw' (1893) rather surprisingly states that he and his wife, being in the second week of their honeymoon, 'naturally' wanted someone else to join them. They encounter a stranger, Elias P. Hutcheson, who has hinted at being alone. Both the narrator and his wife had wanted to invite the stranger to join them but did not want to appear too eager, 'such not being a good compliment to the success of our married life'. When they take Hutcheson on board they find that 'instead of quarrelling, as we had been doing, we found that the restraining influence of a third party was such that we now took every opportunity of spooning in odd corners'. This has a ring of auto-biographical truth about it.

Stoker was not the only interesting character to marry into the Balcombes. When Edward Dowden wrote to Florence's brother-in-law, John Freeman Knott – 'I begin to think you are Dr Faustus, or Mephistopheles, or the Wandering Jew or somebody a little demonic; you bring curious learning on all manners of subjects out of your conjuring bag' – he was describing a man whose polymathic virtuosity made him a natural model for Abraham Van Helsing in *Dracula*, as well as employing demonic imagery appropriate to the Count himself. A fellow doctor, William Taylor, Surgeon to the Meath Hospital in Dublin, said that Knott was someone whom he 'could almost worship' for the extent of his knowledge on subjects other than medicine.[22] Born in County Roscommon in 1853, John Knott decided as a young man to study medicine and became friendly with Thornley Stoker at the Royal College of Surgeons in Dublin. He got a post at Thornley's hospital, the Richmond, and lived near him at 34 York Street. It was presumably through Thornley that he became acquainted with the Balcombe family and, after his first wife died in 1879, he married Philippa Balcombe, Florence's sister. Knott was well connected with the Irish intelligentsia of his day and shared with Stoker and Edward Dowden an enthusiasm for Sir Thomas Browne, the doctor and writer best remembered as the author of a book of reflections, *Religio Medici* (1642), who, while he was concerned to correct popular superstition, also gave evidence that sealed the fate of two women tried for witchcraft in 1665, the last trial of its kind in England. In defence of Browne, Knott pointed out 'how the insights of primitive man entailed a belief in beneficent spirits, baneful demons and witches, pagan ideas still subconsciously nurtured in the minds of the first Christian theologians',[23] the territory which Stoker explored with such effect in *Dracula*.

PART TWO

The Lyceum

SEVEN

An Uncommonly Useful Man

He is a young man, full of energy and talent in his own way,
and of a very faithful disposition.
(*Dracula*, Letter of Mr Hawkins to the Count, apropos Jonathan Harker)

When, in 1878, Henry Irving took over the Royal Lyceum Theatre in London, he had, as we have seen, already been playing there for seven years under the management of the Batemans. Located in Wellington Street, off the Strand in central London, the Lyceum stood on a site occupied as a theatre since the 1780s. Following a fire in 1830, it had been rebuilt on a larger scale, with a magnificent façade which remains a London landmark to this day. Irving's ambition was to establish the theatre as a legitimate art form and dispel the ambiguity which still damaged the respectability of the acting profession. With the beautiful Ellen Terry, the greatest actress of her generation, as his leading lady, he made the Lyceum into a major artistic and social force in the final two decades of Victoria's reign. The Lyceum under Irving had a seating capacity of 2,000 and employed between 450 and 600 people. From 1878 to 1898, Irving played in London a total of 620 weeks, divided into twenty seasons of thirteen to forty-seven weeks each. In this time, he had expenses of £950,000, plus authors' fees of £13,000, huge sums for the era. Irving drew a nominal salary for himself, while Ellen Terry was paid only a third of the salary in London that she received in the provinces and a quarter of that in the United States.

During Irving's management, from the end of December 1878 until he sold his rights to the Lyceum Theatre Company in 1898 (his last performance at the theatre was in July 1902), he produced over forty plays, eleven of them by Shakespeare. Six were inherited from the Bateman era. In a tone that was less than reverential, Stoker described the staple diet of the theatre: 'old plays . . . and a good many "curtain-raisers" whose excellence were old and tried'; even some of the new plays were either old stories told afresh or historic themes treated in a new way. The theatre under Irving's management opened with *Hamlet*, to both popular and critical acclaim for both Ellen Terry and himself. They next played in *The Merchant of Venice* in which Irving's portrayal of Shylock as a man of substance, rather than the usual anti-Semitic stereotype, caused a sensation, not all of it supportive, but the public liked it and the play ran for seven months. The Lyceum aimed at popular success: Stoker commented in *The Mystery of the Sea* 'it's only those who have not tasted popular favour that say they don't like it'.[1]

And Irving certainly tasted popular favour. Some intellectuals may have demurred but Irving's Lyceum dazzled most contemporaries from the late 1870s to the late 1890s. To Joseph Hatton (admittedly an apologist for Irving), writing in 1886, he was 'the best and wisest manager . . . at the head of his profession . . . who . . . has revolutionised the art of the stage'. Irving played this role with appropriate solemnity, always conscious of the fact that he was the outstanding actor of his era, the head of the English stage and heir to a great tradition. One observer commented that the Lyceum was not so much a theatre as a temple to be entered with bated breath, and that there was a sacerdotal air about the entire building; those who entered its precincts were at once absorbed into this rarefied atmosphere. Another observer remarked on the Lyceum's pre-eminent position and on Irving's stature as a national figure occupying a position in public life unattained by any other actor. Irving created an impression of devotion to art, impressing on his patrons that they were supporting a noble endeavour, with vulgar commercial considerations relegated to the background. The sense of grandeur which the Lyceum inspired was immortalised by Arthur Conan Doyle in *The Sign of Four* (1890):

> At the Lyceum Theatre the crowds were already thick at the side-entrances. In front a continuous stream of hansoms and four-wheelers were rattling up, discharging their cargoes of shirt-fronted men and beshawled, bediamonded women.[2]

Henry Irving ran the Lyceum with a rod of iron. His word was law both on stage and off and he brooked no opposition. His success was based on a commanding presence and a conservative formula of carefully chosen plays, allied to the best special effects which the technology of the day could create. He spent lavishly on his productions and on the entertainment which attracted the cream of society. Irving, a man of little education who had overcome the obstacles to his becoming an actor by sheer willpower, was consciously limited in his intellectual horizons: according to Stoker, he never forgot 'that the purpose of stage art is illusion' and that the function of art was 'to do and not to create'. The ultimate aim of acting for him was, according to Stoker, the creation of beauty, of which truth was only an element; to reproduce the vile, the squalid and the mean was a debasement of art.[3] The new theatrical currents of the time, represented by Ibsen in particular, were consciously excluded.

The element of self-creation in Irving's career was caught perfectly by acute contemporaries such as Hall Caine and the painter and illustrator, W. Graham Robertson; the latter saw that 'his artistic life was one long struggle towards perfection; fault after fault he conquered, one by one he laid by his mannerisms, line by line he modelled the beautiful, sensitive face that he had evolved from his original immobile and rather ordinary features. To the hour of his death he worked incessantly, his whole career was a progression and those who witnessed his last performance probably saw him at his best.' The result was a façade which not even his friends could penetrate. Robertson was not sure he ever knew Irving: 'His art was his life – his soul. He had vowed himself to it by a pact as awful as that between Faust and Mephistopheles; like Peter Schlemihl, the subject of Adelbert von Chamisso's *Peter Schlemihls wundersame Geschichte* [1814; *The Wonderful History of Peter Schlemihl*] he had sold his reflection; the memory of the mirror gives back a score of counterfeit images, but the true Irving, the dweller in the innermost, hardly a trace.' As an actor he gave 'expression to everything; as himself he was careful to tell nothing'.[4] Ellen Terry, too, chronicled the evolution of Irving from 1867, when he seemed to possess few of the natural attributes of an actor (which he himself accepted) through to the theatrical majesty of his later years. The result was frustrating for those who encountered him socially: Mary Gladstone left a memorable account in her diary of the tedium of an afternoon walk with him in October 1883: 'Irving came to luncheon . . . Afternoon walked with G.O.M. [Gladstone], L[or]d. Derby and Irving a dead failure – in vain had hoped his long, thin legs would fly over the Park. For an hour and ¼ we dawdled round the house, damp and chilly, the topics never rising above trees, soil, atmosphere. Irving walks ¼ mile an hour. What a brilliant walk it might have been . . .'[5] Even to the companion of his later years, Mrs Aria, he was a man of frustratingly few words. George Bernard Shaw's analysis of Irving's character was that he had become an actor to escape from himself. The price he paid was appalling loneliness. The actor-manager, Sir John Martin-Harvey, who spent fourteen years as an actor with the Lyceum, from 1882 to 1896, commented that 'no man that I ever met was so truly lonely as he'.[6]

The failure of his marriage did not help. After his separation, Irving lived modestly. As Stoker pointed out: 'His own needs were small. He lived in a few rooms, ate sparingly, drank moderately. He had no vices that I know of; he was not extravagant; did not gamble, was not ostentatious even in his charities.' In this, he resembled Count Dracula, whose room is that of a 'lonely bachelor'.[7]

Mrs Joseph Comyns Carr, who designed many of Ellen Terry's dresses for her Lyceum roles, has left a record of the dark side of Irving's character, the man who had a 'morbid passion' for visiting the Morgue in Paris where he would 'scrutinise the incoming visitors, and concoct tales of horror to account for the expressions on the faces of the men and women who inspected the dead bodies'. Terry herself spoke of his fascination with horror and his deep interest in crime – he used to visit the police courts to study the faces of the accused. He had to be persuaded by Mrs Carr's husband, the journalist, theatre manager, playwright and art gallery director Joseph William Comyns Carr, who did not share his fascination with the dead, to go to see the can-can cabaret at the Moulin Rouge, which opened in Paris in 1889, where his imposing, melancholy figure attracted everyone's attention. One of the dancers neatly flicked off his hat with her foot, causing the great man to smile. 'Isn't this better than the Morgue, Henry?' Carr asked, and Irving silently concurred.[8]

Irving proved to be an excellent theatre manager for most of his years at the Lyceum, up to the mid-1890s, adroitly catering to popular taste and assembling an outstanding management team. Stoker, in particular, made an indelible impression on knowledgeable contemporaries such as Horace Wyndham:

> Any mention of Henry Irving leads naturally to mention of one who was for years his faithful watchdog and right-hand man. This was Bram Stoker, to whose unswerving fidelity and marked business aptitude the Lyceum chief probably owed a good deal more than he acknowledged or realized. When Irving was up in the clouds (and where, by the way, he habitually lived), Stoker was down in the box-office, doing unobtrusive, but uncommonly useful, work. As a matter of fact, if Stoker had not been on the bridge, the Lyceum ship would have foundered a lot sooner than it did. The trouble was, Irving – who, despite his general astuteness, was a pretty poor judge of character, and would believe any one who flattered him sufficiently – surrounded himself with a greedy host of third-rate parasites at the expense of the theatre's not inexhaustible revenues. These merchants called themselves 'literary advisers,' or something equally high sounding. They were, however, merely able hacks, whose sole business it was to write speeches full of classical quotations and historical allusions, which Irving delivered to awe-struck gatherings in the provinces and America, and prepare the profound articles which from time to time appeared under his signature in portentous monthly reviews. It was pure dope of course, but the public wanted it, and it

went down. Stoker, who had more brains than the entire pack put together, hated the sight of them. He once told me that if he could have made a clean sweep of the lot, the Lyceum treasury would have been saved some thousands a year. Irving, however, would not listen to such a proposal for a moment. He thought it enhanced his dignity to be surrounded by a courtier-like crowd of sycophants. As a matter of fact, it merely made people laugh at him.

'Stoker' – as he was always called, and whom I knew very well – was a big, red-bearded, untidy Irishman, who had started life in the Civil Service . . . To see Stoker in his element was to see him standing at the top of the theatre's stairs, surveying a 'first-night' crowd trooping up them. There was no mistake about it – a Lyceum *premiere* did draw an audience that really was representative of the best of that period in the realms of art, literature, and society. Admittance was a very jealously guarded privilege. Stoker, indeed, looked upon the stalls, dress circle, and boxes as if they were annexes to the Royal Enclosure at Ascot, and one almost had to be proposed and seconded before the coveted ticket would be issued. The rag-tag-and-bobtail of the musical comedy, theatrical, stock exchange and journalistic worlds who foregather at a present-day *premiere* would certainly have been sent away with a flea in their ear.[9]

From the time he joined Irving at Birmingham in December 1878, the professional demands on Stoker in the quarter-century that he served Irving were enormous and went beyond the normal range of duties of an acting manager. Irving achieved a position as an outstanding figure in British Victorian society, unprecedented for an actor, and much of the hard work which sustained this position devolved on Stoker.[10] He dealt with his huge correspondence, seldom writing fewer than fifty letters per day, the bulk of them admittedly short; he calculated that, overall, he wrote almost half a million letters for Irving. Stoker had two assistants for this office work, Charles Howson, taken on as an accountant in the early days of Irving's Lyceum and another man called Terry (whether he was related to Ellen Terry is not clear). Stoker also scrutinised plays submitted to the Lyceum: he estimated that he read over a thousand, only two of which he regarded as being any good. Stoker's role as the Lyceum's acting manager was defined by theatrical convention and he carried it out with great professionalism and aplomb. He had control of everything on the auditorium side of the curtain, as well as being responsible for the well-being of the company acting in the theatre. His duties included paying the artistes and a permanent staff of forty-eight, supervising the affairs of the box office and acting as host to the guests and patrons of the house. On him also fell the responsibility for making the travelling arrangements for tours, and organising the advance publicity and programme matter. He even represented Irving in court. He was well paid: his salary of £22 per week was almost three times his income as an Inspector of Petty Sessions. For this he was expected to be at Irving's beck and call, shuttling between the Lyceum and his master's rooms at 15A Grafton Street, off New Bond Street (a not inconsiderable distance from the Lyceum at Wellington Street), attending to his needs, both professional and personal.

Stoker deputised for Irving in all sorts of situations. In 1897, for example, when the actor was invited to appear before a select committee of the House of Lords that was considering a copyright bill, three clauses of which dealt with the dramatisation of novels, Irving nominated Stoker to appear in his place. Stoker was the first witness to be heard on 8 July 1897. A contemporary journal declared that Stoker 'speaks as an expert and his opinions will be readily endorsed'.[11] It was a subject close to his heart and he was very strong in his support for the writer and lawyer, Edward (later Sir Edward) Abbott Parry, who took legal action against a publisher over copyright.

In *The Man*, Stoker wrote that a 'good secretary must not be content with doing merely that which his hand finds to do; he must make the work, for so he will aid in development of possibilities'.[12] He carried this philosophy into practice at the Lyceum, where he revelled in its perpetual action; there is just a hint of complaint in his comment to Walt Whitman on the difficulty of arranging a meeting: 'The cares and responsibilities of a theatre are always exacting, and the demands on the time of any one concerned in management are so endless that the few hours of leisure for such a visit [he had promised Whitman] are rare.' Among those who paid lavish tribute to Stoker's professional excellence was Gordon Craig, Ellen Terry's son, who exercised a profound influence on the development of the modern theatre and was therefore in a good position to evaluate Stoker's worth. Ellen Terry's hand can probably be detected in a tribute paid to Stoker's professionalism in T. Edgar Pemberton's *Ellen Terry and her Sisters* (1902). A few years later she was quite explicit about his excellence in her autobiography. Describing him as 'one of the most kind and kind-hearted of men', she said he had filled a difficult position with great tact and was as universally abused as other business managers because he was always straight with the Lyceum Company and never sought to take advantage of them. She also described how Stoker and Loveday, the Lyceum's stage manager, met almost hourly with Henry Irving but wondered whether they, or anybody else, really knew him. Irving enjoyed chaffing his 'valued adjutants', Loveday especially, as his loyalty made him agree with even his boss's most preposterous statements.[13]

If anyone stood to lose by incompetence on Stoker's part, it would have been Terry, so her opinion should carry considerable weight. Another who recognised Stoker's professionalism was Jerome K. Jerome, author of the classic, *Three Men in a Boat* (1889), who found his assistance invaluable in making a play run at a profit. The view of George Bernard Shaw is also illuminating, although his adversarial relationship with Irving and the Lyceum has to be taken into account. In his view, Irving could neither write nor manage:

It was a great merit in him that instead of employing common press agents to write for him, he hired literary men of distinction, notably [the playwright] Frank Marshall, L[ouis]. F[rederick]. Austin [Irving's informal secretary for a number of years from 1882], and Bram Stoker, who were at home in good society, where they turned the conversation on to him and talked him up. Austin was especially active in this way. They wrote his speeches and lectures and crushed his opponents with brilliantly sarcastic letters when this was needed. They made for him an entirely fabulous reputation as a man of profound learning. Like all old actors, he slipped in the most puzzling way from complete illiteracy to the scraps of shrewdness and wisdom he had picked up from Shakespear [*sic*] and the plays he had acted.

As to management, Bram Stoker and others did that for him . . . When H.I. was being robbed, and knew it, he enjoyed the complete mastery of the situation and abject reverence for 'the Governor' which this knowledge gave him. And so he reigned in great dignity and splendour until the final crash came and he had to take perforce to the road, penniless, played out in London, old, and obsolete, but with a tremendous reputation to exploit in the provinces. He had held out in London for thirty years, a quite unprecedented feat . . .[14]

Stoker's thoroughness as a press officer was recalled by the reviewer of his *Famous Impostors* in 1911, who remembered meeting him at Bristol many years previously in connection with an interview with Irving, only to find that Stoker had the 'interview' already prepared; it was published the next day without the 'interviewer' having spoken to the actor. He performed similar functions in relation to Irving's speeches, which were always written out in advance; Irving then used his formidable technique to disguise the fact that he was reading. He learned by heart the texts where he had to speak '*quasi-impromptu*'. It is easy to see why George Bernard Shaw advised Laurence Irving, the actor's grandson, that the difficulty in writing about his grandfather was to avoid making him appear an impostor with a reputation manufactured by those around him.[15] Laurence Irving took this advice to heart, but in a manner hardly foreseen by Shaw, by the simple expedient of laying the blame for the actor's eventual financial crash at Stoker's door.

In 1879, during Stoker's first year as acting manager of the Lyceum in London, Geneviève Ward hired the theatre during August while Henry Irving was yachting in the Mediterranean. Stoker had remained behind to look after the theatre. Ward asked him to be her manager; Stoker refused due to a possible clash of interest with his duty to Irving but promised to do all he could to help. He was as good as his word and Ward was soon in need of his services: her season at the Lyceum was not going well due to poor choice of material. Stoker chose a play, *Forget-me-not*, out of a pile Ward had given him and made the necessary arrangements with the author. The result was 'an enormous success' and Ward played it over a ten-year period 'and made a fortune out of it'. Stoker was not modest about his role in helping Ward but Ward herself confirms it: in her autobiography she described his judgement on the play as 'unerring'.[16] Ward played four parts with Irving at the Lyceum over the years (although she did not rate him highly as a Shakespearian actor). In common with Irving and, indeed, Count Dracula, Stoker wrote, in what was actually a stock description of his, that Ward's eyes could 'blaze'.[17] Like Terry, she was subjected to the interest of George Bernard Shaw who remonstrated with her about her choice of plays. She kept in touch with Stoker and was close enough to his family to write a letter of condolence to Thornley when his wife passed away, signed 'Your sincere old friend'.[18]

At the Lyceum, Stoker worked with many other outstanding personalities of the day, including Charles Villiers Stanford, the composer and conductor. He had, like Stoker, studied at Trinity College Dublin, before moving to England where he became Professor of Composition at the Royal College of Music and Professor of Music at Cambridge University. Stanford provided the music for some Lyceum productions, including *Becket* (Tennyson, the author, had no doubt that Stanford was the right man for the job), and he formed a close professional and personal relationship with Stoker. Contemporaries like Ward and Stanford were at the top of their professions and would have expected the highest standards from those they dealt with. The genuineness of Stanford's regard for Stoker's professional abilities is evident in a letter he wrote to Irving in 1896 asking if Stoker's services could be spared to help him with the theatrical side of mounting an opera: 'My soul yearns for the help of Bram Stoker.'[19] Whether due to Irving's opposition or lack of enthusiasm on Stoker's part, nothing appears to have come of this suggestion. It is clear from the correspondence with

Stanford that Stoker was very much involved in the details of staging Lyceum productions, a point underlined by the fact that Stanford consulted Stoker, not Irving or Loveday, about these matters. Their personal relationship included a mutual love of music: he arranged for Stoker to get a pass for Wagner's *Die Meistersinger* when Hans Richter gave the first ever London performance in 1882.

Stoker's professionalism at the Lyceum is also indicated by the desire of another artist to secure his services. His Chelsea neighbour, the painter, James Abbott McNeill Whistler, approached him at one point to take over his business affairs, offering half his income as commission. It is not clear when this happened as they had long had friends in common. Irving had been less impressed when Whistler painted him as Philip of Spain in Tennyson's *Queen Mary* in 1876: his dislike of it was such that he refused to continue sitting for it or to buy it for a token sum. Stoker's friend, the dramatist, William Gorman Wills, by contrast, testified on Whistler's behalf in his libel trial against Ruskin in 1878. Whistler took up residence at 21 Cheyne Walk, Chelsea, in 1889, and among those he entertained was the London theatrical set. He became close to William Heinemann around this time; Heinemann published his *Gentle Art of Making Enemies* in 1890, when the publisher was also having extensive dealings with Stoker and Hall Caine. By this time Whistler's bankruptcy was in the past and he was a celebrity, although he still had difficulties selling his canvasses and retained significant debt. In any event, Stoker did not accept the offer and his judgement of Whistler was succinctly damning of the foibles of popular fashion: 'He did fine work and created a new public taste . . . and he became bankrupt.'[20]

While Stoker's role as the buffer between Irving 'and mere time-killers and tuft-hunters and fools', as he 'bustled about in his busy but silent and useful way' with 'insinuating adroitness', was recognised by contemporaries, his frustration with the negative side of this role is apparent in the words which he puts into the mouth of Marjorie in relation to her suitors in *The Mystery of the Sea*: 'But the cranks and egotists, and scallywags and publicans and sinners, the loafers that float around one like an unwholesome miasma; these are too many and too various, and too awful to cope with.'[21] Stoker saw himself as relieving Irving of all practical considerations, allowing him to concentrate on his artistic vocation. In casting himself as 'the spirit that denies', he identified with Irving's role of Mephistopheles in Goethe's *Faust*. While Stoker defined himself as the 'chancellor of the exchequer' at the Lyceum, he was more than a mere accountant, although he did exercise control of the theatre's financial affairs, with the treasurer being one of his underlings and only Irving and himself allowed to know the full financial picture. Stoker claimed that, over the quarter-century of their collaboration, Irving confided in him his intentions for productions from the very beginning and kept him in touch with the evolution of his thinking. Irving had, he believed, total confidence in his discretion.

To the staff at the Lyceum, Stoker was a formidable figure. Sir Frank Benson, the distinguished actor-manager who played his first professional role at the Lyceum in 1882, remembered an incident when he decided not to make up for his first part, as he believed that make-up hid the expression. Another leading actor of the era, William Terriss, who was one of the Lyceum company from 1880 to 1883, warned him about the consequences of being caught by 'that devil Bram Stoker, in the front – he can see through a brick wall – God help you!' Benson disregarded this advice and was duly pounced on by Stoker, who brushed aside his theory and insisted that he be given a lesson in make-up. Irving might, however, have had reservations about some of the publicity surrounding Stoker, especially as it seemed to laud Stoker's importance to the Lyceum's success at his own expense. One later description of Stoker stated boldly that he was the power behind the Lyceum productions: 'He is a long, strong, red Irishman, physically as hard as nails, with a keen eye, and a slightly ferocious expression, possessing, as the manager of a great theatre should, an overflowing amount of energy and a forty-horse power of work. One is often led to wonder what Sir Henry would do without this Trojan, whose ubiquity is astounding.'[22] There was occasionally a comic side to Stoker's ubiquity, as when he featured unintentionally in a scene in *The Merchant of Venice*: when a gondola laden with medieval maskers passed across the stage a draught from the wings blew aside the silken curtain hiding the cabin's interior and the audience gasped at the figure of Stoker in evening dress and crush hat working the machinery that propelled the gondola. When the gondola made its next trip, he was not inside!

There was also an element of the comic in the account of Stoker at work in the *Pall Mall Budget* of May 1889 when he was overseeing the preparations for the performance of Irving and Ellen Terry before Queen Victoria at Sandringham:

When the big clock at St Pancras station struck half-past three on Friday afternoon, a business-like gentleman with a beard and a brogue was then chief object of interest on the departure platform. He was performing astonishing evolutions, and seemed to be even more ubiquitous than Sir Boyle Roche's bird [Sir Boyle Roche, an eighteenth-century Irish Member of Parliament given to humorously absurd statements, famously asked: 'How can I be in two places at once unless I were a bird?']. He hurried about – here, there, everywhere; he manipulated bundles of railway tickets; he did conjuring tricks with mysterious documents; and he finally pasted hieroglyphics on the windows of several compartments. It was not until I had carefully deciphered these little *affiches* that it dawned upon me that this individual could be none other than Bram Stoker – the clever and courteous Irishman who knows more of Mr Henry Irving's secrets than any one. And surely he had good reason to be so busily engaged, for was he not piloting the Lyceum Company down to Sandringham, where they were 'billed' to appear before Her Most Gracious Majesty the Queen 'for one night only.'[23]

An excellent vignette of Stoker at work was provided by Sir John Martin-Harvey, who joined the Lyceum at the age of nineteen in 1882. As a young, out-of-work actor, he got a letter of introduction to Stoker whom he saw as having 'something of the power of an ambassador' under Irving and went to see 'the brawny, red-bearded Irishman, whose personality seemed to fill the whole Lyceum with energy and activity'. Even though Stoker was not initially encouraging, he told him to see Harry Loveday, the Lyceum's stage manager, and so began a great theatrical career.[24] Martin-Harvey caught his first sight of Irving during the rehearsals for *Romeo and Juliet* in 1882. There was a hush, and a group emerged from the little passage connecting the stage with the offices: the tall, gaunt figure of Irving, flanked by Harry Loveday and 'by the burly pushing form of Bram Stoker, staunch, faithful, and always in a mortal hurry'. Martin-Harvey detailed the ambiguous relationship which Stoker had with the Lyceum Company:

It is not an uncommon thing for members of a company to dislike the business-manager. Neither he nor they have much sympathy for the other's occupation. Between Bram Stoker and even the amiable Loveday, the artist musician, there was at times an open and often amusing hostility . . . No one could deny Stoker's signal devotion to Irving's interest – that was there for all to see and admire. But we of the company did resent a tendency on his part to herd us here and there in our travels like helpless sheep; which indeed we often were – but we didn't like the fact being rubbed in! We did feel, too, that Stoker strongly fortified the barriers which kept us from our Gov'nor . . . It always thawed any resentment I might feel against Bram Stoker when I noted the conspicuous courtesy with which he always treated my wife, even when she was an obscure little member of the company, and noted, too, the many little considerations he showed her which were scarcely warranted by her position there. It was rather pleasant to see his hat fly off whenever he met her as a small girl. I owe him too, one of the greatest compliments I ever received in my life . . . for, when, some conjectures arose on a certain occasion as to who in the far future would wear the mantle of Irving, and several names were mentioned, he roared in his attractive Irish brogue – 'You're all wrong, it will be Martin-Harvey.' And when the time came for me to set out upon the perilous sea of management no one lent me more courage, more staunch and fatherly help in that initial movement than Bram Stoker.[25]

Martin-Harvey recalled how, on the 1893 Lyçeum tour of the United States, the theatre's head electrician, Briggs, was clapped in jail because American law forbade the importation of 'labour' (as distinct from artists). The rest of the company waited, enjoying a bonus break 'while the ingenious Stoker engaged the local forensic powers in an endeavour to extract Briggs from durance. This was no easy matter and taxed all his resources of persuasion and argument.' He finally succeeded on the grounds that Briggs too should be considered an artist.

Some years later, when the state of Irving's health necessitated the closure of the Lyceum for some weeks, Martin-Harvey took over the theatre. Stoker agreed to act as his business manager on the strict condition that it must attract no publicity. Word did, however, leak out and Stoker retired but left a friend to look after Martin-Harvey. Later still, when Irving had sold out to the syndicate, of which Joe Comyns Carr was managing director, he asked Martin-Harvey to postpone his play, *The Only Way*, because it was too similar to Sardou's *Robespierre*, which was to be the first play under the syndicate. Martin-Harvey went to the Lyceum to see the representatives of the syndicate – Stoker, Loveday and Comyns Carr – with his proposition. They listened carefully, and when he had finished reading the letter, Comyns Carr broke the silence which ensued with the remark, '"Well, that's the most cold-blooded proposition I ever heard." Stoker, however, was more concerned with income than the nature of the plays being put on and broke in: "To hell with that! The point is, we want your rent, my b'hoy; so go ahead with your play."' The proposition was agreed. Martin-Harvey recalled how the information on the Lyceum finances which Stoker went to such great lengths to conceal was preserved by someone who collected the scraps thrown into his wastepaper basket, which revealed that Irving gave himself £60 per week and Ellen Terry £200. There were other scraps: 'insurance policies, appeals to members of the company to be at Euston in good time, the expenses sheets of agents with a passion for cigars, all jumbled together, recall the nervous wear and tear undergone by the faithful Bram Stoker at the time. And among them are notes concerning his blood–and–thunder novel, "Dracula".[26]

Stoker had many delicate personal matters to handle for Irving. When Irving and Ellen Terry ceased to be intimate – whether they had actually been lovers over the years is not clear – their relationship was such that they transacted their necessary theatrical business through him. Ellen Terry commented on Irving's use of Stoker as an intermediary: 'For years he has accepted favours, obligations, etc. *through* Bram Stoker. Never will he acknowledge them himself, either by businesslike receipt or by any word or sign. He "lays low" like Brer Rabbit better than anyone I have ever met.'[27]

Even Irving's children dealt with Stoker about tickets and, in the case of his son, Henry Brodribb Irving in 1898, about whether his father wished him to be part of the Lyceum Company for the following season. Stoker's interaction with Irving's family had long been a complex and difficult one. He had to manage the attendance of the actor's separated wife at the theatre, knowing that she disliked him intensely because of his closeness to her estranged husband. This was evident in Laurence Irving's description of the first night of *The Corsican Brothers* in September 1880:

> In the stalls shirt fronts crackled and lorgnettes flashed like heliographs as the habitués strained and craned to identify and greet each other, making sure that their presence was noted by the press – unaware that Irving's manager, Bram Stoker, had already seen to this . . . As soon as he recognised the tall commanding figure of my grandmother and her young escorts, he disengaged himself and advanced to receive her, his resignation masked by an unconvincing affectation of pleasure. The boys would notice her brusque acceptance of his courtesies as he conducted them to their box, their bright little eyes exchanging mischievous signals as he made much of them and arranged to take them behind the scenes after the second act. For their mother had not concealed from them her dislike of Stoker and of his accomplice, L.F. Austin, Irving's gentle secretary, whom she regarded as conspirators bent on preventing her direct communication with her husband. In fact my grandfather was, as his friend Toole said, 'a Turk' at letter writing that but for them she might have had no communication with him at all. As it was, she attributed any of his sins of omission to their unctuous influence.

At the end of the play, the despised Stoker collected them, explained the workings of the stage and introduced them to members of the cast.[28]

Stoker's engagement with Irving's family did not end with the theatre. When Irving's two sons were sent to boarding-school at Marlborough College, he had to sort out their initial homesickness, dealing at the same time with their feelings of humiliation and the interference of their mother.

It is inevitable that modern criticism should focus on the exact nature of the relationship between Stoker and Irving. In the words of one critic, their friendship 'makes a central issue of the role of the homosocial in his life'. The argument here is not that Stoker was homosexual but rather that he could have been troubled by the intensity of his homosocial relations, especially with Irving.[29] There is no sense, however, either on the part of Stoker or his contemporaries, of awareness of sexual ambiguity in the relationship and it is doubtful that they would have written of the friendship in the terms they did if there had been any grounds for suspicion. At the same time, there is no doubting the intensity of their friendship. In an obituary which appeared in the *Daily Telegraph* on the day on which Stoker was to be buried, Hall Caine wrote:

> His was indeed the genius of friendship . . . never in any other man have I seen such capacity for devotion to a friend.
>
> Much has been said of his relation to Henry Irving, but I wonder how many were really aware of the whole depth and significance of that association. Stoker seemed to give up his life to it. It was not only his time and his services that he gave to Irving – it was his heart, which never failed for one moment in loyalty, in enthusiasm, in affection, in the strongest love that man may feel for man . . . and I say without any hesitation that never have I seen such absorption of one man's life in the life of another.[30]

Stoker himself used marital imagery to convey the closeness of his relations with his boss: 'Irving and I were so much together that after a few years we could almost read a thought of the other; we could certainly read a glance or an expression. I have sometimes seen the same capacity in a husband and wife who have lived together for long and who are good friends, accustomed to work together and to understand each other.'[31] There was also a marital aspect in their taking of holidays together, such as a trip to Southsea in 1880. Given the all-enveloping nature of his job at the Lyceum, one would imagine that Stoker would have been keen to escape and at least take vacations with his family. However, considering that he did so much for Irving that was intensely personal, from sorting out schools for his children to comforting his ancient aunt in Cornwall, it is perhaps not surprising that he should have assuaged the loneliness of his chief, separated from his wife and unable to flaunt his relationship with Ellen Terry too publicly in the years of their partnership.

Nevertheless, Stoker's relationship with Irving had undergone a sea change at the very start, from close friendship to that of a subordinate to a superior. When Irving had written to Stoker in October 1878 from Winchester, before Stoker had actually started working for him, he signed it, 'With love, in great haste, Henry'. The following month, he wrote to Stoker from Sheffield asking him to be with him a week earlier, and the tone was again affectionate: it was signed with 'love' from Irving. The use of this language between two men was unusual for the period and is indicative of a highly emotional, if not homoerotic, relationship between them. Irving, however, having staged a blitzkrieg on Stoker's emotions while he was inducing him to join the Lyceum management team, then retreated to a more distant relationship. A formal and peremptory tone is evident in a letter written to Stoker less than a year later. In August 1879, Irving wrote from the yacht, *Walrus*, at Lisbon, about putting the Lyceum accounts into the hands of accountants: 'Let us begin with our eyes wide open'; he now signed off 'Yours sincerely' rather than 'love'.[32]

In any event, Irving's relationship with his fellow actor and theatre manager, John Lawrence Toole, 'whom he loved with an affection almost passing the love of woman',[33] was more affectionate than that with Stoker. Mrs Aria, the companion of Irving's later years, 'found it difficult to understand the love between these two' and felt that Toole saw her as a 'rival'.[34] Stoker commemorated the 'truly brotherly friendship' between Irving and Toole in an article in the *Daily Telegraph* in 1906. The chapter on Toole in *Personal Reminiscences of Henry Irving* is one of few concerned with Irving on a personal level, revealing how, for example, the two actors indulged in harmless pranks up to middle age. Toole, who was older, is described as totally devoted to Irving. In typical fashion, however, Irving sent Stoker to Brighton to bid farewell to the dying Toole, who became quite emotional: 'Stoker, we have often parted – but this time is the last. I shall never see you again! Won't you let me kiss you, dear!' Stoker had, of course, known Toole since his boyhood, well before he met Irving.[35]

In addition to his normal management tasks, Stoker formed a triumvirate at the Lyceum with Loveday and Irving which influenced the choice and production of plays at the theatre. In *Personal Reminiscences of Henry Irving*, Stoker details how they would converse all night, with Irving reading to Loveday and himself, followed by a discussion of the production. The three of them used the same office, as it was convenient for their perpetual consultations. Stoker claimed that this triumvirate played a vital role in Irving's success. In his first year working at the Lyceum, Stoker was fired with enthusiasm when Irving returned from a summer cruise in the Mediterranean with fresh and sympathetic insight into the character of Shylock and decided he wanted to stage *The Merchant of Venice* as soon as possible. Together with Loveday, he sat up all night with Irving, excitedly talking over the play. When it opened on 1 November 1879, it was a great success and ran for 250 nights, the longest run ever for the play.

There was a fourth controlling influence at the Lyceum in the person of Ellen Terry, who was consulted about everything and had a major input into most arrangements. Stoker's love for Terry shines through the pages of *Personal Reminiscences* with a warmth beyond that expressed for Irving himself. His admiration for his master had a staid, monumental, quality to it; that for Terry was intensely human and light in tone. He remembered a playful creature who would come dancing into his office to ask for help during rehearsals, or even during the play itself.

The tribute paid to her in *Dracula* – 'Our correspondent naively says that even Ellen Terry could not be so winningly attractive as some of these grubby-faced little children pretend – and even imagine themselves – to be' – was echoed in his *Personal Reminiscences*: 'Surely never such a buoyant, winsome, merry, enchanting personality was ever seen on stage – or off it.' Ellen clearly returned Stoker's feelings of 'reverence and regard and love' with an ambiguity about gender sure to fascinate modern psychology: Stoker tells us that she gave him the role of 'big brother' but it seems closer to that of mother as she called him either 'mama' or 'Ma'. She inscribed a photograph to Stoker: 'To my "Ma"! I am her dutiful child Ellen Terry.'[36]

Stoker first saw her on 23 December 1878 at the Lyceum. She was then thirty-one, the same age as himself. Like Henry Irving she had had little formal education but had established herself as a child actress. At the age of sixteen she had contracted a short-lived marriage to the painter, G.F. Watts, after which she lived with the architect and designer, Edward Godwin, who became the father of her three children. After breaking up with Godwin, she returned to the stage to support her family. In 1877 she divorced and married the actor, Charles Kelly, essentially to provide a 'name' for her children. After a successful season at the Court Theatre, she joined the then forty-year-old Irving as his leading lady at the Lyceum Theatre as it prepared to open under his management in 1878. Even the December day could not shut out her radiant beauty for Stoker: 'Her face was full of colour and animation, either of which would have made her beautiful. In addition was the fine form, the easy rhythmic swing, the large, graceful, goddess-like way in which she moved.' Stoker already knew Charles Kelly, her actor husband, from professional visits he had paid to Dublin. Kelly had been several times to Stoker's lodgings there and a close friendship had ensued. This was evident in letters that Kelly sent to Stoker. One, written in 1879, showed that the author and recipient had established an easy intimacy; in another, dated 1878, Kelly was anxious to have Stoker's report on his wife's performance on her first night at the Lyceum.[37]

As was usual with Stoker, those visiting Dublin were put in touch with his family and friends, and Ellen Terry was no exception. Her paternal grandfather may have been an Irish builder but Ellen Terry was unimpressed on her visit there in October 1880. Writing to 'O Father A Stoker', she complained of the dullness of her audience, the tendency to praise lesser actors more than herself, and of the behaviour of his college friends who left their cards but never turned up, adding: 'I can't fancy Florence living here.' The warm relationship with Stoker's immediate family is evident in the manner in which she sent her love to Florence, 'the Babs' (their son, Noel) and Stoker's sister, Matilda. She also referred to the man they both then loved: 'H[enry].I[rving]. is a Magician, his finger writes fire . . .'[38] Stoker was circumspect about Ellen's relationship with Henry Irving in his memoirs. He talked of the 'artistic comradeship' between them which lasted twenty-four years and encompassed twenty-seven plays and of how their 'brotherly affection' remained undimmed to the end of Irving's life. He referred to gossip about them but did not allude to the fact that they may have been lovers until Irving dumped her, late in life, for a Mrs Aria. Stoker acted as an intermediary for Terry in her private affairs, just as he did for Irving. When Winston Churchill, then Under-Secretary for the Colonies, gave a dinner in honour of Ellen Terry in 1906, Stoker was one of the four vice-chairmen. Around the same time, Stoker wrote a glowing appreciation of Terry for the *Northern Echo*, telling its readers: 'She seems to have the happy faculty of spinning gaiety out of the very air, and adds always to the sum of human happiness.'[39]

A less happy relationship was that with Louis Frederick Austin, who acted as an informal secretary to Irving from 1882, having previously filled the same role for the Baroness Burdett-Coutts, an influential supporter of the Lyceum. According to Laurence Irving, Austin's 'intimate contact with the Chief inspired jealousy and suspicion in those who were ever on the alert if they felt their own interests were at stake'. Much has been made of an alleged rivalry between Austin and Stoker and there is little doubt that this is how Austin saw things, initially at any rate, although he wrote to his wife from Quebec in September 1884: 'I have settled down to an understanding with Stoker and he has become remarkably genial and obliging'.

However, a few months later, on Christmas Day, the Lyceum Company passed the time over dinner by satirically reciting verses at their own expense. Stoker's self-satire, beginning with the line, 'I'm in a mortal hurry' brought yells of laughter, as it described his all-action style perfectly. While Stoker had no difficulty laughing at himself, he drew the line, according to Austin, at reading Austin's satire on him: 'Stoker, of course, resented every joke of mine on *his* personality and was in a rage of jealousy because I had done something so successful.' Irving might have been nearer the mark when he told Austin that he was too sensitive and took life too seriously. Austin may also have suffered from a perception that, in the words of an obituary, he 'did not make all the reputation in literature that his talents justified'.[40]

The nub of the problem was probably that Irving indulged his sardonic sense of humour by fanning a sense of rivalry between Austin and Stoker. In 1885, he enlisted the help of Austin to write for him a lecture he was to deliver at Harvard, telling him: 'Poor old Stoker has been trying *his* hand but there isn't an idea in the whole thing.'[41] This reveals Irving at his manipulative worst but there may have been method in Irving's madness: Austin's claim that Stoker had been letting it be known that he had been writing Irving's speeches and articles may have prompted the actor to take countermeasures. George Bernard Shaw, who was in a good position to observe the goings-on at the Lyceum, did not distinguish between Austin and Stoker: to him they were two 'henchmen' involved in the ultimately futile task of writing Irving's letters and speeches for him: 'he did not know how much more creditable to him were his own simple and natural compositions than their displays of cleverness'.[42] Austin saw Stoker as manoeuvring to ingratiate himself with good society, while relegating him to the background. This was probably true but ingratiating himself with good society was a key part of Stoker's role at the Lyceum, both in order to bolster Irving's social skills and to ensure that the Lyceum remained at the pinnacle of fashion by attracting the cream of society. Keeping everyone but Irving in the background would have been part of the public relations magic he was expected to weave. Nor does the surviving correspondence between Stoker and Austin support Laurence Irving's picture of deadly rivalry. In the summer of 1897, Stoker sent Austin two copies of *Dracula*; Austin, who had returned to literary journalism by this time, promised to do his best to 'spread the fame of its gruesomeness'. Stoker would hardly have enlisted Austin's help if his relations with him were really poisonous.

Both Austin and Stoker were involved in Irving's highly successful tours in the United States. Stoker estimated that, between 1883 and 1904, he spent more than four years in the USA on eight theatrical tours with the Lyceum, during which they visited every great town in the Union, travelling more than 50,000 miles on American railways. These tours became something of a fix for the Lyceum's wider difficulties, with the profits being used to subsidise its London activities, although the mushrooming of expenses which so afflicted Irving as time went on also reduced his net takings in America. The Americans themselves credited much of Irving's success in the United States to Stoker, no doubt reflecting, to some extent at least, his superb media-handling skills:

> Mr Irving's great success in this country has been due to a very consid-
> erable extent to the shrewd management of Bram Stoker. We know of
> no manager more vigilant, more indefatigable, more audacious than
> he. He knows how to make friends, how to keep them, and how to
> utilize them. At all times he has an eye to business, yet he is always
> to all appearances a careless, cordial man of the world. In the manip-
> ulation of Mr Irving's intricate and enormous business he exhibits a
> coolness, a shrewdness, and an enthusiasm that are simply masterly
> . . . Irving is fortunate in having so able and so loyal an associate.[43]

Tributes such as this reveal the extent to which Stoker's larger-than-life persona struck a responsive chord with American journalists. In the 1890s, the New York *Commercial Advertiser* declared that 'Bram Stoker, manager for Henry Irving, is rapidly achieving social prominence in this city. He is an eminently good-natured gentleman and handsome, and has received a cordial welcome in New York's highest musical and artistic circles . . . He has been Mr. Irving's manager many years, to the great profit of Mr. Irving . . . He is a tall blond, with large, dark brown eyes. He counts his friends in New York by the hundred.' An Ohio newspaper, in a profile of Stoker, stated that to no other person, not even Ellen Terry, did Sir Henry Irving owe so much of his theatrical success as to Stoker. 'That comfortable giant, with the paw of Hercules and the smile of Machiavelli, has been Irving's agent, emissary and apologist, his manager, his best critic, best advocate, best counsellor and best friend almost from the beginning of his inter-national reputation.' On the other hand, a claim by the *Chicago Daily News* in 1888 that Stoker was as great an artist as Irving might not have gone down too well with his master.[44]

Indeed, whether Irving would have been happy in general to see his subordinate given so much credit is another matter: the purpose of his formidable publicity machine was to make him appear a multi-talented genius and to shore up his weaknesses. Stoker's job was especially difficult as, according to a well-informed contemporary, no man was ever more written of or talked about in America than Henry Irving but, equally probably, no man was more misrepresented. Some saw him as a monster, some as an angel, but he was 'a mystery to untravelled American journalists, and an enigma to the great play-going public of the American cities'.[45]

The mutual love affair of Stoker and the United States was sardonically acknowledged by an English newspaper columnist in 1896 who reported that Stoker had got a hearty welcome on his arrival back from a Lyceum tour of America, 'a continent which according to his account is constructed on the lines popularly associated with heaven'. Stoker's breezy relations with American journalists are evident in his account of going alone to the United States in the winter of 1886 to arrange a tour of *Faust* for the following year. Word of his arrival leaked out and he was met by a 'whole cloud of interviewers', most whom he had known for years. He offered to tell them the purpose of his visit if they would keep it a secret; they said they preferred not to know. The 'whisky' of hospitality was in front of them and a reporter asked Stoker: 'By the way, how do you like American as compared with Irish whisky? – *of course, not for publication!*'[46]

Some of the media misrepresentation with which Stoker had to deal bordered on the grotesque. When he was in Kansas City on a tour with Irving in 1899–1900, the actor, being a firm traditionalist, preferred limelight or calcium light to the newer and cheaper electricity; the gas bottles necessary for this light were outside the Opera House where Irving was appearing and a local reporter, who spotted this, wrote a story that Irving was a dying man, only kept alive by oxygen, so that even the keyhole of his room was stopped up to prevent any escape of the life-giving oxygen! On another occasion, Stoker would not allow a reporter to travel with the Lyceum Company on the train from Chicago to Detroit. Undaunted, the reporter wrote an article describing how the company travelled, even down to the *déshabillé* appearance of some members. At the end, in small type, he added that he could not vouch for its accuracy as he had not been allowed on the train. He described Stoker as: 'an individual who *called himself* Bram Stoker . . . who seems to occupy some anomalous position between secretary and valet. Whose manifest duties are to see that there is mustard in the sandwiches and to take the dogs out for a run; and who united in his own person every vulgarity of the English-speaking race.'[47]

Some of Stoker's experiences on these tours found their way into his fiction. The Atlantic storm in *The Man*, for example, had its genesis in a hurricane which struck when Stoker was crossing the Atlantic on the SS *Marquette* in 1899 with the Lyceum Company. Irving and Ellen Terry were enthralled by this spectacle of nature at its most majestic and Stoker took it upon himself to coach Terry in the arts of riding the storm, holding her against the rail and showing her how to 'look into the wind without feeling it'. His usefulness was almost his undoing. He was sitting on a trunk in the companionway of the *Marquette* 'surrounded by as many of the womankind as could catch hold of me' when the trunk broke loose. He shoved the women away but was caught by the trunk himself and suffered a leg injury which he reckoned could have resulted in the loss of his leg had he been hit slightly differently. Everyone, including a band of American footballers, produced bottles of embrocation or liniment and applied them so vigorously that the skin of the wounded part and the surrounding area was rubbed off! In 1901, Stoker told of an incident in which he chided a passenger who laughed as a ship's pilot put out in a terrible storm. Stoker's manly dialogue on this occasion was worthy of any of his fictional heroes: 'What the devil are you laughing at? Is it to see splendid fellows like that in danger of their lives? You ought to be ashamed of yourself. The men could actually hear you!'[48]

The surviving correspondence from these tours illustrates the different aspects of Stoker's life there. A poem by the American writer, Roswell Field, 'A Night With Sir Henry Irving', dedicated to Stoker, recalls staying up all night with Irving in convivial circumstances. Stoker was generally free to indulge in a bachelor lifestyle as Florence accompanied him to America only once, for the third Lyceum tour, and the storm-tossed crossing of the Atlantic which she endured in 1887 would not have encouraged her to repeat the experience. On one of these tours Stoker and Irving attended the wedding of Gilbert Parker, the Canadian novelist, in New York in 1896, when those present included men of letters such as Edmund Clarence Stedman, the American banker, poet and critic, and Thomas Bailey Aldrich, prolific author and editor of the *Atlantic Monthly*. There were sublime friendships, like that with Clara Louise Kellogg, the American singer renowned for her interpretation of the part of Marguerite in Gounod's *Faust*. Less pleasantly, he had to confront the tensions which emerged within the Lyceum staff, such as when the actor, William Terriss, accused Stoker of bearing ill will towards him, a sign of the strained atmosphere which could develop. Extensive correspondence about the Lyceum tours with William Winter, the influential New York drama critic, illustrates yet another aspect of Stoker's behind-the-scenes work to promote Irving.

EIGHT

Gallant Conduct

We women have something of the mother in us . . .

(Dracula, Mina Harker's Journal)

When Stoker and Florence arrived in London in 1878, they took a suite of six rooms on the top floor of 7 Southampton Street in Bloomsbury, central London, not too far from the Lyceum Theatre, at a rent of £100 per year. Noel, their only child, was born there on 30 December 1879. After two years living at Southampton Street, the Stokers moved to 27 Cheyne Walk, a fashionable address in Chelsea, described at the time as 'a singular hetero-geneous kind of spot, very dirty and confused in some places, quite beautiful in others, abounding in antiquities and the traces of great men'.[1] The writers, Dante Gabriel Rossetti, Hall Caine, Charles Algernon Swinburne and the painter, James Abbott McNeill Whistler, all lived near Cheyne Walk around that time. The 1881 census listed Stoker at 27 Cheyne Walk as head of the family, with Florence and Noel, together with his brother, George Stoker, Elizabeth Jarrald, a nurse, presumably for Noel, Harriett Daw, a cook, and Emma Barton, a housemaid. The Embankment along the Thames, which stretched, conveniently, from Chelsea to central London, had been completed just over a decade previously and provided Stoker with an artery linking his home with the Lyceum. He used both river transport and, in later years, a bicycle, which he pedalled along the Embankment, to get to work. In 1879 the Embankment was lit by electricity, which was then spreading in the capital (the Lyceum would be one of the first London theatres to have electricity installed). Technological change was in the air: the first telephone exchange opened in London the same year, as did Alfred Harman's photographic materials factory in Ilford. Richard D'Oyly Carte's Savoy Theatre on the Strand, just around the corner from the Lyceum, was the first theatre lit by electricity when it opened in 1881. These changes registered with Stoker and would be embodied in *Dracula*: Jonathan Harker brought the Count photographs of the estate, Carfax, when he visited him in Transylvania and Professor Van Helsing waxed lyrical on contemporary advances in electrical science.

It cannot have been easy for Florence having Stoker's youngest brother,

George, living with them at this time, when Noel was an infant. Born on 20 July 1854, George Stoker had qualified as a doctor and filled a number of prominent medical positions, including service with the Red Crescent Ambulance in the Balkans at the time of the Serbo-Turkish and Turco-Russian Wars of 1876–8. His book, *With 'the Unspeakables'; or Two Years of Campaigning in European and Asiatic Turkey* (1878), is of particular interest to Bram Stoker biography, describing, as it does, George's activities in the area where his brother would locate Count Dracula nearly two decades later, although, unlike him, he was sympathetic to the Turks. He later pioneered the idea of using oxygen to treat various illnesses and set up a nursing home to apply this treatment in London. He benefited from his brother's connections with high society through the Lyceum, and Baroness Coutts was among those who supported this venture. George Stoker was a Stafford House Commissioner (the Stafford House Committee was a forerunner of the British Red Cross which provided medical staff in areas of conflict at that time) during the South African War in 1899–1900 and helped organise an Irish Hospitals Corps to serve during the Boer War in South Africa around the turn of the twentieth century. He had, in short, inherited the same ability and energy which characterised his brothers. Like them too, he had a flair for publication, and was the author of a number of books, including *Songs of the Red Cross and Other Verses* (1907).

Bram's elder sister, Matilda, was also part of the Stoker family circle in London in the years following the move of Florence and Bram from Dublin. Matilda, who had studied art in Rome while her parents lived in Naples, lived in the 1880s in lodgings off the King's Road, Chelsea. As this was close to Stoker's home, it might be assumed that he was instrumental in helping her settle in London. In an 1880 letter to Stoker, Ellen Terry sent her love to 'Miss Matilda', so Matilda was presumably either staying with Stoker and Florence or was living nearby.[2] Stoker may have helped Matilda too with publishing outlets in London; the April 1887 issue of the *London Illustrated Magazine* featured her article on the relationship of Richard Brinsley Sheridan and his wife, Eliza Linley, which attracted favourable comment from Oscar Wilde. On 5 March 1889, at the Rathfarnham Church of Ireland parish church, Matilda married Charles Petitjean, a French administrator, son of a civil engineer who was a chevalier of the Légion d'honneur. Both their ages were rather tactfully described as 'full' on the marriage certificate: Matilda was in fact forty-two. Charles may afterwards have been commissioned by Stoker to do some translation work for the Lyceum, presumably to supplement his official income.

* * *

Stoker's duties at the Lyceum allowed him little time to spend at home with his family. He left for work in the forenoon and returned about 4 p.m. He dined at 6 p.m. before returning to the theatre. He used a bus, train or hansom cab for transport and would get home about midnight, by which time the rest of the family had gone to bed, and he ate the supper which had been left waiting for him in the fireplace. He breakfasted in bed at about 10 a.m. Florence once 'complained that her lord rarely came home to dinner' and would be more troubled if Henry Irving died than his own son; Stoker is reputed to have replied that he could have another son but not another Irving.[3] His relative lack of engagement in family life is corroborated by Noel's reminiscence that '. . . my father's life was spent away from home, the theatre, social life, & writing books. He would never have discussed the first of these with a youth, anyway.'[4] While he remembered him as absent a good deal, Noel had positive recollections of his father, recalling him lying full-length on the drawing-room carpet before leaving for work at the Lyceum in the forenoon and allowing his son to climb on his chest. Later Noel would listen to him as he got into his dress suit, telling tales of pixies 'and about a delicious Compound called Quasheroo'. One episode Noel remembered was of arriving at a railway station with his parents to find the train already leaving. Stoker let out a bloodcurdling yell and everything stopped, including the train, and they were able to get on board, an illustration of his father's booming voice and generally larger-than-life personality. The experience of fatherhood is reflected in Stoker's fiction. In *The Man*, for example, there is a marvellous description of a big man holding a baby for the first time:

> Like all men unaccustomed to babies, he feared it . . . In addition there was a physical fear . . . It was so helpless, so wee, so frail. At first he could never take it into his arms without suffering a fear that its head would drop off. He was himself so big, so strong, so rough . . . he feared he might unwittingly do it an injury.[5]

A less sentimental view of babies is to be found in 'Chin Music', one of the stories in *Snowbound*, where a widower is attempting to deal with a squalling baby on a train:

> All babies are malignant; the natural wickedness of man, as elaborated at [sic] the primeval curse, seems to find an unadulterated effect in their expression of feeling . . . This baby was a particularly fine specimen of its class. It seemed to have no compunction whatever, no parental respect, no natural affection, no mitigation in the natural

virulence of its rancour. It screamed, it roared, it squalled, it bellowed. The root ideas of profanity, of obscenity, of blasphemy were mingled in his tone. It beat with clenched fist in its father's face, it clawed at his eyes with twitching fingers, it used its head as an engine with which to buffet him. It kicked, it struggled, it wiggled, it writhed, it twisted itself into serpentine convolutions, till every now and then, what with its vocal and muscular exertions, it threatened to get black in the face.[6]

The chin music of the title is, of course, the baby's crying.

In his 1887 story, 'The Dualitists', Stoker addresses these words to a character on the brink of parenthood:

Ah! Ephraim Bubb, little thinkest thou that another moment may for ever destroy the peaceful, happy course of thy life, and open to thy too-craving eyes the portals of that wondrous land where childhood reigns supreme, and where the tyrant infant with the wave of his tiny hand and the imperious treble of his tiny voice sentences his parent to the deadly vault below the castle moat. As the thought strikes thee thou becomest pale. How thou tremblest as thou findest thyself upon the brink of the abyss! Wouldst that thou could recall the past! But hark! The die is cast for good or ill.[7]

Stoker's playful ambiguity about the havoc wreaked on the lives of parents by the birth of a child may well have reflected his own reaction to the birth of Noel and any lack of enthusiasm for further children may have derived from him as much as from Florence.

Neither Stoker nor Florence seems to have been particularly sympathetic parents. Stoker's ham-fisted attempt to teach Noel to swim at Whitby when he was about seven years old had the effect of putting him off swimming for life. According to her granddaughter, Florence was a distant parent when Noel was small. At birth he had a wet-nurse, who apparently starved him. Noel was actually christened Irving Noel Thornley Stoker as a tribute to the actor, who was also his godfather, but he never used the Irving part of his name as he resented a man who had, he felt, worn his father out. He was christened in 1880 at Howth, a seaside village to the north of Dublin city. He was entrusted to a French governess whom he adored, which was just as well as he spent much of his time with her, in the absence of his sociable parents. As a result, he spoke French before English. He never lost his ability in French to the extent that, in later life, people in France thought he was a Frenchman who had been out of France for a while. Stoker had no more than a smattering of French but Florence, who went to see *Hamlet* in French in Paris, presumably had a reasonable command of the language.

Noel spent a good deal of time in his youth with his uncle, Thomas Stoker and his wife, Enid. She told her grandson (and Bram Stoker's biographer), Daniel Farson that Florence had not been especially fond of Noel; Farson characterised her attitude as one of lack of interest rather than providing maternal warmth.[8] The sense of distance between Noel and his parents is caught by George du Maurier's cartoon, 'A Filial Reproof', which appeared in *Punch* in September 1886, with the caption, '*Mamma to Noel (who is inclined to be talkative)*. "Hush, Noel! Haven't I told you often that little Boys should be *Seen* and not *Heard*?" Noel. "Yes Mamma! But you don't *Look* at ME!"' The setting is the lawn of a country house, with Stoker and Florence relaxing in easy chairs. Noel is standing behind his mother, who remains absorbed in her reading, and his barbed wit is directed at Florence: Stoker is seated to the right of the drawing, a tennis racquet at his feet, giving his son his attention.

Noel was with his mother when they survived the sinking of the Channel steamer, *Victoria*, off the French coast, in mid-April 1887. The *Victoria* had run aground at a quarter to four in the morning on rocks off Cap d'Ailly and Stoker spent agonising hours waiting for news before it was established that both Florence and Noel were among the survivors. Stoker's prestigious place in London society was reflected in the prominence given to his family in the media coverage of the tragedy. A number of newspapers quoted criticism by Florence of the alleged incompetence of the *Victoria*'s sailors. This was hastily retracted, with the retractions variously attributed to Florence and her husband. The hand of Stoker, the master publicist, can be seen at work here, killing a negative story which he may have feared could have led to a lawsuit or generated unfavourable publicity either for himself or for the Lyceum. Some of the publicity certainly had been taking on the lurid hue of a Gothic novel, with foreign cowardice contrasted with English bravery. More positively for Stoker, Florence's brush with death was linked to his attempt to save the drowning man in the Thames and she featured prominently in a dramatic front-page picture of the wreck in the *Illustrated London News* of 23 April 1887.

Noel went to a preparatory school, Summerfield, in 1889 at the age of ten and attended a public school, Winchester College, from 1893 to 1898. His absence from home at boarding-school did little to encourage intimacy with his father. Even allowing for the conventions of the time, the 'Dear Sir' opening and general bureaucratic stiffness of Stoker's reply to a letter of congratulation from Noel on the publication of *Dracula* does not convey any sense of warmth or intimacy. When Noel finished school, Stoker asked

if he would like to become a chartered accountant. Noel agreed, as he wanted
to earn his own money. He started in the profession in January 1899 when
he was articled to Westcott & Co., the firm which audited the Lyceum
accounts. He married Neelie Moseley Deane Sweeting in 1910, to whom
he had become engaged three years earlier; her lively personality provided
a contrast to his generally withdrawn nature. He was, in fact, so shy that
he designed walks to avoid meeting other people.

While he was living at Cheyne Walk Stoker performed a feat of heroism
that won him wide publicity. On September 1882, the *Dublin Evening
Telegraph* reported on how Stoker, 'a clever young Dublin man', had
attempted to rescue a drowning man from the Thames. A passenger on
board a ferry decided to commit suicide, climbed over the rails and leapt
into the river. Stoker threw off his coat and jumped in after him; he managed
to get the man back on board and took him to his house nearby but despite
medical assistance, the man died. The coroner's jury in the case added a
rider to its verdict of suicide recognising 'the gallant conduct of Mr. Stoker
in attempting to save life'. Stoker's 'manly & generous' conduct was widely
reported. A Bedford newspaper stated that the country needed to be
governed by an honest and intelligent despot who would reward men like
Stoker. *The Entr'acte* of 23 September featured a large illustration of Henry
Irving congratulating Stoker on the rescue, stating that actors pretended to
be heroes but Stoker was a real hero. Whether the real-life Irving would
have uttered these sentiments is open to question.

Heroic rescue features repeatedly in Stoker's fiction and it is tempting
to see it as a recurrent re-enactment of his moment of glory, although the
rescue theme in Stoker's fiction actually predates the episode in the
Thames. The most extended treatment in Stoker's fiction is his ''Eroes of
the Thames, The Story of a Frustrated Advertisement' which appeared in
the *Royal Magazine* in October 1908. It is the story of a professional
swimmer, Peter Jimpson, who dreams up a stunt whereby he would throw
his son, also called Peter, off London Bridge and stage a dramatic 'rescue'
in order to gain publicity. He is, however, outmanoeuvred by Tom Bolter
and his friend, Polter, a pair of champion swimmers from the North of
England who hijack his attempted stunt for their own publicity purposes.
In this story, Stoker subverts the heroism of the rescue episode, usually
played straight in his fiction.

It is generally believed that the Stokers moved from Cheyne Walk to
17 St Leonard's Terrace after 1884 as a result of Florence's revulsion from
the body of the drowned man being laid out on the dining-room table
following Stoker's rescue attempt of 1882. Apart from the question of

whether the authorities would have allowed a drowned body to remain in a private house overnight, there was in fact a two- or three-year gap between this episode and the move to St Leonard's Terrace, where the Stokers were ensconced by the mid-1880s. Stoker was not, incidentally, moving up in the world by this change of address: Cheyne Walk's greater social cachet was reflected in a rateable value almost double that of St Leonard's Terrace. He was listed at 17 St Leonard's Terrace until 1896 when he moved next door to number 18. He stayed at this address until 1906–7, when he moved to 4 Durham Place, around the corner. Stoker was again head of the family at 17 St Leonard's Terrace in the 1891 census. The domestic staff consisted of Mary A. Dunhunter, the cook, and Ada B. Howard, a parlourmaid. Noel Stoker remembered his parents having two domestic staff, Maria Mitchell, the cook, and Louisa Baiden, the maid, both of whom 'worshipped the master'. These names do not square with the census returns, so this cook and maid must have been employed later. As the rateable value was higher at 18 St Leonard's Terrace, Stoker's motive in changing from the house next door in the mid-1890s was not to save money: it was probably part of the contemporary middle-class pattern of moving every few years and a sign that he rented rather than owned the properties in which he lived.

As if he did not have enough to keep him busy, Stoker decided, in 1886, to qualify as a barrister (Jonathan Harker in *Dracula* is a solicitor). He may have been fulfilling a wish of his dead father and had, in any event, developed some legal expertise in a Civil Service career dealing with the administration of justice. It may also have been a further sign of ingrained restlessness, an inability to focus indefinitely on a single occupation, which had manifested itself previously in relation to his Civil Service position in Dublin. As his period of legal study was also the heyday of his friendship with Henry Irving, his motive could hardly have been disillusionment with Irving and the Lyceum. Stoker made no secret of his legal studies: they were referred to in one journal in May 1889 which made it clear that there was no conflict of interest with his Lyceum duties: 'However, Mr. Stoker looks after his chief's affairs, carries on his legal studies, contributes to periodical literature, and turns up fresh and smiling at social functions as if he had nothing whatever to do.'[9]

Stoker was admitted to study for the Bar on 3 May 1886. Becoming a barrister was not an unduly demanding business in that era: it required evidence of a liberal education and statements from two sponsors that the entrant was the right sort of person for admission (a university degree was generally sufficient proof of that). The entrant then followed a process of 'reading in chambers', which involved a form of apprenticeship to an established barrister and the use of the library, together with the 'keeping of terms' (eating a certain number of dinners with legal colleagues to develop the appropriate social and professional ethos). Qualification generally took about three years by the late nineteenth century. Stoker took four years: he was called to the Bar at the Inner Temple on 30 April 1890, which again generated media interest: 'Mr. Stoker is a genial good fellow, most popular in the theatrical profession, and we have no doubt that he will become equally so amongst his new associates who are engaged "in the law".'[10]

Stoker once told his son that he would have liked to have practised at the Bar and it is hard to disagree with Noel's belief that he would have made a good barrister. He was also proud of his legal qualification: he listed his occupation as 'Barrister, Theatrical Manager, Author' in that order in the 1891 census. It is probably a sign of his identification with the character of Van Helsing in *Dracula* that he is a qualified lawyer. If the form in which *Dracula* is presented bears similarities to a Civil Service file, it is also the manner in which evidence is gathered for a trial. Yet, despite his keen interest in the law (he had a fine collection of statutes in his library) and the fact that he had been involved in its administration as a civil servant, Stoker's attitude towards it, as revealed in his fiction, is deeply ambiguous. This has long been recognised in the case of *Dracula* where 'behaviour generally attributed to the vampire – the habit of attacking a sleeping victim, violence, irrational behaviour – is revealed in the behaviour of the civilized Englishman also'. Van Helsing, the moral pillar of *Dracula*, is, for example, willing to countenance euthanasia for Mina Harker to prevent her becoming a vampire and she, in turn, contemplates either suicide or being murdered by one of the men. It is all right for brave men to kill their 'womenkind' to prevent them falling into the hands of the enemy. The attitude of his heroes in defying the law, in believing that their moral imperative overrides mere legal niceties, is also evident in *The Mystery of the Sea* where the hero declares: 'We were, one and all of us, prepared to set at defiance every law – international, maritime, national or local.'[11] In *Dracula*, Lord Godalming declares grandly that his title will make house-breaking all right with the locksmith involved and any policeman who happened to come along. The attitude towards the law of *Dracula*'s supposedly virtuous characters is encapsulated in Quincy Morris's declaration: 'I have a kind of belief in a Winchester when there is any trouble of that sort around.'

NINE

Lyceum Literati

I have asked my friend Arminius, of Buda-Pesth University, to make his record . . .

(*Dracula*, Mina Harker's Journal)

While some of Stoker's work for Irving was personal, or even menial, he did benefit greatly from their collaboration. Horace Wyndham remembered the Stokers as knowing everyone worth knowing and being exceedingly hospitable in their Chelsea home. Their guests included such figures as Jerome K. Jerome, a neighbour who lived at Chelsea Gardens, a short walk from the Stoker home. Invitations have survived to J. Bernard Partridge, an artist with access to the Lyceum who drew both Irving and Ellen Terry, and to Percy FitzGerald. The fact that much of his social life derived from his Lyceum connections overturns the notion that Stoker would have felt exploited and therefore 'vampirised' by Henry Irving. (In this view of their relationship Stoker, angry and frustrated by the subservience of his subordinate role, created the vampire Count both as reflection of, and protest against, the imperious Irving.)

His position at the Lyceum also made Stoker a man about town. *Vanity Fair* mentioned Florence and himself as attending a private view at the New Gallery in 1891, together with a number of pretty people, if not the usual number of smart ones. The *World* described Stoker as 'a tall man with an amiable manner and a red beard' who was present at another private view at the same gallery in 1892. Arthur Sullivan, the composer, Oscar Wilde and Comyns Carr were also present. The *Gentlewoman* noted Florence's attendance at private view teas at the Argonauts Club whose members included Hall Caine, Arthur Conan Doyle, Justin McCarthy, Anthony Hope and other literary luminaries of the time. The perception of Stoker and Florence as enjoying an active social life is reinforced by private family correspondence. Margaret D. Thomson, Stoker's sister, wrote to his brother, Tom: 'Stoker & Flo are flourishing & very gay I hear.'[1]

Of all the literary figures with whom Stoker came into contact at the Lyceum, he respected none more than the poet, Alfred, Lord Tennyson. His feelings for the Poet Laureate bordered on the reverential. Tennyson's influence on

Stoker's generation was evident in the structure of Dowden's English course at Trinity, which featured him as the successor to the major Romantic poets. Stoker addressed meetings of the Trinity Philosophical Society after the reading of papers on 'Seven Poems of the Laureate' in February 1871 and again in 1873 after a paper on 'Tennyson's Treatment of the Arthurian Romance'. He met the great man in person when James Knowles introduced them at the Lyceum in March 1879. Stoker was impressed by Tennyson's large and strong physique and his propensity for 'manly games' in his youth. They shared an interest in the macabre, with Stoker noting that Tennyson regarded Poe as 'the most original genius that America had produced'.[2] Stoker and Florence lunched with the poet and Lady Tennyson, while his sons, Hallam and Lionel, spent Sunday evenings at the Stoker home in Cheyne Walk. The Poet Laureate may, to some degree, have been a model for the character of Dracula. Stoker compared his 'lifting of the upper lip which shows the canine tooth, and which is so marked an indication of militant instinct' to the same characteristic in the explorer Richard Burton.[3]

Stoker carried out research in the British Museum for the production of Tennyson's *The Cup* at the Lyceum. As in *Dracula*, the period of the play was 'semi-mythical' and stood between East and West, when the old gods still commanded real belief. Stoker was intrigued by the dichotomy between the gorgeous pagan effects created by Irving for the play and the large number of High Church clergy who attended. *The Cup* opened on 3 January 1881 and was a great success. Tennyson followed with a trilogy on the struggle between the British people and the Papacy: *Becket*, *Harold* and *Queen Mary*. Irving refused *Becket* when Tennyson offered it in 1879 but asked permission to mount it in 1891. Stoker acted as intermediary between Irving and Tennyson and found that the poet was familiar with every line of his play and was alive to even the smallest change.[4] In *Dracula*, Van Helsing uses the phrase '*In manus tuas, Domine!*' as he is about to enter Lucy's tomb; translated as 'Into thy hands, O Lord', it echoes closely the final phrase spoken by Becket in Tennyson's play.[5]

In October 1890, Stoker and Irving visited Tennyson at his home in Aldworth, Surrey. Stoker found it a haven of peace after the strenuous world of London. He went for a walk with Tennyson, who began to tell 'Irish anecdotes'. In return, Stoker made Tennyson laugh with 'some Irish dialect stories' and tales of extravagant toasts of the Orange Order. In 1892, he was again with Tennyson and thought him 'full of insight into the Irish character'. On this occasion, Tennyson asked Stoker if he was Irish; when Stoker replied in the affirmative, Tennyson apologised: 'You must forgive me. If I had known that I would not have said anything that seemed to belittle Ireland.'[6] On the 1892 visit, the poet asked Stoker if he had read his poem, 'The Voyage of Maeldune', based on an Irish legend; Stoker had not, so Tennyson gave him a description, spiced with quotations. The poem of Tennyson's that most obviously influenced *Dracula* was not, however, 'Maeldune' but 'Demeter and Persephone'. In using the name, *Demeter*, for the ship which carries Dracula to England, Stoker is consciously recalling a poem whose dualistic landscape of good and evil, of gods and demons, shares much with his novel. The determination of the God of Dreams that Persephone 'Should be for ever and for evermore/The Bride of Darkness' matches that of Dracula that Lucy and Mina should be his dark brides for evermore.

Stoker sent Tennyson copies of both *Under the Sunset* and *The Snake's Pass*. He wept as he left Tennyson after his 1892 visit, knowing it would be the last time he would see him; the poet died eleven days later. *Becket* was produced in February 1893. In 1897, Irving read *Becket* at Canterbury Cathedral, holding his audience spellbound, to raise money for a restoration fund. Stoker handled the arrangements, which included having a letter publicising the event 'facsimiled' and sent to 400 newspapers, as well as arranging special trains from London to Canterbury.

Irving's masterful creation of horrific leading roles must have influenced Stoker but they were only one stream of many which flowed into his eventual masterpiece. Stoker was an intensely literary man whose position at the Lyceum brought him into contact with the leading artistic and literary figures of the day. The way that he is mentioned by the contemporary magazine editor, Frank Harris, in his autobiographical *My Life and Loves*, for example, demonstrates that he was very much a public figure who Harris assumed would be known to his readership. His dealings with the literary elite were not always easy; in 1895 he found himself having to mediate with a touchy George Moore when *Journey's End and Lovers' Meeting* was produced at the Lyceum and Moore demanded that his name be restored to what he regarded as its rightful place on the playbill.[7] Stoker was, in fact, caught in the middle of one of Moore's celebrated interlinked literary and personal quarrels over the question of the authorship of the play. Moore had originally produced a scenario (borrowed from the French of Caraquell) and some dialogue which he gave to the beautiful American heiress and writer (under the pen-name, John Oliver Hobbes), Pearl Craigie (1867–1906), and with whom he was having a flitation. She developed it and submitted it to the Lyceum through Ellen Terry for production as a curtain-raiser under her own name. A furious Moore appeared at the Lyceum and was seen by Stoker who agreed to print new playbills to meet his concerns on authorship. Terry, however, seems to have persuaded Moore to climb down and allow Craigie the title of sole author while being paid half the fee.

Moore was, incidentally, the author of an 1870s poem echoing Baudelaire, 'The Metamorphoses of the Vampire'. Given that Moore had been a childhood friend of Oscar Wilde's, Stoker may have known him prior to his departure from Ireland through his connection with the Wildes. Moore may have used the London-based, Dutch artist, Lawrence Alma Tadema (1836–1912), a good friend of Stoker's, as a model for the central character of Lewis Seymour in his 1883 novel, *A Modern Lover*, so the two Irishmen moved, to some extent at any rate, in similar circles in London. Julian Hawthorne, for example, was a friend of both men. Moore would have joined the Irish Literary Society in London but was blackballed by the Liberal lawyer and politician, Charles Russell who, as 'An Amazed Catholic Parent', had strongly objected to Moore's use of a convent where his daughter was at school in the opening chapter of his novel, *A Drama in Musin* (1886).[8] They would, however, have been divided by their respective attitudes towards the acting profession, Moore describing it in 'Mummer Worship' as the lowest of the arts, if it were an art at all. His particular target was the star system of the West End which produced celebrity actors like Henry Irving and the Kendals. Irving counterattacked effectively, quietly using his contacts in the press to denigrate Moore, with Stoker probably acting on his behalf. In this difference with Moore, Irving had a trump card: his rejection out of hand of Moore's play, *Martin Luther*, when the author approached him over breakfast in a Liverpool hotel in 1878, thus making Moore appear to be settling scores for a previous snub.

The conflict between Moore and Irving was, however, much deeper than personal antagonism. The Lyceum entertained the Establishment; it did not challenge it. Moore, by contrast, consistently pioneered new forms of art in various media and this took no little courage in late Victorian England. In particular, he was instrumental in interesting the publisher, Henry Vizetelly (1812?–89) in publishing Emile Zola's novels in English, the first of which, *L'Assommoir*, came out in 1884 in a translation that was partly Moore's work. Vizetelly attracted the attention of the National Vigilance Association, set up in 1885 to promote, among other things, the adherence of both sexes to 'the law of chastity' and the 'importance of personal purity of all good citizens', language which could have come from a Stoker novel. A sub-committee was set up to police literature (a cause which Stoker would promote in the first decade of the twentieth century). In 1888, Vizetelly was charged before the Chancery court with publishing obscene books, three of them by Zola. Herbert Asquith, the future Prime Minister, prosecuted, describing the novels as the three most immoral books ever published. The elderly publisher escaped with a fine on this occasion but was not so lucky the following year when he was again prosecuted, with the Solicitor General leading for the Crown, denouncing Zola's *La Terre* as 'filthy' and 'bestial obscenity'. This time the ill old man was sent to Holloway prison for three months where he was visited by a shocked Moore whose efforts, through petition to the Home Secretary, for remission of sentence, were unsuccessful. Extending the boundaries of art was a risky business in this climate and it was not attempted at the Lyceum. Any subversion in *Dracula* would be carefully coded and its author would avoid the fate of those who drew down on themselves the wrath of the moral guardians of the time; indeed, he was among the most vocal in promoting a virtuous public morality.

Moore was connected with the progressive developments in the theatre, which would increasingly challenge the position of Henry Irving's Lyceum in the 1890s. His friend, the critic, William Archer, was instrumental in the mounting of Ibsen's *A Doll's House* at the Novelty Theatre in June 1889. To some, such as A. B. Walkley, it was exhilarating, evidence that the great intellectual currents of the day had at last reached the theatre. The Lyceum loyalist, Clement Scott, by contrast, was antagonistic, horrified at the modernity of the central character of Nora. In October 1889, Moore contributed an article on the English playwrights of the day to the *Fortnightly Review* in which he analysed critically the output of various dramatists, some of them friends of Stoker, including W. S. Gilbert and Arthur Wing Pinero and found them wanting. In 1890, fired with enthusiasm following a trip to Paris with Arthur Symons during which they had seen Ibsen's *Ghosts*, Moore outlined plans for a free theatre in London in a series of articles in the *Hawk*. The freedom was to be from commercialism, censorship and convention; in other words, it was to represent the antithesis of everything the Lyceum represented. The type of drama envisaged by Moore – free of virtuous heroes and fortuitous accidents to move the plot along – was also the antithesis of the staple elements to be found in much of Stoker's fiction.

Another Irishman – and Ibsen enthusiast – who challenged the status quo in the London of that period also proved problematic for Stoker. George Bernard Shaw referred to the Lyceum's first nights, in which Stoker had a starring role, disparagingly as Irving's 'direct bribery'. Shaw was invited to these occasions as a drama critic but did not accept, although he did attend the plays at the Lyceum often between 1895 and 1898. Stoker had grittier work to do on Irving's behalf with Shaw. It fell to him to tell Shaw when Irving finally decided, after much prevarication, not to produce his *Man of Destiny* at the Lyceum. The manuscript was returned with a curt note of rejection written by Stoker. Shortly afterwards, Shaw told Terry that he would like to see her as Portia, but 'the Lyceum would fall on my head, and bury me with the fainting Stoker & the prostrate Henry if I presented myself'.[9]

Stoker did, however, keep open his lines of communication with Shaw. In May 1898, he invited Shaw to attend the first night of *The Medicine Man* at the Lyceum, asking if he would come 'personally' although he was no longer on the critics' list. Shaw replied that he had only one personal desire and that was to see the theatres of London, with actors, managers and critics, plunged into hell until only a virgin art remained. However, it would not be 'decent' to have a first night at the Lyceum without him and would create the impression of a vendetta. Again he denied that he had meant to imply that Irving had been drunk in a production of *Richard III*, two years previously, an implication at which Irving had taken mortal offence. So he added a formal acceptance at the end of his letter to Stoker in a manner which implied an element of collusion between them.

They had, in fact, a good deal in common. Also from a Protestant Dublin background, Shaw too was an admirer of Shelley and was saturated in Shakespeare and the Bible from an early age. He was a regular at the Theatre Royal in Dublin as a child, and Barry Sullivan was his hero, as he was for Stoker. He first saw Henry Irving in *The Two Roses* at the Theatre Royal in Dublin in 1872 and envisaged Irving and Terry as his ideal leading couple. When he failed in this objective with Irving, he began a correspondence with Ellen Terry, designed to undermine her faith in the actor, not a difficult task after the sundering of their personal relationship, when she had come to the conclusion that Irving did not appreciate anything.

In 1895, Shaw replied ironically to Stoker's reaction to criticism that the actor is a parasite upon the play: 'The courteous and indefatigable Mr Bram Stoker – just as all majesties are "gracious" so are all acting-managers "courteous and indefatigable" – has, it appears, been taking his turn at the popular sport of chastening the dramatic critics. No doubt he thinks that long experience of putting them in their places qualifies him, *a fortiori*, for putting them in their place.'[10] Here Shaw used his wit to deadly effect and there was an element at least of the jocose in his relationship with Stoker. Florence Stoker remembered a story of Shaw going to first nights as a theatre critic in tweed knickerbockers and jacket; when Stoker stipulated that he must wear tails, the playwright complied but still wore a flannel shirt! The belief in his family was that Stoker, in turn, regarded Shaw in a humorous light.

Shaw and Stoker were two of a triumvirate of Dubliners who exercised considerable influence on the London theatre in the latter years of the nineteenth century. The third was Oscar Wilde. He had long been a fan of Irving, having seen him perform the title role of *Macbeth* in December 1876 and enjoyed it immensely. Wilde's son later remembered both Irving and Ellen Terry having been frequent visitors to his parents' receptions at their Tite Street home, the décor of which was designed by Edward Godwin, Terry's lover and the father of her chidren.[11] Reviewing *Olivia*, a play adapted by his kinsman, William Gorman Wills, from Oliver Goldsmith's *The Vicar of Wakefield*, Wilde waxed lyrical about Irving's management of the theatre: 'The Lyceum under Mr Irving's management has become a centre of art. We are all of us in his debt. I trust that we may see some more plays by living dramatists produced at his theatre, for *Olivia* has been exquisitely mounted and exquisitely played.' Of the play itself, he wrote that it was 'a very exquisite work of art. Indeed, I know of no other dramatist who could have re-told this beautiful English tale with such tenderness and such power . . . The sentiment of the poet and the science of the playwright are exquisitely balanced in it.' He was also enthusiastic about the performance of Ellen Terry – 'a very great artist' – and Henry Irving, whose performance was 'a masterpiece of fine acting'.[12] Shaw was less impressed, feeling that the Lyceum production was inferior to the original 1877 production at the Court Theatre, when her creation of the role of an innocent girl seduced had been a milestone in Ellen Terry's development as an actress and had convinced Henry Irving to make her his partner. Although Stoker excised all mention of Oscar Wilde in *Personal Reminiscences of Henry Irving* (as he did of George Bernard Shaw), he was very much part of the social scene surrounding the Lyceum: he was, for example, a guest at the supper to celebrate the hundredth performance of *The Merchant of Venice* in 1880 and he tried, unsuccessfully, to get Irving to stage *The Duchess of Padua* in 1891.

Oscar continued to be fond of Florence Stoker. In 1881 he wrote to Ellen Terry wishing Florence success in Tennyson's *The Cup* at the Lyceum in which she had a small part. He sent two crowns of flowers, one of which she was to give to Florence from herself, with blithe indifference to the potentially embarrassing situation in which he was placing Terry: 'I should like to think that she was wearing something of mine the first night she comes on stage, that anything of mine should touch her. Of course, if you think – but you won't think she will suspect? How could she? She thinks I never loved her, thinks I forget. My God how could I!'[13] Wilde was captivated by Ellen Terry around this time and was so impressed by her playing of Queen Henrietta Maria in W.G. Wills's *Charles I* that he sent her a privately printed sonnet in 1880. She accepted the dedication of two sonnets from him in 1881 and made clear her pride in having inspired Wilde in her 1908 autobiography, at a time when his name could not be mentioned in polite society. Wilde was among those who saw the Lyceum Company off from Liverpool on the *Brittanic* on its first American tour in 1883.

An early poem of Wilde's, 'The Rose of Love, and with a Rose's Thorns', featured an unhappy suicidal lover but Wilde seems to have been able to carry on a normal relationship with Florence and Stoker. In 1885 he wrote to Philippa Knott, Florence's sister, that it would be a pleasure to call on her and to see Florrie again. He accepted a supper invitation from Stoker in 1889 for himself only, stating that his wife was not well and had gone to Brighton.[14] Stoker provided Lyceum tickets for the Wildes and both Stoker and Florence attended, on 20 February 1892, the première of *Lady Windermere's Fan*. Wilde sent Florence a copy of his book of fairy tales, *The Happy Prince and Other Tales*, published in 1888 and, in 1893, a copy of *Salome*, together with kind regards to Stoker.

Irving's knighthood was announced in 1895, on the day Wilde was convicted at the Old Bailey; Laurence Irving stated that his father did not know Wilde well but that his sons delighted in Oscar's company. Laurence Irving believed that Ellen Terry was the veiled lady with the violets at Wilde's trial and that the violets were a joint gesture from Irving and Terry, pointing to the fact that when Wilde was released from prison, one of the few messages of encouragement came from Irving. There is, however, no solid evidence to support the conjecture that Ellen Terry was the veiled lady at the trial. Nor is there any real evidence for the speculation in recent biography that Stoker, encouraged by Florence, went to Paris with money for Oscar after his release. The source for this latter claim was Ann Stoker, Bram Stoker's granddaughter. Ann heard the story from her mother, who was on good terms with her mother-in-law, presumably the original source.

One small indication that there may be substance in the story is a reference in a letter written by Wilde from prison in 1897 about his finances in which he asks that 'whatever Mr Stoker is owed be paid to him from the same fund in Leverson's hands'. It has been assumed that this refers to a firm of solicitors but it is not impossible that the Mr Stoker referred to was in fact Bram Stoker.[15] As against that, while Oscar Wilde touched all his acquaintances for money at the time of his release from prison, he was punctilious in writing letters of thanks and no such letter to Stoker has come to light.[16] Oscar Wilde was never mentioned by Florence in front of Ann; he was still a taboo subject.[17] Stoker was certainly aware of the distress that Oscar's downfall caused in the Wilde family: Oscar's brother, William (known as Willie), wrote to him in July 1895 of how 'poor Oscar' had been 'led astray by his vanity & conceit' but was now taking his punishment with manly fortitude which would help to purify him in body and soul.[18]

Stoker had maintained a close friendship with Willie Wilde after he moved to London, following the relationship of their student days at Trinity College Dublin. Willie Wilde was very different to Oscar; sporting a black beard, he was 'less a clever fellow' but was an amusing companion capable of good conversation and some wit. He married a wealthy American lady under the mistaken notion that she would support him in 'luxurious idleness', while she 'expected him to work in the fiction factory she owned in Fifth Avenue'. Declaring that 'the man who married for money jolly well earns it', he returned to England to ply his trade at the *Daily Telegraph*, with which Stoker was also connected. The tone of the surviving letters between Stoker and Willie is affectionate.[19] Willie, a neighbour in Chelsea was, like Stoker, an active member of the Irish Literary Society in London until his death in 1899. Lady Wilde was also a neighbour of Stoker's in Chelsea – her London home in Oakley Street was around the corner from his and their friendship continued until her death in 1896. On one occasion, when Stoker introduced a girl as half English and half Irish at one of her literary gatherings, Lady Wilde responded: 'Glad to meet you, my dear, your English half is as welcome as your Irish bottom.'

Probably the most discordant literary relationship was that between Stoker and Florence and one of Florence's sisters, Alice Grace (1861–1901), who married the writer, Frank Frankfort Moore. While Alice may have been deemed by contemporaries not to have had 'the wonderful beauty' of Florence, she was pretty, attractive, highly intelligent and well read. Moore himself was seen as one of the liveliest of spirits, 'full of that radiant and laughing optimism which accounted for much of the brilliant success of his writings'. One newspaper found it hard to associate such a lively couple with death, when Alice Grace died at a comparatively early age in 1901.[20] Frankfort Moore was born in Limerick in 1855; a few years later his family moved to Belfast. Forced to abandon plans to attend Trinity College Dublin, he travelled to South Africa and India before returning to Ireland and publishing a volume of poems in 1874. He turned to fiction and also became a drama and art critic. In 1881 he was appointed assistant editor of the *Belfast News Letter* and began a career as a prolific writer of fiction. Stoker's friend, Geneviève Ward, appeared in his drama, *Forgotten*, at the Grand Theatre in 1889 but it was in 1892, with *I Forbid the Banns*, that he made his reputation. He had moved from Belfast to London in the early 1890s. In 1891, a piece in *Piccadilly* stated that Irish journalists were proud of Frankfort Moore and his drama, *The Queen's Room*, noting that Mrs Moore was a sister of Mrs Bram Stoker and of Mrs Knott, 'that famous patron of the drama in Dublin'.[21] As Moore and his wife became figures in London literary circles, the connection with Bram Stoker and his wife was often commented upon.

Moore was a great admirer of Henry Irving, claiming to have seen his *Hamlet* seventeen times; to him, Irving represented 'the utmost limits of art'. He was present at the supper in the Lyceum after *Othello* in 1881 in which Irving alternated the principal parts with the American actor, Edwin Booth. Moore's description of Irving and Booth clasping hands as 'an emblematic tableau of the artistic union of the Old World and the New' could hardly have been more in tune with Stoker's views on Anglo–American relations.[22] While, however, all might have seemed to be well between Stoker and his brother-in-law, tensions lurked beneath the surface. Moore claimed, with bitter irony, in an 1894 book, that although he was a 'nonentity' who had published a mere nine books, he had had to be invited to post-*Merchant of Venice* celebrations at the Lyceum in 1880 as he had written a 'comedietta' produced there.[23] The implication is that the invitation was reluctant and the finger of blame can only have pointed at Stoker, the key figure in distributing invitations to the social events at the Lyceum.

After Stoker's death, Moore was explicit about his resentment in private correspondence. Commenting to Douglas Sladen on the latter's *Twenty Years of My Life*, he contradicted Sladen's impression that when he arrived in London, his connection with the Bram Stokers would have resulted in a lot of introductions:

> Nothing could be more remote from accuracy, though it might reasonably have been expected that it should be as you assumed. The truth is that on coming to London we received not a single introduction from the Stokers. They were mortally afraid we intended to look on them as our sponsors in society, and they took good care that they should not be compromised. They had literary and artistic luncheons almost every Sunday, but to none of them were we asked. Not until three years had passed, and our position was secure, did we have so much as a cup of tea in the Stokers' house, except on one occasion when we came in from Kew (at a cost of 4/-) to meet a couple of nameless friends [?] . . . The truth is that the whole Stoker family were among the most ardent time-servers in London. Stoker's brother, George, the Doctor, who professed the greatest friendship, would not allow his wife to call lest we should set about borrowing half-a-crown! The whole attitude of the family was a constant source of fun to us, especially as it changed materially after four years, when our positions were reversed.[24]

Yet Stoker, who loomed larger than Moore on the London social and literary scene in the 1890s, seems to have gone out of his way to recognise his brother-in-law, as evidenced by Horace Wyndham's memoir of the era:

During the latter period of his life, and after Irving's death, I saw a good deal of Bram Stoker. There was some sort of connection between him and Frankfort Moore. I am not very clear on the subject, but I fancy he had married Moore's sister. This was probably the case, for 'Mrs. Stoker' was a charming woman and brim full of Irish wit and impulsiveness.[25]

Similarly, when Stoker was interviewed in the *British Weekly* after the publication of *Dracula*, he mentioned that he was a brother-in-law of Frankfort Moore, 'one of the popular young writers of the day'.[26]

Some of the difficulties that Moore saw in their relationship may have been due to political differences. While Stoker was a Home Ruler who treated Ulster Orangeism with ironic detachment, Moore was a staunch defender of the 'excellent Presbyterians of Ulster' who claimed never to have met a nationalist in the society he frequented there and referred to 'the poisonous snake of Home Rule Government'. He returned to his roots in his fiction, and his novel, *The Ulsterman* (1914), the story of a Protestant mill owner whose sons marry into poor Catholic families, was described by the *Times Literary Supplement* as a portrayal of 'the unsympathetic materialism, the drab ugliness of a life which finds its chief recreation in religious strife, and much of its consolation in strong drink'. Moore was scathing about Gladstone's conversion to Home Rule, in contrast, of course, with Stoker's devotion to the English statesman.[27]

Stoker's friendship with Hall Caine was a happier affair. Caine's early work as a journalist with the Liverpool papers included dramatic criticism, and he was greatly influenced by Irving's acting. His close friendship with Irving began in 1874 when he reviewed Irving in *Hamlet* at the Lyceum for the Liverpool *Town Crier*; his review made reference to the language of 'terror and pity' in the play. He was invited to the glittering opening night of the Lyceum under Irving's management on 30 December 1878: Harry Loveday, the Lyceum stage manager, told him to make contact with Bram Stoker, who had a box for him. Caine was in good company on this occasion: others present included the Prince of Wales and Lillie Langtry, Gladstone, Disraeli, Tennyson, Swinburne, Whistler, Millais, Gilbert and Sullivan.

Six years younger than Stoker, Caine had passed a sexually ambiguous youth in the Isle of Man and Liverpool, determined to escape provincial confines and establish himself as a writer in London. Sharing many of Stoker's enthusiasms, including the cause of Anglo-American friendship, the poetry of the English Romantics and Walt Whitman, and the acting of

Henry Irving (he gave lectures in Liverpool on Irving's *Richard III* and *Macbeth* in 1877–8), he began a correspondence with Edward Dowden in October 1877 and got the professor to chair a meeting on 'The Supernatural in Literature' in July 1878. He also wrote an essay on 'The Supernatural Element in Poetry' in these years. Caine's intellectual interest in the occult was reinforced by his hypnotic stare which gave people the impression that he had the power of a medium. As Stoker had done with Whitman, Caine's letters to idols like Dowden, Dante Gabriel Rossetti and John Ruskin, the writer and artist who was championing the Gothic revival in England, were reverential in tone. In August 1881, he achieved his ambition of establishing himself in London when he moved in as an assistant and general factotum with the declining, drug-addicted Dante Gabriel Rossetti, a nephew of John William Polidori, originator of the modern literary vampire story. Rossetti's house was 16 Cheyne Walk, just down the street from Stoker, who was then living at number 27. Caine and Stoker became the closest of friends, swapping tales of the weird when he visited the Stokers at weekends and on tour when they often stayed up with Irving till dawn. Caine produced, at Stoker's suggestion, many sketches, drafts and scenarios for Lyceum productions but none were produced; he attributed this failure to the dominant nature of Irving's personality and the increasing limitations which advancing years imposed on his range of roles. The actor asked Caine to write a new *Vanderdecken*, as he believed the Manxman had great potential as a writer of 'weirdness', but it never materialised as Caine was then too busy. A bizarre manifestation of the weird occurred in real life when the trio of Stoker, Irving and Caine were strolling in the zoo in Regent's Park and Irving was attacked by a monkey which appeared to have turned into 'a veritable, red-eyed, restrainless demon'.[28] Strange goings-on in London Zoo would feature in *Dracula*.

Stoker arranged a publication deal for Caine, who had asked him to sort out a tangle of offers and commitments. Stoker, in fact, played an important behind-the-scenes role in several of the major successes which catapulted Caine to fame as one of the most popular fiction writers of his era. In 1889 he introduced Caine to Wolcott Balestier, the resident representative of a New York publishing firm in London and brother-in-law of Rudyard Kipling, who was setting up a publishing house with William Heinemann and was looking for a suitable novel to launch the imprint. Balestier accepted Stoker's view that Caine's *The Bondman* was the best candidate. He was proved right when Heinemann published it in January 1890 and it was an immediate and huge success, setting Caine and Heinemann on the road to lasting prosperity. Stoker drafted the contract for the dramatised version of the novel later that year. He edited *Cap'n*

Davy's Honeymoon (1893), admittedly one of Caine's least successful novels, and his suggestion that the last section needed rewriting was accepted by the author. This accounts for the effusive nature of the book's dedication to Stoker:

> . . . I confess that I publish it because I know that if any one should smile at my rough Manx comrade, doubting if such a man is in nature and now found among men, I can always answer him and say 'Ah, then, I am richer than you are by one friend at least, – Capt'n Davy without his ruggedness and without his folly, but with his simplicity, his unselfishness and his honour – Bram Stoker.[29]

Stoker, in turn, dedicated *Dracula* to him, using Hall Caine's pet name, 'Hommy-Beg', the Manx for 'Little Tommy'.

Stoker also collaborated with Caine on his biggest success, *The Manxman* (1894), which sold 400,000 copies and excited the admiration of Gladstone. The author sent Stoker a presentation copy 'with love and greeting' in 1895. Stoker provided an introduction to the 1905 edition of Caine's first Manx novel, *The Deemster* (1887), and a presentation copy of *My Story* (1908) carries the inscription 'To my dear Stoker, to whom this book owes much'. He was not exaggerating: Stoker had suggested extensive editorial changes, including a new title, which Caine accepted, and he acted as agent for the book. When Caine's play, *Pete*, was being produced in 1908, Stoker wrote a three-page letter of detailed advice.

Caine, in turn, gave Stoker practical assistance, including a loan of £600 in 1896, secured by a £700 insurance policy, when he was in financial difficulty. Caine could well afford it: he was by now a best-selling author, who left an estate of £250,000. He received $100,000 in royalties from his play, *The Christian*, which, as a novel (1897), had sold over a million copies. It was staged at the Lyceum in 1907, after Irving's death, when the venerable theatre had been rebuilt as a music hall. Stoker acted as an informal business manager for Caine in these years: when Caine sued Wilson Barrett over the dramatisation of *The Christian* in 1899, Stoker retained the lawyer, Sir George Lewis, to act for him (Lewis had acted for Whistler in the legal action over his 1890 book *The Gentle Art of Making Enemies* but refused to act for him in a later action against George Du Maurier, who was also a friend of his). He visited Caine at his magnificent home, Greeba Castle in the Isle of Man to discuss the case, which was settled out of court. He and Lewis were again active on Caine's behalf when he was threatened with legal action over the serialisation of *The Eternal City* in 1900. Lewis would later act for George Moore when he was sued for libel by an actor in 1917. Apart from his friendship with Stoker, Hall Caine was not a popular man. William Heinemann regarded him as one of his most difficult authors, who might have been called 'Hell Caine' but who had to be indulged because of his popular appeal. He was not shy about his success, describing himself in 1895 as 'the best paid man in my profession at the moment' although he moaned to Stoker: 'The penalties of success are terrible. Every base & low down dodge . . . seems to have been practised on me.' With Stoker he could relax and be himself. Stoker described visits from his friend to his Chelsea home, when they would sit in front of a blazing fire on a Sunday afternoon with Florence, and Caine's big eyes would shine like jewels.

Stoker was deeply involved with Hall Caine's business affairs in the 1890s as a partner with William Heinemann in publishing English-language works in Europe. Heinemann set up the English Library in an attempt to wrest some of the distribution of mass-circulation English-language books in continental Europe from the Baron Tauchnitz, whose firm reigned supreme in this area. The rationale, as explained by Stoker to Mark Twain in 1891, was that the authors would benefit as well as the publisher. The plan was to publish fifty of the most popular authors in Britain and America, offering royalties of five cents for single-volume works and ten cents for those sold in two volumes. Stoker hoped to get authors like Twain to commit all their work for the next ten years (or five, if they were more cautious), trading on his personal reputation with these writers while trying to create the impression that a sufficient number had been signed up to develop an unstoppable momentum behind the venture.

Heinemann was joined by Wolcott Balestier in this undertaking. A small limited company was set up with four directors: Stoker, Heinemann, Balestier and W. L. Courtney, a *Daily Telegraph* journalist who would later review *Dracula* with great insight. Arthur Waugh, father of Evelyn, of the firm of Chapman & Hall, was the company secretary. The English Library was launched in 1891 with Kipling's *The Light that Failed*. A torrent of other works followed, including reprints of books by George Meredith, Henry James, Hall Caine, Robert Louis Stevenson, J.M. Barrie, Jerome K. Jerome, Oscar Wilde and S. Baring Gould, whose book on werewolves so influenced Stoker. In one letter, Chatto & Windus, Caine's publisher, accepted with bad grace Stoker's offer of £70 for two of Hall Caine's books, saying that they would have expected more but did not care to haggle. Stoker was not sentimental in dealing with business affairs, even those of a close friend.[30] Hall Caine had been equally unsentimental in turning down a project he had discussed with Stoker in 1883, of writing 'a critical work on

Irving's impersonations' on the grounds that the sum offered by the prospective publisher was insufficient.[31]

Balestier died in December 1891, and although Waugh continued to run the English Library, the returns for the first year were discouraging; none of the books, except Kipling's, had made a profit. This may explain why Stoker, having offered a large sum of money for the rights to some of Tennyson's work, seemed to go to ground and attracted letters both from the poet's publisher, Macmillan, and his son, Hallam, over progress (or lack of it) in closing the deal in late 1892. They decided instead to come to terms with the Baron Tauchnitz. Much the same thing happened with Chatto & Windus, who were initially willing to come to terms with Stoker over Twain's work and, indeed, offered some other of their authors for the English Library. They too were disappointed at his tardiness in closing the deals offered. Stoker must, incidentally, have been engaged in this enterprise with the knowledge, if not the blessing, of Henry Irving, as some of the correspondence was addressed to him at the Lyceum. By the middle of 1893, Heinemann was forced to wind up the venture. Stoker had invested more than he could afford in it and the loss he suffered affected him for the rest of his life.

Stoker remained close to Heinemann, often calling at his office in Bedford Street, a few minutes' walk from the Lyceum. Along with Florence, he attended the publisher's brilliant dinners where they met the *crème de la crème* of the literary world. Heinemann published five of Stoker's novels and his *Personal Reminiscences of Henry Irving*, between 1902 and 1909. He also published two books by Irving's son, Henry Brodribb, a study of French criminals in the nineteenth century, and a life of Judge Jeffreys, the seventeenth-century Lord Chancellor who was perhaps the most notorious 'hanging judge' in English history, as well as work by Edward Dowden. Ironically, perhaps, he also offered £150 for the rights of Ibsen's *Hedda Gabler* in 1890, a sign that he was in touch with the currents of the time which would, within a decade, render outmoded the Lyceum and the kind of theatre managed by the nineteenth-century actor-managers like Irving.

The friendship of Bram and Florence Stoker with the writer, William Schwenk Gilbert, the librettist of the D'Oyly Carte operas, also came through Henry Irving, who had got to know Gilbert in the 1860s when they stayed up late at night discussing their common love of the theatre. Gilbert frequented the Beefsteak Room at the Lyceum, as did his artistic partner, Sir Arthur Sullivan. He did, however, object to Irving's practice of cutting Shakespeare and disagreed with the critic, Clement Scott, who was devoted to Irving's approach to this subject. Once, when asked if he had seen an Irving production at the Lyceum, he replied acidly that he went to the pantomime only at Christmas. Gilbert became friendly with Stoker and Florence and frequented their social gatherings, although the impression created in the mind of the writer, Horace Wyndham, who also attended these parties, was of irascibility and bad temper.

Gilbert formed a special friendship with Florence. We find him writing to her in 1887, sending her tickets for *Ruddigore* and inviting the Stokers to his country place at Grim's Dyke, Harrow Weald. Florence's friendship with Gilbert may not have been anything other than amiable flirtation but he was secretive about it, telling her that he did not want it to be known that they were in correspondence. He regularly invited her to the Savoy Theatre but when he sent her some tickets in 1899 he added, '*This is strictly in confidence*' at the end of his letter. The following year he expressed gratitude for her 'self-denying kindness in spending three days with a helpless invalid – you, whose society is so much sought – & who can spend your time as agreeably as any lady in London'. Mrs Gilbert sent her love.[32] Daniel Farson was puzzled by a letter of instruction from Gilbert to Florence about caring for an animal; this was, in fact, a monkey that he gave her. The monkey did not distinguish itself in the Stoker household and Florence's patience with him finally snapped when he defecated into a bowl of fruit on a table underneath the chandelier from which he was swinging. Florence loved animals and had several dogs – but the monkey was banished.

Gilbert was disturbed by Florence's engagement with Roman Catholicism (she converted in 1904); he wrote to her in 1901, 'God bless you & make you a good Protestant some day'. They fell out soon after and, in December 1902, Gilbert wrote twice within two days to Florence asking for reconciliation: in the second letter he expressed a desire to escort her to functions. They made up and, within a month, he was suggesting that she might come for outings in his motor car. Cars were then increasing in popularity: the first Highway Act regulating their use had been passed in 1896. There is no way of knowing if Stoker was jealous of Gilbert's attention to Florence but the motor car does feature in *Lady Athlyne* (1908) as an erotic aid when, for example, Joy quivers in languorous ecstasy while being driven at high speed by Athlyne in his big red car. Later that year Gilbert asked if Florence was going to the Oaks, a horse race, stating that he and his wife would not go unless she did too: 'for what is life without you?' He wrote again the following day, saying that he hated the Oaks 'but I am quite happy when you are there'. The earlier chill which had afflicted the relationship returned, however, and in July 1904 Gilbert wrote to Florence: 'What we have done we don't know. It used not to be so.'[33]

Nevertheless, the relationship between the Gilberts and the Stokers did not break down completely. In 1908 Stoker presided at the New Vagabonds

Club when Gilbert and his wife were the principal guests at the January dinner to celebrate his knighthood. Stoker paid a notable eulogy to Gilbert as having done good work 'for the civilised world'. Florence acted as hostess. Stoker interviewed Gilbert for the *Daily Chronicle* around the same time. Even so, cool feelings seem to have persisted between Florence and Gilbert. A *rapprochement* was effected in March 1911, on Florence's initiative, clearly driven by the need to seek help to overcome the Stokers' difficult financial situation. Gilbert agreed to see her to talk things over and assured her that he would be at Stoker's service if he applied for a Civil List pension.[34]

Stoker's dealings with Arthur Conan Doyle, whom he knew both through the Lyceum and the Irish Literary Society, were altogether more straightforward and modern criticism sees parallels between their writings. When Irving gave Stoker a copy of Doyle's play, *Waterloo*, to read, Stoker's reaction was that the Lyceum must have it at all costs. It opened in September 1894 and was an extraordinary success for Irving, then at the height of his powers. Critical interest was so great that Stoker arranged special trains for the reviewers. In 1897 Irving staged a special performance of *Waterloo* as part of Queen Victoria's Diamond Jubilee celebrations; some 2,000 troops marched to the Lyceum from Chelsea Barracks, with the public cheering them all the way. In the literary sphere, *The Parasite* (1894), a novel by Doyle, was published by the Acme Library in the same series as Stoker's *The Watter's Mou'* and included a soul-sucking vampire in the shape of a spinster. However, in 'The Adventure of the Sussex Vampire', Doyle, in sending up vampirism in Hungary and Transylvania through the character of Sherlock Holmes, may be poking fun at his old friend.[35] Doyle's own fascination with the supernatural is clear both in his account of his mother's ability to convey the horror of stories so dramatically that it made him 'goose-fleshy' to recall even as an adult, and in his three books on spiritualism and spirit photography published in the 1920s. Indeed, his credulity on these subjects would cause him considerable embarrassment in his later years. Doyle's personal relationship with Stoker was close. When Irving died, he wrote a letter of condolence to Stoker, and both Florence and Stoker attended Doyle's wedding in 1907, along with their in-laws, the Frankfort Moores.

At a more mundane level, Stoker was used by many of his acquaintances, like John Butler Yeats, as a means of gaining access to the Lyceum Theatre. The relationship between Stoker and the Yeats family went back to John Butler Yeats's student days at Trinity College Dublin, where he was active in the Philosophical Society and, like Stoker, was made an honorary member, a distinction reserved for those who had rendered outstanding service. John

Butler Yeats and Stoker would have known each other through this channel and had many friends in common. In a letter of 17 March 1879, Yeats expresses appreciation to Stoker for providing a box at the Lyceum, stating that he is bringing a party including his son, a small boy who is very fond of Shakespeare. The theatre trip was recalled by W. B. Yeats in his *Autobiographies*: 'When I was ten or twelve my father took me to see Irving play Hamlet, and did not understand why I preferred Irving to Ellen Terry, who was, I can now see, the idol of himself and his friends . . . I was not old enough to care for feminine charm and beauty.' Yeats was, in fact, fourteen, not ten or twelve, and he must have been a rather backward fourteen-year-old if he was unable to understand the sexual chemistry of Ellen Terry, then at the height of her beauty. Not that he was particularly impressed with Irving either; he tells us elsewhere in his *Autobiographies* that 'Irving . . . never moved me but in the expression of intellectual pride . . .'[36]

As his prowess as a poet developed and he became established in London literary circles, W.B. Yeats's relationship with Stoker evolved. This is attested by a volume in Stoker's library of *The Countess Kathleen*, dedicated 'To Bram Stoker with the compliments and best regards of W.B. Yeats, Sept[ember] 1893'. They moved in the same circles in London; both, for example, frequented the literary salons of Lady Wilde in Oakley Street, Chelsea. Their most sustained contact was through the Irish Literary Society in London in the 1890s. Both men shared the horrific connection with the West of Ireland, their mothers being Sligo women who were affected as children by the cholera epidemic of 1832. Yeats's memories of his youth in Sligo featured many ghost stories, together with visions and haunted houses. It was in Sligo that his brother died at the age of three and his mother fancied that she had heard a banshee the night before. Yeats's interest in the occult caused Aleister Crowley, the magician and fellow member of the Order of the Golden Dawn, to describe him as 'a lank dishevelled demonologist'.[37] Yeats also dabbled in mesmerism, as did Henry Irving, and some see Dracula's mesmeric powers as deriving from this; cipher played a role in the Order of the Golden Dawn and it is central to Stoker's *The Mystery of the Sea*. Egyptian rites featured in the Order's ritual and Stoker's *The Jewel of Seven Stars* (1903) revolves around the resurrection of a long-dead Egyptian priestess.

While he visited the United States in his capacity as Irving's acting manager, Stoker made an impression in critical and literary circles there, one of the most important, from his own perspective if not from Irving's, being on Walt Whitman. They finally met in the flesh in March 1884, when Stoker and Irving called on the poet in Philadelphia. Stoker was not disappointed in his idol:

I found him all that I had ever dreamed of, or wished for in him: large-minded, broad-viewed, tolerant to the last degree; incarnate sympathy; understanding with an insight that seemed more than human . . . A man amongst men! . . . To me he was an old friend, and on his part he made me feel that I was one. We spoke of Dublin and those friends there who had manifested themselves to him. He remembered all their names and asked me many questions as to their various personalities.[38]

Stoker called on the poet again in November 1886 when he was in America to make preparations for the *Faust* tour the following year. Whitman asked Stoker about London and they spoke of Abraham Lincoln for whom they shared an 'almost idolatrous affection'. Thomas Donaldson, Whitman's friend, has left a vivid account of this visit and of the deep impression that Stoker made on Whitman:

Mr. Stoker, a man of intelligence and cultivation, having had the advantage of association with the most cultivated in all walks of contemporary English intellectual life, was at his best. Mr. Whitman was captivated . . . 'Well, well; what a broth of a boy he is! My gracious, he knows enough for four or five ordinary men; and what tact! Henry Irving knows a good thing when he sees it, eh? Stoker is an adroit lad, and many think that he made Mr. Irving's path, in a business way, a smooth one over here.'[39]

On this visit Stoker discreetly raised with Whitman's friend, the journalist, Talcott Williams, the vexed question of cutting some controversial lines and passages from Whitman's work to enable it to enjoy wider circulation. On his third visit to Whitman in December 1887, he again broached the subject, first with Williams and then with the poet himself, who rejected the notion out of hand. This was the last time that Stoker, who did not visit the United States again until 1893, saw Whitman. The poet, however, left what Stoker termed a 'Message from the Dead' in the form of notes for his Abraham Lincoln lecture, which were given to Stoker by Donaldson in 1894. (Stoker, in turn, gave the typescript of *Dracula* to Donaldson as a gesture of friendship some years later and may have meant the name of Captain Donelson of the *Czarina Catherine* in *Dracula* to echo that of his friend.) Stoker, incidentally, could have had little idea of the value of his gift to Donaldson: the typescript was sold in 2002 for $941,000. Stoker had earlier arranged his own memorial to Whitman. After his 1886 visit, he saw in New York the sculptor, Augustus Saint-Gaudens, who had been born in Dublin a year after himself, and asked him to do casts in bronze of the face and hands of the poet; Whitman agreed but died before the work could be completed. Twenty people agreed to buy sets, including both Stoker and Henry Irving. Through Donaldson, Stoker kept in touch with Whitman up to his death in 1892. In a letter of October 1889, Donaldson acknowledged £15 – then equal to $78 – from Stoker and expressed the poet's appreciation of his kindness. Henry Irving sent money at the same time, probably at Stoker's suggestion.[40]

Another outcome of the Lyceum tours of America was Stoker's friendship with Mark Twain, whom he met in Chicago in 1883 and who attended a farewell banquet for the company in New York in 1885. Stoker was corresponding with Twain as 'Mr Clemens' in the early 1890s when he asked him to join in his publishing venture with Heinemann and traded on the fact that they knew each other well. Twain's reaction was to send a copy of Stoker's letter to his own publisher, Chatto & Windus, and to tell Stoker to deal with them directly.[41] Stoker's friendship with Twain survived the failure both of his publishing venture with Heinemann and of an investment scheme that Twain had persuaded Stoker and Irving to back in 1894. Following the death of his daughter, Susy, in August 1896, Twain and his family settled in London, taking a house at 23 Tedworth Square, close to the Stokers' Chelsea home. Two years later, Stoker agreed to act as his London agent. Although he had to smooth over a fit of pique on Twain's part when the American felt that the Lyceum staff had been less than attentive to his family, social activity between the two families continued, with Stoker providing Lyceum tickets and copies of his books, not only to Twain, but also to his wife and daughters. Both Stoker and Irving were also friendly with Brander Matthews, the writer, critic and academic who edited Twain's collected works. In 1907 Stoker attended a dinner for Twain given by the American Ambassador; the other guests included Arthur Conan Doyle and the novelist Anthony Hope, author of *The Prisoner of Zenda* (1894). When Stoker, Twain and the American writer, Eugene Field, gathered at Brown's Hotel in London in 1907, where they discussed literary witchcraft, it must have felt like a flashback to the happy gatherings on the Lyceum tours in America. Hints of a deeper, if obscure, involvement are to be found in a letter from Twain to Stoker in 1908, introducing George Robinson, a friend of forty years' standing, asking that Stoker 'tell him the things he wishes to know, for Clara's [Twain's daughter] sake and mine'.[42]

As well as his literary work for the Lyceum, Stoker indulged his personal interests in his role as a founding member of the Irish Literary Society, established in London in 1892 and itself a significant development in the

Irish literary revival of the late nineteenth and early twentieth centuries. Its objectives were to bring together Irish people in London and to promote the study of Irish literature, history and art. Politics were to be eschewed as members included both Unionists and Home Rulers. The initial membership, which was open to women as well as men, attracted more than a hundred names, including political and literary luminaries such as Sir Charles Russell, a Liberal Attorney-General who was leading counsel for Charles Stewart Parnell before the Parnell Commission (1888–90) and was Lord Chief Justice of England from 1894; the Young Irelanders, Sir Charles Gavan Duffy and John O'Leary; the labour leaders, Michael Davitt and William O'Brien; John Redmond, later Leader of the Irish Nationalist Party; Douglas Hyde, Gaelic League activist and later President of Ireland; Justin McCarthy, politician and writer; as well as literary figures like George Bernard Shaw, Arthur Conan Doyle, Percy FitzGerald, Louis F. Austin, Oscar Wilde, W.B. Yeats, Alfred Perceval Graves, T.W. Rolleston, John Todhunter, Lady Wilde and Katharine Tynan, the Irish poet and novelist.

Despite its desire to be non-political, the Irish Literary Society drew fire from proponents of both British and Irish nationalism. In 1892, the *Morning Advertiser* was critical of the fact that its members wrote in English and were published in London: 'Nor do we remember the particular contribution to Irish literature of Mr Bram Stoker . . .'; the *Freeman's Journal*, a leading Dublin newspaper, launched an attack on the society eight years later, describing Conan Doyle as 'narrowly and even arrogantly British' and criticising Stoker for giving 'to Sir Henry Irving's managerial affairs what was meant for the English-speaking portion of mankind'.[43] These criticisms did not deter Stoker, who remained active in the society.

TEN

Political Animal

Mr. Morris, you should be proud of your great state. Its reception into the
Union was a precedent which may have far-reaching effects hereafter, when
the Pole and the Tropics may hold allegiance to the Stars and Stripes.
The power of Treaty may yet prove a vast engine of enlargement, when the
Monroe doctrine takes its true place as a political fable.

(*Dracula*, Renfield to Quincey Morris)

Irving's audience consisted of two distinct elements: the working class, which
had tripled in London between 1810 and 1850, and wanted mainstream
theatre with outstanding scenery and the latest technology; and the upper
classes, to whom Irving looked to realise his dream of social respectability
for the theatre. This social balancing act was based on alternating a diet of
serious theatre with popular melodrama and was wrapped in a policy of
respect for the status quo (Irving even had an invisible choir sing the national
anthem when he proposed the Queen's health on occasion).

The monarchy formed the apex of Irving's social world. An important
part of the mystique which surrounded the Lyceum was the ability of Irving
to attract royal patronage, especially from Edward, Prince of Wales, during
the latter part of Queen Victoria's reign, and this inevitably involved Stoker
in dealings with the monarchy. Irving was elected to the Marlborough Club
on the proposal of its founder, the Prince of Wales, and, in October 1880,
when the Prince visited the Lyceum for *The Corsican Brothers* he was taken
behind the scenes to observe the workings of the theatre. In 1883 Stoker
was used as an intermediary by Sir James Mackenzie in sounding out Irving
as to whether he would accept a knighthood. The actor refused but later
accepted and was knighted on 18 July 1895. The royal household was also
in touch with Stoker about other matters over the years, through Sir Richard
Quain, Physician-Extraordinary to Queen Victoria and Sir Dighton M.
Probyn, Keeper of the Privy Purse to King Edward VII. In July 1906, Stoker
sent King Edward VII 'The Theatrical Book' of coronation addresses by
figures associated with the theatre, including himself.[1]

Irving played at Sandringham in 1889 and again in November 1902 for
the Kaiser's visit. In 1893 Irving mounted a performance at Windsor Castle

at the Queen's request, which Stoker saw as the point at which Queen Victoria 'broke the gloom of more than thirty years and began the restoration of something like the old happy life of the earlier years of her reign' before the death of her consort, Prince Albert. The press approached Stoker to write an account of the performance and the Queen ordered the telegraph office at Windsor to be kept open for Stoker's convenience until he had finished his dispatch. Getting Irving there was a major logistical challenge for Stoker as the actor was playing *Faust* in Belfast the previous evening. Needless to say, Stoker succeeded and he again acted as press officer. He was allowed only to give the pre-agreed formula, 'Programme adhered to', although some papers managed to extend this to a column!

Reminiscing about the Lyceum after Henry Irving's death, Joseph Comyns Carr recalled that many of the most notable people of the era were to be met in its Beefsteak Room, the Lyceum's private entertainment area. His wife too remembered Irving presiding there, always conscious of his role as the pre-eminent figure of the English stage. The Beefsteak Club as a theatrical adjunct had its origins in London in the eighteenth century, when it attracted the patronage of many outstanding personalities. Thomas Sheridan, father of Richard Brinsley Sheridan, formed a 'Beefsteak Club' at his house adjoining the Smock Alley theatre in Dublin. A Beefsteak Room had formed part of the Lyceum in the early nineteenth century and, when Irving took over the theatre, it was refurbished. The décor included four Gothic doors and a Gothic alcove. Larger social gatherings, following first nights for example, were accommodated on the Lyceum stage, which was transformed into a room by ringing it with supper tables, but the Beefsteak Room remained the holy of holies of the Lyceum, where Irving worked his magic on the great and the good, ably supported by his acting manager.

Stoker's intelligence and charm were obvious in his dealings with the Liberal statesman, William Gladstone who, over a period of fourteen years, from 1881 to 1895, was a regular visitor to the Lyceum and took a great interest in Irving's career. Stoker noticed that the statesman seemed to come to the Lyceum at times of great crisis, such as on 10 April 1886, just two days after the introduction of his controversial Irish Home Rule Bill. Stoker was proud that Gladstone seemed to like to discuss current political developments with him. In March 1887, via James Knowles, he sent Gladstone 'an exhaustive note' on Rule XII of the new Rules of Procedure of the House of Commons. The rule was dropped shortly afterwards.

Stoker sent a copy of *The Snake's Pass* to Gladstone, 'whose magnificent power and ability and character I had all my life so much admired'. He received a postcard in response from Gladstone, dated 18 November 1890,[2] and, shortly afterwards at the Lyceum, they discussed *The Snake's Pass*: 'Mr Gladstone was then full of Irish matters' and was particularly interested in the oppressive role of the 'gombeen man', or moneylender, in Irish rural life. In general, he spoke of the book 'very kindly and very searchingly' and said that the scene set in Mrs Kelligan's was 'very fine indeed'. The court verdict in the divorce case of Parnell's colleague, O'Shea, in which Parnell was cited as co-respondent and which would sink him politically, had been delivered the previous day. Although he described himself as 'a philosophical Home-Ruler', Stoker expressed surprise and anger at a recent attack by Parnell on Gladstone. He replied: 'I am very angry, but I assure you I am even more sorry.'[3] The episode provides some insight into Stoker's political views. By siding with Gladstone, he was aligning himself with Liberal opinion in England which decreed that Parnell's moral irregularity made impossible a continuation of the political alliance between the Liberals and the Irish Parliamentary Party as long as Parnell remained its leader. The Party split on this issue, precipitating a deep and lasting rift in Irish political life. Stoker had friends on both sides of the divide but he was not a Parnell loyalist.

When Gladstone came again to the Lyceum on 25 February 1893 to see *Becket* he discussed with Stoker his second Home Rule Bill, recently introduced, and made the mistaken prediction that, in four or five years, those who opposed it would wonder why they had done so. Stoker's admiration for Gladstone was typical of many Irish literary intellectuals in the London of that era. Oscar Wilde had written to him in 1877, congratulating him on his protests against the massacres of Christians in Bulgaria and sending him a sonnet he had written on the subject. Percy FitzGerald published *An Apology for the Life of the Rt. Hon. W.E. Gladstone; or The New Politics* in 1885. Whilst Hall Caine had been much influenced by direct personal contact with the Liberal statesman as a young man (his first employer, a relative of Gladstone's, was a passionate supporter of the Liberal cause), his attraction for FitzGerald and Stoker, as Irishmen, would have been his Home Rule politics.

FitzGerald's reference to the 'wonderful management' of the Lyceum in his memoirs could be taken as a pat on the back for Stoker.[4] Born in 1834, he was a graduate of Trinity College Dublin. An associate of Dickens and a prolific novelist, he produced biographies of Irving, Garrick and the Sheridans, among others. Like Wills and Stoker, he had a fascination with the macabre, evident not just in his collaboration on *Vanderdecken*, but also in his *Chronicles of the Bow Street Police-Office* (1888), the famous police station which stood close to the Lyceum Theatre. The *Chronicles* featured details of hideous eighteenth-century cases, such as 'The Story of Sarah Metyard and her Apprentice Ann Naylor', about a parish child apprentice murdered by an evil haberdasher and her daughter, both of whom were executed, and 'The Resurrection Men' about men who dug up bodies from graveyards. The ambiguities of sexuality and identity which would later mark Stoker's *Famous Impostors* (1910) surfaced in 'The Female Personators', the case of two young men who went dressed in drag to theatres and other places of amusement.

Another influential figure to cross Stoker's path in his capacity as acting manager of the Lyceum was the Baroness Angela Georgina Burdett-Coutts (1814–1906), who had inherited the banking fortune of her grandfather, Thomas Coutts. Much of it she spent on philanthropic projects, largely under the influence of Charles Dickens. Her interest in Stoker's native country was intense and, over five decades, she attempted to relieve distress in Ireland. She prompted an inquiry into the terrible poverty in south-western Ireland in 1862 which resulted in those hardest hit being assisted to emigrate to Canada. In 1880 she offered to advance £250,000 to the British government for the supply of seed potatoes for Ireland, which stimulated the government to act. The Baroness was an habitué of the Lyceum. While Stoker disputed reports that she had financed it, Hannah Brown, her lifelong friend, had pressed a loan of £1,500 on Irving and had left him £5,000 in banknotes on her death. The Baroness's enthusiasm for Irving's work was evident in a letter she wrote to Thornley Stoker in November 1879 saying that she was sure he would rejoice in the success of *The Merchant of Venice* as it had exceeded the most ardent expectations.[5]

Thornley had actually been involved in the events which formed the character of Shylock in Irving's mind, when he joined Burdett-Coutts and Irving on a sailing trip in the Mediterranean in July 1879 aboard her yacht, the *Walrus*. The experience of seeing real Jewish merchants in the Levant inspired the actor's sympathetic portrayal of a character generally much maligned. Thornley, who at that time was earning the then very considerable income of £1,600 per year, had insisted on being paid a fee for participating in the cruise as medical officer. Burdett-Coutts, who was friendly with both Stoker and Thornley, wrote to Thornley in December 1879 that she had seen the pregnant Florence Stoker: 'She looked very pretty but rather delicate I thought.' In another communication, she wrote of having called at Stoker's home in Southampton Street, where she had seen both Mrs Stokers. She had also been asked to meet a lot of Florence's cousins but could not attend on that occasion.[6] When Hannah Brown died, her portrait was sent to Thornley on the instructions of Burdett-Coutts. Thornley responded in the florid style which marked their correspondence, saying that he would carry the soul of the picture in his heart while its body would have an honoured place on the wall; he knew she would not have given the picture to anyone she considered unworthy. She clearly wanted him to know of her good works in Ireland as she sent him a newspaper cutting describing her efforts to combat the 'prevailing distress in Ireland', which included paying off the debts of Cape Clear fishermen and giving £500 towards a harbour on the Sligo coast.

Burdett-Coutts married a Mr W.L. Ashmead Bartlett in 1881 when she was sixty-seven and he was thirty; he took her name by royal licence. The marriage caused some outrage: Thornley received a letter from a mutual friend, Mr H.S. Braddyll, the day after the marriage, alleging that the couple had nothing in common except obstinacy and the desire to make a sensation. At the same time, Ashmead Bartlett sought to enlist Thornley's assistance in combating adverse publicity in the 'virulent radical press'. Thornley, in turn, sought to use his connection with Bartlett and the Baroness to secure his appointment to the post of royal physician. There was much toing and froing: she attended his parties when in Dublin and he sent her a present 'which may sometimes remind you of your Irish doctor'.[7]

In 1879 Henry Irving asked the playwright, Frank A. Marshall, to write a play on the Irish patriot, Robert Emmet, who had been hanged for treason in 1803. Both Irving and Stoker had personal associations with the subject. As a schoolboy, Irving had been given a speech in defence of another Irish patriot of the same era, Hamilton Rowan, to recite by his headmaster. In Dublin as a young actor, he discovered that his resemblance to Robert Emmet made him popular with many Irish people. They suggested that he present a play on the subject and he found the idea attractive; shortly after he took over the Lyceum, he commissioned Marshall to start on the play. He wrote to Stoker from *Walrus*, in the Mediterranean: '*Emmett* [sic] is good, will act well and I would have played it sooner had the woman's part been better', and he hoped to mount it in the 1879–80 season at the Lyceum.[8] It actually took another five years for the play to be finalised to Irving's satisfaction but, just as he was about to announce the production in 1884, the Lord Chamberlain intervened on political grounds and Irving abandoned the project. He gave it to his old mentor, Dion Boucicault, who produced it in New York, where it was not a great success. Irving, who had given a good deal of time and thought to the character of Emmet, was very disappointed. Stoker had been closely involved in preparations for the Emmet play, planning its production at meetings in the Beefsteak Room with Irving and Marshall and believing that it would be highly successful.

The circumstances surrounding the withdrawal of the Lyceum production are somewhat confused. While Stoker states that Irving was 'debarred' from playing it, the Lord Chamberlain did, in fact, license the play, so the decision not to proceed was made by Irving, formally at any rate. This was acknowledged by Stoker when he gave evidence before the Joint Parliamentary Committee inquiring into the censorship of plays in 1909. He recalled the Lord Chamberlain's intervention with Irving on the 'grounds of public policy' in respect of the Emmet play: 'he suggested that it should not be brought forward. Mr Irving said he was only too willing to do anything that was right, and accordingly shelved the play.'[9] Yet Irving was not happy with this turn of events and may have been less of a free agent than Stoker allowed: a journalist who interviewed Irving when the play was being rehearsed was led to believe that it 'was peremptorily interdicted by the Lord Chamberlain or official Censor', which Irving attributed to the intervention of the Chief Secretary for Ireland.[10] In other words, Irving was keen, on artistic grounds, to mount the play at the Lyceum but succumbed to subtle political pressure not to proceed. His dilemma illustrates the constraints imposed by his stature as an establishment figure.

In his statements on the Emmet play, Stoker never revealed his own family connection with the subject. His brother Thornley owned the table on which Emmet's head had been cut off after he was hanged 'in accordance with the horrible code for treason of penalties attaching to conviction for high treason'.[11] This suggests that Thornley's nationalism may have had stronger emotional roots than might otherwise be assumed and that their Home Rule sympathies were a vital part of the bond between Bram and his brother. In creating a fantasy aristocratic world in *Lady Athlyne*, Stoker paralleled in fiction what Thornley had done in real life. A highly successful surgeon, he lived in great style in a mansion in the centre of Dublin. Probably few better illustrated the dramatic potential for middle-class upward mobility in nineteenth-century Ireland than Thornley Stoker, although his siblings, including his brother Bram, were also affected by the process. A large and growing commercial and professional class made good the loss of the city's political life as a capital to London in the nineteenth century, with the middle class occupying roles formerly reserved for the gentry. Standish O'Grady caught well the power of new money in this era: 'The rich shopkeeper sails out from Kingston in his gorgeous yacht, and his sons hunt with the Wards. The brewer and distiller, the successful manufacturer and contractor, the stock-broker, and even the well-to-do tenant – National Leaguer though he be – they all love pleasure as much as we and spend their incomes in its pursuit quite as regardless of general consequences.'[12] Given the propensity of modern critics to describe the family as Anglo-Irish and Ascendancy, implying aristocratic lineage, the truth is that

Thornley recreated himself as an eighteenth-century grandee on the basis of his self-made, middle-class income.

Like the aristocrats he had displaced, Thornley patronised the arts. Walter Osborne, an outstanding painter, was an especial favourite. He was a constant visitor at Thornley's magnificent home at Ely Place which features in James Joyce's *Ulysses*.[13] Osborne, however, fulfilled a more important function for Thornley than that of dinner guest: he was employed in the creation of lineage. In the years 1894–5 he had Osborne paint, not just his wife and himself, but also his mother and, posthumously, his father. Osborne also painted Stoker's wife, Florence, at this time. It is interesting, in the context of the Stokers' connection with the Home Rule movement, that Osborne had painted its leader, Charles Stewart Parnell, in 1889; he also painted Professor Edward Dowden in 1891.

George Moore the novelist was a neighbour after he moved back to Ireland in 1901 and Thornley has been described as the only person whom Moore really understood in Ireland.[14] Oliver St John Gogarty recalled Thornley vividly in *As I Was Going Down Sackville Street* (1937) and gave an account of his wife, when elderly and ill, bursting in on a dinner party and running around the table, in the nude, crying, 'I like a little intelligent conversation' before she was seized by two female attendants and bundled, screaming, from the room.[15] The story first appeared in an English newspaper in 1933. George Stoker alerted Florence Stoker to it and suggested that an explanation be sought from Gogarty. While it has been claimed that the scene as described by Gogarty was well attested by the two lady attendants present, Betty Webb and Florence Dugdale, Betty Webb in fact angrily denied it. She suggested that a solicitor's letter be sent to restrain Gogarty and expressed her indignation that: 'Sir Thornley *made* this fellow [when] he was a Richmond student – they were both very fond of him, & that's friendship . . .'[16] No legal action followed, however, and the story remained on the record. Sir Thornley's mansion was also the scene of a Moore family falling out, when George Moore, who had by this time become an enthusiastic Protestant, visited and, finding his Catholic nephew there, declared to Lady Stoker in a loud voice that he could not remain in the same room as a 'papist'. Moore would later situate his story, 'Sarah Gwynn', in the house of a doctor in Ely Place.

Thornley's standing had been greatly enhanced when he was knighted in 1895, during his term as President of the Royal College of Surgeons. He had, however, declined the title when it was first offered to him on the grounds that nothing less than a baronetcy, the honour that was accorded to the President of the Royal College of Surgeons in England, would be acceptable. Stoker encouraged Thornley to accept the knighthood, pointing out, accurately, that 'the Bart' could be added later. He had been active behind the scenes in London and had induced Sir James Blyth (whose connections included the Prince of Wales), to approach the Earl of Rosebery, Liberal Prime Minister from March 1894 to June 1895, on Thornley's behalf. Stoker's advice that Thornley should parade his Home Rule credentials in a forthcoming election was somewhat ironic in view of the fact that Rosebery later fell out with his party over the issue of Home Rule as well as that of the Boer War. At a celebratory dinner at the Royal College of Surgeons in Dublin on 2 November 1895, the entire Stoker family could bask in the reflected glow of Thornley's honour. A host of dignitaries attended and laudatory references were made to the Stoker family, including Bram.

Stoker, Florence and Thornley continued to be active in Home Rule politics up to Stoker's death. Florence dined with John Dillon and his wife at the House of Commons around the time that Dillon became leader of the main anti-Parnellite movement in 1896 and joked about the Dillons raising their newborn son as a little patriot. In 1910 it was Florence who wrote to Thornley, introducing a M. André Gérard, the London representative of the *Echo de Paris*, who was coming to Ireland to do an article on its political situation. Thornley then wrote to John Dillon, on the basis of Florence's introduction, suggesting that Gérard be granted an interview.

Bram Stoker's political views were formed as a young man and were probably strongly influenced by his friendship with the Wilde family and their political connections. Isaac Butt, the original advocate of Home Rule and a former Professor of Political Economy at Trinity, frequented the Wilde household, and Sir William Wilde was a Home Ruler. Nevertheless, Butt appeared for Mary Travers, with whom Sir William had had an affair, in the 1864 court case which undermined Sir William's reputation. From their early days together at the Lyceum, Irving liked to rib Stoker about his Home Rule views. Stoker claimed that Irving had no fixed political convictions himself but loved to draw out anyone about anything. When they talked of Home Rule, Irving would take the 'violently opposite side'. In the midst of a debate on the subject while they were on holiday together in 1880, they heard the heavy tramp of a policeman coming down the road. Irving said: 'Here comes the Voice of England' and asked the policeman for his view 'on this trouble in Ireland,' before getting the answer: 'Ah, begob, it's all the fault iv the dirty Gover'mint!' 'His brogue might have been cut with a hatchet . . . Home Rule was of little moment to that guardian of the law; he was an out and out Fenian.' Stoker used the 'Voice of England' when he was chaffed by Irving about Home Rule afterwards.[17]

After his move to London, Stoker formed a close literary and political friendship with Justin McCarthy, the Irish nationalist writer and politician who lived for many years in Cheyne Gardens, near Stoker and who included among his friends Henry Irving, Ellen Terry and John Lawrence Toole. While McCarthy made his name as a novelist, it was his *History of Our Own Times* which made him famous: Chatto & Windus sold thirteen editions of the first edition in 1879–80, a major publishing feat. In 1879 he became involved in Irish politics and was vice-chairman of the Irish Parliamentary Party, dedicated to the achievement of Home Rule, under Charles Stewart Parnell. In the split over the leadership, McCarthy became chairman of the anti-Parnellite faction. Notwithstanding an excellent result in the 1892 general election, he resigned the leadership to John Dillon, another friend of Stoker's, in 1896.

McCarthy's concept of Home Rule, and the economic development which he believed would follow its implementation, was similar to Stoker's beliefs on the subject. Stoker was well acquainted with McCarthy by the mid-1880s; he wrote to the American theatre critic, William Winter, in 1886, formally introducing him as his friend.[18] Quite an extensive correspondence between Stoker and McCarthy survives. The most interesting item is a note from McCarthy asking to be excused for not having turned up the previous evening: 'Just as we were on the point of starting, Parnell suddenly came in on his way back to prison. We had so much to say to each other, and he did not leave until half past eleven. So I am sure Mrs Stoker will forgive us.'[19] This was probably in October 1881 when Parnell was imprisoned for verbal assaults on Gladstone's Land Act of that year. Other correspondence concerned minor influence-peddling, with McCarthy promising to assist in any way he could with Stoker's brother's candidature (which brother and what post was involved is not clear), while cautioning that he was out of favour with the government.[20] McCarthy, in turn, asked Irving to put in a 'word of recommendation from you to your stage-manager' for the employment on the stage of a young friend of his.[21] McCarthy was evidently something of a fixture at the Lyceum throughout Irving's tenure there and included 'The Gombeen Man' section from *The Snake's Pass* in his massive 1904 anthology, *Irish Literature*. Among the editors of this volume were Douglas Hyde and Lady Gregory, the writer and playwright who played a prominent role in the Irish literary renaissance of the late nineteenth and early twentieth centuries.

Stoker collaborated with McCarthy's son, Justin Huntly, who was also a novelist, in the multi-author serial novel, *The Fate of Fenella*, which appeared in the *Gentlewoman* in 1892 and was published in book form later the same year. Stoker's chapter was 'Lord Castleton Explains' and, given that Stoker was working on *Dracula* at the time, the gaunt cheeks and deadly pallor of the character of Lord Francis Onslow, together with reference to marks on the dead man's throat, are of interest. Arthur Conan Doyle was among the other contributors. In the course of a generally negative review in August 1892, the *Speaker* described it as a very long joke.[22]

Valentine Blake Dillon was Lord Mayor of Dublin in 1894 when Irving and Stoker visited the city. Stoker later recalled: 'At that time the long-continued feuds between Conservatives and Liberals, Home Rulers and Unionists, Catholics and Protestants, which had marked with extra virulence – for they had been long existent – the past decades, were still operative. Still, improvement was in the air; only opportunity was wanting to give it expression.' In contrast to the divisive nature of Irish society, Irving and Ellen Terry 'had no politics, and what religion either professed was not even considered; their artistic excellence shadowed all else'. The occasion was a happy one: 'Ever since 1876 my native city had a warm place in Irving's heart. And very justly so, for it had showered upon him love and honour.' Three thousand people attended the reception given by Dillon for Irving on 29 November 1894: Irving and Terry shook hands with all. Stoker also waxed lyrical about the public address – almost certainly written by himself – which Irving gave at the theatre after his performance on 1 December, the audience for which included Dublin's leading figures. Irving was very moved and gave the not inconsiderable sum of £100 for 'the use of the poor'.[23]

Stoker was proud that Lord Mayor Dillon was a boyhood friend and that he was a man of broad views. A leading figure in the Land League, Dillon came from a Roman Catholic, nationalist background. He was born in 1847, and died less than two months before Bloomsday, on 31 March 1904 (he was, indeed, immortalised in Joyce's *Ulysses*, in which Leopold Bloom cites him as a potential referee, stating, 'I have moved in the charmed circle of the highest').[24] The son of a Sligo solicitor, Valentine Blake Dillon graduated from university the same year as Stoker and became a Dublin solicitor. In that capacity, he defended Parnell when he was arrested in 1880 and acted for William O'Brien, MP and John Dillon, MP – both of whom were well known to Stoker – following an incident in Tipperary in 1890, when a crowd was baton-charged by the police. He was active in helping to get Nationalist candidates elected to Parliament. He took Parnell's side following the split in the Irish Parliamentary Party and fought a by-election on his behalf in 1891. Thornley Stoker attended him during his final illness at Baggot Street Hospital in Dublin. Dillon's funeral attracted a large and representative attendance, including the Archbishop of Dublin and many other Roman Catholic clergy, as well as the Master of the Rolls, the Lord Mayor, John Redmond MP, and a number of other MPs including

Tim Healy, later the first Governor-General of the Irish Free State. Despite, however, his connection with Valentine Blake Dillon, Stoker's links were mainly with the anti-politicians like John Dillon and Justin McCarthy.

Perhaps the most unlikely of Stoker's political friendships was with the Russian revolutionary, Sergius Stepniak, to whom he devoted a chapter of his *Personal Reminiscences of Henry Irving*. He heard Stepniak speak at Speakers' Corner in Hyde Park, London, on 1 May 1892, an interesting illustration of how Stoker spent his free time. In July of that year, Stepniak attended a supper at the Beefsteak Room after a performance of *Faust* and he and Stoker conversed at length, chiefly about the situation in Russia. Hall Caine had been staying with Stoker for a week in June 1892, during which they discussed Caine's forthcoming visit to Russia and Caine suggested to Stoker that he pump the Russian revolutionary for information. Stoker did so and was moved by Stepniak's tales of innocent deportees being sent to Siberia by the Tsar. Stepniak followed up in August by sending him copies of his paper, *Free Russia*, and noted that Stoker had read all his books, indicative of Stoker's prodigious capacity for absorbing information. Stoker did not, incidentally, mention the connection between Stepniak and Mark Twain, who was involved with Stepniak as a supporter of the cause of revolution in Russia.

When he toured in the United States, Irving's stature was such that American dignitaries, from the President down, received him. On his first visit to Washington, in 1884, he and President Chester A. Arthur stayed up till the early hours of the morning together. He met Grover Cleveland, as President-elect, in 1887 at a charity performance (although the occasion was marred for Irving by a clown sending up his performance as Shylock). He called on McKinley in 1899, at the time of the war in the Philippines, and was much taken by the excitement.

Stoker, of course, benefited from these contacts. He met Theodore Roosevelt in 1895 when he was New York Commissioner of Police and found him 'a person of extraordinary interest'. Roosevelt invited Stoker to a hearing of complaints against the police and, when he asked Stoker to guess his judgments, found that they agreed in every case. Roosevelt's views are unlikely to have been liberal in any modern sense of the word: when he visited police shelters for tramps in New York he decided that something had to be done about 'the willful-idle class' he found there. His solution was that they be indelibly marked and sent to a labour colony set in a remote fastness, initially for a year, then two years and, finally, for life. Stoker wrote in his diary that Roosevelt must be President some day. And, in turn, Stoker made quite an impression on his hosts. Elihu Root, the American Secretary for War, invited his 'desirable and delightful personality' (together with Irving and Terry) to supper in 1899; Irving, incidentally, directed Stoker to turn down the same invitation to Ellen Terry on the grounds that she could not go out in the evening and do her work properly. In 1902, Stoker sent a copy of *The Mystery of the Sea*, the American aspects of which may well have had their origins in these contacts, to Root, who told him that *Dracula* had made a powerful impression on him but, being of serene disposition, he had not lost any sleep over it.

Both Stoker and Henry Irving believed in the cause of Anglo-American friendship: the actor was a member of 'The Kinsmen', a small dining club of literary and artistic men of British and American nationality, and Stoker's activities left little doubt as to his views on the subject. The first Lyceum Theatre tour of the United States in 1883–4 fired Stoker's enthusiasm for that country and convinced him that most British people did not know or care much about it. He decided to rectify matters himself and a second American tour by the Lyceum in 1884–5 gave him the opportunity to pursue his research. He accumulated a collection of books covering such diverse subjects as the American constitution and American history and statistics, as well as Congressional reports, census information, school books, and books of etiquette. He also consulted a wide range of experts, including political, economic and academic figures. The result was a lecture, 'A Glimpse of America', given at the London Institute on 28 December 1885 before a large audience and published by Sampson Low the following year. Stoker focused on the social and political aspects of his subject while peppering his talk liberally with statistics, for example on the comparative railway networks of the UK and USA. He spoke glowingly on various aspects of American society, from the advanced position of women to the virtues of its political system (which would, he predicted, influence the world) and the outstanding human qualities of the American people. He saw the future in terms of an alliance between America and England, based on ties of culture and blood.

In December 1888, Stoker lectured on the related theme of 'Abraham Lincoln: How the Statesman of the People saved the Union, and abolished Slavery in the American Civil War' to the Sunday Lecture Society, a small but appreciative audience. It is possible to see a measure of identification between Stoker and his subject in terms of Lincoln's personal appearance and qualities, as well as his favourite books, such as the Bible and Bunyan's *Pilgrim's Progress*. Stoker's emphasis on Lincoln's contribution to the abolition of slavery is noteworthy, given a negative attitude towards black people in his fiction. The following year, he lectured again at the North Islington

Liberal Club on the lessons to be learned from Lincoln's life, reciting Walt Whitman in the process.

Many in Stoker's circle shared his views on the United States. Ellen Terry calculated that she had spent five years touring in the USA and felt herself to be American. Arthur Conan Doyle (now Sir Arthur, having been knighted in 1902 for his activities in the Boer War), in an interview with Stoker in 1908 made it clear that he was a great admirer of America, although he was critical of anti-British feeling there, claiming that America would find, when it became a world power, that it could rely on Great Britain, its own kin. Similarly, in an interview the same year, Stoker quoted Winston Churchill's positive views on America's potential to influence the future of politics. Hall Caine revealed his enthusiasm for the United States and his belief that the Americans represented the English nation transplanted in *My Story*, also published in 1908. These views had already emerged in Stoker's fiction: in *The Man*, Mr Stonehouse tells how he had prospered in the United States through his parents' values and hard work, although Stoker struck a more critical note in *Lady Athlyne*: 'The American in him was clamorous for movement, for speed and progress! . . . we are but children and the new toy but renews the old want and the old impatience; bringing in turn the old disillusionment and the old empty-hearted discontent.'[25] In his essay, 'Americans as Actors', published in the *Fortnightly Review* in 1909, Stoker heaped praise on America as a nation of specialists, but concluded that strenuousness and attendant self-consciousness made Americans admirable in smaller parts but not as well suited to the 'higher walks': 'The perfect Hamlet or Ophelia must not have a brogue, a twang or a lisp.'

ELEVEN

Pre-Echoes of Dracula

Then I had a vague memory of something long and dark with red eyes, just as we saw in the sunset, and something very sweet and very bitter all around me at once.

(*Dracula*, Mina Murray's Journal)

Stoker did not neglect his own creative work in the midst of all the Lyceum-generated and other activity. Some of the short stories that he had written in Dublin found their way into his first book of fiction, *Under the Sunset*, which was published in London late in 1881, although the official publication date was the following year. 'The Castle of the King' appeared in the *Warder* in 1876 and the other stories seem to have been written spasmodically over the next few years, making it unlikely that they were conceived as children's stories to entertain Noel, who was not born until three years after the publication of this story. The genesis of the book is therefore more likely to have been Stoker's wrestling with the emotional and psychological legacy of his own childhood.

Under the Sunset shares preoccupations with Stoker's other fiction of the early to mid-1870s, as well as looking forward to his later work, *The Snake's Pass*, *The Lair of the White Worm* and *Dracula*. One can only speculate about the emotional imperatives which impelled Stoker to some of the writing in *Sunset*. The early deaths of parents and children are a feature, especially in 'The Shadow Builder', a tale of a mother's ultimately successful search for her lost son which culminates in her snatching him from a procession of the dead. It is tempting to see autobiographical elements also in 'How 7 Went Mad', a slight story otherwise interesting mainly for its Lewis-Carroll-style nonsense element. It features the Nurse from the Grammar Village who is trying to bleed the subject of the story and may reflect Stoker's experience at the hands of the medical profession as an invalid child. The biblical concepts and language of the stories may also provide a clue to the moral earnestness of Stoker's childhood. Autobiographical concerns are evident in 'The Wondrous Child', about the three children of the Lord of the Manor in a village lying on the edge of a creek that stretches inland from an endless sea, which mirrors the locale of Stoker's Dublin childhood.

Under the Sunset was published by Sampson Low, Marston, Searle &

Rivington at a then high price of 10s. 6d. Stoker's contact at Sampson Low was Edward Marston, a partner in the firm and one of the most popular men in the London publishing world; he accepted the drawings by Stoker's friend and fellow Trinity graduate, William Fitzgerald, and commissioned additional ones by W.V. Cockburn. Edward Marston also published Stoker's later work, *A Glimpse of America*. Louis Frederick Austin, Stoker's colleague and sometime rival at the Lyceum, claimed that Stoker had spent £700 getting *Sunset* published, a considerable sum indeed for those days. This seems unlikely, given Stoker's position in London's artistic world at the time and his personal friendship with Marston. Whatever the truth of this claim, the book was widely reviewed by over two dozen journals in Britain and Ireland, including some of the most prestigious. The *Saturday Review*, for example, stated that

> Mr. Bram Stoker has produced a book which may please grown-up children as well as the smaller readers to whom it is specially addressed. The writer has a graceful fancy, the forms of which he expresses in excellent English, an accomplishment by no means too commonly met in children's or, indeed, in other books. *Under the Sunset* is well illustrated by Messrs. Fitzgerald and Cockburn, who have caught and expressed the author's delicate fancies with keen perception.

The reviewer in the Dublin *Daily Express* may have unwittingly connected with the autobiographical elements in the book when he wrote: 'We feel as we read it that the shades of the prison-house have not closed about the author – that he has succeeded in retaining much of the child-spirit, and that, therefore, both in his humorous and romantic stories, he understands what children like.'

The illustrator, William Fitzgerald, was a lawyer who became a clergyman in the year that *Under the Sunset* was published. He was the son of the Right Reverend William Fitzgerald, DD, the Church of Ireland Bishop of Cork, later Bishop of Killaloe, and brother of George Francis Fitzgerald, Professor of Philosophy at Trinity College Dublin since 1881 and the author of various scientific works. The latter lived at 7 Ely Place in Dublin from where William wrote to Stoker looking for theatre tickets for his sister and exclaiming:

> I will do anything for you, but illustrate your next book, which I fancy would be about as bad a turn as I could do you. Illustrations have so [?] much to do with the first glance at a Christmas Book in a shop, & a first glance has so much to do with the selling of such books, that I

fancy the illustrations in the 'Land under the Sunset' [*sic*] had *something*, at least, to do with any want of success it had in the market.

One cannot, however, take Fitzgerald's throwaway remark as proof positive that *Under the Sunset* did not sell well; indeed, Stoker was congratulated by Hallam Tennyson on its success. The theatrical journal, *Entr'acte*, featured Irving sticking up for Stoker when he was attacked by a Mr Merivale: Stoker was no ordinary manager but an author 'and a very good one too. The children's book called "Under the Sunset" is one of the very best works of its kind.'[2]

Stoker employed the short story medium throughout most of his adult life, from his days as a young civil servant in Dublin through to his final days in London, albeit with mixed results. It was the means by which he maintained his literary activity in the mid-to-late 1880s, when he was most immersed in his duties at the Lyceum and his fictional output was at its lowest. 'Our New House' appeared in *The Theatre Annual* of 1886. A slight story, it employs some of Stoker's perennial themes: a lost family, surrogacy and hidden treasure. Another story, of a very different kind, appeared in *The Theatre Annual* the following year. 'The Dualitists' featured a married couple in opposition to two murderous young boys living close by. Stoker continues his sardonic negativity about children with a satirical account of the boys' destructive tendencies, as they ultimately graduate to murder while enjoying the favour of society. It is an extraordinarily vicious story, devastating in its cynicism about human nature. There are parallels with some of the Lyceum plays; *The Bells*, for example, where Mathias is esteemed by society but has a secret murder in his past. It prefigures the infanticide which would feature in *Dracula*. It also reflects the influence on Stoker of the work of the contemporary criminologists, Cesare Lombroso (cited in *Dracula* as an authority on the Count as a criminal type) and Guglielmo Ferrero, who propagated the notion of the inherent criminality of women and children.[3]

Another of Stoker's horrific short stories, 'The Judge's House' (written in 1891), which has already been mentioned, was described by a contemporary source as 'a creeper of the first water'. Modern critics agree on the quality of this story of the disintegration and death of a student under the malign influence of a long-dead judge and also on the obvious influence of Sheridan Le Fanu, especially his 'Mr Justice Harbottle' and 'An Account of Some Strange Disturbances in Aungier Street'.[4] The notion that another horror short story, 'The Secret of the Growing Gold' (1892) – the growing gold of the title being a dead woman's hair – was inspired by the exhumation of Dante Gabriel Rossetti's wife, Elizabeth Siddal, gains credence from the fact that Hall Caine was shown some of her hair, recovered from the perfectly preserved body, by Rossetti. He might have been aware that Alfred Perceval Graves, who was also a great admirer of Rossetti, had to deal, in his capacity as a Home Office official, with the granting of permission for Siddal to be exhumed.

In 1892, the year that 'The Secret of the Growing Gold' was published, Stoker found inspiration for another story, 'The Coming of Abel Behenna', in the small fishing village of Boscastle on the west coast of Cornwall, which he discovered by chance on a long walking tour of the area during Holy Week in 1892. He fell in love with it and gave such a glowing account to Irving that the actor spent two vacations there. Boscastle became Pencastle in Stoker's tale of two fishermen in love with the same girl, ending sentimentally with the body of Abel Behenna washed up on rocks, a hand outstretched towards his beloved Sarah, at the hour of her wedding to the other man.

It has become generally accepted in Stoker biography that another story, 'The Squaw' – which features a cat impaling in an ancient torture instrument the man responsible for the death of her kitten, and was published in the Christmas 1893 number of the *Illustrated Sporting and Dramatic News* – was also the product of a trip by Stoker, this time to Nuremberg. Certainly Irving did take a party, including Ellen Terry, Comyns Carr and Hawes Craven to Nuremberg and Rothenburg, prior to the production of *Faust* in 1885, as part of the preparation for mounting it. Stoker did not claim that he had been included in the party and he is not mentioned as having been there by any of the other accounts of the visit.[5] Stoker would have heard descriptions of the visit from those who did participate and probably used his ability to describe places he had never actually visited, so ably demonstrated in *Dracula*, to paint a convincing portrait of the medieval German city. Continental European travel featured in another story from this era, 'The Burial of the Rats', set in the rubbish dumps of Paris. Stoker had, of course, visited Paris in the 1870s when he stayed with Geneviève Ward and her mother. Stoker, like Le Fanu, was fond of the image of the rat and used it in this story as well as in 'The Judge's House'. More unusual was Stoker's narrator taking an interest in an underclass: 'So I determined to investigate philosophically the chiffonier – his habitat, his life, and his means of life.'

Stoker continued the horror theme with 'The Man from Shorrox'', published in the *Pall Mall Magazine* in February 1894 but this time leavened with his particular brand of sardonic humour. The story of a bumptious Englishman becoming the butt of sly Irish rural humour by being put into the same bed as a corpse, 'The Man from Shorrox'' was well received by contemporaries. The *Yorkshire Post* described it as the amusing adventure of an Englishman in Ireland: 'and Mr. Stoker's patriotism naturally makes him give the Englishman the worst of it; but his many friends all over the country will not shun him on this account'.[6] The inspiration for 'Shorrox'' may have derived from correspondence with William H. Ridenig, editor of *Youth's Companion* in Boston, who had published Stoker's poem, 'One Thing Needful', an earnestly Christian piece based on the Gospel story of Mary and Martha, in 1885 and encouraged him to write short stories, 'full of incident and dialogue', based on the life of the Irish countryside that he had experienced as a civil servant.[7] Nothing would have amazed the editor of this wholesome Victorian journal more than the suggestion of a modern critic that the story he may have helped inspire suggests homosexuality (waking up in bed with a male corpse), as well as necrophilia.[8]

Stoker's next story, 'A Dream of Red Hands', published in the London *Sketch* in July 1894, is in essence a Christian morality tale which was again well received by contemporaries although its pietism seems risible today. The tone of 'The Red Stockade', published in *Cosmopolitan Magazine* in September 1894,[9] is more Kiplingesque. The genesis of the story may have been Stoker's contact with Admiral Erben of the American Navy when the USS *Chicago* visited London. 'The Red Stockade' is told in the first person by a matey narrator on the frigate, *George Ranger*, ordered to the Straits of Malacca to put down Malay pirates – 'yellow devils', in Stoker's description. The Straits of Malacca were a favourite location of nineteenth-century writers, including Herman Melville, Jules Verne, Rudyard Kipling and Joseph Conrad who, in *Lord Jim*, refers to 'the awful Malacca Portuguese'. The story combines effective horror with demonisation of the Oriental pirates. The 'red' of the title, emblematic of their intimidatory use of blood, links it to the preoccupation with blood in *Dracula*, then in gestation: '. . . there, on the spikes of the stockade, were the heads of all the poor fellows that we had lost the day before, with a cloud of mosquitoes and flies already beginning to buzz around them in the dawn. But beyond that again, they had painted the outside of the stockade with blood, so that the whole place was a crimson mass. You could smell it when the sun came up!' It ends, predictably, with the Western sailors killing all the Malays – 'We didn't leave a living thing within the Red Stockade that day, and we wouldn't if there had been a million there!' – and its final note is jingoistic: 'He died for his Queen and country, and for the honour of the flag! And what more would you have him do!'

'Crooken Sands', which appeared in the Christmas number of the *Illustrated Sporting and Dramatic News* in 1894, was a welcome change to a more humorous theme. Its central character, Mr Arthur Fernlee Markam, is a London merchant who dresses up in Highland costume when he goes on his summer holidays to Scotland. There is a reference to 'Crooken Sands' in *Dracula* and it might be possible to link the unflattering portrait of Hildesheim, 'a Hebrew of rather the Adelphi Theatre type, with a nose like a sheep, and a fez', in the novel[10] with a clearly Jewish duo in this story as borderline anti-Semitism on Stoker's part, but his real target was pseudo-Celticism. It has been suggested that Stoker got the inspiration for Arthur Markam on his own holidays in Scotland from the elderly nineteenth Earl of Erroll who was in the habit of walking around Cruden Bay, the east Scottish seaside village where Stoker took holidays in the 1890s, in a 'tweed suit of antique cut and high Glengarry bonnet with the Hay falcon in silver on it'.[11] He may also have been inspired by the story of a real-life Londoner, familiar to Henry Irving, who liked to assume a Celtic Welsh persona. It is more likely, however, that Stoker had in mind the true story of the two Bohemian brothers, calling themselves James and Charles Sobieski Stuart, who had published a pattern book *Vestiarum Scoticum*, in the early 1840s, supposedly linking the Scottish tartans to specific clans. Although it was as much a hoax as James Macpherson's Ossian poems in the previous century, it ignited the nineteenth-century passion for tartans and was an element in the vogue for the reconstruction of the Celtic past so beloved for the Victorians.

In 1893, Stoker expressed the desire to bring out a volume of his stories, an ambition which was not realised in his lifetime.[12] In January 1899, when he sent three stories to *Lloyd's Weekly Newspaper* for publication in forthcoming Sunday issues ('Chin Music', to appear on 19 February; 'A Young Widow' for 26 March; and 'A Yellow Duster' for 7 May), he was, as usual, fussy about the copyright.[13] 'Chin Music' would later appear in *Snowbound*. The plot of 'A Young Widow' is banal and the story is of interest mainly as an illustration of the themes of dead and surrogate parents being carried through from Stoker's earliest to his later fiction.

Stoker's use of his Irish background finds its most sustained expression in his first novel, *The Snake's Pass*. It is narrated by Arthur Severn, an Englishman who comes to visit friends in Clare, on the west coast of Ireland, as he had determined to improve his knowledge of 'Irish affairs' after he had inherited his great-aunt's wealth. At the Widdy Kelligan's shebeen (drinking establishment), he encounters an idyllic view of peasant life and is introduced to Irish storytelling, specifically the legend of the Snake's Pass.

The King of the Snakes had to have a live baby brought to him every year; he would wait for the full moon to enjoy his feast, when a wild wail would be followed by 'black silence' in much the same manner as Dracula would provide for his lady vampires. The King of the Snakes shares some other characteristics with the Count: he is legalistic and is capable of altering his shape. There are too, parallels between the Snake and Black Murdock, the gombeen man, or moneylender, and villain of the novel. Like the upstart Jason in Maria Edgeworth's *Castle Rackrent* (1800), Murdock is a ruthlessly accumulative Irish peasant, representative of a new breed of unattractive, ambitious, native entrepreneurs as seen by unimpressed Protestant observers. As a 'human-shaped wolf', Murdock is linked to Dracula, whose basic characteristics are those of a werewolf. Parallel with this intrusion of the past into the present is the development of contemporary themes. Dick Sutherland, an engineer who is working for Murdock, hopes for government measures to reclaim the Bog of Allen, the kind of developmental idea which characterised Stoker's thinking about Ireland and derived from the thinking of mid-nineteenth-century Irish nationalists such as Thomas Davis. Dick is carrying out magnetic experiments to try to locate metal hidden in the ground at the behest of Murdock, who is looking for treasure believed to have been buried locally by a French force which came to the west coast of Ireland in 1798 to aid the abortive revolution in which Stoker's great-uncle, George Blake, had actually participated. Arthur Severn decides to buy Knockcalltecrore, the land at the centre of the novel, which Dick believes can be developed through the application of power and electric light. Arthur also transforms the farm of Norah Joyce, the book's heroine, loved by both Dick and Arthur, into an aristocratic country house, a reversal of the actual practice of peasants buying land from their landlords in the late nineteenth century and a throwback to earlier experiments in creating ideal communities in Ireland. Norah's father's declaration that he will move to Glasgow is, by contrast, in line with the reality of emigration patterns of the time.

Dreams feature prominently in *The Snake's Pass* and function as a means of bringing together the various plots: the conflicts between good and evil; Murdock and the virtuous band, led by Dick and Arthur, who ultimately defeat him; St Patrick and the King of the Snakes; primitive conditions and large-scale economic development.

Norah Joyce is to be remodelled educationally and socially to make her worthy of Arthur Severn's exalted social station. Stoker may have been inspired in this by the real-life action of Hall Caine in educating a young girl, Mary Chandler, with whom he lived and who later became his wife. The education of young girls to enable them to contract socially superior marriages was a theme of Caine's fiction and Caine did take an intense interest in the evolution of *The Snake's Pass*, sending Stoker several pages of criticism of a draft in 1890. The transmogrification of sexual rivalry into a sibling relationship is accomplished when Arthur tells Dick, the loser in the contest for Norah's love, that he is to look on him as a brother. Murdock hatches a terrible scheme either to murder or to compromise Norah and is assaulting her in the middle of a great storm when Arthur comes to the rescue. Murdock gets his just deserts when his house, with him inside, sinks into the bog, which then sweeps through Shleenanaher to the sea, as presaged in Arthur's dreams. Norah departs to spend two years at school in Paris, promising to try to be worthy of Arthur.

The French treasure is discovered and Dick prevails on Norah's father to take the gold. Treasure of a more prosaic kind is discovered when the discovery of pottery clay and limestone enables Dick to transform Knockcalltecrore into a 'fairyland'. Benign landlordism and assisted emigration are the solution for the tenants who stand in the way of this fairytale transformation. Dick is best man at the wedding of Arthur and Norah, who declares that she would otherwise not feel properly married.

On 13 July 1890, the *People*, then a new and highly successful weekly, announced that its next issue would see the start of the serialisation of *The Snake's Pass*, which was 'of a very striking character, the scene being placed in Ireland, while the plot is interwoven with a local tradition which dates back to the very long ago. Whether for originality, strength of characterisation, or continuous interest, the story may challenge comparison with the best novels of modern times.'[14] The novel duly appeared in serial form in the *People* and a number of provincial journals in the second half of 1890. Its publication had been trailed in the London newspapers as far back as September 1889, when Stoker had let it be known that he was writing a novel, the plot of which he had thought out in the course of a walking tour through Ireland, and that he had started on it as soon as the final curtain had fallen on the production of *Macbeth* at the Lyceum on 29 June 1889.[15] Stoker fed media interest in the background and development of the novel over the next few months, repeating that it had been written during a holiday spent in the West of Ireland.[16] He did not explain that elements of the plot had been in his mind for years, having been sketched out in his notebooks. *The Snake's Pass* was published in book form in November 1890 and reprinted by Sampson Low in 1892, with a new, cheaper edition appearing in the 'Collier's Shilling Library' in May 1909. Stoker later listed the publication date as 1891, but this was a lapse of memory on his part.[17]

Much of the background to the novel was real enough. Bog-slides were well documented in Irish records as far back as the eighteenth century: rare and unexpected occurrences, they were mysterious and terrifying to the local people. An article in the *Dublin Evening Mail* of 18 November 1873, which Stoker may well have seen, gave an account of a moving bog at Dunmore: 'the impounded mass has burst its barrier, "blown out," and made its way down the valley in a sluggish but broad and destructive stream of dark mud'.[18] In 1896, a few years after *The Snake's Pass* was written, a bog-slide at Knocknageeha near Killarney swept away and buried a family of eight, with their home and livestock.

If the bog-slides were firmly entrenched in the imagination of the country people, so too was the concept of the giant serpent. Lough Brin in Kerry, where Stoker's brother-in-law's family, the McGillycuddys of the Reeks, had extensive holdings, was believed to be inhabited by a 'wurrum' called Bran. This 'wurrum' was half-fish, half-dragon and lived in a mountain lake, where it was seldom seen but often heard. Local legend had it that on the opposite side of Kenmare Bay a 'wurrum' of enormous size had been slain by St Patrick and turned to stone and now formed a worm-like ledge of rock winding along the side of Coom na Peastha or 'the Valley of the Worm'. Great serpents featured in Sir William Wilde's *Irish Popular Superstitions* (1852).[19] Lady Wilde speculated that the May dance in Ireland imitated movements of the serpent and wrote of serpent worship in Ireland and of the legend of St Patrick hewing down a serpent idol, with the serpent a symbol of the Evil One which had to be propitiated. *A House of Tears* (1886) by her publisher, Edmund Downey, featured a half-man, half-snake as well as a character called Stoker.[20]

The symbolism of the snake had featured in Stoker's earliest published work – the heading of the final instalment of 'The Primrose Path' in 1875 was 'The Trail of the Serpent' – and would recur indirectly in *Dracula* when Arthur Holmwood is compared to Thor as he stakes Lucy. Thor is the enemy of the world serpent, Jormungand, the symbol of evil in Norse mythology and they are destined to kill each other in the Ragnarok, or end of the world. The snake is a symbol of evil in Judaeo-Christian belief, from the fall of man in the Garden of Eden onwards; the Bible states: 'And he laid hold on the dragon, that old serpent, which is the Devil, and Satan, and bound him a thousand years.' Elsewhere in the Bible, we are told: 'for out of the serpent's root shall come forth a cockatrice, and his fruit shall be a fiery flying serpent.'[21] The cockatrice is a legendary snake with a deadly glance, linking him with Count Dracula's hypnotic – and often fatal – stare.

If Black Murdock's roots lie partly in the symbolism of the snake, they also derive from the social conditions of nineteenth-century Ireland. Eviction was a fact of life in the landlord–tenant conflict that had convulsed the country in the years before *The Snake's Pass* was written. There were those who had over-extended themselves by borrowing money at high interest to buy the land of evicted tenants and, in most cases, found themselves without sufficient means to continue farming. Moneylending at exorbitant rates flourished and Black Murdock was representative of a very real social problem that existed in the Irish countryside of that time. The moneylender was an established fictional type in Irish novels of the nineteenth century, featuring in William Carleton's 1847 novel, *The Black Prophet*, and in Dion Boucicault's *The Shaughraun* (1875), a play which unites an English hero and Irish heroine in opposition to a local gombeen man. In *When We Were Boys*, published at the same time as *The Snake's Pass* by Stoker's friend, William O'Brien, Hans Harman, a landlord's agent, shares Black Murdock's propensity for vampiric exploitation of weaker victims. Stoker, indeed, wrote to O'Brien, expressing admiration for the book and O'Brien responded on 30 July 1890 suggesting that it might be dramatised and produced at the Lyceum by Henry Irving, in which case it 'would be of priceless value in the Home Rule fight'. O'Brien added that, while he had been given 'a most enthusiastic account' of Stoker, he 'was not prepared for kindness so amazing'. Stoker had to disabuse O'Brien of the idea that Irving would produce a political play, after what had clearly been an embarrassing misunderstanding, and O'Brien withdrew although he was still keen to enlist Stoker's help in getting a professional opinion on the dramatic possibilities of his work.[22]

The wider economic aspects of *The Snake's Pass* were also rooted in contemporary perceptions. Great hopes were entertained of large-scale economic development following the achievement of Home Rule; indeed, it was believed that Ireland possessed great mineral wealth that the British government was not allowing to be exploited and which could be developed under self-rule. Stoker's thinking was influenced by Robert Kane's 1844 work, *The Industrial Resources of Ireland*. Kane was concerned with the developmental potential of Irish natural resources – for example the harnessing of water power through turbines – which he saw as being facilitated by the marriage of English capital and of Irish enterprise. This, of course, is precisely the solution adopted in *The Snake's Pass* and, years later in the Balkan context, *The Lady of the Shroud*. Kane's ideas were adopted by the mid-nineteenth-century Irish nationalist leader, Thomas Davis, who was, like Stoker, a Protestant educated at Trinity College Dublin, and they became a staple element in the Irish nationalist economic thinking which informed Stoker's views on his native country for the rest of his life.

The clearing of the peasantry from estates is another feature of life in late nineteenth-century Ireland which Stoker portrays in his fiction. In *The Snake's Pass* it is a benign phenomenon and this reflects one strand of contemporary reality. For example, Sir Robert Gore-Booth of Lissadell in County Sligo, a friend of the Baroness Burdett-Coutts, chartered vessels to send people, free of charge, to America after the Famine, and the government initiated a number of state-aided emigration schemes. However, the attempts by some landlords to reduce the number of smallholdings as a prelude to the introduction of a more highly commercialised agriculture led to unrest and violence in the countryside. Stoker was not unaware of the realities. He had, after all, written of the Irish people 'seething in revolt' in the context of the cancellation of the Robert Emmet play in 1881.[23] Indeed, when William Fitzgerald was corresponding with Stoker about the illustrations for *Under the Sunset* he included, for Stoker's private amusement, a full-page cartoon of two men fighting furiously, meant to represent the state of Ireland at that time.[24] But Stoker was concerned to create reconciliatory scenarios in which idealistic solutions triumphed over the sordid realities of division and violence, and economic development revitalised a stale and underdeveloped economy.

The Snake's Pass impressed contemporaries of differing political viewpoints. Not only did Gladstone respond favourably, but Michael Davitt, who founded the Land League which championed tenants' rights in opposition to landlordism, to whom Stoker sent a copy, replied in November 1890 promising to say a 'not unkindly word' in the *Labour World*. He was as good as his word, and the resultant review described it as a

fresh, powerful, dramatic, intensely interesting story, the scene of which is set amid the wild scenery of Galway . . . The way in which the story is interwoven with an old legend which declared that at this very spot St Patrick drove the snakes into the sea reveals great artistic power. The characters are all firmly and clearly outlined, and around all is the feeling of the wild western Irish scenery, the driving mists, the tremendous rains, the bare mountain sides, and the thunder of the sea.[25]

Four years after the publication of *The Snake's Pass*, Stoker completed *The Watter's Mou'* at Cruden Bay, where he was on a summer holiday with Florence and Noel. He dedicated it to his mother 'in her loneliness'. Regarded by Stoker as a 'story' rather than a novel, it is a romantic morality tale set in a world of smuggling and intrigue in the harsh natural environment of Cruden Bay on the east coast of Scotland. *The Watter's Mou'* was published in 1894 in London by the Acme Library and in New York by L. DeVinne & Co. It appeared under the Constable imprint in London in January 1895. It was published simultaneously in paper wrappers at a price of one shilling by the Acme Library and in New York by Appleton at 75 cents in 1895.

The leading male character, William Barrow ('Sailor Willy'), a customs officer, is a manly chap, strong and handsome, but easily touched by a woman's distress. Maggie MacWhirter, the heroine who loves Willy, also represents another staple theme in Stoker's fiction, that of doubleness: she seems to herself to be two people and is capable of behaviour that is predatory as well as sweetly feminine. The harsh side of her character derives from her sturdy Berserker blood. The historical Berserkers, savage warrior gangs of Norse and Germanic history, had contributed to the development of the werewolf legend in Europe. In *Dracula*, the Count proudly identifies his Szekely ancestry with them and personally shares many of the attributes of a werewolf. In Stoker's mind, the Berserkers represented both the evil of the werewolf and the regenerative influence of their vigorous blood on flaccid contemporary society.

The dark side of Maggie's character expresses itself in sexual advances which sometimes anticipate those of the female vampires towards Jonathan Harker in Castle Dracula, as well as in an attempt to lure Willie into wrong-doing for her father's sake. His fishing boat is mortgaged to Solomon Mendoza of Hamburg and Aberdeen, a grasping villain whose combination of avarice and general unpleasantness makes him a lineal descendant of Black Murdock in *The Snake's Pass*. Stoker's description of Mendoza – 'an elderly man with a bald head, keen eyes, a ragged grey beard, a hooked nose, and an evil smile'[26] – runs perilously close to the anti-Semitic stereotypes of the literature of the era. Mendoza's foreign obnoxiousness is counterpointed by the home-grown aristocratic wholesomeness of the Earl of Erroll, a real person, whose castle at Slains was a feature of Cruden Bay. Where Mendoza is remorselessly grasping, the Earl is a benefactor. Maggie is a great favourite with the ladies at the Earl's Slains Castle and he awards her father master-ship of the harbour. He comforts Willy with pietism and establishes a hearty male relationship with him. Willy's masculine nature is not susceptible to the moral weakness urged on him by Maggie and nothing can tempt him from his duty. Maggie attempts desperate measures of atonement and goes missing at sea. Sailor Willy joins in the search but pays for his heroism with his life. Willy and Maggie are found dead together in a boat, their requiem being the roar of the waves and the screams of the circling white birds, symbolic of the soul of the lost girl, a suitably sentimental end to a Victorian tale of redemption through death.

Stoker published another of his lesser stories, *The Shoulder of Shasta*, in 1895 and dedicated it to his brother, Thornley, then President of the Royal College of Surgeons in Ireland, 'with love and esteem'. Its setting in the Rockies was inspired to some extent by E. Marston's 1886 book, with which Stoker was familiar, *Frank's Ranche or My Holiday in the Rockies*. Stoker would have known the scenery around San Francisco, well described in the book, from his travels in the United States with the Lyceum. The experiences of his brother, Dick, who settled in a log house on Vancouver Island, had some parallels with this novel.

The central character, Esse Elstree, is a seventeen-year-old English heiress who has been brought by her widowed mother to an estate in the Rockies. While the Rockies suggest both ghostliness and nightmare, the picturesque and romantic setting enables Esse to feel 'like some barbaric empress'.[27] The theme of the improvement of a primitive landscape by the injection of benign capital and technological ingenuity, present in *The Snake's Pass*, is now developed further, with the creation of an idyll by Westerners in an exotic wilderness, hitherto peopled by Indians. In this contrast between primitivism and development, Stoker places the mediating figure of a tall and handsome mountaineer, 'Grizzly Dick', who is counterpointed by Reginald Hampden, a refined young English painter. They are rivals for Esse's affection, with Reginald the eventual winner. The ending is similar to that of *The Snake's Pass* where the rivalry of two males for the heroine is resolved by friendly acquiescence on the part of the loser. Although *Shasta* was scathingly reviewed in the *Athenaeum* in November 1895, not all notices were bad and it fared well in the *Spectator* in February 1896.[28]

PART THREE

Dracula

TWELVE

Dracula

'We are in Transylvania; and Transylvania is not England. Our ways are not
your ways, and there shall be to you many strange things.'

(*Dracula*, the Count to Jonathan Harker)

In 1897, when Stoker signed the memorandum of agreement with the
publisher, Constable, for the publication of *Dracula* it was still entitled *The
Undead*. The memorandum provided that at least 3,000 copies were to be
published in that year; he was to earn no royalties until 1,000 copies had
been sold, after which he was to receive 1s. 6d. from the selling price of six
shillings. The agreement was to remain in force for ten years.[1] It was
published by Doubleday in the United States: this company told Florence
in 1931 that *Dracula* had never been out of print since its publication there
in 1899.[2] Stoker personally edited the text for the sixpenny mass-market
edition in 1901.

Because the widespread awareness of *Dracula* derives more from movies
than from reading the novel, there is often a lack of appreciation of its length
and complexity. There is also a tendency in many of the movies to isolate
a limited number of the clearly defined themes and sections of the novel,
rather than trying to convey a sense of Stoker's original intentions.

The first section features a young English solicitor, Jonathan Harker (whose
surname Stoker borrowed from the Lyceum scenery painter, Joseph Harker
(1855–1927)), travelling to the isolated castle of Count Dracula in remote
Transylvania to finalise the purchase by the Count of a large property in
England. As the vampiric nature of the Count is revealed to Harker, so is the
fact that he himself is a prisoner at the castle. Having survived the attentions
of three seductive female vampires, Harker manages to escape, waking up in
a hospital in Budapest a much shaken man. The grimness of these opening
chapters is counterpointed by the pleasant, intertwined English lives of two
friends, the worthy Mina Murray (who will marry Jonathan Harker) and the
heiress, Lucy Westenra. Lucy, bright and flirtatious, has received three
marriage proposals: from Dr John Seward, director of a mental asylum; from
the Texan, Quincey Morris; and from Arthur Holmwood, heir to a title and
wealth, whom she accepts. Depressed by his rejection at the hands of Lucy,

Seward throws himself into his work and is especially interested in a 'zoophagous (life-eating)' patient, Renfield, who eats small creatures and speaks of devotion to a Master who will turn out to be Count Dracula. Seward's hospital is close to Dracula's newly acquired English property, Carfax.

The action of the novel moves to Whitby, the North of England seaside resort where Mina and Lucy are on holiday. A less welcome visitor is Count Dracula who, having murdered the crew of the ship which brings him to England, comes ashore in the form of a huge dog and begins to vampirise the sleepwalking Lucy. Her health declines and Dr Seward calls in from Amsterdam Professor Abraham Van Helsing, an expert in obscure diseases who combines scientific with occult knowledge. While he is able to diagnose that she is the victim of a vampire, he cannot save her. In undeath, the pure, if coquettish, model of Victorian virtue develops the wanton sexuality of the vampire and is staked in her tomb by her putative husband, Arthur Holmwood (now Lord Godalming). The Count, meanwhile, has taken up residence in London, looking younger than ever from his depredations, and is about to unleash a vampire plague on the unsuspecting English population. Jonathan Harker and Mina Murray are now married. Under Van Helsing's tutelage, they, together with Dr Seward and Arthur, accept the reality of vampirism and form a band of pursuers dedicated to the destruction of Dracula. The bonds uniting the group are primarily those of male friendship. Mina is included, though with her 'man's brain' allied to a woman's heart, she straddles the male/female divide somewhat ambiguously (which some see as reflecting suppressed homoerotic impulses on the ostensibly heterosexual author's own part). She is a woman but also one of the chaps, fashioned by the providential hand of God for a great purpose, developing finally into the group's most effective member.

Together with Seward, Mina begins to correlate the disparate materials which provide vital information on the Count and the clues which, combined with Roman Catholic ritual and folkloric wisdom, will ultimately enable his destruction. Showing a fine disregard for the law, they break into his houses at Carfax and in London to destroy the vampiric lairs, boxes of the blood-enriched soil of Transylvania the Count has laboriously transported to England, so that he has nowhere to return to during daylight hours. The critic, Terry Eagleton, sees parallels between the position of Dracula, running out of land, and that of the Irish aristocracy, similarly afflicted as land reform measures transferred ownership to their tenants. Tension is added to the hunt for Dracula: he has exchanged blood with Mina, who begins the transition into a vampiric state. If they cannot destroy him in time, Mina, the novel's most powerful symbol of pure Victorian womanhood, will become a debased undead creature of the night.

The Count decides to retreat to his Eastern Transylvanian fastness, with the band of righteous Western Christian pursuers, likened by Van Helsing to the Crusaders of old, in hot pursuit. The theme of a complex but ultimately backward East, opposed by an up-to-date, technologically impelled West, is maintained from beginning to end in the book. The individualism of the accomplished Eastern Count is finally no match for the collectively applied modernism of his Western pursuers. Dracula, the foreigner who had the temerity to invade the heart of the West's most powerful empire, will now be eliminated by a justified Western invasion of his remote homeland.

The final section of the book is largely occupied with the pursuit of Dracula, a horror-driven grand chase reminiscent of some earlier Gothic fiction, Ann Radcliffe's novels especially. It also recalls the movement and exotic locations of *Melmoth the Wanderer* (1820), a Gothic masterwork by the Irish Protestant clergyman, Charles Maturin. The novel reverts once again to a travel narrative, with the band of pursuers following Dracula back to Transylvania. There are false steps along the way and Mina comes perilously close to succumbing to the vampiric state but, unlike the hapless Lucy, she is able to turn her partial vampirism against her undead seducer and use their affinity to track his movements. Epitomising the theme of Christian redemption that runs through the book, Renfield, Dracula's adherent, is affected by Mina's goodness and is murdered by the furious Count.

The information which Dracula had given to Jonathan Harker at his castle about his exploits as a mortal leader hundreds of years before, when he fled from the field of battle against the Turks to the safety of his home territory, leaving his followers to be slaughtered, now gives Van Helsing and his band a vital clue to the Count's likely course of action. Here we see the advanced Western ability to store and analyse data being used to deadly effect against the more instinctual, essentially medieval, vampire. The commanding figure we meet in his castle at the beginning of the book is now the possessor of a 'child brain' and the limitations of his imperfectly formed criminal mind are clear to Van Helsing and Mina, the more intellectually impressive figures in the band of pursuers. The seasonal setting of the novel reflects this downturn in the fortunes of its central character, who is dominant in the earlier summer of the book's opening chapters but is an increasingly diminished figure in the wintry landscape of its close.

Dracula is interdicted on the final leg of his journey back to his castle and killed by the knives of Jonathan Harker and Quincey Morris, a look of peace crossing his face in his final moment. His vampire brides have been dispatched by Van Helsing who, though elderly, is nevertheless affected by their beauty. All find peace in death and Mina is released from her partial vampiric state. Christian redemption is shown to be available to all, even the most depraved. The novel ends seven years after these events, with the Harkers having named their son after Quincey Morris, who was killed in the assault on Dracula. They are struck by the lack of authenticity in the mass of material which constitutes the record but decide that proof of their strange tale is irrelevant, their own faith in it being sufficient. At the last moment, Stoker playfully subverts the very basis of the text's credibility which he has painstakingly built up over hundreds of pages, leaving the reader to ponder his own willingness to suspend rational belief, as the novel's characters have also done.

This credibility derives from the narrative structure of *Dracula*, the importance of which to its success is recognised by critics. Given the inherently unlikely nature of the events, the use of multiple narrators employing seemingly objective documents, which acknowledged that very incredibility, enabled the reader to perform the necessary suspension of disbelief sufficiently to be drawn into the story. It is commonplace to attribute the inspiration for this device to Wilkie Collins's *The Woman in White* (1860). Stoker knew Collins, who attended the Lyceum and also accepted an invitation from Stoker to join the Honorary Committee of the Westland Marston Testimonial Fund in 1887. Marston, now obscure, was a Victorian poet whose work attracted the attention of Charles Dickens to the extent that he contributed a prologue to Marston's *Patrician's Daughter* in 1842. Stoker was in possession of the original manuscript of the dramatised version of Collins's *The Woman in White*, which fetched £20 at the auction of Stoker's books and papers after his death. The fact that the undead Lucy in vampiric form was being dubbed 'The Woman in Black' in the novel may have been a conscious reference on Stoker's part. While, however, Stoker would have been aware of the effectiveness of Collins's technique in *The Woman in White*, the epistolary form was much older and Stoker was probably aware that its use in the English novel dated back through Samuel Richardson's *Pamela; or, Virtue Rewarded* (1740–1) to the seventeenth century. A similar technique was employed by Maria Edgeworth in *Castle Rackrent* (1800), where the novelist is supposedly simply the editor of an invented character's memoirs. Having enjoyed a great vogue across Europe in the eighteenth century, the epistolary form was, ironically, in decline from the 1880s, precisely the point at which Stoker revived it with such vigour and originality. It also functioned to help keep Stoker's own larger-than-life personality, often reflected in the impossibly wonderful virtues of his autobiographically inspired heroes in much of his other work, out of the novel. As Franco

Moretti has pointed out, Stoker's narrative technique drags the reader forcibly into the text and the characters' fears are also theirs.[3]

After his death, a former administrative subordinate of Stoker's at the Lyceum, called Jarvis, was appointed literary executor. Going through Stoker's papers, he discovered a manuscript that was assumed to be a chapter of *Dracula* that Stoker had omitted in order to shorten the book. 'Dracula's Guest' features a narrator staying in a hotel in Munich who goes for a coach ride on Walpurgis Nacht, the Witches' Sabbath, when the Devil is supposed to be abroad, graves are opened and the dead arise. As the driver refuses to take him down a particular road, he decides to explore it alone, ignoring the pleading of the coachman: 'Go home, Johann – Walpurgis Nacht doesn't concern Englishmen.' Groping through a snowstorm, he comes across the graveyard of a depopulated village. In it is the tomb of a suicide, with an iron stake running through it, bearing the inscription: 'Countess Dolingen of Gratz in Styria Sought and Found Death 1801'. Inside the tomb he discovers a beautiful woman, obviously the dead Countess, with rounded cheeks and red lips, on a bier, seemingly asleep. In a distinctly Wagnerian manner, lightning strikes the iron stake through the tomb of the Countess: 'The dead woman rose for a moment of agony, while she was lapped in the flame . . .' He is finally rescued from a nightmare scene of walking dead by searchers alerted by Dracula, who states in a telegram: 'He is English and therefore adventurous.'[4]

In her preface to Stoker's posthumously published story, Florence stated that it was being presented 'practically as it was left by him', which raises the question of whether some revision took place, possibly at the hand of Jarvis. Any such editing would be important, as the role of 'Dracula's Guest' in relation to the published novel is one of the most vexed questions in Stoker scholarship and critics rely mainly on textual analysis for their conclusion. Harry Ludlam, Stoker's first biographer, believed that it was dropped from the novel because the parallels to Le Fanu's *Carmilla*, which anticipated its aristocratic female vampire theme and Styrian location, could have been misconstrued as overly derivative. Stoker's son, Noel, thought that *Dracula* had been judged to be too long 'and the Incidents at Munich, which came at the beginning, were omitted'. As he was eighteen when the book was published, he might have been expected to know what was going on. This explanation has been supported by the author, Peter Haining, who claims that Stoker made the cut at the request of the publisher, Constable, as the book needed to come in under 400 pages, otherwise sixpence would have been added to the price. In *The Undead: The Legend of Bram Stoker and Dracula*, with his co-author, Peter

Tremayne, he attributed the deletion to the suggestion of Otto Kyllmann, Constable's chief editor.[5]

Some scholars feel that 'Dracula's Guest' is the draft of an early chapter, since passages which referred to it further in the text were changed or deleted, although one of the female vampires encountered by Jonathan Harker has been identified as the Countess Dolingen. Sir Christopher Frayling, Rector of the Royal College of Art in London and author of *Vampires, Lord Byron to Count Dracula*, by contrast, thinks that 'Dracula's Guest' was written as a free-standing story based on Stoker's manuscript notes; Clive Leatherdale, a Stoker scholar and publisher, has also provided cogent arguments against the deleted chapter theory.[6] None of the competing theories can be definitively proved or disproved. While it is possible that the chapter was a draft which Stoker chose not to work into the final version, it is difficult to see it as being part of the novel more or less up to publication. Its locale in Austria represents an earlier stage of Stoker's approach to the setting of the novel, as evidenced by his notes; and the use of a single narrator is at odds with the style of the published novel, which eschews this convention in favour of an epistolary, multi-narrator approach. The possibility that it was edited after Stoker's death further muddies the waters.

By contrast with the disagreement about the nature of 'Dracula's Guest', a number of paragraphs featuring a Wagnerian *Götterdämmerung*-style ending for *Dracula*, in which, following Dracula's death, his castle self-destructs in a majestic, volcano–like explosion, are generally accepted to have been an excised final section of the novel. These were included in the setting typescript given to his publisher but not incorporated in the published text. It has been suggested that Stoker deleted this final section because of parallels with Edgar Allan Poe's 'The Fall of the House of Usher'. An alternative explanation is that because the passage offered incontrovertible proof of Dracula's 'final death', it may have been deleted to allow Stoker the possibility of writing a sequel. It may also, of course, have been deleted because of its obvious derivation from the destruction of Valhalla, the home of the Gods, in *Götterdämmerung*, at the climax of Wagner's *Ring* cycle of operas, the German composer being a favourite of Stoker's and an influence on Irving's style of staging at the Lyceum.[7]

Few works of literature have their genesis as well documented as *Dracula*. Stoker's working notes have survived and are now in the Rosenbach Museum and Library in Philadelphia;[8] they provide a fascinating insight into the development of the novel. They contain source material and reveal changes in plot and characterisation from 1890 onwards. Most importantly, perhaps, they prove that, far from whipping up a hasty potboiler, Stoker worked on the novel for several years prior to its publication in 1897. As one note, dated 14 March 1890, contains an outline of chapters divided into four books, it can be seen that Stoker's concept of the novel was already quite developed at this stage and indicates that its conception was earlier, perhaps stretching back into the late 1880s. Interviewed by the *British Weekly* in 1898, Stoker said that the story of *Dracula* had been on his mind a long time and that he had spent about three years writing it.[9] It is difficult to square this with the length of time we know he worked on it from his notes. Stoker may have wished to differentiate the actual writing of the final text over three years from the research and outline plotting or he simply may have wanted to downplay the amount of effort he had put into it. In this interview, Stoker makes no mention of the explanation of the origins of *Dracula* given by his son, Noel, to Harry Ludlam and accepted by early biographers: that *Dracula* was born of a nightmare, following a supper of dressed crab. Stoker himself meant this as a joke, as is clear from the first draft of a letter from Noel Stoker to Ludlam in which he states that '*In a flippant mood* [italics added], my father attributed the genesis of "Dracula" to a surfeit of dressed crab . . .' This phrase was removed from the letter actually sent.[10]

Stoker stated that his knowledge of vampire superstition came from a good deal of miscellaneous reading, especially Emily Gerard's 'Essays on Roumanian Superstitions'[11] which had appeared in 1885 and were later expanded into a couple of volumes (Gerard's 'Transylvanian Superstitions' appeared in the *Nineteenth Century* in 1885; her book, *The Land beyond the Forest*, was published three years later). Stoker certainly took extensive notes from Gerard, including on the identification of St George's Day as the Witches' Sabbath; on the Scholomance (where Dracula would imbibe the Devil's teachings in Stoker's novel); on thirteen being an unlucky number; and on the 'Vampire or Nosferatu'. If Stoker had been influenced by Gerard's article as far back as 1885, it strengthens the case for locating the origins of *Dracula* in the latter half of the 1880s. Indeed, a reference by Mina Harker to the 22nd of September being a Thursday limits the years in which the novel is putatively set to 1887, 1892 or 1898 in the late nineteenth century if Stoker had an actual year in mind. As 1898 was the year after it was published and Stoker had been working on it for at least two years by 1892, there is a case for locating it in 1887, even if there are references to subsequent events in the text.

The only other book mentioned by Stoker in the interview was Sabine Baring-Gould's *The Book of Werewolves*. Werewolves do feature in Stoker's notes but not in the final novel (other than some isolated general references) although many of Dracula's characteristics derive from them rather than from vampires *per se*. Stoker's own sardonic reaction to over-enthusiastic excavation of his work was summed up in his reply to an American who sent him a memorandum on *Dracula* in 1906, to the effect that his correspondent knew a lot more about the book than he did!

Stoker also said that Van Helsing was founded on a real character, without specifying the identity. In the working notes, he was originally a German professor, which underlines the dangers of overstating the importance of his Dutch identity in the novel. Stoker refused to comment on an editorial in a provincial newspaper which claimed that 'high moral lessons' might be gathered from the book, on the grounds that readers should find out for themselves. Stoker referred to the effect of the vampire myth in the Middle Ages when the terror of the vampire had depopulated whole villages and speculated that the legend may have had its origins in a person being buried alive in a death-like trance; the trance concept was one he would develop further in *The Jewel of Seven Stars*. Asked to list the parts of Europe in which vampire belief was most prevalent, he mentioned Styria first as the place where it had survived longest and with most intensity; Styria was, of course, the location of his story, 'Dracula's Guest', as well as of Le Fanu's earlier *Carmilla*. Styria features prominently in the Rosenbach notes. In an early draft, the solicitor's clerk in the novel, Jonathan Harker, visits Styria; this was later crossed out by Stoker and 'Transylvania' written in. Similarly, the Count was originally 'Count Wampyr', later changed to Dracula. This weakens the case for seeing Vlad the Impaler, who is conspicuous by his absence from the notes, as the basic inspiration for the Count. The notes list Dracula's attributes, including connections with immortality and, obscurely, with Gladstone (Stoker may have been linking Gladstone with the Count in the sense that both had achieved a form of immortality, Gladsone in the political sense; he returned to the theme in the covering note with which he sent a copy of *Dracula* to the statesman in 1897).

The Rosenbach notes include a book list for Stoker's sources, much more extensive than he admitted in the *British Weekly* interview. Stoker's notes include quotations from Sir Thomas Browne, on 'Necromancy – divination by the dead' and from his *Religio Medici* on sleep as a middle way between life and death. This explains why Dracula's victims are afflicted by horrific dreams as they slip into vampirism: they are halfway between life and death. Stoker used Bishop Robert Gray's 1808 work, *The Theory of Dreams*, as another source, and his notes from it include information on the *Insomnium*, a phantasm called *visio* by Cicero, which arises between sleeping and waking and may have helped inspire the appearances of Dracula to Lucy and Mina. He also took notes on Philo Judaeus, a Jewish philosopher at the time of Christ, who believed that the prophet Abraham was the first skilful interpreter of dreams; in *Dracula*, Abraham Van Helsing, an occasional administrator of religious rites, is the interpreter of Mina's dreams about the Count. Stoker took notes from *Golden Chersonese* (1883), by the Orientalist, Isabella Bird, about Malay superstitions, in which she connected monotheism with demonology. Among the beliefs she described was that of a bird as the ghost of a dead woman, which relates to Dracula as a bat. The Malay belief in men who were tigers by night and men by day bears more than a passing resemblance to the Count as does the *polong* or bottle imp which lives on the blood of its owner and the vile fiend called *penangalan* which takes possession of women, turning them into witches who fly away at night to gratify cravings for human blood. Bird repeatedly used the image of the vampire to describe the Korean official class, sucking the life-blood of their people, in her *Korea and Her Neighbours*, published in the same year as *Dracula*.[12]

From Elizabeth Sarah Mazuchelli's *Magyarland* (1881), Stoker derived information on the arrival of the Huns under Attila and noted the Hungarian words for Satan, *Ordog*, and hell, *Pokol*, which would be used by the crowd at the inn as they try to dissuade Jonathan Harker from undertaking his fateful journey to Dracula's castle. From Andrew F. Crosse's *Round the Carpathians* (1878), he gleaned details of local colour which he later used in the novel, such as a description of the leiter-wagon seen by Jonathan Harker on his journey to Castle Dracula, and the Golden Mediasch wine which produced 'a queer sting' on Harker's tongue, following Crosse's description exactly. He also described how the Szgany, or gipsies, hung around Magyar castles and adopted the faith of the owner, as they would serve Dracula in the novel. Whether Stoker was familiar with the gypsy element in George Borrow's *Lavengro* (1851) and *The Romany Rye* (1857) is a moot point.

The description of the Carpathians' appearance used in Jonathan Harker's journal of 5 May was based on notes taken by Stoker from *On the Track of the Crescent* (1855) by Major C. Johnson. Other sources for Transylvania included Charles Boner's *Transylvania: Its Products and People* and William Wilkinson's *An Account of the Principalities of Wallachia and Moldavia with Various Political Observations relating to them* which he found in Whitby public library when he holidayed there in 1890. Wilkinson was Stoker's source for the historical Dracula and it was from here that he derived the name. Stoker also noted Wilkinson's description of the town of Galatz, where the boat, *Czarina Catherine*, lands with Dracula in the novel, and the calèche, a type of carriage used by the Count to take Jonathan Harker to Castle Dracula. More mundane sources found in Stoker's notes included R.H. Scott's *Fishery Barometer Manual* (1887) and F.K. Robinson's *Whitby Glossary* (1855).

One of the books in Stoker's library, *British Goblins: Welsh Folk-lore, Fairy Mythology, Legends and Traditions* by Wirt Sikes, the United States Consul for Wales, published in 1880, contained concepts which, coincidentally or otherwise, found their way into *Dracula*. Sikes wrote about the Welsh belief in Gwerddonau Llion, the abode of some Druids, not wicked enough to be condemned to hell nor holy enough for the Christian heaven, a kind of nether world similar to that in which Dracula exists. A bat features in the tale of the Ellylldan elf, which causes other creatures of the marsh to fall silent at his approach. The Bwbach is a terrifying phantom that transported mortals through the air in the service of troubled ghosts who cannot sleep on account of treasure they want removed (Dracula is an avid collector of treasure). Then there is Gwylli, Dog of Darkness, a frightful apparition of a huge mastiff with baleful breath and blazing red eyes that shine like a fire in the night. Dracula, of course, comes ashore in the form of a fearsome dog at Whitby.

Stoker retained a cutting from the *New York World* of 2 February 1896 about a nineteenth-century belief in vampires in New England (where the symptoms of tuberculosis were sometimes confused with vampirism), as well as cuttings about the vampire bat. In addition to the clearly documented sources for *Dracula*, there are others less certain but nevertheless worth investigating. One key phrase in the novel, 'For the blood is the life', in addition to being biblical, was used in an advertisement for 'Clarke's Blood Mixture' which appeared in the *Era*, a theatrical journal which Stoker would have seen and which may have stirred memories of similar advertisements in Dublin newspapers of the 1870s. Further source material preserved in the Rosenbach notes, which found its way into *Dracula*, came from Stoker's brother, Thornley, who provided medical information on the effects of head injuries, together with a diagram. This was used in relation to the fractured skull inflicted on Renfield by the vengeful Dracula. Thornley's description of stertorous breathing is also used in Stoker's depiction of Renfield's state following the attack.

Thornley, who had been educated at a grammar school in England and then at the Royal College of Surgeons in Dublin, before taking his M.D. degree at Queen's College, Galway, in 1866, had had experiences relevant to the undercurrent of insanity prevalent in *Dracula*. A Freemason, like Henry Irving, he had held appointments at the Royal City of Dublin Hospital and various other Dublin medical establishments. The most interesting, from the perspective of Bram Stoker biography, was Thornley's appointment as visiting surgeon to 'Dean Swift's Hospital for the Insane' (St Patrick's Hospital, Dublin) in 1876. He held the position for a number of years. While Thornley's influence on the development of *Dracula* is well documented, his connection with a mental hospital has not hitherto been known; this is of particular

interest in relation to the characters of Dr Seward and Renfield, the psychiatrist and his patient in *Dracula*, and, indeed, in the broader context of the
theme of madness which permeates the book (Van Helsing states that 'All
men are mad in some way or the other . . .') and is now attracting critical
attention. In 1873 Thornley took up a position as surgeon at the Richmond
Hospital in Dublin and remained connected with it for thirty-seven years.
Some years previously, its lunatic department had been moved to a separate
location in Dublin under the care of a Dr Stewart, a former governor of the
Richmond whose name suggests that of Dr Seward in *Dracula*. As President
of the Royal College of Surgeons in 1894, Thornley warned of the sudden
appearance of 'a grave Eastern disease', beri-beri, at the Richmond Asylum
in Dublin, at the same time quoting the Bible: 'Out of evil cometh good.'
Like the cholera epidemic in Sligo during his mother's youth, the concern
here is about a threat of contagion from the East. A similar fear is evident in
Dracula, on which his brother was engaged at this time.

As a young man, Thornley was an assiduous applicant for medical
positions. Later in life, the appointments seemed to come of their own
accord and from the highest levels, including the Lord-Lieutenant. He
was President of the Royal College of Surgeons 1894–6, for which he was
knighted, and President of the Royal Academy of Medicine in Ireland –
'the blue ribbon of the profession' – from 1903 to 1906. Patrick Hennessey,
MD, MRCS, LKQCPI, the obviously Irish doctor who reports to Seward
in *Dracula*, has qualifications from the Royal College of Surgeons as well
as the King's and Queen's College of Physicians in Ireland. Just as Stoker
kept up to date and had his characters employ the latest technology in
Dracula, so Thornley is described as having 'kept his mind receptive to
every scientific advance, and utilised the latest developments of the humoral
pathology as readily as the youngest of his colleagues'.[13] He was indeed a
pioneer in the field of surgery in Ireland, including brain surgery. When
Van Helsing says of the injured Renfield in *Dracula*: 'we must trephine [an
operation for opening the skull] at once' he was reflecting Thornley's
expertise in this area. In fact, when Augustine Birrell, the British Chief
Secretary for Ireland from 1907 to 1916, asked about his brother, Bram
Stoker, Thornley replied, according to Oliver St John Gogarty, that he was
engaged in scientific research somewhere. 'Not on the habits of Dracula?'
was Birrell's rather obvious rejoinder.[14]

The holiday which Stoker took in 1890 at Whitby, the fishing port and resort
on the north-east coast of England, was of crucial importance to the early
development of *Dracula*. Stoker showed an awareness of the town's ancient
history in the novel:

Right over the town is the ruin of Whitby Abbey, which was sacked by the Danes, and which is the scene of part of 'Marmion,' where the girl was built up in the wall. It is a most noble ruin, of immense size, and full of beautiful and romantic bits. There is a legend that a white lady is seen in one of the windows.

In Walter Scott's poem, 'Marmion', Constance of Beverley is bricked up alive in Whitby for forsaking her nun's vows to go with the false knight, Marmion. The white lady supposedly seen in one of the Abbey's windows is Saint Hilda, its seventh-century founder who supported the Celtic Church at the Synod of Whitby (663–4), which settled the date of Easter in the Western Christian Church. Among the members of Hilda's abbey was the poet, Caedmon. Whitby was also the place where Henry Irving enjoyed his last holiday with his companion, Mrs Aria, in 1905. Various addresses in Whitby have been mooted as the place where Stoker and his family spent that fateful vacation in the summer of 1890,[15] but there is no doubt that they lodged close to the scenery in *Dracula* which Stoker described with extraordinary fidelity. Joseph Hatton had referred to the red roofs of Nuremberg in his account of the trip there by Henry Irving and others of the Lyceum Company (they featured on the sets of the Lyceum *Faust*) and this finds an echo in *Dracula* when Mina compares the red roofs of Whitby to those of the German city.

Stoker recast some of his diary entries for the holiday in Whitby in *Dracula*. For example, the entry for 11 August 1890 describing a grey day, with a brool over the sea and men like trees walking, is reproduced in Mina Murray's Journal for 6 August. Similarly, a description of lights scattered over Whitby in his diary of 18 August 1890 features in Mina's Journal for 24 July. Stoker also found raw material in the inscriptions on Whitby's tombstones. The name of the old sailor, Swales, who tells Mina Murray that he is nearly a hundred years old, derived from Stoker's note of the tombstone of Ann Swales, which recorded that she had died in 1795, aged a hundred years. In the case of Braithwaite Lowrey, one of the drowned sailors mentioned by Mr Swales in Mina Murray's Journal for 1 August, Stoker simply took his name and that of his ship from the tombstone of Braithwaite Lowrey, who was lost in the ship, *Lively*, that foundered off Greenland in 1857. The details of other drowned sailors mentioned by Swales to Mina Murray, Andrew Woodhouse, John Paxton and John Rawlings, were similarly taken from their gravestones.

Stoker also kept a 'Memo' of a meeting with three old fishermen in the churchyard on the cliff at Whitby, on 30 July 1890, when they told him of the sinking of the whaler, *The Esk*, with the loss of all lives except three.

Its master, a powerful man who had fought an American on an ice floe and had vowed to find 'Hell or Whitby tonight', knocked down the crew, one by one, as they came to implore him to take a less risky course; this may have been part of the inspiration for Dracula's gradual murder of the crew of the *Demeter*. Further inspiration came in a conversation, on 11 August 1890, with the Whitby coast guard, William Petherick, who told him of the wreck of the Russian ship, the *Dimitry*, five years previously, on 24 October 1885. It had run in to the harbour with full sail, just as the Dracula-bearing *Demeter* would do, at nearly full tide; it put out two anchors in the harbour, one of which broke, causing the ship to slew around. The *Dimitry* was ballasted with silver sand, as was the *Demeter*. Another ship also got in to the harbour, quite how, Petherick never understood as all hands had been below deck praying; the *Demeter* also arrived with no crew on deck, all hands having been taken care of by the Count.

A widely held belief in *Dracula* commentary is that the character of the Count was modelled on Henry Irving. Some go further and see the cast of the novel as reflecting the personalities of the Lyceum Company. While there are some obvious similarities, there are also emphatic differences between the Count and Irving, who, among other things, did not share the werewolf characteristics which Stoker so obviously attributed to his vampire (although Ellen Terry did compare Irving playing Macbeth to a great famished wolf). The case for seeing Irving as Dracula, apart from any physical resemblance (they were both tall) and dramatic personality, is based largely on his nocturnal habits (although these are inevitable in the acting profession) and an alleged feeling on Stoker's part (for which there is no supporting evidence) that he was exploited by the actor; this is a variation on the Marxist identification of vampirism with economic exploitation. Dracula's reinvention of himself as an English gentleman does parallel Irving's recasting of his unpromising attributes to become a great actor through a supreme effort of will. However, Stoker's descriptions of Irving do not generally suggest the supernatural; by contrast, the drugged appearance of Sarah Bernhardt's husband, Jacques Damala, who frequented the Lyceum, made Stoker think that he was a living dead man. Other aspects of Dracula recur in Stoker's fiction without any obvious link to Irving; the furious cat in his short story, 'The Squaw', for example, bears more than a passing resemblance to the Count: the very incarnation of hate, her green eyes blaze with lurid fire and her sharp white teeth shine through the blood around her mouth.

Some at least of Dracula's characteristics may have come from contem-poraries other than Irving, Sir Richard Burton being an obvious example.

Stoker first encountered Burton in Dublin and maintained contact with him at the Lyceum. They first met when Burton visited Ireland in 1878 to lecture in Dublin on ogham, the early Irish alphabet, at a time when his star was very much in the ascendant. Irving was in Dublin at the same time, on his way to give a reading at the Samaritan Hospital in Belfast and he introduced Burton when Stoker met him off the train at Westland Row Station. Stoker's attention was riveted by the explorer's air of dark, forceful ruthlessness. In January 1879, Stoker met him again at the Green Room Club, where he sat between Burton and James Knowles, editor of the *Nineteenth Century* magazine.

In the following few weeks, Stoker met Burton and his wife at supper several times. His first impression of Burton as a man of steel was confirmed. He also noticed that, when Burton laughed, his face seemed to lengthen, with the upper lip rising, showing the right canine tooth, just like Count Dracula. Burton enthralled Stoker with his tales of the East: 'As he talked, fancy seemed to run riot in its alluring power; and the whole world of thought seemed to flame with gorgeous colour.'[16] There is a reference in *Dracula* to the *Arabian Nights*, which Burton had translated and which he had, indeed, suggested might provide the material for a play at the Lyceum. Like Dracula himself, Burton arrogated to himself the power of life and death with a casual imperiousness. He told Stoker of how he had murdered an Arab lad who had recognised him as a foreigner in Mecca, without being troubled; as he recounted the tale, his canine tooth gleamed like a dagger.

Burton was a generation older than Stoker, having been born in Torquay, in the west of England, in 1821. He had family roots in Tuam, County Galway, where his paternal grandfather had been the Church of Ireland rector and owner of an estate. Like Stoker, Burton had definite ideas on the issue of Home Rule and advocated the adoption of the Austro-Hungarian constitution as a model for Ireland. He wrote on the parallels between the Irish and the Magyars and was familiar with the life and work of Arminius Vambery, the Hungarian writer and traveller who some believe first interested Stoker in Vlad the Impaler, the historical Dracula. When Stoker met Burton in London in 1879, the explorer told him of a planned expedition to reopen the old Midian gold mines in Arabia; Stoker asked him to take his adventurous brother, George, with him as a doctor to the party and Burton was agreeable but Arabi Pasha's 1882 revolt led to the indefinite postponement of the project.

Stoker shared an interest in the supernatural with Burton, whose analysis of 'The Praeternatural in Fiction' featured in Justin McCarthy's ten-volume *Irish Literature* (1904). Stoker and Irving subscribed to the private publication of Burton's five-volume *Persian Tales* but the most interesting of

Burton's literary efforts from the perspective of *Dracula* is his *Vikram and the Vampire or Tales of Hindu Devilry* (1870). It is fair to assume that Stoker read it and while the evildoer of the tale is the character, Jogi, not the vampire (who saves the King's life), the concept of the vampire and the horrific descriptions in the book may well have influenced Stoker. It features blood-sucking demons among a ghastly crew and the manner in which Jogi raises his hand to silence nature anticipates Dracula's ability to control the wolves by a similar gesture. The decapitation of Jogi also resembles the fate met by the Count.

Another man of action who inspired Stoker was the explorer, Henry Morton Stanley, for whom Irving gave a dinner at the Garrick Club in October 1882. Stanley had just returned from the experiences he would later chronicle in *In Darkest Africa* and had been in close consultation with the King of the Belgians about the foundation of the Congo Free State. He held his audience at the Garrick spellbound and Stoker sat up until 4 a.m., enthralled by the traveller's tales. At the same time, Stoker recognised a darker side in Stanley: in 1882, he saw horror ingrained on Stanley's face, feeling that there were times when he looked less like a living than a dead man, a real-life example of the living dead. Stanley returned Stoker's admiration, telling him in 1890 that he had mistaken his vocation and should devote himself to literature. Stanley's opinion was based on Stoker's least significant work from a literary perspective; his pamphlet on the United States, *A Glimpse of America*, was one of very few books the explorer had taken with him to Africa. They shared the same publisher around this time: Edward Marston published *Under the Sunset* and *A Glimpse of America*, as well as Stanley's *Through the Dark Continent*.

In some respects, Stoker himself is closer to the Count than Irving. Like Dracula, and in marked contrast to the actor, Stoker was a man of many parts, willing to turn his hand to more or less anything. Just as Stoker tackled a multiplicity of roles for Irving, so the Count made himself generally useful, acting as coachman, cook and domestic servant. He also arranges travel and transport (his boxes of earth resembling the theatrical baggage which Stoker looked after), reading reference works and dabbling in the law. Like Stoker, too, he is immensely strong physically. If Stoker did contract syphilis, it might reflect a dualistic nocturnal existence on his part not entirely dissimilar to the Count's sexual adventures which are cloaked in darkness.

Much of Irving's stage repertoire impacted on Stoker's writing, his productions of Shakespeare especially. The allusions in *Dracula*, for example, to Shakespeare's work, including *Hamlet*, *The Merchant of Venice*, *Twelfth*

Night and *King Lear*, show his influence. This is not surprising as Sigmund Freud, in 'The Uncanny', noted how Shakespeare stages his action in a world peopled with spirits, demons and ghosts, not just in *Hamlet* and *Macbeth* but also in plays such as *The Tempest* and *A Midsummer-Night's Dream*. Of course, not all of Shakespeare's influence was due to the Lyceum: Stoker had immersed himself in Shakespeare well before he went to work for Irving, a point underscored by the reference in his serial story, 'The Chain of Destiny' (1875), to Shakespeare's *Much Ado about Nothing* and to his *Pericles* in another early story, 'The Castle of the King'.

Irving's forte was supernaturally tinged melodrama: he established his reputation in *The Bells* as far back as 1871 as the guilt-stricken murderer, Matthias, who is haunted and ultimately destroyed by the sound of the sledge bells of his victim. To the leading contemporary critic, Clement Scott, the spell created was irresistible: 'the young actor had held his audience fast as in a vice, and, most wonderful of all, in a scene probably the most risky and exhausting in the long catalogue of the modern drama'. His Vanderdecken was, like Dracula, 'haunted by the despair of an eternity of love'.[17] The supernatural in Shakespeare was of particular interest to Stoker: he was struck by the wonderful way in which Irving handled the ghost in *Hamlet* and related it to one of Shakespeare's sources of inspiration, François de Belleforest's *Histoires tragiques*, which described how, in Hamlet's time, northern Europe lived under Satan's laws and the Prince had been instructed in the devilish arts by his father, enabling him to know of things past (but not future). Stoker saw this as the essence of Hamlet's patient acquiescence in the ways of his time, inspired by a mixture of pagan fatalism and Christian belief. Given that Irving's lack of education makes it unlikely that he would have read sources such as Belleforest himself, Stoker probably played a mediating role in conveying insights gleaned from them to the actor. Some of the Shakespearian elements which impinged on *Dracula* may have been conveyed by Stoker to Irving in the first instance. It has been suggested that Van Helsing's name may derive from the Danish name for Elsinore, Helsingør, or 'the island of Helsing'. Even a romantic play like *Romeo and Juliet* struck a horrific chord with Stoker, with the bloodthirstiness of the Italian petty states ingrained in it making an unusually strong impact on him.

It was, however, *Macbeth* that interested Stoker the most of all the plays performed by Irving and it was a favourite subject of discussion between them from 1876, before he began working for the actor, until 1888 when it was performed at the Lyceum. As with *Hamlet*, Stoker researched the sources for *Macbeth*, especially the work of Andrew of Wyntoun, the Scottish chronicler whose *Orygynale Cronykil* is the original source for the encounter

Stoker, as Auditor, with the other officers of the Trinity College Dublin
Historical Society for the 1872–3 session.

Stoker, an outstanding athlete, featured prominently in the Trinity College Dublin Races in the
late 1860s and early 1870s. This drawing of the 1874 College Races shows the Lord Lieutenant
of Ireland, the Duke of Abercorn, and Lady Georgiana Hamilton in the foreground.

Bram Stoker, *c*.1890

(*Left*) Florence Balcombe from a drawing by Oscar Wilde, as she would have looked when Stoker fell in love with her. (*Right*) Florence Stoker with Noel as a child.

Cartoon in *The Entr'act* 23/9/1882 of Stoker being congratulated by Henry Irving on his efforts to save a drowning man from the Thames.

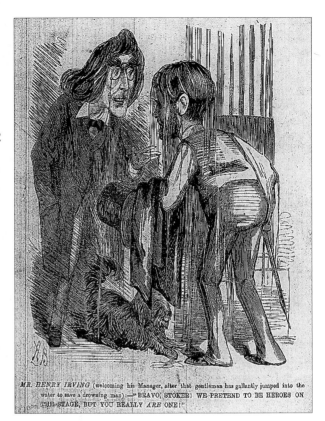

MR. HENRY IRVING (welcoming his Manager, after that gentleman has gallantly jumped into the water to save a drowning man):—"BRAVO, STOKER! WE PRETEND TO BE HEROES ON THE STAGE, BUT YOU REALLY *ARE* ONE!"

A humorous view of the logistical difficulties Stoker had to deal with on Lyceum tours in a silhouette drawing by Pamela Colman Smith.

Henry Irving about to get into a cab, followed by Stoker, emerging from his private door at the Lyceum Theatre in Burleigh Street, London.

Henry Irving (left) and Stoker (centre) on board ship. Long tours, provincial and American, were an important source of income for the Lyceum Theatre.

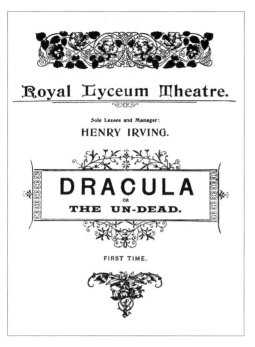

The programme for the play version of
Dracula mounted at the Lyceum on
18 May 1897 for copyright purposes.
It was the only stage performance of
the novel in Stoker's lifetime

Ellen Terry (left)
and Henry Irving
(right) in a scene
from the Lyceum
production of *Faust*
(1885), the theatre's
greatest ever
financial success.

Frank Sutcliffe's nineteenth-century photographs of Whitby
(*Above*) Sailor telling a story to a group of children

(*Below*) The ship, *Agnes and Mary*, being pounded in a storm off Whitby on
24 October 1885. Dracula arrived in Whitby by ship in the midst of a storm

Sketched suggestion, by William FitzGerald, for the illustration of 'How 7 Went Mad', included in *Under the Sunset*, in an 1881 letter to Stoker.

THE IRISH "VAMPIRE."

(*Left*) 'The Irish Vampire' by John Tenniel featured in *Punch* on 24 October 1885 (*Below left*) The reply, 'The English Vampire', by an unknown artist, appeared in the *Irish Pilot* of 7 November 1885. The use of vampiric images to stigmatise the opposition by both English and Irish nationalists may well have influenced the politically minded Stoker in his creation of Dracula. (*Below*) 'La Lanterne', drawing of Church as Vampire in a French anti-clerical journal of 1898

Two original Dracula posters:
(*Above*) 'Taste the Blood of Dracula'(1970)
(*Left*) 'Le Cauchemar de Dracula' (1958)

between Macbeth and the weird sisters, and of Raphael Holinshed, the English chronicler whose work was such a source of inspiration for Shakespeare. Whether Stoker ghosted Irving's lecture on the subject to Owens College, Manchester, six years after the second production at the Lyceum, is not known although Stoker did claim that Irving was able to hold his own in sophisticated discussion on Shakespeare with the poet, Robert Browning (Browning, incidentally, gave Edmund Kean's purse to Irving, a handing down of a totemic symbol in the succession of great actors). According to Clement Scott, the witches' scene in the Lyceum production of *Macbeth* conveyed forcefully the gloom and horror that Shakespeare had wished to inspire in the audience. Hawes Craven, the great Lyceum scene painter, excelled himself in recreating Macbeth's forbidding Scottish castle in the scenery for Irving's production.

Stoker may have been instrumental in developing another of Irving's key roles, that of Mephistopheles in *Faust*, adapted from Goethe's German version by William Gorman Wills, a fellow Irishman and graduate of Trinity College Dublin. He was related to the writer, Violet Martin (who, with her cousin, wrote under the joint pseudonym, Somerville and Ross). One of Oscar Wilde's middle names, Wills, was a tribute by his parents to the family of the playwright. Stoker had been familiar with Wills's work from his own Dublin days when he had been present at the production of one of Wills's plays and they were sufficiently good friends to have spent a holiday together at Étretat on the Normandy coast. Like Irving and Stoker, Wills had a strong ghoulish streak in his nature and found employment for these horrific talents at the Lyceum where he collaborated with Percy FitzGerald in writing *Vanderdecken*. He was a German scholar and the imprint of his version of Goethe's *Faust*, like his *Vanderdecken*, is visible in *Dracula*. Irving had had Wills's *Faust* in his possession for several years, and had thought and talked of mounting it before taking the plunge. The playwright wrote to Stoker occasionally enquiring about Irving's plans to produce it.[18] Stoker would have been acutely aware of Irving's preoccupation with the Faust drama as not alone had he had Will's version of it for several years, but his room was crowded with Faust paraphernalia for months before the Lyceum production.

Goethe's *Faust* had exercised a fascination on audiences in the West for many years before Irving mounted it at the Lyceum. Indeed, the Faust legend was long embedded in literature: the *Faustbuch* (1587), notable for its creation of the fiendish Mephistopheles, caused a Europe-wide sensation in the sixteenth century. An English prose translation inspired Christopher Marlowe's *The Tragicall History of Doctor Faustus* (1604), which cast the central character as a doctor and necromancer who sold his soul to the devil in return for knowledge. The legend found its most powerful expression in J.W. von Goethe's *Faust* (1808/1832), which represented the legend as an expression of the eternal battle of good and evil, a basic theme of Stoker's novel. Hector Berlioz followed his *Huit scènes de Faust* (1829) with *The Damnation of Faust* (1846), based on Gerard de Nerval's French version of Goethe's poem which interpreted Mephistopheles as a darkly romantic anti-hero.

Charles Gounod's opera *Faust* followed in 1859 and Schumann's *Scenes from Goethe's Faust* was performed for the first time in 1862. Boito's *Mefistofele* was premièred at Milan in 1868. It is no surprise therefore that Faust was very much in the air when Stoker was active in the Philosophical Society at Trinity College. Papers on the subject were read under the Presidency of his friend, John J. Robinson, in 1874 and again in 1877. Interest at Trinity would have been stimulated by the fact that the influential translation (1835) in English was by a Trinity man, John Martin Anster, a friend of the Le Fanu family and a popular poet in Dublin in the generation before Stoker's. Anster's translation of *Faust* provided the basis of William Gorman Wills's adaptation of the story for Irving.

The Lyceum production of *Faust* was set in Nuremberg around 1550. The plot revolves around the devilish Mephistopheles who tempts the ambitious Faust with the prospect of renewed youth in exchange for his soul, making him sign the bargain in his own blood. Mephistopheles promises to allow Faust to triumph over the maidenly virtue of a young woman, Margaret, whom he covets. He gives Faust a potion to make her sleep while he makes love to her but her mother is killed by it, just as the Count would bring about the death of Lucy Westenra's mother in *Dracula* as he drained the blood of her daughter. At the end of the play, Margaret is condemned to death for killing her baby but refuses to flee with Faust. Her soul is saved while his is lost, borne away by a triumphant Mephistopheles. Irving's *Faust* contains other elements which recur in *Dracula*. At one point in the play, men in a tavern rush at Mephistopheles with knives to kill him but find, as Jonathan Harker would discover with Dracula, that they are powerless to harm him. Like Dracula's victims, Margaret has horrific dreams of Mephistopheles trying to claim her soul. In the play, lights appear floating above the grounds on Walpurgis Nacht like the flames under which the Count finds money, also on Walpurgis Nacht, in *Dracula*. A hound is transformed into a phantom or demon in Wills's text; the demonic Dracula takes the form of a great hound in Stoker's. A scene of wild devilry on the Brocken Mountain in Irving's production had an immense effect on those who saw it, with Irving the focus of attention as Mephistopheles as a bright-red figure of kingly splendour and familiarity with evil, his face calm and pale, with glittering eyes and shining white teeth.

The Lyceum production of *Faust* opened in December 1885. It ran for 792 performances and made over £250,000 – the Lyceum's greatest ever financial success. Stoker later told a parliamentary committee that the Lyceum *Faust* had stimulated big sales of Goethe's work. Stoker was intrigued by the technology employed in the Lyceum production: the fight between Faust and Valentine was the first time electric flashes were used in a play and he found the effects of light and flame startling. Not everybody was impressed: the Irish novelist, George Moore, whose own work would be staged at the Lyceum, was dismissive of the 'fricassee of Faust, garnished with hags, imps, and blue flame'.[19] Henry James and, later, George Bernard Shaw may also have been dismissive but Gladstone wrote to congratulate Irving. Rather bizarrely, when Stoker brought his seven-year-old son to see the play, Irving made him up as Mephistopheles.

Stoker is therefore more likely to have been influenced by Irving's performances in his great horror roles than by the man *per se* and his *Faust* may have been the most potent of these. Dracula's affinity with Faust, who sold his soul to the Devil in exchange for knowledge and power, as well as with Mephistopheles (the role played by Irving) is obvious. The Draculas – Stoker sees them as 'a great and noble race', of whom the Count in the novel is but the latest incarnation – had had dealings with the Evil One and learned their secrets in the Scholomance, with the Devil claiming every tenth scholar – including presumably the subject of the novel – as his due.

The Faust influence on Stoker may have been compounded by the attraction of Edward Dowden to Goethe; at one time he intended to make a full study of Goethe's life and works. He wrote of Faust's bargain with the Devil in his study of Shakespeare and believed that Romantic literature had turned towards the East, whence Dracula came. He wrote approvingly of Southey's *Thalaba* and of how, for Byron, the East was a source of boundless beauty and passion. Faust was a clear influence on Stoker's *Dracula* but the temptation to pinpoint a single major source of inspiration should be resisted.

Dowden's continuing influence on Stoker should not be underestimated, in the *Dracula* context especially. He kept in touch with Stoker after his move to London, sending him copies of his poems – as Stoker sent him copies of his own work – and visiting the Lyceum on his trips to London. Yet when he wrote to Stoker in 1879, shortly after Stoker's move to join Irving in London, he urged that Stoker was 'not to be cut off from Ireland' and added playfully: 'You will be pleased to hear that all your friends are engaged in writing dramas which through your influence are to be acted immediately at the Lyceum. I am myself at work on three tragedies, two melodramas, & a farce. It will I am sure be a pleasure to you to read these, you will see their merit, & I will need not say any more.'[20] He even sent a Miss Sara de Groot, an aspiring Dublin actress, to Stoker armed with a letter of introduction, before explaining that he really did not know her very well. Stoker's hand can be seen behind Dowden's continuing connection with Irving and the Lyceum. When Frank Marshall, who was collaborating with Irving in producing Shakespeare's work in eight volumes, died before the last volume was complete, the task was finished by Dowden before being seen through the press by Arthur Symons. When Irving and Ellen Terry made a triumphant visit to Dublin in 1894, the address given by the Lord Mayor, Valentine Dillon, was written by Dowden. In the same year, however, Dowden responded negatively to a proposal, conveyed through Stoker, that he undertake a lecture tour in the United States.

Dowden wrote poems on Salome, also the theme of a play by Wilde, and on Edgar Allan Poe and he was certainly well versed in the horrific in literature. Stoker was familiar with Poe in the years of his closest friendship with Dowden and in 1872 considered writing a play based on Poe's 'The Fall of the House of Usher'. Around the same time, he was pained when an attempt to recite 'The Raven' by an ill-educated local man produced only laughter from the audience at a poetry reading in Greystones, a seaside village outside Dublin. In his life of Shelley, Dowden wrote knowledgeably of Matthew Lewis and the Gothic tradition and of how 'some overpowering horror laid hold of Shelley's imagination'. Shelley had, in fact, written two youthful Gothic novels, *Zastrozzi* (1810) and *St Irvyne* (1811). Dowden also covered the fateful events of 1816, crucial to the birth of the modern horror tradition in literature, when conversations involving Mary and Percy Bysshe Shelley, Lord Byron and his physician and secretary, John Polidori (1795–1821), at the Villa Diodati in a suburb of Geneva in Switzerland, resulted in the writing of Mary Shelley's *Frankenstein* and Polidori's *The Vampyre*.[21]

The literary interests Dowden shared with Stoker are evident in his *Puritan and Anglican: Studies in Literature*, in which he devoted chapters to the seventeenth-century Puritan writers, Sir Thomas Browne and John Bunyan, both critical influences explicitly recognised by Stoker in his work. However, it is in Dowden's analysis of the difference between the Roman Catholic and Puritan views of the supernatural that we approach most closely the dualistic psychological geography of *Dracula*, with the Evangelical or Puritan belief placing the natural and the spiritual in irreconcilable contradiction, allowing each 'to exist only by the extinction of the other'. From this grew the Puritan belief 'that the order of the world is a divine order . . . that a great contention is in progress between the powers of darkness and light, that the victory will be the Lord's.' God and the soul were the chief actors in this drama, 'but for the Puritan imagination a world of magic lay around the human soul – blessed angels, demons of the pit, special inter-positions of Providence, miraculous words of Scripture, preternatural voices echoing in the heart . . .' There were grave dangers for the soul, including that 'it might pass into a diseased fascination', the fate suffered by Count Dracula and avoided so narrowly by his pursuers.[22]

Patrick Leigh Fermor's savagely ironic description of Dracula tourism in Romania – 'People who should know better exploit the confusion between the two figures [Vlad the Impaler and Dracula] and when "Dracula's Castle" is pointed out to a charabanc-load of tourists, I suspect that it is not the historical figure that appears before their mind's eye . . . but a natty Count in an opera-hat, a satin-lined cape and a queer look about his incisors; someone who might equally well be advertising after-shave lotion, teaching the tango or sawing a boxed lady in half at a matinee'[23] – captures well the absurdity involved but it also touches on the troubled question of the relationship between Stoker's fictional Count and the real-life 'Vlad the Impaler'. This relationship has been explored in a series of books by Radu Florescu and Raymond T. McNally, two Americans of Romanian and Irish background respectively. The historical figure most often identified with Dracula is Vlad Tepes (1431–76), who ruled Wallachia (not Transylvania) as Vlad III briefly in the fifteenth century (1448, 1456–62 and 1475–6) and who attempted, unsuccessfully, to halt the principality's slide under Turkish domination. Whether or not it reflected the bias of his German chroniclers, Vlad's reputation was synonymous with cruelty, espe-cially a penchant for putting his enemies to death by impalement. Among the atrocities attributed to him was forcing mothers to eat their own babies. Vlad's father was known as Vlad Dracul, his name deriving from an Order of the Dragon into which he was initiated in Nuremberg in February 1431. As the son of Dracul, Vlad was called Dracula. However, Vlad the Impaler was not regarded as an undead vampire following his death in 1476 and Florescu and McNally accept that the Dracula of Romanian literature does not correspond with Stoker's Count. They also acknowledge the paucity of sources for a true biography of Vlad.[24]

The note on Dracula which Stoker took from William Wilkinson's *An Account of the Principalities of Wallachia and Moldavia with Various Political Observations relating to them* was not strictly accurate but captured the essence of what the Wallachians meant by the term: 'Dracula in Wallachian language means DEVIL. Wallachians were accustomed to give it as a surname to any person who rendered himself conspicuous by courage, cruel actions or cunning.'[25] Wilkinson gave information on the defeat and decapitation of the Voivode (ruler) Dracula of Wallachia following the Battle of Varna in 1444 and the subsequent defeat of another Voivode, also called Dracula, some years later at the hand of the Turks who then appointed his brother, Bladus, to rule in his place. This is the figure to whom the Count refers when he gives a heroic account of Transylvanian history to Jonathan Harker: 'Who was it but one of my own race who as Voivode crossed the Danube and beat the Turk on his own ground? This was a Dracula indeed! Woe was it that his own unworthy brother, when he had fallen, sold his people to the Turk and brought the shame of slavery on them!' The real Vlad's brother, Radu, was indeed involved with the Turks and replaced him on the Wallachian throne. At another point in the story, Van Helsing says, 'He must, indeed, have been that Voivode Dracula who won his name against the Turk . . . he was spoken of as the bravest of the sons of the "land beyond the forest".' Stoker's Dracula is, however, a man of great ability and learning – 'in life, he was a most wonderful man. Soldier, statesman, and alchemist . . . He had a mighty brain, a learning beyond compare, and a heart that knew no fear and no remorse.'[26] So while some of the qualities which Stoker ascribes to the Count might be applicable to Vlad – a soldier and, perhaps, statesman – others clearly are not: there is no record that Vlad was a man of great learning. And there is no reference either in Wilkinson or in Stoker's notes to Vlad the Impaler or to his notorious cruelty. Dracula in the novel is not a sadistic mass murderer in the manner of Vlad; he leaves his relatively small number of victims undead, not squirming on top of poles. Stoker's Dracula is a composite figure, possibly borrowing some elements from Vlad, in the same way that in *The Lady of the Shroud* he borrows some elements from Danillo II, a ruler of Montenegro, but he cannot be simply equated with Vlad.[27]

The issue is further clouded by the uncertainty surrounding the influence exercised by Arminius Vambery on Stoker and whether he provided him with information on the historical Vlad. Vambery (1832–1913) was a Hungarian philologist, traveller, Orientalist, political theorist and writer who held the position of Professor of Oriental Languages at Budapest University from 1865 to 1905. Disguised as a dervish, he had travelled across central Asia, learning the languages and exploring an exotic area hitherto barred to Westerners. From the time of his first arrival in London in 1864, Vambery's knowledge on this region, especially of Russian activity there, ensured him a welcome in political and official circles. He was taken up by the Conservatives, who were more attuned to his warnings of Russian expansionism and the threat it posed to British India than Gladstone's Liberals. His network of relationships with Eastern rulers, including the Persian

shahs, his wide reading of indigenous newspapers and indefatigable correspondence with sources of information throughout the region gave him a
role as an adviser in the shaping of British government policy. His friendship with Edward, Prince of Wales (later King Edward VII) ensured his
acceptance in the highest social circles, his humble Jewish origins notwithstanding. He repaid the debt by acting as an apologist for Edward in Edward
Legge's 1912 volume, *King Edward in his True Colours*.

It has been claimed that it was through contact with Vambery that the
concept of Dracula fired Stoker's imagination. In *Dracula*, Van Helsing does
indeed quote 'my friend Arminius' as a source of, admittedly, rather imperfect knowledge on the historical Dracula, or, as it should have been, Draculas.[28]
Those who put forward this view admit that Vambery never refers to Vlad
the Impaler, Dracula or vampires in all his writings but still claim that, in the
course of conversation, Stoker became impressed by the professor's stories
about his homeland. Others believe that Stoker already had enough material
on Transylvania not to need Vambery's input.[29] However, as Vambery had
come to the Lyceum just months before Stoker's holiday in Whitby where
he researched and sketched out notes for *Dracula*, it is possible that his conversations with Vambery touched on Transylvania and developed his interest
sufficiently for him to have consulted books by such authorities as William
Wilkinson during his holiday. Vambery does refer in one work to Transylvania
as still asserting its independence and forming a bulwark against the Turks,[30]
which is very similar to Stoker's view of it. Stoker included a short chapter
on 'Arminius Vambery' in his *Personal Reminiscences of Henry Irving* and it is
clear that he was greatly impressed by the Hungarian 'Professor at the
University of Buda-Pest', whose visit to the Lyceum on 30 April 1890 was
to see, appropriately enough, *The Dead Heart* by Watt Phillips (1825–74). He
stayed to supper and Irving too was delighted by this man who was full of
fascinating experiences. Stoker presumably met Vambery the previous year
when he was present at the entertainment put on by Irving for Queen Victoria
at Sandringham in 1889 although Stoker does not mention him in his account
of it. When Stoker saw Vambery at the 1892 Trinity College Dublin ter-
centenary, the Hungarian seemed to him to shine like a star even in the most
exalted company. Stoker was not the only contemporary impressed with
Vambery. Isabel Burton devoted a long paragraph to him in her biography
of her husband, *The Life of Captain Sir Richard Burton* (1893), which Stoker
almost certainly read (she was on sufficiently good terms with Stoker to have
sent him a presentation copy of another of her books).[31]

While the story of Vlad the Impaler continued to shock and enthral for
hundreds of years after his death, there was, from the early eighteenth

century onwards, quite separately, a vampire scare in Central and Eastern Europe.[32] In France, in 1746, Dom Augustin Calmet, a Benedictine monk, published a treatise on ghosts and vampires. In *The Phantom World*, Calmet included chapters on 'Revenants, or Vampires of Moravia' and 'Dead Men of Hungary who suck the Blood of the Living', in which he recorded tales recounted by Comte de Cabreras, at Freiburg im Breisgau, in 1730. These included a Moravian woman who, having died and been buried, appeared after four days in the shape of a dog and reduced people to 'extreme weakness'. Then there was a shepherd in a village in Bohemia whose ghost walked abroad; when staked by the locals, he uttered loud cries and a great quantity of bright vermilion blood flowed from him. A man on the Hungarian frontier who had been dead for ten years appeared and caused the death of another man. When his body was exhumed it was found to be in the same state as that of a man who had just expired. His head was cut off. Another tale told of opening the grave of a man who had been excommunicated and whose body was found to be uncorrupted, his veins swollen with blood. When the rite of absolution was performed, a great noise came from the coffin and the body decayed as if it had been dead for several years.

This fascination with vampirism evident in popular tales extended to European intellectual circles in the eighteenth and nineteenth centuries. Elements of vampirism are to be found in the works of writers such as Goethe, Coleridge, Scott, Byron, Southey and, of course, John Polidori. To some writers, vampirism was synonymous with social and economic exploitation. In *The Citizen of the World* (1760–1) Oliver Goldsmith had named a social parasite 'Major Vampyre', and depicted a corrupt magistrate as sucking 'blood like a vampyre'. In *Questions sur l'Encyclopédie* (1772) Voltaire equated businessmen, among others, with vampires. Karl Marx later embodied a similar concept in *Das Kapital*, claiming that capital was dead labour which, vampire-like, subsisted by sucking living labour.

While Stoker was acquainted with the horrific elements in the works of the Romantic poets, he would also have been well aware of the vampiric literary tradition which had its roots in the Villa Diodati in 1816, when the interaction of the Shelleys, Byron and John Polidori led to the creation of Mary Shelley's *Frankenstein* – which contains a reference to the monster as vampire[33] – and an 1816 fragmentary tale by Byron which in turn inspired Polidori's *The Vampyre*. A scene in Byron's 'fragment of a novel' is set in a cemetery once Christian, now Turkish, anticipating the Christian/Turkish conflict which forms part of the backdrop to *Dracula*. Polidori's tale, published in the *New Monthly Magazine* in April 1819 (and wrongly attributed to Byron), concerns the vampiric Lord Ruthven who becomes involved with a young man, Aubrey, and his sister. This slight piece ends with Aubrey dead and his sister having fallen prey to Ruthven. Polidori's work enjoyed a vogue at the time, helped enormously by the assumption that Byron was the author. It made quite an impression in France where, in 1820, Cyprien Bernard published anonymously a follow-up, *Lord Ruthven ou les Vampires*. Just like the original, this too was attributed to another author, in this case to the playwright, Jean Charles Nodier, who had in fact written a preface for the French edition of Polidori's work. Nodier did dramatise the Lord Ruthven story under the title, *Le Vampire*, and the play was successfully staged in Paris in 1820. This inspired no fewer than four further plays on the Lord Ruthven theme, which were produced in Paris soon after. Lord Ruthven was exported back to England when James R. Planche's *The Vampire, or, the Bride of the Isles* was staged in London in the same year. Later in the decade, the vampire made his appearance in Germany in Heinrich August Marschner's opera, *Der Vampyr* (1828), which influenced Wagner, especially his *Flying Dutchman*. Alexandre Dumas's dramatisation of the story was produced in Paris in the middle of the century. Dion Boucicault's play, *The Vampire*, opened in London in June 1852 and featured Alan Ruby, a Restoration vampire who meets his doom at the hands of Dr Rees, a student of the supernatural who employs a charmed bullet. Boucicault would later be closely connected with both Stoker and Henry Irving.

A few years previously, Emily Brontë's *Wuthering Heights* (1847) had included a speculation by one of its characters that the evil, irredeemable, Heathcliff might be a vampire. Also published in 1847 was the 'penny-dreadful', *Varney the Vampire or, The Feast of Blood*, by James Malcolm Rymer or Thomas Pecket Prest, containing over 800 pages of text. Like *Dracula*, it features a central European vampire aristocrat, Baron Stolmuyer of Saltsburgh, who becomes master of a grand English house. With glittering eyes that fascinate his victims and fang-like teeth, he has a taste for the blood of young virgins. The state of Flora Bannerworth, one of his victims, who has the appearance of someone who has suffered long illness rather than a young girl in the prime of life, has obvious parallels with Lucy's symptoms in *Dracula*, as does the staking of Clara Crofton, another victim. Admiral Bell, an elderly man full of courage and good sense, could be seen as a prototype for Van Helsing. Just three years after the appearance of *Varney*, an English translation of Augustin Calmet's *The Phantom World* was published in London. The alternating currents of sexual charge and death so evident in Stoker's *Dracula* were previously and pungently expressed in Charles Baudelaire's 'Les metamorphoses du vampire', included in *Les Fleurs du Mal* (1857).

While Calmet was promoting belief in vampirism as a real phenomenon, it was already being satirised. In his story, 'The Canterville Ghost', first published in 1887, Oscar Wilde had poked gentle fun at the genre, with the ghost turning himself into a great black dog and resting in a coffin, as well as impersonating 'Gaunt Gibeon, the Blood-sucker of Bexley Moor' and 'The Vampire Monk, or, the Bloodless Benedictine'. Count Eric Stenbock's short story, 'A True Story of a Vampire', published in 1894, opens in highly ironic fashion, sending up the Western tradition of locating vampires in Eastern Europe and was probably aimed particularly at Sheridan Le Fanu's *Carmilla*, underlining the point by naming the narrator 'Carmela':

> Vampire stories are generally located in Styria; mine is also. Styria is by no means the romantic kind of place described by those who have certainly never been there. It is a flat, uninteresting country, only celebrated for its turkeys, capons, and the stupidity of its inhabitants. Vampires generally arrive at night, in carriages drawn by two black horses. Our Vampire arrived by the commonplace means of the railway train, and in the afternoon.[34]

A note of similar, if more hesitant, irony was struck by the Frenchman, Jules Verne, in his *Carpathian Castle*, also published a few years before *Dracula*: 'nobody would invent legends at the close of this practical and positive nineteenth century; not even in Transylvania, where the Carpathian scenery lends itself so naturally to all sorts of supernatural imaginings. But it is well to note that Transylvania is still much attached to the superstitions of the early ages.' The owners of this castle, the barons of Gortz, had, like Dracula, been the lords of the country and fought in the Transylvanian wars, pouring out their blood for the cause of independence. Verne's general tone, however, is dismissive of the 'evidence' produced by the priest and scholmaster in support of local superstitions, 'that werewolves prowled about the country; that vampires . . . quenched their thirst on human blood . . . If ever a building were a fitting refuge for the creatures of this Roumanian mythology, was it not Carpathian Castle? On that isolated plateau, inaccessible except from the left of Vulkan Hill, no doubt there lived dragons and fairies and vampires, and perhaps also a few ghosts of the Gortz family.'[35] Not all contemporaries were as sceptical: a vampire picture by Philip Burne-Jones, the son of Sir Edward and known to Stoker, was shown in a London gallery in 1897 and inspired a poem on the subject by Kipling, a cousin to Burne-Jones, in 1906. According to Ellen Terry, Burne-Jones was one of the Lyceum's greatest admirers.

In the eighteenth century, Jean-Jacques Rousseau saw vampires as miraculous phenomena which required obscurantist dogmas to explain them because common sense was insufficient. In the twentieth century, the vampire phenomenon has attracted the attention of various schools of thought, including Freudians and Marxists. The psychoanalyst, Ernest Jones, one of Sigmund Freud's closest associates, included a chapter on the subject in his classic, *On the Nightmare* (1931), in which he argues that the fear of the dead has its source in childhood and the vampire superstition is the product of conflict with one's parents. He also noted the Irish concept of a vampire as *Dearg-dul*, which he translated as red bloodsucker. The historian and folklorist, Patrick Weston Joyce, had made the connection between Abhartach, an undead, blood-consuming, Irish chieftain of the early Christian era and vampirism in a book published in Dublin in 1880. This theory has recently been revived, with the suggestion that Stoker might have been aware of these Irish legends of the vampire-king and the blood-drinking dead. He might also have been aware of the Irish folk tales concerning the Tuatha De Danán, a divine race which would not die, from Standish O'Grady, who wrote of them in his Bardic *History of Ireland*. In our own era, Franco Moretti argues that Marxism and psychoanalysis converge in defining the function of vampire literature as presenting fears in different forms from their real ones, thus allowing readers to avoid facing up to what might really frighten them. The literature of terror is born of the terror of a split society, and literature, having produced the terror, must also erase it and restore peace. The monster seeks to displace the antagonisms and horrors, evidenced within society, outside it. This literature is full of protagonists brushing aside the awareness that the perturbing element is within them: that they themselves produce the monsters they fear. The repressed returns disguised as a monster.[36]

The origins in English of the Gothic novel – so called because of its attempt to create a fusion of medievalism and terror – are generally traced back to Horace Walpole's successful, if mediocre, *Castle of Otranto* (1764). William Beckford's *Vathek* (1786) brought an Oriental flavour to the genre. The 1790s were its heyday, with works such as Ann Radcliffe's *Mysteries of Udolpho* (1794) and *The Italian* (1797) and Matthew Lewis's *The Monk* (1796) enjoying great popularity. The anti-Roman-Catholic, anti-Spanish sentiments so evident in Lewis's work are also to be found in John Dryden's play, *The Spanish Fryar, or, The Double Discovery* (1680), a copy of which was in Stoker's library. While these do not feature in *Dracula*, they are to be found in Stoker's later work, *The Mystery of the Sea* especially. Other elements derived from the mainstream Gothic tradition are evident in *Dracula*: the Count's great and gloomy castle is a linear descendant of those found in the eighteenth-century classics of the genre and the grand trans-European chase which culminates in the Count's death has obvious parallels with those in Radcliffe's work.

In the 1790s, French revolutionary subversion replaced these older phobias as the main threat to the established social order in England. T. J. Mathias's *The Pursuits of Literature* (1794) linked the French Revolution with Gothic horror. Mathias had been influenced by Edmund Burke's *Reflections on the Revolution in France* (1790), which has been seen as interpreting the revolutionary event in Gothic terms. From this perspective, Burke could be seen as a joint fountainhead of the British and Irish Gothic traditions. His philosophical treatise, *A Philosophical Enquiry into the Origin of Our Ideas of the Sublime and Beautiful* (1757), explored the concepts of pleasure and pain in a way which united philosophy with psychology and, by positing that pain and danger were the most powerful of all the passions, created a philosophical basis for the effectiveness of horror literature. *Melmoth the Wanderer* (1820), the work of another Irishman, Charles Robert Maturin, had an enduring influence throughout Europe and is regarded by some as the greatest work of the Gothic genre.

Professor Roy Foster sees a line of supernatural fiction encompassing Maturin, Le Fanu, Stoker, W.B. Yeats and Elizabeth Bowen, the creation of marginalised Irish Protestants, generally of clerical and professional background, often living in England but looking back to Ireland. Their preoccupation with the occult reflects a sense of displacement, a loss of social and psychological integration and an escapism motivated by the threat of a take-over by the Catholic middle classes. This engagement with the occult is linked with an interest in folklore, seen as embodying secret truth. For the English critic, David Glover, it is *Dracula* that goes furthest in establishing Stoker's pedigree as a distinctively Irish writer. It belongs within an insular Gothic tradition, in which commonplace Gothic tropes could acquire disturbing new resonances in the hands of a remarkable line of Irish Protestant writers, from Maturin to Stoker: 'compounders of fantasies and tales of the grotesque, set everywhere save in Ireland'. Terry Eagleton too links *Dracula* with other works by Irish writers, Jonathan Swift's *Gulliver's Travels*, Maria Edgeworth's *Castle Rackrent*, Maturin's *Melmoth*, Le Fanu's *Uncle Silas*, and Joyce's *Ulysses* in a 'literary tradition . . . [of] largely unrealistic works', with Stoker and Maturin transcending realism altogether. This Irish Protestant Gothic might be dubbed the political unconscious of Anglo-Irish society, the place where its fears and fantasies most definitively emerge. While agreeing that Irish Gothic writing is an essentially Protestant tradition, W. J. Mc Cormack, a noted critic of the genre, sees it as a distinctive version of a wider Victorian crisis in Christian belief.[37] While not linking it to any particular Irish tradition, James Joyce, in *A Portrait of the Artist as a Young Man*, has Stephen Dedalus give a definition of terror: 'Terror is the feeling which arrests the mind in the presence of whatsoever is grave and constant in human suffering and unites it with the secret cause.'[38]

A nineteenth-century Irish writer who may have influenced Stoker directly was the Reverend George Croly, a friend of his father's. In Croly's *Salathiel the Immortal* (1829), there are similarities of predicament between Salathiel and Dracula (and Melmoth the Wanderer). Salathiel had led the mob which had urged the death of Jesus, in return for which he was 'condemned to know the miseries of life interminable'. He was in essence the Wandering Jew (as was Maturin's Melmoth), appearing from time to time in Europe, 'a mysterious individual – a sojourner in all lands, yet a citizen of none; professing the profoundest secrets of opulence, yet generally living in a state of poverty, astonishing every one by the evidence of his intercourse with the eminent characters of the age, yet connected with none'.[39] The family connection with Croly – a fiery proponent of the status quo of Protestantism in the then United Kingdom of Great Britain and Ireland in both the religious and political spheres – may be of significance, given the other elements of the Protestantism with which Stoker was imbued as a child and which surface in *Dracula*. Like Faust, Dracula seems to have involved himself with the Devil but, more than that, in some respects he resembles either the Antichrist (identified with the Papacy by leaders of the Reformation, Martin Luther especially) or the Devil himself. One of the obvious clues to Stoker's own view of Dracula's character and origin is the manner in which he begins to capitalise the personal pronouns referring to the Count as the book progresses. Since such capitalisation is generally reserved for God, its use for Dracula is surely intended to represent him as emblematic of the Manichaean Devil, on a par with God. In pre-modern times there was widespread belief in the ability of the Devil to assume the form of any animal and, at the Witches' Sabbath, to have carnal intercourse with the witches. The Antichrist, the chief enemy of Christ, was, like Dracula, seen as a worker of wonders and a seducer.

Some of the ideas underlying *Dracula* were embedded in societies professing Christianity although they actually derived from non-Christian sources. The medieval European superstition of demons and humans becoming lovers was a survival of the ancient belief in the cohabitation of the gods with mortal women. Medieval superstition encompassed belief in demons whose special mission it was to seek carnal relations with mortals. The incubus was a male demon which haunted women in their sleep, *à la* Lucy and Mina, while the succubus was a demon in woman's guise which visited men in their dreams, *à la* Jonathan Harker and the three female vampires. A similar mixture of pagan and Christian beliefs existed in the

Irish countryside, and these were explored by Sir William and Lady Wilde. In 1887, Lady Wilde published *Ancient Legends, Mystic Charms, and Superstitions of Ireland, with Sketches of the Irish Past* and followed it in 1890 with *Ancient Cures, Charms, and Usages of Ireland, Contributions to Irish Lore*. Much of the research for these works had been done by Sir William Wilde prior to his death in 1876. He had been making notes on these subjects all his life, of which his *Irish Popular Superstitions* was the result. To W.B. Yeats, Lady Wilde's tales represented the innermost heart of the Celt, pondering on the soul and on the dead. The world explored by the Wildes had many resonances for the writers of the time: Lafcadio Hearn's phrase, 'the divinely beautiful' had, for example, occurred previously in Lady Wilde's work.[40] It was probably the Wildes who first imbued Stoker with an interest in folklore and Van Helsing's spirited defence of superstition in *Dracula* – 'And to superstition must we trust at the first. It was man's faith in the early, and it has its root in faith still' – may well have reflected values absorbed by the author from them.

There is much in Lady Wilde's work which anticipates the world of *Dracula*: she wrote of giant dogs devouring souls; Dracula would later take the form of a great and murderous dog. The story of 'The Horned Women', recounted by Lady Wilde, bears more than a passing resemblance to Stoker's masterpiece: it concerns witches who take over a woman's house then draw blood from her sleeping family and mix it into a cake that they bake. The woman restores her family by putting some of the cake into their mouths as they sleep. Blood is a recurrent theme in Lady Wilde's books: her spirits love blood: its colour excites them, giving them the power and semblance of life. Drinking blood could ward off the evil abroad in early May, when the dead roam the land. According to Lady Wilde, because the spirits loved it, blood must be spilled. If blood gives her spirits power, the rituals of Roman Catholicism are the reverse. Like Stoker, Lady Wilde was an Irish Protestant recounting popular belief in the power of Roman Catholic objects, such as the scapular, which were anathema to her religion. The concept of a circle of holy water to keep the undead at bay, found in her work, is similar to the 'Holy circle' of sacred wafers used by Van Helsing to keep Mina safe in *Dracula*. Jonathan Harker's struggle between a belief in the practical efficacy of these elements of Roman Catholicism and his Protestant values is echoed in Lady Wilde's attitude to 'Popery'.

Lady Wilde's 'A Wolf Story', about the transformation of people into wolves, has clear parallels with the opening chapters of *Dracula*: a man goes to a lonely house and the door is opened by a tall, thin, grey-haired old man with keen, dark eyes. His welcome is later echoed by that of Dracula to Jonathan Harker: 'Come in, you are welcome.' His wife has long sharp teeth and terrible glittering eyes. The children, who enter as wolves, are transformed into dark, slender, handsome youths, also with glittering eyes. The evil eye, a major preoccupation of the Transylvanians in *Dracula*, features a good deal in Lady Wilde's work, as does the evil influence of fairies, whose glance does not kill 'but throws the object into a death-like trance' and whose music is enchanting. Fairies were, in fact, fallen angels and they were greatly tempted by the beauty of mortal women, desiring them as wives, a concept central to *Dracula*. 'The Witch Lady', in Lady Wilde's story, was reputed to have sold her soul to the Devil in return for earthly power; like Dracula she could go out only at night and could change into human shape. This story also features enchantment in sleep and has as a theme the possession of a man's wife by a powerful superhuman figure and the struggle to reclaim her from the powers of darkness. 'November Eve' and 'The Dance of the Dead' both concern that special night when the spirits of the dead are abroad and have power over all things, similar to Walpurgis Night in Stoker's work, 'Dracula's Guest' especially.[41]

Lady Wilde drew parallels between ancient ritual and belief in Ireland and that of the Slavic nations. Her husband had been aware of Transylvania many years before, mentioning it a number of times in his 1843 book *Austria, its Literary, Scientific, and Medical Institutions*. He may have piqued Stoker's interest during the years of their friendship in the 1870s, especially in relation to Transylvania's status as a military frontier between the Christian and Muslim worlds and the existence of '*Wallachian* people, half-Christian, half-Mohommedan [*sic*], resident in Transylvania and on the Turkish borders'.[42] Lady Wilde went further, drawing attention to parallels between Transylvanian and Irish legends. Referring to Emily Gerard, whose book on Transylvania, *The Land Beyond the Forest*, had been published not long previously, she declared that many of the Transylvanian legends 'will be found identical with the Irish'. Here, surely, lies the origin of one, at least, of the strands of *Dracula*: Stoker's substitution of Transylvanian popular legends for the Irish ones he had used in *The Snake's Pass*. As a close friend, Stoker would have read Lady Wilde's work and may well have listened to her holding forth at her literary salons on the subject of Irish and Transylvanian horrific superstition. The timing matches perfectly: *Dracula*'s intellectual roots can be located in the late 1880s, when Lady Wilde published the first of her volumes of legends and superstitions. The fact that a phrase used by Count Dracula about the 'Children of the Night' is to be found in Lady Wilde's book may be proof of her direct influence on Stoker (it is used by Saint Augustine in his *Confessions* but Stoker is unlikely to have found it there). Indeed the very concept of the Prince of Darkness is to be found in Lady Wilde's work.[43]

Lady Wilde also intertwined politics and horror in her poems. 'A Servian Song', published in *Poems* (1864), underlined her long-standing interest in the Balkans. Another poem from the same volume, 'The Brothers', the story of the Sheares brothers executed for revolutionary activities in the Ireland of 1798, ends with a vision of the martyrs undead, their severed heads lying in coffins and kept from decay by angels. Stoker is likely to have read all of Lady Wilde's work, including her translation from the German of Johann Wilhelm Meinhold's novel, *Sidonia the Sorceress* (1849), concerning the trial and execution for witchcraft of the Lady Cantoness of Pomerania, Sidonia von Bork, in 1620. Sidonia was a favourite subject of the Pre-Raphaelites, Rossetti and William Morris especially, and was painted by Sir Edward Burne-Jones in 1860. Lady Wilde's translation gives an account of how Sidonia yielded to the temptations of Satan and learned the secrets of witchcraft, as Dracula does in Stoker's novel. There are other anticipations of *Dracula* in the story; for example Sidonia is in a carriage pursued by wolves that tear a foal to pieces, much as the wolves do to the distraught mother in the vampire tale; wolves also follow Jonathan Harker's carriage on its way to Dracula's castle. There is a more exact anticipation of *Dracula* when we are told that the Duke of Pomerania would drink blood in place of wine after he had decided on Sidonia's sentence of death. Lady Wilde also tells the story of how, in 1731, when the coffin of Duke Bogislaff, the last Duke of Pomerania, was broken open, his body was found to be perfectly preserved. Lady Wilde had visited the vault on 6 May 1840, the anniversary of his burial in 1637.

Lady Wilde may also have exercised an influence on Stoker through Dr John Todhunter, whose play, *The Black Cat*, first acted by the Independent Theatre in London in 1895, was based on a story she had written for a collection of Irish folk tales edited by Alfred Perceval Graves. The product of a respected Dublin Quaker family, Todhunter was an outstanding member of the group of writers and admirers of Whitman who surrounded Stoker in his Trinity years. He was regarded by Alfred Perceval Graves as one of the finest contemporary Irish poets and as a leader of the Irish literary renaissance in Dublin. Standish O'Grady contributed a foreword to Todhunter's posthumously published *Essays* in which he recalled the impact the older man had made on Stoker's generation of undergraduates as a representative of culture and intellectual refinement. Todhunter's literary output ran to over two dozen books, including a translation of Goethe's *Faust*, and a biography of Shelley. A shared fascination with the macabre is suggested by Stoker's *The Banshee and Other Poems* (1888). Dedicated to Standish O'Grady, its contents included 'The Coffin-Ship', a highly charged patriotic poem featuring a mother who sees the ghosts of her children, drowned when a coffin-ship (used to transport poor Irish emigrants to

America) sank, walking along the shore in a manner reminiscent of the parade of the dead in Stoker's *The Mystery of the Sea*. Todhunter settled in London and was part of Stoker's circle there, frequenting the Lyceum and joining with him in the foundation of the Irish Literary Society in the early 1890s. He presented a copy of his *The True Tragedy of Rienzi, Tribune of Rome* (1881) to Stoker with his kind regards.

Irish superstition also interested Alfred Perceval Graves, who was intrigued by the theory that fairies are outcasts who 'occupy intermediate space' between heaven and hell, as Dracula seems to do. Graves described Irish churchyard demons, which include a beautiful phantom that waylays a widower at his wife's tomb and poisons him by her kiss 'when he has yielded to her blandishments', rather in the manner in which Dracula seduces Lucy in Whitby churchyard and the female vampires had hoped to vampirise Jonathan Harker.[44] Graves's *Irish Songs and Ballads* (1880), on which he collaborated with the composer, Sir Charles Villiers Stanford, featured a poem, 'The Song of the Ghost', about a girl who is visited by the ghost of her dead love, and calls on the cocks not to proclaim the dawn and send him back to the dead; in the morning she herself is found dead.

Speculation about Stoker's political intentions in relation to *Dracula* continues to the present day. Debate rages as to whether Dracula is emblematic of the Anglo-Irish absentee landlord or whether he represents the opposite, the atavistic violence commonly attributed to the landlords' opponents in the Land League. It has even been suggested that Dracula may represent the Irish nationalist leader, Charles Stewart Parnell, or that the origins of the book may lie in a Land League demonstration at Mitchelstown in the south of Ireland in the late 1880s. *Punch*'s Irish political cartoons of that era feature monsters, some of which shared characteristics with the vampiric Count. For example, in February 1881 *Punch* featured a drawing of Gladstone strangling the three-headed monster of Irish terrorism, anarchy and sedition; the middle head, of terrorism, has long canines, just like Dracula. An 1885 *Punch* cartoon by Sir John Tenniel features a sleeping figure of Erin (Ireland), in a swoon, menaced by the giant vampire bat of the Irish Land League bearing the face of Parnell. An unknown artist responded the following week in the *Irish Pilot* with an heroic, warrior-queen figure of Ireland squaring up to the giant 'English Vampire' bat.[45] Given Stoker's Home Rule sympathies and his readership of *Punch*, these cartoons provide an obvious inspiration for aspects at least of Dracula.

Lucy Westenra's surname was the family name of Lord 'Derry' Rossmore (b. 1853), a prominent and controversial figure in Irish Unionist politics in Stoker's era. He was the leader in 'The Rosslea Incident' of 1882 when, as co-Grand Master of the Orangemen of Monaghan, he organised a counter-demonstration to one held by nationalists at Rosslea, a village on the border of Fermanagh and Monaghan. Rossmore wrote to all the principal English newspapers to give the Unionist perspective on events. Dismissed from his position of magistrate by the government, he was celebrated as a Unionist martyr. Fêted by Unionists as the man of the hour, he was given a banquet in the Rotunda in Dublin and an enormous meeting was held in his honour in the Ulster Hall in Belfast. He was on good terms with Edward, Prince of Wales and discussed Irish affairs with him. He must have impinged on Stoker's consciousness and the appropriation of the name for the vampirised Lucy could be seen as a hearty political joke on Stoker's part. Charles Lever's novel, *Charles O'Malley, the Irish Dragoon* (1841), with which Stoker was almost certainly familiar, features a ballad, 'The Irish Dragoon', concerning a banshee claiming the life of Lord Rossmore:

> The day was declining,
>   The dark night drew near,
> And the old Lord grew sadder,
>   And paler with fear.
> Come listen, my daughter,
>   Come nearer – oh! near,
> It's the wind or the water
>   That sighs in my ear.
>
> Not the wind nor the water
>   Now stirr'd the night air,
> But a warning far sadder –
>   The banshee was there.
> Now rising, now swelling,
>   On the night wind it bore
> One cadence, still telling,
>   I want thee, Rossmore!
>
> And then fast came his breath,
>   And more fix'd grew his eye;
> And the shadow of death
>   Told his hour was nigh.
> Ere the dawn of that morning
>   The struggle was o'er,
> For when thrice came the warning –
>   A corpse was Rossmore![46]

Stoker may have seen the memorial to Lady Rossmore by Thomas Kirk (1843) in St Patrick's Church in Monaghan in which Lord Rossmore, restrained by his son, takes a last look at his deceased wife; this has been seen as reminiscent of the deathbed scene of Lucy Westenra in *Dracula*. Stoker would amost certainly have been aware of the social sensation surrounding George Moore's quarrel with Rossmore in the early 1880s when politically motivated insults and blows were traded at a Mayfair dinner party in London.

In a wider context, *Dracula* is viewed as a late nineteenth-century narrative of reverse colonisation in which the 'civilised' world is threatened with being overrun by 'primitive' forces. This links to perceived problems in Britain itself, with disruptive figures, mirroring imperial practices in monstrous form, coming from the periphery of empire to threaten its troubled metropolis. Following the sensation caused by Sir George Chesney's 1871 novel, *The Battle of Dorking*, the invasion novel was established in English-language fiction, in which an interest in the primitive is linked with the occult and paranormal and, by extension, the Gothic. This form of 'imperial Gothic' produced divided narratives, symptomatic of the anxieties seen by some as having been gnawing away at the superficial confidence that attended the climax of the British Empire. Like Robert Louis Stevenson in *The Strange Case of Dr. Jekyll and Mr. Hyde* (1886) and Oscar Wilde in *Dorian Gray* (1890), Stoker achieved a dramatic effect by bringing the terror of the primitive, or the peripheral, 'other' home to the heart of empire. While we can probably take for granted that Stoker read everything by Wilde, his familiarity with *Dr. Jekyll and Mr. Hyde* is known from a reference to it in his essay on 'Dramatic Criticism' of 1894. This is not surprising, as a play based on the story was put on at the Lyceum by the actor, Richard Mansfield in 1888. Although Irving was unimpressed by the contemporary realism of Stevenson's horror, preferring a histrionic variety less likely to upset his audience, Stoker was on good terms with Stevenson, who sent him a copy of his *Father Damien* (1890). Stoker had in his library a copy of Stevenson's short story, 'The Body Snatcher', as published in the *Pall Mall Gazette* in 1884, a supernaturally tinged tale of digging up the dead, murder and the reappearance of a dissected corpse. The *Pall Mall Gazette* posters advertising it were so ghoulish that they were suppressed by the police. In *Dracula*, Dr Seward speculates that a body snatcher may have taken Lucy Westenra's corpse when her tomb is found empty.

Nineteenth-century Anglophone writers often described Transylvania as 'Oriental' and Count Dracula comes from a landscape which Jonathan Harker finds is outside the pale of Western civilisation. On the very first page of the novel, he feels that he is leaving the West as he goes east of

Budapest, to a country as yet unmapped which will become more sinister and threatening as time goes on. Stoker had been concerned with the notion of British and American decline since his auditorial address to the Historical Society in Trinity College Dublin, in 1872, allied to a belief that the supposedly less developed Irish could reinvigorate these cultures. *Dracula* presents a nightmare vision of a reverse reinvigoration, with an energetic, undead Count from the periphery spreading contagion in Piccadilly, the heart of the metropolis, and growing younger in the process. Count Dracula also undermines England's sense of its own centrality. As an 'Occidentalist' scholar studying British culture with a view to subverting it, he also reverses the role of Western Orientalists in the expansion of empire. His Western adversaries cannot compete with him in purely personal terms and he is ultimately defeated only when the band of pursuers use their collective abilities to harness superior Western technology, financed by Lord Godalming's wealth and powered by Mina's bureaucratic expertise, in welding disparate fragments of information into a coherent and, to Dracula, deadly narrative.

A strong sexual element had permeated the Faust story since its origins in sixteenth-century Germany. Sodomy was an element in the tissue of legend surrounding one of the historical characters who inspired the legend, following his death around 1540. At the conclusion of Goethe's drama, Faust's soul is able to escape as Mephistopheles makes sexual advances to the angels which have come to redeem it. The powerful sexual charge which runs through *Dracula* has caught the attention of modern commentators, who see in it deviant and taboo forms of sexuality, including rape, incest, adultery, oral sex, group sex, sex during menstruation, bestiality, paedophilia, venereal disease and voyeurism, among other things. These readings are often based on the assumption that Stoker himself was unaware of the sexual element in his work, unconsciously revealing both inner tensions and anxieties and external concerns about contemporary issues such as female empowerment and liberation. Certainly, there were overtly sexual aspects of *Dracula* which Stoker's late Victorian audience seems to have handled with greater maturity than some modern commentators. The most celebrated sexual scene in the novel, the staking of the vampiric but virginal Lucy, does not require too much imagination to be transposed to sadistic orgasm, especially as the staking is performed by the man who was to be her husband and on what was to have been their wedding night. Van Helsing's instruction that her putative husband should kiss her dead lips adds more than a hint of the necrophiliac. Yet if Lucy represents a newly liberated female sexuality, which is violently suppressed at source, she is counterbalanced by Mina's wifely rectitude. Due to the bungling of the men who were supposed to protect her, Mina, the novel's strongest and most effective character, apart from Dracula himself, comes partly under the Count's spell but does not lose her determination to protect her virtue. After she has been made by Dracula to drink blood from a slit in his chest – suggesting to some a bleeding vagina and menstrual taboo – she declares herself unclean and determines to touch her husband, Jonathan, no more. The theme of non-consummation of conjugal relations, so common in Stoker's fiction, is thus woven into *Dracula*.

The scene where the three female vampires approach Jonathan Harker in Castle Dracula is certainly suffused with sexual energy: 'There was something about them that made me uneasy, some longing and at the same time some deadly fear. I felt in my heart a wicked, burning desire that they would kiss me with those red lips.' Parallels between these women and the prostitutes whom Stoker would have seen nightly on the streets of London are obvious: their approach to Harker is overtly sexual and yet they are not interested in real sexual relations, only in extracting blood, as prostitutes are in extracting money, from their victim. Dracula's thunderous intervention with the female vampires, claiming Harker as his own, has been seen as homosexual in intent. Homoerotic undertones might be detected in Van Helsing's recognition of 'the strong young manhood' in Jonathan Harker and in his invitation to him to come to the drawing room so that they can lie there on adjacent sofas to comfort each other. He proposes that they should become as one and tells Harker that he has 'grown to love you – yes, my dear boy, to love you . . .' Yet, in real life, Stoker recoiled with horror when, at the Lyceum, it seemed as if the visiting French painter, Jules Bastien-Lepage, having clasped both his hands and shaken them hard, was going to kiss him.

The attribution to Stoker of the insecurities and neuroses of his characters is surely specious: as the tough acting manager of the premier London theatre of the era, he had to deal with the problems – including no doubt sexual ones – thrown up by the scores of actors and actresses who came under his care. He could not have been unaware of the sexual irregularity in the lives of his closest friends and colleagues, such as Hall Caine, Henry Irving and Ellen Terry. Far from suffering from obvious insecurity in dealing with women, he was capable of deep friendship with some of the strongest and most distinguished women of the era, like Terry and Geneviève Ward. He had had the confidence to woo and win one of the most beautiful women of the time from Oscar Wilde. We have to assume therefore that Stoker was aware of the sexual elements he was weaving into the tapestry of his masterwork and that they did not necessarily represent his own desires and impulses.

* * *

Once *Dracula* was published in 1897, Stoker set about tapping into his extensive network of contacts in the publishing world to promote reviews; these
included the newspaper magnate, Alfred Harmsworth (later Lord
Northcliffe), James Knowles, Lord Glenerk, proprietor of the *Morning Post*,
F.H. Field, editor of the *Literary World*, and Sir Wemyss Thomas Reid,
editor of the *Speaker*. Robert Leighton, the journalist and author who was
to review the novel in the *Daily Mail*, asked Stoker to provide a few paragraphs about himself for use in the 'Bookchat' column. Edgar Pemberton,
who had previously reviewed *The Snake's Pass* and would later review *The
Mystery of the Sea*, promised to do all he could for *Dracula* at the
Birmingham *Daily Post*.[47] Sir Henry Lucy, the Conservative Member of
Parliament and *Punch* author, wrote to Stoker in July 1897 attaching his
'London Letter', published in the *Keighley News* of 10 July 1897:

> Mr Bram Stoker is well and favourably known in two hemispheres as
> Sir Henry Irving's business manager. He aspires beyond the success
> achieved on that line, and enters the lists held by the modern novelist.
> For a man of suave manner and blameless life, a kind husband, a good
> father, and an obliging friend, he has written the most blood-curdling
> novel of the paralysed century. With subtle, if unsigned, appropriate-
> ness, 'Dracula' is published by Constable. I have to confess that as I
> breathlessly turned over its pages (which ought to have been printed
> in blood) I was wondering all the time where were the police. The
> hero is, not to put too fine a point on it, a vampire . . . The nature of
> Count Dracula's adventures may not even be hinted at in this domestic
> column. Suffice it to say the story is written with a grim power, a swift
> succession of graphic touches, that make it terrible. If anyone wants
> his flesh to creep Bram Stoker is the boy to accomplish the desire.[48]

From the critics in mainstream newspapers, *Dracula* received a generally
favourable, if somewhat mixed reception. *Punch* described it as the very
weirdest of weird tales and the *Pall Mall Gazette* found it 'excellent'. The
Daily Mail ranked Stoker's powers above those of Mary Shelley and Edgar
Allan Poe, as well as Emily Brontë's *Wuthering Heights*. The *Spectator* too
related Stoker to his predecessors in the Gothic tradition, feeling that he
had set out 'to eclipse all previous efforts in the domain of the horrible',
including those of Wilkie Collins and Sheridan Le Fanu but was critical of
Dracula's 'mawkish' sentimentality. The *Bookman* declared it 'something of
a triumph'. The reviewer in the *Lady* found its 'fascination . . . so great
that it is impossible to lay it aside'.[49] The issue of the credibility of *Dracula*
dominated two of the most penetrating reviews, in the *Athenaeum* and the

Daily Telegraph.[50] The reviewer in the *Athenaeum* was critical of the construction, literary skills and characterisation of the book. He saw *Dracula* as part of a trend of using the supernatural as a reaction against 'late tendencies in thought', presumably scientific rationalism, and objected to Stoker's 'way of presenting his matter' as 'too direct and compromising', lacking 'the essential note of remoteness and at the same time subtle affinity that separates while it links our humanity with unknown beings and possibilities hovering on the confines of the known world'. The reviewer commented archly: 'Isolated scenes and touches are probably quite uncanny enough to please those for whom they are designed' but found the novel 'wanting in constructive art as well as in the higher literary sense', while acknowledging the great energy which propelled the story and accepting that, at times, Stoker seemed almost to succeed in creating a sense of the possibility of the impossible.

W. L. Courtney, who reviewed *Dracula* in the *Daily Telegraph*, was the author of a variety of books and edited the *Fortnightly Review* in succession to Frank Harris. For him, the book had two aspects: 'the first is the confident reliance on superstition as furnishing the groundwork of a modern story; and the second, more significant still, is the bold adaptation of the legend to such ordinary spheres of latter-day existence as the harbour of Whitby and Hampstead-Heath'. Courtney guessed, correctly, that Baring-Gould's 1865 book on werewolves had influenced Stoker and wondered if 'the were-wolf was in reality a metaphorical figure for the outlaw . . . a man with a price set on his head as an enemy to society, whom at all hazards a developing civilisation had to destroy'. He paid tribute to Stoker's ability to make the reader suspend disbelief:

> Never was so mystical a tale told with such simple verisimilitude. We are not allowed to doubt the facts because the author speaks of them as mere matters of ascertained truth. Such is Mr. Stoker's dramatic skill, that the reader hurries on breathless from the first page to the last, afraid to miss a single word, lest the subtle and complicated chain of evidence should be broken; and though the plot involves enough and to spare of bloodshed, it never becomes revolting, because the spiritual mystery of evil surmounts the physical horror.

He preferred the first part of the book, partly because he feared that 'if goodness can be turned into vice by a purely extraneous agency, the mystery of evil becomes too awful for us to contemplate' and he had difficulty in accepting that innocents like Lucy and Mina could be contaminated; Macbeth and Faust were susceptible to evil because they were already flirting with it: 'Such, at least, is our modern ethical principle, which we are reluctant to relinquish even in dealing with the sphere of transcendental mystery.' The juxtaposing of the everyday and the supernatural also caught the attention of the reviewer in Dublin's *Freeman's Journal* when *Dracula* was reprinted in Constable's cheap series. It was seen as 'weird and fascinating' and 'a powerful romance which combines in a wonderful way the supernatural with the human, and the gloomiest of phantoms with domestic concerns of the lightest and most practical quality'.[51]

Despite her poor health, Stoker's mother wrote two letters of congratulation to her son when she read the book. In the first, dated 1 June 1897, she told him that it was 'splendid/a thousand miles beyond anything you have written before & I feel certain will place you very high in the writers of the day – the story being deeply sensational exciting & interesting'. She wrote again the following month, prompted by a positive review in a London newspaper, stating that 'no book since Mrs Shelley's Frankenstein or indeed any other at all has come near yours in originality, or terror [;] Poe is nowhere. I have read much but I have never met a book like it at all in its terrible excitement [–] it should make a wide spread reputation and much money for you.' Arthur Conan Doyle wrote in similarly enthusiastic terms to Stoker from the holiday resort of Eastbourne in August 1897:

> I think it is the very best story of diablerie which I have read for many years. It is really wonderful how with so much exciting interest over so long a book there is never an anticlimax. It holds you from the very start and grows more engrossing until it is quite painfully vivid. The old Professor is most excellent and so are the two girls. I congratulate you with all my heart for having written so fine a book.[52]

The values of another lady who wrote to Stoker in praise of *Dracula* could hardly have been more different from those of his earnestly moralistic mother: Mary Elizabeth Braddon (1837–1915) was one of the most successful sensational novelists of the nineteenth century and a good friend of his. He would probably have read her vampire story, 'Good Lady Ducayne', published in 1896, which had some elements in common with *Dracula*, like blood transfusion and a young girl failing in health as she comes under the vampiric spell. Experiments with blood transfusion also featured in H.G. Wells's *The Island of Doctor Moreau*, also published in 1896.

Another friend of Stoker's, the painter, John Singer Sargent, sent an enthusiastic note of congratulation on a card from Palermo. An unlikely source of praise was the Reverend Dr Lisdall, Chancellor of Christ Church

Cathedral, Dublin, who wrote to Irving: 'Tell Stoker that I have just finished the reading of his "*Dracula*", and that it reminds me of the time when I saw Boucicault in his drama as "The Vampire" at the Prince of Wales [?] . . . Stoker's work is very cleverly written, & will, I hope, have extensive circulation. He certainly makes his readers "soul/ample [?]-full, with horrors."' Gladstone responded graciously to an early copy of *Dracula* sent by Stoker, telling him that he had been very successful in maintaining the reader's interest in the story.

Stoker was probably especially pleased at the plaudits he won from Sir Melville Macnaghten of Scotland Yard, who told him that he had revelled in *Dracula*: he was particularly interested in the werewolf aspect and was revolted by Mina being forced to drink Dracula's blood.[53] This, incidentally, was from a man who had been very much involved in the Jack the Ripper case less than a decade before. Whether this lurid series of murders in 1888 had, in turn, an influence on Stoker is a subject of debate. Hall Caine's close friend, Dr Francis J. Tumblety, an American quack doctor, was a prime suspect in the killings and this gave Stoker a direct connection to the case. Tumblety fled from Britain after his arrest on charges of gross indecency in November 1888, after he had been granted bail. Macnaghten, Assistant Chief Constable of the Metropolitan Police and deputy head of its Criminal Investigation Department (CID), was the author of an 1894 report on the murders. Stoker's preface to the 1901 Icelandic edition of *Dracula* alludes to the Jack the Ripper killings;[54] whether this means that Stoker was genuinely influenced by Jack the Ripper when he was writing the book or was merely attempting to add verisimilitude to the alleged 'facts' of the novel, a few years after its publication, is open to question.

Within a few years of the publication of *Dracula*, Stoker's name became inextricably linked with it and the mixed nature of its reception in England was forgotten. As the American edition was being prepared by Doubleday & McClure in 1899, the *Commercial Advertiser* in New York stated that it had 'met with a cordial reception in England and is said to be a daring work of the imagination'. The following year the *Literary World* claimed that Stoker had 'earned considerable fame as a novelist. "Dracula," from his pen, is worthy of E.A. Poe, and is probably the best vampire story extant', while the *Echo* commented that 'his "Dracula," though uneven, has earned a place for him in the outer circles of novelists'. In 1904, the *Washington Post* declared that in *Dracula* Stoker had written a story that none who read could forget: 'The story had a grewsomeness [*sic*] that has not been equalled in the literature of the century.' It 'murdered sleep'. The next year the *Literary World* noted that *Dracula* had brought Stoker lasting fame, the anonymous author stating that it was the most borrowed book in his library. A year later, the *Sketch* prophesied, correctly, that *Dracula* 'will be reprinted in the cheap series of 2000 A.D.'[55]

While *Dracula* had to wait two years before an American edition was published, its reception on the other side of the Atlantic was generally favourable. Whitelaw Reid, the proprietor and editor of the New York *Tribune*, and later American Ambassador to the UK, wrote to Stoker: 'Congratulations on your imaginative powers, which were heartily appreciated before, but the full scope of which could never have been guessed till this book was written.' Thomas Aldrich Bailey of the *Atlantic Monthly*, who had been a friend for some years, wrote to Stoker as he was reading *Dracula* and said there was not a drop of blood in his body which did not feel as if it had been in cold storage.[56] The reviewer in the *Free Press of Detroit*, who clearly knew Stoker, found it hard to believe that he had actually written *Dracula*:

> And Bram Stoker wrote it!
> Think of him.
> He – a great shambling, good-natured, overgrown boy – although he is the business manager of Henry Irving and the Lyceum Theatre – with a red beard, untrimmed, and a ruddy complexion, tempered somewhat by the wide-open, full blue eyes that gaze so frankly into yours! Why, it is hard enough to imagine Bram Stoker a businessman, to say nothing of his possessing an imagination capable of projecting Dracula upon paper.
> But he has done it. And he has done it well.[57]

The *Home Journal* of New York was positive in the extreme: 'Edgar Allan Poe never wrote a story more purely imaginative, more profoundly spectral, more decidedly ghoulish than "Dracula."' One Washington journal stated that *Dracula* was causing a tremendous sensation in spite of its gruesome nature: 'Reading it on a stormy night in one's room alone, the shadows take on the shapes of hideous devils, the slightest noise in the room makes one jump, and the moaning of the wind outside only echoes the hideous voices of the soulless maidens, the vampires of the weird Carpathian forest.' The *Chicago Daily News*, while critical of the book's literary qualities, acknowledged its strong attraction: 'a grewsome [sic], weird and diabolical story which is cheerfully recommended to all who are bored with ordinary books'.[58]

Stoker had long been assiduous in cultivating influential Americans and he sent copies of *Dracula* to contacts such as Wayne McVeagh, the American Attorney-General, as the book was being published in the United States in

1899. He had kept up contact with American diplomats in London since the 1880s and was part of the Embassy's social circle, which also included Mark Twain. Stoker had corresponded with William Cody, 'Buffalo Bill', in the 1880s and 1890s, providing tickets for the Lyceum and receiving tickets for the frontiersman's show in return, as well as a photograph which Stoker had requested. American readers would no doubt have been particularly interested in the Texan, Quincey P. Morris, in *Dracula*, one of Lucy Westenra's unsuccessful suitors and one of the dedicated band of comrades who track down Dracula. When Dr Seward declares of Morris that if 'America can go on breeding men like that, she will be a power in the world indeed', he was uttering sentiments very close to its author's heart. Stoker even places a positive speech about the United States in the mouth of Dracula's unfortunate minion, Renfield. Up to the end of the novel, Dracula has been held at bay only by the symbols of religion and superstition; he is finally ensnared by the efficient application of modern technology and is dispatched both by Jonathan Harker's great kukri knife, a 'Ghoorka' implement of empire and Quincey Morris's bowie knife, that symbol of the American frontier.

Morris has aroused a good deal of critical interest, with some seeing him as representative of an expansionist America, an ambiguous threat to British interests who had to be killed off and who may even have been in league with the Count. Another view is that he represents the enterprising spirit of the English race, reinvigorated by transplantation to the United States. Yet others hold that, through Quincey Morris, Stoker may have been trying to advocate an end to American isolationist policies or that Renfield's reference to the Monroe Doctrine may represent a longing on Stoker's part for American intervention in European affairs.[59] As a Texan, Morris occupies a somewhat ambiguous place in Stoker's value system. In his fiction generally, language plays an important role in determining the place of his characters in the order of things. As a general rule, those speaking in dialect, while they can be virtuous, are outside the sphere of metropolitan propriety. Quincey is well educated, with exquisite manners, but is able to talk in slang, much to the amusement of Lucy Westenra. She is not sure if she herself could ever use slang and wonders if Arthur, her successful, aristocratic suitor even likes it. As well as embodying Stoker's admiration for the United States and its people, Quincey may reflect Stoker's own ambiguous position in London society, well integrated but differentiated by his Irish brogue.

The only dramatised performance of *Dracula* to take place in Stoker's lifetime was a production at the Lyceum on 18 May 1897 at 10 a.m., in the form of a prologue and five acts, under the title, *Dracula or the Un-Dead*.

The admission cost of one guinea was expensive and, together with the early hour at which it was staged, the intention was clearly not to encourage attendance by the general public (two tickets were sold). In fact the performance was mounted for copyright purposes, to establish Stoker's title to *Dracula* in dramatic form and prevent future unauthorised adaptations for the stage. The text had been cleared, just nine days previously, by George Redford, the Lord Chamberlain's examiner of plays, who told Stoker that he had read the 'very remarkable dramatic version of your forthcoming novel' and was sending a provisional licence, as he saw nothing 'unlicensable' in it.[60] The contrast with the much more restrictive attitude on the part of the Lord Chamberlain's office in the 1920s to play texts based on *Dracula* is probably indicative of Stoker's close relations with Redford rather than changing social attitudes. According to Noel Stoker, Irving dismissed the performance as 'dreadful'. The novel went on sale eight days after this performance, on 26 May 1897. The dramatic possibilities of *Dracula* were spotted early by one unlikely source: Viscount Halifax, President of the Church Union, wrote to Stoker, in October 1897, suggesting that a dramatisation of the novel, with Henry Irving playing the part of the Count, 'could inspire awe in even the boldest'.[61] It has been claimed that Stoker 'planned to bring Dracula over to America in another story' but there is no evidence that he ever had any great interest either in developing the dramatic possibilities of *Dracula* or in writing a sequel. Besides, *Dracula* was not the only one of his novels for which Stoker arranged a copyright performance in the theatre.[62] The full dramatic – and financial – potential of *Dracula* would be achieved by others, but only after the author's death.

PART FOUR

Fading Splendour

THIRTEEN

The Lyceum Theatre Company

I am beginning to feel this nocturnal existence tell on me. It is destroying my nerve. I start at my own shadow, and am full of all sorts of horrible imaginings. God knows that there is ground for my terrible fear in this accursed place!

(*Dracula*, Jonathan Harker's Journal)

In 1898, its financial state necessitated the temporary closure of the Lyceum. This failure was the result of a number of reverses which struck in the late 1890s. Stoker identified the opening night of Irving's production of *Richard III* in December 1896 as the turning point. After this night of unqualified success, the high-water mark of his career, Irving and a friend, Professor James Dewar, enjoyed the Lyceum's hospitality, then detoured to the Garrick Club and on to the Royal Institution, both social venues. Dawn was breaking by the time Irving reached home; he slipped and ruptured ligatures under his kneecap, which kept him out of action for ten weeks. According to Ellen Terry, his general health began to fail at this time, making the last decade of his life a struggle with a weakening heart and lungs.

In fact, Irving's problems may have had their origin immediately prior to the performance of Richard III. George Bernard Shaw was among the critics on the first night and his review gave rise to a furious row with Irving – with Stoker acting as intermediary – over the actor's belief that Shaw meant to imply that he had been drunk on stage. It may have been that Irving had, in fact, taken drink before he went on stage but Shaw claimed that he had naïvely described Irving's performance without perceiving what was the matter with him, an explanation which rings a little hollow. According to Shaw, Irving was not a heavy drinker – in the sense that Edmund Kean, for example, had been – but he did go on stage in his later days 'in the condition in which many London clubmen who are not teeto-tallers are after dinner'.[1] The brush with Shaw was unfortunate, especially in its timing; as the champion of Ibsen and the new theatre of ideas, his depiction of the Lyceum as outmoded was damaging, while Irving's enmity only served to underline Shaw's credentials as an agent of change.

In February 1898 the Lyceum suffered a hammer-blow when fire destroyed more than 2,000 pieces of scenery, worth more than £30,000, in storage at Southwark. Stoker had had the scenery insured for £10,000 but, shortly before the fire, Irving had instructed him to reduce the insurance cover to £6,000, to avoid 'wasting money'. In Stoker's words, for Irving 'it was checkmate to the "repertoire" side of his management . . . The effect of the fire on Irving was not only this great cost, but the deprivation of all that he had built up. Had it not occurred he could have gone on playing his repertoire for many years, and would never have had to produce a new play.'[2] Fresh disaster struck several months later, in October, when Irving was struck down with pleurisy and pneumonia in Glasgow. Stoker attributed the follicular pharyngitis, or 'clergyman's sore throat', which Irving suffered afterwards to these attacks, although syphilis can be one of its causes. Its effect on Irving was that for the next six years he was coughing up pus on such a scale that he used 500 handkerchiefs per day.

To add to these problems, Irving's touch in the choice of material deserted him and the final two plays produced under his own management at the Lyceum in January and May 1898 respectively were disasters. It was ironic that, having devoted so little time to his family, and worked so hard to keep his sons off the stage, his path to ruin was compounded by indulging his son, Laurence, at the Lyceum. In 1897 Laurence Irving completed a play, *Peter the Great*. His father purchased it and decided on a lavish production, sparing neither pains nor expense. Although the Prince of Wales loved it and saw it three times, the general public thought otherwise. On the first night, New Year's Day 1898, people left the theatre when a conspirator was tortured off stage but with his screams being heard before he was brought in, pale and bloody. Stoker was diplomatic in his choice of language but there was no mistaking the scale of the disaster which the father–son combination had wreaked on the Lyceum when he said that the dramatist was not 'at his full skill' and that the tone of the play did not suit the public taste, adding ominously that the spectacle of a father hounding his son to death was enough to cause a shudder in those 'whose instincts and sympathies are normal'. The play had to be taken off within the month.[3] Irving's next production, *The Medicine Man*, a curious melodrama in which he played a medical specialist who was secretly using his patients for experimentation, was mounted in May 1898. Described by Ellen Terry as a quite unworthy production, it turned out to be another flop and had to be withdrawn after twenty-four performances, a failure made all the worse by the fact that Irving had turned down an offer from Conan Doyle to write a Sherlock Holmes play for him which would have been virtually guaranteed success. Stoker was clearly appalled by Irving's behaviour but he seems to have lost influence to the father–son axis now in the ascendant at the Lyceum. His situation was akin to that of Mina

Harker in *Dracula* when Van Helsing tells the other men that 'she must be no more of our counsel'.

There was, however, no disguising Irving's lack of judgement over what proved to be the ultimate débâcle of his career. Joseph Comyns Carr visited Irving at the Bournemouth boarding-house to which he had withdrawn following the temporary closure of the Lyceum in 1898 with a proposition that he should sell his interest in the theatre to a consortium. Carr could raise the necessary funds to reopen it, but the backers involved (who included two of Carr's brothers, a solicitor and a financier) would not entrust its management to him. As Carr had long been associated with Irving, he clearly had credibility with the actor. He had written the text (on the basis of an earlier draft by W.G. Wills) of the highly successful *King Arthur*, staged at the Lyceum in 1895 with Irving, Ellen Terry and Geneviève Ward in the cast (it was one of the many plays put out of commission by the warehouse fire which destroyed the theatre's scenery). As Director of the Grosvenor Gallery, he exhibited many of the Pre-Raphaelite painters, one of whom, Edward Burne-Jones, was responsible for the artistic design of the production of *King Arthur*. Carr was a central figure in the artistic nexus of which the Lyceum was part and the actor's willingness to rely on his advice, rather than Stoker's, has a certain logic to it, even if it proved to be most unfortunate. Irving accepted the proposition, 'but with a sore heart and a wholly human resentment at his change of state . . . and his acting was never the same again'.[4]

Stoker protested to Irving about the terms of the offer which, he believed, were deeply unfavourable to Irving, and suggested an alternative. It can be seen from his account of the formation of the new company that he was poorly treated by Irving. As he put it, even though he was 'Sir Henry Irving's business manager . . . from first to last I had absolutely no act or part in the formation of the Lyceum Theatre Company – in its promotion, flotation, or working. Even my knowledge of it was confined to matters touched on in the contract with Irving. From the first I had no information as to its purposes, scope or methods, outside the above.' In fact, he was on the Atlantic or in the United States when the parent company or syndicate was formed. When he returned he found the Lyceum Theatre Company was a *fait accompli*. He did not even see a copy of the prospectus for nearly a year.

The Lyceum Theatre Company lasted from the beginning of 1899 to the end of the 1902 season. Irving featured in three plays in this period: *Robespierre* (1899), *Coriolanus* (1901), and *The Merchant of Venice* (1902). The arrangement he had entered into was, as Stoker said, an excellent arrangement for the Lyceum Theatre Company but was in no way beneficial to Irving and he was able to show in *Personal Reminiscences of Henry*

Irving just how much the actor lost by the deal. The contract between Irving and the company was eventually cancelled because the company was unable to fulfil its obligations. Stoker was left to clear up the mess. Notwithstanding the fact that he had had no part in the setting up of the company, it was he who faced the shareholders' wrath and, indeed, had to endure heckling at directors' meetings: these turned to cheers from those present when he produced figures showing what Irving's contribution to the failed enterprise had been.[6] Stoker's account of this sorry episode has never been controverted and he pulls no punches in placing on the record his view that Irving's ruin was, to a certain extent, brought about by his own dismal judgement and deviousness.

Not deterred by the example of *Peter the Great*, in April 1899 Irving produced Laurence's translation of *Robespierre*, which the French playwright, Victorien Sardou, had written expressly for him. Commenting that Irving 'could be very secretive when he wished', Stoker decided not to argue with his boss, to spare him upset, but did distance himself from the play, noting that the arrangements for *Robespierre* were made in Paris, presumably by Laurence Irving, but not through him. A peremptory note from Irving to Stoker on 4 April 1899, the day before the production opened, reprimanding him for not having attended properly to the publicity, was a sign of a now-strained relationship. Irving insisted that, in future, he would supervise the advertising lists, hitherto one of Stoker's core functions.

Irving's decline was apparent to discerning observers. When Lady Gregory saw him in Shakespeare's *Coriolanus*, yet another late, unsuccessful effort in 1901, she commented: 'Went to see "Colioranus" with Yeats – but poor Irving's voice is quite gone, & sounds as if coming from a phonograph.'[5] The fact that Irving was now failing with Shakespeare, hitherto a key element in his formula for success, was indicative of the extent of his decline. Stoker loyally stood by his master. Although he accepted that *Coriolanus* and Victorien Sardou's *Dante*, mounted in 1903, were costly and unsuccessful and were rejected by the various publics in London (Ellen Terry, however, claimed that it had done fairly well at Drury Lane), the provinces and the United States, (Terry fully agreed on its failure there) he maintained that Irving had been a success; the fault lay with the plays. Presumably Stoker was not finding fault with Shakespeare but was more likely hinting at the disastrous influence of Laurence Irving on the choice of inferior plays such as *Peter the Great*, *Robespierre* and *Dante*.

Irving apologists have claimed that, had he been better served by his subordinates, he would not have succumbed to disaster. This line of argument began a few years after Irving's death when Sir Squire and Marie Effie Bancroft, the influential theatrical couple, in their *Recollections of Sixty Years*

(1909), while allowing that his judgement began to fail late in life with the production of plays like *Coriolanus*, *The Medicine Man* and *Dante*, nevertheless stated: 'Had Irving been in partnership with a capable comrade, to whose guidance he would sometimes have submitted, he might have lived and died a man of fortune.'[7] Stoker was actually only too aware of the potential for disaster in Irving's behaviour in his later years but his loss of influence rendered him powerless. This is apparent in his account of Irving's production of *Dante*, which the actor read to his company, now without a theatre of their own, in January 1903. Stoker had not previously read the play or even the scenario, translated from the French and adapted by Laurence Irving, and his heart sank as he listened to what he knew would be a fresh disaster. He found the play difficult to comprehend which, he noted savagely, helped it with the less cultured part of the audience. The play opened on 30 April 1903 at the Theatre Royal, Drury Lane, despite Stoker's efforts to persuade Irving not to proceed with what he considered 'a venture of fearful hazard'. He remonstrated with Irving over the costs and the likely 'immense loss' but, as 'Chancellor of the Exchequer to his Absolute Monarchy', had to be content with Irving's irresponsible reply which was that, as a gamble, it was better than Monte Carlo![8] When Van Helsing says in *Dracula*, 'We must obey, and silence is a part of obedience', it may have reflected Stoker's final response in situations such as these.

The real assault on Stoker's reputation had to wait until Irving's grandson, Laurence Irving, published a biography of his grandfather in 1951. He claimed, in the face of all evidence, that Stoker's 'emotional impetuosity handicapped him in dealing with Irving's business in a forthright and sensible manner'.[9] Laurence Irving does not appear to have used the Lyceum archives, preserved at Leeds and Stratford, which detail Stoker's work for his grandfather. Quite apart from Stoker's role in attempting to save Irving from the disastrous Lyceum Theatre Company and the subsequent illjudged *Dante*, the factual references in Laurence Irving's biography show that Stoker did stand up to Irving when necessary and that his advice was sound.[10] One point on which Laurence Irving probably was reliable was his grandfather's reaction to the situation in which he found himself at the end of his life: 'He was not a man to admit a mistake [about the Lyceum Theatre Company]. Yet the knowledge that he had done so in the face of Stoker's earnest opposition – to say nothing of Stoker's natural pique at his Chief's disregard – clouded a little their relationship to one another.'[11]

Another source of possible friction was Irving's hiring of Austin Brereton as his press agent, after the fire which destroyed the Lyceum scenery in 1898. This was done over Stoker's head and, given the fact that media management was part of his job, it is not surprising that Stoker was not best pleased.

Brereton had been secretary to the critic, Clement Scott, in which capacity he was well known to Stoker who was, indeed, his channel of communication to the actor in the 1880s and 1890s. He had previously been associated with the Lyceum: in 1883, when he was a young journalist, Irving sent him to the United States to do advance work before the theatre's first tour to that country. He published *Henry Irving, A Biographical Sketch*, in the same year.

Yet Stoker's role at this time was appreciated by some well-placed observers. After the collapse of the Lyceum Theatre Company, Henry Labouchère, the English ex-diplomat, Liberal Member of Parliament and journalist, who had offered to finance Irving as far back as 1878 and, when he refused, had begged him to save so that he would be independent in all circumstances, commented: 'Had it not been for his old friend Bram Stoker, Irving would have been eaten out of home and theatre very speedily.'[12] Labouchère, incidentally, had proposed an amendment to legislation which made male homosexuality illegal for the first time in 1885 and was instrumental in exposing Richard Piggot as the forger of politically damaging letters ostensibly written by Charles Stewart Parnell in 1889.

Irving had lived for his art and had, from the beginning, been contemptuous of financial considerations in the operation of the Lyceum. Joseph Hatton observed, as far back as 1884, that there was 'no commercial consideration at work when he is mounting a play though his experience is that neither expense nor pains are lost on the public'. The financial recklessness inherent in Irving's Lyceum was apparent to observers. This attitude carried over into his personal life: when they visited Nuremberg in 1885 with some members of the Lyceum Company, Mrs Joseph Comyns Carr found that Irving was annoyed by her attitude of haggling and often paid more than the price asked.[13] Such spendthrift ways were sustainable only as long as the Lyceum retained popular favour in both Britain and the United States: when Irving's ability to support the inflated costs he generated declined, his *modus operandi* was no longer viable. Hall Caine had offered perspicacious advice about the Lyceum's excessive costs when it was still at the height of its success in 1897: 'If Irving would or could lower expenses & take a few of the second towns he would make a pile of money, I think.'[14] By this time, such sound advice was already too late: the years of Irving's success were behind him and ruin lay ahead.

While the Lyceum was imploding, competition in the London theatrical world had been growing for years. Three new theatres had opened in 1881 alone and six theatres would open on Shaftesbury Avenue in the twenty years after its completion in 1886. In September 1892, the first in what would become a nest of theatres opened in St Martin's Lane, not far from the Lyceum. Oscar Wilde and George Bernard Shaw, both of whom had yet to taste popular acclaim, had plays produced in London in this year, albeit with widely differing results. Wilde's *Lady Windermere's Fan* opened with a glittering première at the St James's Theatre on 20 February and was both a critical and a commercial success. Wilde made £7,000 from it in a single year and *The Importance of Being Earnest* would open to an even more rapturous reception on St Valentine's Day, 1895. Shaw's *Widowers' Houses*, which had its première at the Royalty Theatre on 9 December 1892 was, by contrast, a flop and was abandoned within the month, to be replaced by *Charley's Aunt* by Brandon Thomas, a hugely successful farce. Shaw's presentation of social themes in a realistic manner may have had to wait another few years to capture popular success but his arrival, as well as that of Wilde, on the London theatrical scene was indicative of the rise of a type of drama which was the antithesis of the fare provided by Irving's Lyceum. Meanwhile Shaw would use his position as drama critic of the *Saturday Review* from 1895 to 1898 to excoriate Irving and all that he represented. In 1897, the last in a nineteen-year run of success for the Lyceum, yet more theatres opened in London. Some, like Herbert Beerbohm Tree's Her Majesty's Theatre, provided direct competition in central London. Others, like the Grand in Fulham, the Bedford in Camden Town, the Metropolitan on the Edgware Road and the Alexandra in Stoke Newington, were evidence of the spread of entertainment centres outside the traditional concentration in the orbit of the Lyceum. There was a certain irony inherent in Ellen Terry opening the huge Camden Theatre, with its capacity of nearly 2,500, in December 1900 as Irving struggled to keep the Lyceum afloat.

Irving therefore faced rising challenges both from new theatres and new types of theatre, challenges he was increasingly ill equipped to handle. The Lyceum was also facing competition from new forms of entertainment: music halls mushroomed in Britain in the second half of the nineteenth century, after the Theatre Regulations Act of 1843 had allowed drinking and smoking in them while banning it in legitimate theatres. Henry Wood opened his first series of Promenade Concerts, 'The Proms', at the Queen's Hall in August 1895. Even the movies were beginning to gain a toehold in the entertainment business. Thomas Edison's kinetoscope made its first appearance in London in 1894 and the technology would improve rapidly in the remainder of the decade. Also that year, Alfred Harmsworth (later Lord Northcliffe) and his brother began the creation of modern mass-market journalism in England by purchasing the London *Evening News*, and, two years later, launching the *Daily Mail*, taking advantage of the mass literacy created by the inauguration of compulsory elementary education in 1870. Wireless telegraphy and radio too were on the horizon, with the pioneering Guglielmo Marconi filing his first patents in Britain in 1896.

FOURTEEN

'Wholesome, Healthy, and Stirring Fiction'

I do not know how I am writing this even to you. I am afraid to stop . . .
and I don't want to stop, for I do so want to tell you all.
(*Dracula*, Lucy Westenra to Mina Murray)

The growing turbulence at the Lyceum did not deflect Stoker from his literary activity; on the contrary, the mounting difficulties in his professional life seemed to act as a spur to his creativity. There may, of course, have been an element of desperation in this, a realisation that he needed an alternative source of income, as his future with Irving looked increasingly uncertain. The bulk of Stoker's literary output came after the apogee of Irving's career in the late 1890s and, indeed, after Stoker had created his single masterpiece. He knew that the Lyceum's best days were over and, as a man in his fifties, without the means of comfortable retirement but too old to start a new career in the theatre, he renewed his vocation as a writer. In the period between the start of Irving's long decline, which coincided with the publication of *Dracula*, and the actor's death in 1905, he crammed in five novels. There was a frenetic air to this literary activity and predictably its quality was uneven.

Less than a year after the appearance of *Dracula*, in February 1898, Stoker published another novel, *Miss Betty*, which had been written some years earlier. It was the first in a series of 'Latter-Day Stories' by the publisher, C.A. Pearson. On 31 January 1898, it was given a copyright performance at the Lyceum as a play in four acts, with a Miss Suzanne Shelton playing the title role. The performance took place early on a Monday afternoon. The theatre was 'not quite packed to overflowing' – not surprising perhaps as admission was two guineas – but it was judged to have passed off successfully. Dedicated to Florence, *Miss Betty* was a romance which could hardly have been more different to its predecessor in content or quality. The evil which permeates *Dracula* is almost entirely absent except for the well-intentioned highwayman activities of its hero, Rafe Otwell, who is, in any event, morally regenerated by the novel's coy heroine, Betty Pole. From a literary point of view it is, rightly, regarded as the weakest of Stoker's romances, but from a biographical perspective it is not without interest.

In choosing an eighteenth-century setting, Stoker did not stray far from his own experience: the house of Betty Pole, the heiress to a considerable fortune, is in Cheyne Walk where the Stokers lived in the 1880s. It is filled with beautiful pieces given to her grandfather by a Dutch minister when he was on a diplomatic mission for William III; thus the Dutch influence evident in the character of Van Helsing in *Dracula* carries through to its successor. Lord Rossmore, the Irish peer from whose Dutch-originated family Stoker borrowed the Westenra surname in *Dracula*, had an ancestor, Lady Hester Westenra, who had an encounter with Freyney, a famous highwayman whose chivalry bears more than a passing resemblance to that of Rafe Otwell; when Freyney attempted to rob Lady Hester Westenra, she challenged him to a race, which she won. She then tried to give him her purse as she felt that she had had all the luck but he refused on the grounds that it would contravene his honour as a 'Gentleman of the Road'. The fictional Rafe makes an equally unlikely highwayman.

Miss Betty features a boat race on the Thames, which starts at the Old Swan near London Bridge and finishes at the White Swan Inn at Chelsea. The White Swan Inn did exist and was located at the bottom of Swan Walk; it was a popular resort for river parties in the eighteenth century and was the finishing point of Doggett's Coat and Badge Race for watermen, which still took place in Stoker's era and, indeed, survives to this day. The boat race gives Stoker the opening to introduce his hero, Rafe Otwell, a darkly handsome young man with a proud bearing, 'lithe as a panther and strong as steel'. Betty falls into the water and Rafe jumps in to save her, performing the rescue which is almost obligatory in a Stoker novel and which parallels closely Stoker's own heroics in the Thames. Equally predictable is the theme of inheritance, with Dudley Stanmore, her grandfather, leaving his considerable fortune to Betty, along with a good deal of pietistic moralising. From this point, the novel revolves around the romance of a well-to-do young woman with a penniless young man, reversing the gender roles of *The Snake's Pass*. Stoker now introduces the historical figure of the statesman, Sir Robert Walpole, a distant relative of Rafe, who wants him to marry an heiress. Stoker may have been inspired by the fact that Walpole had a summer house on the site of the Royal Hospital in Chelsea, which Stoker could see from the front windows of his house in St Leonard's Terrace. Walpole is presented as a bully and a generally unpleasant character who would have used Rafe's lack of moral courage to mould him to his own purposes, had Rafe been willing to follow his dictates. Sir Robert was, of course, the father of Horace Walpole, author of the landmark Gothic novel, *The Castle of Otranto*. Horror dreams feature, as they had done in Stoker's earlier work, when Betty finds herself sitting up in bed wide awake, terrified, with a scream frozen on her lips. Another echo of *Dracula* is Rafe's battle against the Turks. The ending of *Miss Betty* is similar to that of *Dracula*, with domestic bliss and children in store as they were for Mina and Jonathan Harker.

Stoker had tried to publish *Miss Betty* as early as 1894 but had met with a devastating rebuff at the hands of the Bristol publisher, J.W. Arrowsmith, who, having read the manuscript, told him: 'I should do neither you nor myself any good by putting it on the market.'[1] There do not appear to have been any hard feelings between Stoker and Arrowsmith who, the following year, offered to introduce him to Anthony Hope. While Arrowsmith's reaction seems eminently sensible to a modern reader (Hall Caine, too, had been critical of the manuscript when Stoker gave it to him to read), the book was widely and almost universally well reviewed. Sir Henry Lucy wrote to Stoker in March 1898 that he would find a notice of *Miss Betty* in *Punch*: 'I found it quite a charming book. How do you find time to write these masterpieces, with two plays on the nightly bill, matinees on Wednesday & Saturday, & stage properties aflame in the warehouse?' Lucy was as good as his word: the *Punch* review was positive, stating that Stoker, having written one of 'the most blood-curdling novels of the age, makes amends by giving us . . . one of the prettiest'.[2] The *Era* found it 'a pretty little tale, well told', and thought it 'should be widely read'. The *Irish Times* declared that the novel would add to Stoker's reputation and, indeed, that the mantle of Robert Louis Stevenson had fallen on him: 'It is a specimen of wholesome, healthy, and stirring fiction such as is seldom placed upon the modern bookshelf, and we commend it to all readers of cultivated literary taste.'[3] Stoker himself made a compilation of quotes from the reviews and he had an embarrassment of praise from which to choose. The metropolitan journals, both heavyweight and popular, loved it, as did their provincial counterparts. In addition, it drew admiration from reviewers from religious publications as disparate as the *Catholic Times* and the *Freemasons' Journal*.[4]

In 1893, when he travelled alone exploring the east coast of Scotland on the advice of friends who praised the quality of its air, Stoker discovered Cruden Bay, a small village in a bay of the same name, in the Banff and Buchan district of the Grampian region. Captivated by it, he booked into the Kilmarnock Arms Hotel. He became friendly with the fishing people and returned with Florence in later years, staying in a small, cliff-top cottage, 'The Crookit Lum', at Whinnyfold, a fishing hamlet a few miles south of Cruden Bay. It was an excellent location for his writing: 'From the bedroom windows of the cottage, white-plumed waves roar and crash against the black rocks on a winter's day. A perfect setting for a thriller.' It has been claimed that an invitation to Slains Castle, near the village, then occupied by the Earl and Countess of Erroll, inspired Castle Dracula. Victor Hay, their eldest son, wrote a novel, *Ferelith* (1903), featuring a young girl haunted by a spectral visitor, based on a local legend about the appearances of the 'undead' body of man whose soul had gone before him to the other world. However, apart from the fact that Stoker had begun *Dracula* before he visited Cruden, the castle is an unlikely model for Dracula's as it had been rebuilt in 1836 more in the style of a mansion than a grim Transylvanian fortress. Samuel Johnson, and his companion, James Boswell, were entertained at Slains Castle by an Earl of Erroll on their celebrated tour of Scotland in 1773 and witnessed a great storm which Johnson described in dramatic terms: 'From the windows, the eye wanders over the sea that separates Scotland from Norway, and when the winds beat with violence must enjoy all the terrifick grandeur of the tempestuous ocean. I would not for my amusement wish for a storm; but as storms, whether wished or not, will sometimes happen, I may say, without violation of humanity, that I should willingly look out upon them from Slanes [*sic*] castle.'[5]

Mrs Cruickshank, proprietrix of the Kilmarnock Arms when Stoker stayed there, recalled him with affection: 'He was one of the nicest men I ever knew . . . A big, cheery, handsome Irishman; and his wife was the most beautiful woman I ever set eyes on.' Stoker told her that he got inspiration for his stories when he was out around Cruden Bay. Mr George Hay, another inhabitant of the area, remembered well how Stoker would lie for hours at a time in a hammock, looking across to the Skares, those 'jagged rocks which seemed like fangs rising from the deep water'. At other times he was more active, especially when the wind was high:

> Then the tall, bearded Irishman, his cloak flying in the wind, stamping about the heavy sand, prodding it with the heavy stick, waving his arms and shouting at the great rollers as they thundered up the beach, and altogether behaving in such an outlandish way that George's second cousin, Eliza, who worked at the Kilmarnock Arms, was afraid to walk home across the sands to Whinnyfold, and took the long way round.[6]

Stoker intertwined his personal reaction to Cruden Bay with his fiction: 'When first I saw the place I fell in love with it. Had it been possible I should have spent my summers there, in a house of my own, but the want of any place in which to live forbade such an opportunity. So I stayed in the little hotel, the Kilmarnock Arms.'[7] The narrator of his story, 'The Seer' – published in the *London Magazine* in November 1901 – comes back each year; taking a 'feu' at Whinnyfold and deciding to build a house there. 'The Seer' formed part of the genesis of *The Mystery of the Sea*, published the following year. Most notably, it also featured the sinister Gormala MacNiel, based on an encounter Stoker had in Cruden Bay, in 1901, with an old woman, believed to have supernatural powers and so generally shunned by the locals. Stoker may have been encouraged to persevere with the material in 'The Seer' by Arthur Conan Doyle's opinion that the material in it was beautifully handled.

A local legend, that the bodies of those drowned in the previous twelve months rose from the waves to join their spirits in heaven or hell, probably inspired the procession of the dead in *The Mystery of the Sea*. The chapter titles of the novel: 'Second Sight', 'The Cipher', 'Secret Service', 'The Secret Passage', 'The Pope's Treasure', 'The Duty of a Wife', 'The Redemption of a Trust,' 'Danger', 'The Eyes of the Dead', etc., give a fair indication of Stoker's preoccupations in his writings. Indeed, a cardinal weakness of a book with some excellent individual elements was its author's inability to resist including a multiplicity of his favourite themes. Stoker put a good deal of himself into *The Mystery of the Sea* – his youthful pantheism, secret codes and dreams of wild doings at sea, including pirates and buried treasure. Just as in *The Snake's Pass* and *Dracula*, the narrator has chaotic dreams mingling the past, present and future. In the early part of the book especially, there is some excellent horror writing, with the narrator's consciousness balanced between rationalism and belief in the supernatural, rather like Jonathan Harker in *Dracula*. One of the protagonists is the fisherman, Lauchlane MacLeod, who, like Stoker himself, is over six feet tall, with a bushy beard; he is a son of the Vikings, speaks in biblical language, and has a simple purity which is placed by Stoker in opposition to the soulless work of modern trawlermen.

The novel begins when its narrator, Archibald Hunter, has just arrived in Cruden Bay for his annual visit. Through the medium of a Van-Helsing-like learned professor at Aberdeen, full of astronomical learning, Stoker introduces his interest in syzygy, the paired emanations in Gnosticism, the duality of God and the Devil, of good and evil. Under this system, mathematical principles, expressed in number symbols, are used to organise the world of gods, spirits and demons. The number three, important in *The Mystery of the Sea*, represents divine triads, the Trinity, and the body–soul–spirit structure of man. Gnostic thought includes the concept of discovery of the unconscious self or spirit in man which sleeps in him until awakened by the Saviour, very similar to the process undergone by Archie Hunter: 'The spirits of the earth and sea and air seemed to take shape to me, and all the myriad sounds of the night to have a sentient cause of utterance . . . I was becoming wrapped in the realisation of the mightier forces around me . . . my own heart seemed to stand still, to be a part of the grim silence of the waiting forces of the world.'[8] Into this philosophical mix, Stoker adds an idea of the Fates derived from Scandinavian/Germanic mythology.

The second major strand of *The Mystery of the Sea* is introduced when Hunter buys an old oak chest with Spanish papers in it, dating from 1598 to 1610, together with a cipher. A third strand is introduced soon afterwards, when Hunter meets two American ladies marooned after their boat has drifted away, whom he duly rescues. The latter two strands of the novel are neatly linked when Hunter and Marjory, the younger American, agree to work together to unravel the 'Mystery of the Sea'. This being the period of the Spanish-American War of 1898, Marjory's professed hatred of Spaniards chimes with Hunter's English historical feelings of enmity towards the same race. Hunter's work in cracking the ancient Spanish cipher gives the author an opportunity to indulge his interest in the subject. Stoker's recommendation of secret writing (he had a book in his library on the 'Bilateral Cipher' of Francis Bacon) as an antidote to boredom and his caution that it can become an obsession is indicative of his own personal engagement with it. Breaking the cipher reveals the text of a letter from the sixteenth-century Spaniard, Bernardino de Escoban, to his son, enjoining him to fulfil 'the Trust', essentially a plot involving the Spanish and the Pope, to bring about the downfall of Queen Elizabeth I of England. Stoker had done considerable research into Tudor history; in *Famous Impostors* he would later use an impressive range of sources on Queen Elizabeth I and reveal a profound admiration for her. Bernardino de Escoban has built and manned, at his own cost, one of the flagship vessels of the Armada, which has a figurehead by Benvenuto Cellini, the great Renaissance artist, as well as carrying the enormous hoard of treasure amassed by the Pope for the subjugation of the 'heretical' Elizabeth. After the conquest of England, the figurehead of the *San Cristobal* was to be set over the High Altar at Westminster. The treasure is buried on the Aberdeen coast, after the ship is crippled, for fear that it might fall into English hands.

In resurrecting in fiction the threat to the hybrid political and religious state of Tudor England, represented by the intertwined threat of the Papacy and Spain, Stoker is following in the tradition of the English and Irish Gothic writers, Matthew 'Monk' Lewis and Charles Maturin, whose major works, *The Monk* and *Melmoth the Wanderer* respectively, relied for much of their effect on stoking latent English anxiety about the horrors of the Church of Rome, allied to Catholic Spain. He was also echoing the views of his friend, Edward Dowden, who declared that 'in the days of [Queen] Elizabeth [I] the [English] nation had sprung up to a consciousness of new strength and vitality, and its political and religious antagonists, Spain and the Papacy, were identical.'[9] Stoker may have been conscious of the activities of Francis Hay, the ninth Earl of Erroll, who attempted to use Spanish money and arms to restore Roman Catholicism in Scotland in the late sixteenth century. He died in 1631 at Slains, and Stoker was acquainted with his descendant, the nineteenth Earl. He may have been aware too of the wreck of three ships of the Spanish Armada off the coast of Sligo in 1588 and the account of his travels in Ireland by Captain Francisco de Cuellar, a notable survivor of that ill-fated enterprise. Like Count Dracula, Francisco de Escoban, another continental European nobleman, wants to become assimilated in Britain, in order to subvert it. Marjory connects herself and the Spanish-American War with England's struggle of three centuries previously, when her ancestors, including Francis Drake, had swept the Spanish from the seas. Bellicose politically, she is personally submissive to Hunter, whose chaste wife she becomes. Mrs Jack, Marjory's older companion and surrogate mother, acts as Stoker's mouthpiece for conservative views on the role of women.

There is more than a passing resemblance between Castle Dracula and Crom Castle which Marjory, an heiress in the best Stokerian tradition, rents from a gentleman who turns out to be a descendant of Don Bernardino de Escoban. Stoker may have derived the name of Crom Castle from the similarly named seat of the Desmonds, one of the most noble of Irish families, in County Limerick, or from Crom Castle on the shores of Upper Lough Erne in County Fermanagh. While Archibald and Marjory enjoy a fairytale existence, the action in the novel culminates with the latter-day Don Bernardino turning up at Crom. A worthy successor to Dracula, his eyes have 'a cavern of fire within'. Like many of the best families of Spain, he has Moorish 'black blood' in his veins: 'The old diabolism whence had sprung fantee and hoo-doo seemed to gleam out in the grim smile of incarnate, rebellious purpose.'[10] Don Bernardino outlines the vast wealth of his family and offers all his possessions to Archibald in return for being allowed to reclaim the Spanish treasure. Hunter is tempted but realises that this treasure was amassed for the purpose of destroying England's polity, with which he identified the liberty of the entire human race. Stoker now piles horror upon horror, including the threat of the violation of Marjorie by a repulsive Negro kidnapper, but the book ends with Don Bernardino dying nobly and the evil conspiracy to subvert Britain finally laid to rest. In according Don Bernardino an honourable death, Stoker was adhering to the Gothic tradition which distinguished between the capacity of the individual for goodness and the depravity of the system, Spanish Catholicism, which had shaped him.

The Mystery of the Sea was published in London by William Heinemann in 1902 and in New York by Doubleday, Page & Co. A British Empire edition appeared in Heinemann's Colonial Library and it was reprinted in Leipzig by Heinemann and Balestier for sale in continental Europe. It was given a copyright performance at the Lyceum on 17 March 1902, which prompted speculation in a British newspaper that a public production of the play would take place in the United States but no play was produced in Stoker's lifetime.

The Mystery of the Sea impressed a good friend of Stoker's, John William Brodie-Innes (1848–1923), a Scottish lawyer and writer much involved in the occult and active in organisations such as the Golden Dawn and the Theosophical Society who would later dedicate a novel to Stoker.[11] Stoker showed his usual energy in promoting the book. Lord Glenerk, the proprietor of the *Morning Post*, politely informed him that he would be delighted to read another work by Stoker: he had not forgotten past experiences. The author, Edgar Pemberton, who had reviewed *The Snake's Pass* in 1890 and had been helpful after the publication of *Dracula*, told Stoker that he was doing a review for the *Birmingham Daily Post*. Sir Wemyss Thomas Reid, editor of the *Speaker*, to whom Stoker had sent *Dracula* for review in 1897, responded most enthusiastically: 'It is really a fine bit of work, a first-rate story, full of substance & feeling, & it ought to have a great success. I am, as you know, an old critic & I mean what I say when I give my opinion that you have written a novel infinitely above the average of English fiction.' The Crown Prince of Siam, an habitué of the Lyceum, did not, on the other hand, even pretend to have read the book when he thanked Stoker for having sent him a copy in September 1902.[12]

At that time, Stoker still benefited from his association with Irving and *The Mystery of the Sea*, its clear weaknesses notwithstanding, was widely and well reviewed. The publishers were able to take positive snippets from heavyweight journals such as the *Scotsman*, and *Pall Mall Gazette*, as well as from Conan Doyle, to promote the book. It was well reviewed in *Punch* in August 1902 ('a rattling good story') and the *Bookman* the following October: 'Altogether a thrilling and absorbing romance, ingeniously constructed and exceedingly well written.' By and large, other reviewers were also positive, especially in the mass-circulation newspapers such as the *Daily Mail* and the *Daily Graphic*, as well as in journals such as the *Era*, which termed it an excellent specimen of the romantic novel and heartily commended it to all lovers of sensational fiction. The *Topical Times* of London declared that Stoker had 'given us one of the most terrifically exciting novels that has seen the light since *Treasure Island* while the *Westminster Gazette* thought it an admirable story for the holiday season and a great advance in Stoker's powers as a writer of fiction. Provincial journals, such as the *Northern Whig* of Belfast and the *Liverpool Courier*, were also complimentary. Not everyone was equally convinced. The *Sunday Special*, in its review on 10 August 1902, was generally negative and the New York *Sun* commented that, while *Dracula* protested nothing and was impossibly real, *The Mystery of the Sea* was really impossible.[13]

In these opening years of the twentieth century, Stoker maintained an extraordinary level of literary fecundity, even if its quality was variable. In 1903, the year following the appearance of *The Mystery of the Sea*, he published another novel, *The Jewel of Seven Stars*. William Heinemann brought out the original text in London in June and an American edition by Harper & Bros appeared in February 1904. It was dedicated to two American sisters, Elinor (misspelled by Stoker as 'Eleanor') and Constance Hoyt, whom Stoker had met when they visited London in 1903. Elinor Morton Hoyt, who later achieved prominence as a poet and novelist under the name Elinor Wylie, was a noted beauty. Stoker may have been impressed by her looks but they may also have found common ground in their shared literary interests, including the work of Shelley, whose influence is evident in *The Jewel of Seven Stars*; Wylie's novel, *The Orphan Angel* (1926) imagines the poet's life as it might have been if he had not drowned.

The opening of *The Jewel of Seven Stars* has the distinct feel of a Sherlock Holmes story about it: a messenger arrives with a summons for the barrister, Malcolm Ross, who is the narrator of the novel: his Jermyn Street chambers recall Holmes's Baker Street rooms. The character of Superintendent Dolan, who had worked with Ross on the 'Brixton Coining' case, suggests the same provenance (Stoker had originally sketched out a detective character in his working notes for *Dracula*). Ross answers the summons of Margaret Trelawny whose father, Abel, is in a deep sleep from which he cannot be awakened, seemingly either drugged or under hypnotic influence. Dr Winchester, ministering to Trelawny, recalls the hypnotic sleep he had seen in the 'Charcot Hospital' in Paris. Stoker was here paying tribute to Jean-Martin Charcot, the nineteenth-century founder of modern neurology who was associated with Salpetrière Hospital in Paris and whose employment of hypnosis in investigating hysteria stimulated the interest in the psychological origins of neurosis by his pupil, Sigmund Freud in the 1880s. Charcot also described the symptoms of the medical condition, *locomotor ataxia*, resulting from syphilitic infection.

Through the character of Mr Corbeck, a seasoned traveller in the desert and expert in Egyptology, who has a Van-Helsing-like collection of fantastic academic qualifications, Stoker was able to display his considerable knowledge of ancient Egyptian religion and his familiarity with the work of the great Egyptologists, including Wallis Budge, the Keeper of Egyptian and Assyrian Antiquities in the British Museum. Stoker was a keen student of Budge's work and had in his library Budge's *History of Egypt* in nine volumes, his *Egyptian Ideas of the Future Life*, *Easy Lessons in Egyptian Hieroglyphics* and *The Egyptian Book of the Dead*. In 'The Primrose Path', published in 1875, Stoker had referred to Isis, an indication that he was familiar with Egyptian theology from his youth, probably under the influence of Sir William Wilde. Trinity College Dublin was a principal centre for the study of Orientalism in Britain and Ireland, with scholars like Edward Hincks (1792–1866) being among the leading pioneers in the field of Assyriology and Egyptology.

There was a fascination with the occult lore of ancient Egypt in Dublin literary circles of the later nineteenth and early twentieth centuries, evident in the use of Egyptian esoterica by the Hermetic Society of George William Russell (AE) and Yeats's absorption in Helena Blavatsky's *Isis Unveiled* (1877), which fused it with Irish nationalist sympathy for Ahmed Arabi Bey's efforts to free Egypt from Franco-British control. Egyptian themes also featured in nineteenth-century literature. 'Alciphron', by the Irish poet, Thomas Moore, a close friend of Byron and Shelley, was later elaborated into his novel, *The Epicurean* (1827), which dealt with the adventures of a young Athenian duped by the artifice of Egyptian priests. *A Strange Story* (1862) by Edward Bulwer-Lytton, whose work included a novel based on the story of Eugene Aram, featured a hero driven by a luminous evil spirit to rise at night in his sleep and take up a strange Egyptian wand. Arthur Conan Doyle's 'Lot No. 249' (1892) was concerned with the reanimated mummy theme. Stoker would have been aware both of the publication of Richard Burton's findings on Egypt in 1879 and of H. Rider Haggard's use of Egyptian material, including his novel, *Cleopatra* (1889). In *The Jewel of Seven Stars*, Stoker invents an ancient Egyptian Queen, Tera, who has claimed all the privileges of masculinity and dresses as a man, a not uncommon occurrence with Stoker's female characters, while the Egypt of her time is dominated by an ambitious priesthood. Tera has learned black magic but has also 'seen through the weakness of her own religion' and aspires to be resurrected in the North, 'whence blew invigorating breezes that make life a joy'.[14]

As a revived Abel Trelawny gives an outline of Egyptian theology, Ross quotes Shelley's 'Prometheus Unbound': 'The Magus Zoroaster . . . /Met his own image walking in the garden.' The passage quoted continues:

For know there are two worlds of life and death:
One that which thou beholdest; but the other
Is underneath the grave, where do inhabit
The shadows of all forms that think and live
Till death unite them and they part no more;
Dreams and the light imaginings of men,
And all that faith creates or love desires,
Terrible, strange, sublime and beauteous shapes.

The imagery here, of the Zoroastrian dualism of the Wise Lord, Ahura Mazda, and his opponent, Ahriman, the embodiment of evil, and of a world of undead spirits and dreams, recalls the spiritual landscape of *Dracula*. Abel Trelawny responds: 'Shelley had a better conception of ancient beliefs than any of our poets', a clear indication of the influence of the poet on Stoker's philosophical development. Stoker then connects these ancient beliefs with those of Christianity, when Ross speculates that death might not be final and the dead could rise again, with the 'Old Forces' coming into contact with the 'New Civilisation': 'Were those primal and elemental forces controlled at any time by other than the Final Cause which Christendom holds at its very essence? . . . Whence came that stupendous vision of the Evangelist which has for eighteen centuries held spellbound the intelligence of Christendom? Was there room in the Universe for opposing Gods . . .?'[15] Stoker is undermining the assumptions of his Christian readers by positing that there may be a duality of good and evil in the universe and that their God, the repository of their faith, may not be all-powerful after all. The fact that Ross's mind is 'brooding on the mysteries of the occult' hints at spiritual possibilities beyond conventional religion. As in *Dracula*, Stoker's audience is cautioned against assuming that they are possessed of definitive wisdom: 'We must not . . . believe too much in our present state of knowledge.' Abel Trelawny states that astrology was an exact science with the Egyptians two thousand years before Tera and speculates that the time may not be far off when astrology will be accepted on a scientific basis. He hopes to 'let in upon the world of modern science such a flood of light from the Old World as will change every condition of thought and experiment and practice'.[16]

On these philosophical foundations, Stoker builds a dual love and horror tale. Ross loves Margaret but she has become possessed by the spirit of Queen Tera, who is now determined to be resurrected, millennia after her death. Her tomb, which had been investigated by Abel Trelawny, was designed for this purpose and contains, among other wondrous objects, the Jewel of Seven Stars of the title, carved into the image of a scarab or dung beetle, a very common form of Egyptian amulet, which symbolises life and echoes the seven fingers on the hand of the mummified queen. Abel Trelawny's wife had died giving birth to a daughter who bears a remarkable resemblance to Tera. As she becomes possessed by the spirit of the dead Queen, Margaret begins to exhibit a duality similar to that of Dracula's victims, becoming increasingly aloof and dangerous. Abel Trelawny's well-fortified ancestral house in Cornwall is the scene for the denouement of the novel. It has a secret cavern in which Abel rigs up an electric light to illuminate the 'Great Experiment', an attempt to bring about the resurrection of Tera which Trelawny hopes will bring the knowledge of the ancient world back to the service of the present. There is more than a hint of necrophilia, as the un-wrapping of her mummy reveals the beauty of the nude Tera. A great storm, which appears to Ross to be almost a wrathful, living thing, rages and leaves Margaret sprawled dead on the ground.

Unlike *Dracula*, there is no happy ending, although public revulsion at its horror caused a more anodyne conclusion to be appended to a later edition. *The Jewel of Seven Stars* was natural cinematographic material and influenced the mummy movie genre. The films most obviously based on it include *Blood from the Mummy's Tomb* (1972), directed by Seth Holt, who died during filming, as did Peter Cushing's wife, causing him to withdraw from his role, and *The Awakening* (1980), directed by Mike Newell and featuring Charlton Heston and Susannah York. *Bram Stoker's The Mummy* (1997) was set in San Francisco.

Modern critics see a range of meanings in the novel, from articulation of contemporary political anxieties, to a fusion of the Whig and scientific narratives of history, to an exploration of the fascination with sexually aggressive women, as well as an unresolved allegory of female power.[17] Contemporaries were more straightforward in their reaction. J. Brodie-Innes told Stoker that he had read *Jewel* to his whole household and it was not just a good but a great book: 'It seems to me in some ways you have a clearer light on some problems which some of us have been fumbling in the dark after for long enough.'[18] While there were dissenting voices, reviewers on both sides of the Atlantic were fairly positive. Flattering comparisons were made to Poe, Jules Verne and H. Rider Haggard.[19] The New York *Herald* picked up on the seeming contradiction between Stoker's writing and his character:

How does Mr Stoker come by this quality, so eerie yet so edibly [*sic*] convincing? His is the heartiest of material existences. To see him active in his role of theatrical manager is to be aware of a vital, virile personality. Shut his bank book, close his theatre, end his colloquies with his satellites, send him home for the night, and, behold, he is off to some 'misty midregion of Weir,' between moonland and dreamland. Then must it be that the geist of Sir Henry Irving enters into him, compounded of Hamlet, Matthias, Macbeth, the Courier of Lyons and Louis XI, and the result, when he takes his pen in hand, is a novel where the ink marks run from the 'writing fluid' of commerce into transcendental blues and greens and lurid reds of the phantom worlds between dusk and dawn.[20]

In September 1905 Stoker published one of his longest romantic novels, *The Man*; it ran to 436 pages, divided into forty chapters, and cost six shillings. A British Empire edition appeared at the same time. He later shortened the text by 19,000 words for newspaper serialisation, in which form it was published in the American market, under the title *The Gates of Life*, by Cupples & Leon Co., in New York, in 1908, at 75 cents. A heavily abridged, rewritten version was published in London by Robert Hayes in the early 1920s.

The Man marked a change of tone from Stoker's previous two books, being largely concerned with the issue of the parameters of the relationship between the sexes. By creating a female character who challenged the conventions of the time, Stoker attempted to break new ground, for him at any rate, even if his conclusions ultimately collapsed into banality. The protagonist Stephen Norman, a middle-aged widower and owner of a great estate, Normanstand, is the father of a daughter called Stephen, a family name from time immemorial. By the age of fourteen, the female Stephen Norman has grown into a striking beauty and attracts the attention of Harold An Wolf, a broad-shouldered, six-foot two-inch, idealised version of Stoker himself. Harold's masculine superiority over the heroine is established by statements such as, 'Well, because after all you know, Stephen, you are only a woman and cannot be expected to know,' and he is allowed to have the better of the argument, beginning the book's agonised consideration of the respective roles of men and women and their relationship to each other. A rival, Leonard Everard, wins Stephen's heart by standing up to her. As sexual awareness stirs in her for the first time, Stephen starts to review her femininity and to see its 'defects' and decides that she will base her life, not on 'woman's weakness' but on 'man's strength'.[21]

In *Dracula*, Mina Harker noted tartly that the 'New Woman' would take it upon herself to propose marriage to the man in the future, reflecting the preoccupation with female empowerment and changing women's aspirations of the time. Legal, as well as psychological change was in the air. Changes to the Married Woman's Property Act in the later nineteenth century gave a woman the right to own her own property for the first time. An Act of

1907 would allow women to sit on borough and county councils. The modern critic, Elaine Showalter, has described the New Woman as 'an anarchic figure who threatened to turn the world upside down and to be on top in a wild carnival of social and sexual misrule'.²² Stephen Norman was not a full-blooded New Woman but she had definite ideas on challenging accepted male prerogatives, including the right to propose marriage. She proposes to Leonard Everard but he brutally rejects her. She then, in turn, rejects Harold. Harold changes his name to John Robinson, borrowed by Stoker from an old Trinity friend, and sets off for Alaska to start a new life in the wilderness.

On board ship for New York he encounters Andrew Stonehouse, an embodiment of American success, who has amassed a great fortune by unremitting work (he may have been modelled on Stoker's friend, James McHenry, an American railway magnate). Stonehouse is happily married and has a daughter, Pearl, aged six, who insists on playing with Harold, despite his general air of reserve. She calls him 'The Man'. Stoker's description of a great storm at sea drew on his many experiences of crossing the Atlantic with Irving; Harold, like Stoker, takes the storm in his stride but Pearl is swept overboard and Harold saves her. This incident of caring for a child in rough seas may have taken some inspiration from a real-life incident when Ellen Terry had put her son under Stoker's stewardship on a rough night on board the yacht of a Clyde shipyard owner in 1883. Pearl's father offers Harold a partnership in his business but Harold refuses. Surrogacy surfaces again when Stonehouse tells Harold that he is what he would wish his son to be.

While Harold is in Alaska making his fortune, Stephen succeeds to the title of the Earl de Lannoy and inherits the Earl's castle on the north-eastern coast of Britain. Stoker's description of Stephen's solitary state there, communing with nature, surely reflects his own experiences on holiday in Cruden Bay:

> Sometimes she would walk, all alone, far down to the sea-road, and would sit for hours on the shore or high up on some rocky headland where she could enjoy the luxury of solitude. At this time of her life there was an enjoyment in loneliness, so long as the forces of nature were around and apparent to her. At home with curtains drawn . . . loneliness was horrible. It seemed to fill the very air with ghosts; with memories; with vain, hopeless, helpless fears. But out in the open she felt free and at one with untrammelled things . . . After every such excursion she returned; fairly wearied in body, but with an inward calm and satisfaction which she had begun to fear would never be hers again.²³

After two years in northern Alaska, Harold boards a ship, the *Dominion*, for London with an ill-defined plan of seeing Stephen again. The *Dominion* runs aground in wild weather near Stephen's castle, and Harold's heroics enable the other passengers to be rescued. He, in turn, is saved and brought into the castle. Stephen does not recognise him but has 'a sort of idea that the stranger was God's guest who was coming to her house . . . Some great weight seemed to have been removed from her. Her soul was free again!'[24] Meanwhile the Stonehouses, who have read of 'Robinson's' feats in the Canadian papers, are convinced that he must be 'The Man' and visit Stephen, telling her of 'Robinson's' heroic rescue of their daughter. Discovering who he is, Stephen realises that she loves him and, at the end of the novel, waits for him to come to her at the edge of a cliff: 'She was all woman now; all-patient, and all-submissive. She waited for the man; and the man was coming!'[25]

Following its publication, the *Daily Illustrated Mirror* of London noted that *The Man* was 'meeting with strangely conflicting judgements from the Press'. Like a number of other reviewers, the critic in the *Daily Illustrated Mirror* knew Stoker personally and, possibly in extenuation of the bad reviews, described him as a hard worker, writing in what was supposed to be his leisure time, away from his duties to Irving. The *Bystander* too took a personal approach; while noting that *The Man* was written with Stoker's 'unfailing grace and vivacity of manner', it concentrated on a profile of him, complete with a photograph, claiming that he was chiefly a literary adviser to Henry Irving and was a 'splendid specimen of the brawny Irishman . . . His long residence in London has not robbed him in the least of his rich Irish brogue.' The *Literary World* also profiled Stoker in November 1905, as a follow-up to the review of the novel in September. It too featured a photograph and biographical information which obviously came from the subject himself.[26]

These highly positive personal profiles show how Stoker's position as a power in the theatrical world continued up to the death of Irving, even though his Lyceum was no more and the great actor was but a shadow of his former self. However, there were a number of deeply critical reviews of *The Man*, in the *Outlook*, and the *Saturday Review* as well as further afield, in the Chicago *Record Herald*, and the *Tasmanian Mail* which described it as a 'disheartening mass of unprofitable verbiage'. A female reviewer in the *Bristol Times* was strongly critical of Stoker's views on male–female relation-ships and thought the book 'almost incredible'.[27] Other reviewers were less negative, seeing both strengths and weaknesses in the novel: the *Yorkshire Post* felt that despite its blemishes it was readable. To *Vanity Fair* it was too carefully written but a notable book in its way, showing sympathetic insight into its female characters. The *Speaker* commented ambiguously that people who liked sentimental scenes and original situations would like the novel. For the *Manchester Guardian*, Stoker was a very unequal writer, who in *The Man* was at his best and his worst, having the gift to make the improbable seem plausible but failing with the commonplace and making Stephen Norman less believable than Dracula. A similar point was made by the reviewer in the *Birmingham Post* who took the view that the characters were too far removed from ordinary life.[28]

This negativity about a work which strikes the modern reader as quite incredible was more than balanced by a spate of positive reviews in significant London as well as provincial journals. A number of reviewers were very supportive of Stoker's seemingly clean-cut morality, of the absence in *The Man* of any hint of 'the salacious or the unwholesome', contrasting the 'enervating, neurotic atmosphere of the modern decadent novel' with 'the heartsome, tingling ozone which blows from the exciting pages of Mr Stoker'. The *Irish Times* applauded the 'powerful moral' that 'Woman is and must remain in the scheme of creation as Providence has placed her, and that if in her efforts at "emancipation" she oversteps certain rigidly defined limits she must be prepared for a troubled future.'[29] This interpretation of Stoker's work is indicative of the support which its reactionary societal messages enjoyed in the mainstream media of his time while modern criticism is also fascinated by it, albeit for entirely different reasons.[30]

FIFTEEN

The Final Curtain

And if I work, as work I shall, no matter trust or no trust, without my friend
trust in me, I work with heavy heart and feel, oh so lonely when I want all
help and courage that may be!'

(*Dracula*, Van Helsing to Dr Seward)

The combined effects of the Lyceum disasters in the years around the turn
of the century undermined Irving's acting ability, resources and health and
Stoker had now to soldier on with the increasingly forlorn and out-of-touch
figure, deprived of a theatre in which to act, consumed by a bitterness which
was, in Stoker's phrase, 'all for himself'. In his last seven years, from the
collapse of the Lyceum under his control to his death in 1905, Irving gave
up his old pleasures, including sitting up late with friends and associates,
and 'fostered that bitterness which had struck root already'. His happy
moods became 'rarer with his failing health' and Stoker did not see as much
of him in these last years as he had done previously. Stoker stated: 'We each
of us had his own work to do,' although how he was occupied, other than
working with Irving or writing, he does not make clear. With lavish entertainment now a thing of the past, Irving's isolation increased: 'When in
London he would linger and linger; the loneliness of his home made it in
a degree a prison house. My work became to save him all I could.'[1] Stoker's
own health was not always robust in these years: he was suffering from
pneumonia when Irving received an honorary degree at Glasgow in 1899,
the only time in their twenty-seven-year association when he was unable to
be present when the actor was being honoured in this way. His situation
was now akin to that of Van Helsing in *Dracula* when he declares: 'My life
is a barren and lonely one, and so full of work that I have not had much
time for friendships . . . and it has grown with my advancing years, the
loneliness of my life.'

Even falling back on old favourites like *Faust* could not rekindle the magic
of the past. Irving was now in his sixties and, like Ellen Terry, too old to
be convincing in many former roles. When Irving was reviving *Faust* in
1902, Terry was given to understand that she was too old to play Margaret.

Unwilling to undertake the lesser roles suggested, she went to play Queen Katherine in Frank Benson's *Henry VIII* at Stratford-upon-Avon. Shaking the dust off her feet, she noted tartly that the Lyceum reign was dying and taking an unconscionably long time about it.

Irving, however, could not afford to take a break: 'to fall back or to lose one's place in the running is to be forgotten'.[2] To keep going, he resorted to the use of stimulants, using burnt brandy to energise a weakening heart. His after-dinner speeches were now rambling and obscure, to the embarrassment of his audiences. The theatrical critic, George Goodale, saw Irving for the last time in February 1904 and his account of the actor underlined the difficulties Stoker must now have faced in keeping the show on the road: 'He [Irving] was then feeble in voice and limb, a fact that was painfully obvious to me, who had for twenty years been accustomed to associating his name and person with tremendous work and of course equally tremendous endurance. I felt then that the end was coming.'[3]

Irving decided on a two-year farewell tour, starting in June 1904, but by the time the second leg started in the spring of 1905 he was 'alarmingly ill' and Stoker was forced to postpone a later tour of the United States. Irving could not stop, however, because of his financial state of affairs: he stood to make a fortune from his farewell tours; the alternative was a poverty-stricken old age. An autumn tour began on 2 October 1905 and Irving arrived in Bradford a week later. The Mayor of Bradford gave a lunch at the Town Hall and presented a public address. Irving looked feeble: 'He seemed tired, tired; tired not for an hour but for a lifetime.' That evening he played Becket, his part ending with the line: 'Into Thy hands, O Lord! into Thy hands!' After the performance, Irving, unusually, shook hands with Stoker and left him with the words: 'God bless you!' echoing what he had written on his photograph all those years earlier, after his fateful recitation of 'Eugene Aram' for Stoker in Dublin. Shortly afterwards, Stoker received word that Irving was ill. He hurried to the Midland Hotel to find that Irving was already dead, having collapsed in the foyer at 11.50 p.m. In a macabre detail, Stoker closed his master's eyes but had to ask the doctor who arrived on the scene to straighten the eyelids.

As befitting a national figure, Irving was given a public funeral, on 20 October 1905; the Prince and Princess of Wales attended and the King and Queen were represented. Lady Irving, ignored in his substantial will (as were Stoker and Loveday), asked George Bernard Shaw's help in blocking his burial in Westminster Abbey. He replied that, as the widow of a famous actor buried in the Abbey, she could get a pension but as the widow of an exposed adulterer (his estate was divided between Mrs Aria and his sons), no Prime Minister would dare put her on the Civil List; she accepted his advice. Immediately after Irving's death and even before his funeral, his family demanded that Stoker hand over all matters to Irving's executors. It is difficult not to see a strong dislike of Stoker in this move, with almost indecent haste, to freeze him out of the picture. According to Shaw, Lady Irving was driven by an 'implacable Irish hatred' of her husband. Stoker's name was conspicuous by its absence from the funeral arrangements, prompting a kind and affectionate note from Ellen Terry: 'I do want to see your kind old face – but I am ill and scarce able to get on with my work . . . To think that you and poor L[oveday] were not more closely associated with the last scene at Westminster grieves me.'[4] Shaw, ironically, was invited to the funeral but refused. His view of the actor did not change: he wrote to the distinguished actor-manager, William Poel, in 1916 that 'Irving was an illiterate mutilator of every piece of fine dramatic literature he laid hands on.'[5]

In October 1906, a year after the actor was laid to rest, Stoker published his *Personal Reminiscences of Henry Irving* in two volumes at 25 shillings for the set. It was dedicated to Irving's loving friend and fellow actor, John Lawrence Toole, to whom Stoker devoted a chapter of the book. The American edition appeared a few weeks later, published by Macmillan at $7.50 for a boxed set. A single-volume revised edition was published in London by Heinemann in October 1907 at six shillings. A review of *Personal Reminiscences* in the *Times Literary Supplement* a few weeks after its publication set the tone for much subsequent comment. It was critical of Stoker's intrusion of his own personality and his 'Grand Ducal' manner, while making fun of his unconscious self-revelation. The tale he told of the Lyceum was 'of banquets and convivial suppers by the score. It reads like an account of one of the later Roman Emperors – life one long panorama of gorgeous display. The viands are of the choicest, the band is always playing, and the crowd is always cheering without . . . It was a dazzling time for both.'[6]

There was some truth in the *TLS*'s review but it was not the full picture by any means and flawed interpretations of the work, usually dismissing it as hagiography, continue to this day. Little effort has been made to understand the context in which it was written. Irving had just died, a shattered, anachronistic, embarrassing wreck who was still, nevertheless, a national icon. One of Stoker's main objectives was to explain how Irving came to such a tragic end while upholding the actor's national iconic status and defending his own role in Irving's affairs. Yet, for a supposed work of hagiography, there was little real warmth towards its subject apart from set-piece declarations of the depth and longevity of his friendship with Irving.

By contrast, Stoker displayed extraordinary affection in dealing with Ellen Terry. True, he does claim to have been Irving's most intimate friend – 'I knew him as well as it is given to any man to know another' – and he describes how a lifelong bond was formed at the time of their meeting in Dublin – 'a loving and understanding friendship' which lasted unbroken until Irving's death. Yet some of the references to Irving, as an 'ambitious young clerk'[7] for example, might well have given rise to resentment on the part of Irving's family and admirers.

Stoker laid bare some of the technique by which Irving disguised his lack of education by laboriously writing out and learning by heart speeches which appeared to be impromptu. Stoker's statement that 'there was always a possibility of creating a wrong impression somewhere' when Irving spoke, hints strongly that he was not very articulate. Other, somewhat condescending passages, convey a sense of Irving's lack of formal education and his inadequate expression of his philosophy. Complimentary references to Irving's intellectual, as opposed to his acting, ability, such as his ease in discussing Shakespeare with Browning, were rare enough. He was discreet about the relationship between Ellen Terry and Irving and his claim that their 'brotherly affection' remained undimmed until the end of Irving's life was disingenuous, to say the least, and was not fully accepted even by contemporaries.[8] Stoker's portrait of the great actor in decline in his later years, while not truly unvarnished, was sufficiently revealing to have been uncomfortable to contemporaries. He was, for example, forthright about Irving's spendthrift ways but it was in his coverage of Irving's handling of the disposal of the Lyceum and the establishment of the Lyceum Theatre Company that he was most critical of his erstwhile boss.

When Irving was buried at Westminster Abbey, Stoker described the scene in suitably Gothic terms: 'Slowly, imperceptibly, like shadows in their silence, the crowds gathered; a sombre mass closing as if with a black ring the whole precincts of the Cathedral [sic].' The muffled drums 'seemed to recall us to a life that has to be lived on, howsoever lonely or desolate it may be', a good description of Stoker's own dilemma. The final words of the *Personal Reminiscences of Henry Irving* were indicative of Stoker's need to steel himself to face an uncertain future: 'Duty calls. March! March!'[9] It was Stoker's fate to be associated with Henry Irving for the rest of his life. Stoker's 1912 obituaries in the London newspapers, *The Times* and the *Evening News*, stated confidently that, while he was the master of a particularly lurid and creepy kind of fiction, represented by *Dracula*, 'his chief literary memorial will be his *Reminiscences of Henry Irving*, a book which with all its extravagances and shortcomings – Mr Stoker was no very acute critic of his chief as an actor – cannot but remain a valuable record of the workings of genius as they appeared to his devoted associate and admirer.'[10]

Once *Personal Reminiscences* was published, Stoker went about getting it reviewed in his usual energetic fashion and it garnered some very encouraging notices. The *Sketch* pronounced it a triumphant success, a model of its kind. It sold well, with one survey of the books of 1906 stating that it had been among the most popular books of the autumn season. Another reviewer commented that it was on the shelves of most people who took any interest in theatrical matters. Stoker was, however, no longer the power he had been in the theatrical world and the book did not generally attract the sycophantic reviews he had achieved, when the Lyceum was at its zenith, for his least memorable fiction, such as *Miss Betty*, although he could still count on some favourable personal references in the media. Probably the most commonplace criticism was that Stoker had allowed too much of his own personality to intrude on the work, to the detriment of Irving. One satirical columnist invented an imaginary 'Who's Who for 1909': 'Stoker, Stoker; friend of the late Henry Irving and man of letters. Publication: Vol. I., Stoker. Vol. II., Stoker; in each of these volumes he found it impossible to omit all allusion to Henry Irving. Recreations: Stoker-Jitsu. Address: Stoker-Poges.'[11]

Reviews of the book also brought out some insightful reminiscences of both Irving and Stoker. A reviewer in Sheffield recalled that Stoker had lectured on Irving to the Sheffield Literary and Philosophical Society, making the point that the Cornish household in which Irving had been brought up 'was, to a large extent, moulded by the narrowing characteristics of the little sect of Bible Christians, and the only literary food for the child's imagination was the Bible, a book of old ballads, the *Pilgrim's Progress*, Foxe's *Book of Martyrs*, and *Don Quixote*'.[12] The theatrical critic, George Pomeroy Goodale remembered interviewing Irving on tour in the United States in 1884 when Stoker

> bustled about in his busy but silent and useful way, and so succeeded in keeping back other callers till my own time had expired. I did not then realize how diplomatically and unobtrusively this was accomplished; but in the light of subsequent experiences I learned how necessary such protecting interference was in the interest of Mr. Stoker's bedeviled and much-sought chief. Likewise I learned to appreciate the insinuating adroitness of the Stoker management of the situation.[13]

Stoker revisited the Lyceum in fictional form when he published *Snowbound, The Record of a Theatrical Touring Party*, in December 1908, stating that the truth or accuracy of the sketches might be accepted or not as the reader pleased; they were given as fiction. He was hinting strongly that they had a basis in reality and this was indeed the case. As early as 1884, Joseph Hatton gave an account of the Lyceum's train stuck in snow on a tour of the United States. Percy FitzGerald in his *Henry Irving, A Record of Twenty Years at the Lyceum* (1893), described the sight of the huge theatrical trains containing companies like the Lyceum, with a 'Pullman Car' in which the performers relaxed suggesting a deceptive luxury and prosperity. Austin Brereton's *Life of Henry Irving* (1908) also probed the often grim reality behind the seeming glamour of the long theatrical train rides in North America.[14] In his *Personal Reminiscences of Henry Irving*, Stoker had recounted how the trains were often delayed by minor accidents. In *Snowbound*, he uses the situation of a theatrical party marooned on board a train, stuck in American snowy wastes, as the vehicle for a series of sketches, a literary mechanism not unlike the dinner party for thirteen people, where each guest has to make up a strange incident, which Stoker had sketched out in his working notes for *Dracula*. Stoker also reused previously published material in *Snowbound*. For example, 'A Baby Passenger', which had appeared in *Lloyd's Weekly Newspaper* in February 1899, was used as the basis of the 'Chin Music' chapter in *Snowbound* with elements added, mainly to keep the continuity of *Snowbound*'s theatrical stories format. 'At Last' was written about 1903, on Stoker's last visit to America with Irving, where he sold it to *Collier's magazine*.[15]

The collection was published around the same time as *Lady Athlyne* and contained similar elements of Stoker's exploration of the nature of the Irish and Irishness. By having the narrator of one story, 'A New Departure in Art', recite Sheridan Le Fanu's poem, 'Shamus O'Brien', which 'went like wildfire' with the audience, Stoker calls on the ambiguity of his own Irish roots. Le Fanu's patriotic ballad centred on the rebellion of 1798. Alfred Perceval Graves explained that the later died-in-the-wool Tory, Le Fanu, wrote a 'rebel poem' based on his mother's admiration for the 1798 revolutionaries, Lord Edward FitzGerald and the Sheares brothers, both of whom were executed, but his experiences during the tithe war later 'drew him away from the people's side in politics'.[16] Le Fanu's family had much the same ambiguous political position as Stoker's own. Stoker was known to recite the poem as a party-piece for the Lyceum Company.

Personal experiences of a different sort underlay another story in *Snowbound*, 'Mick the Devil', in which the title character, Mick Devlin, was also an Irishman. Stoker seems to have amalgamated two real-life adventures of the Lyceum Company to create the basis for it: one was the story of the Lyceum train rushing over flooded bridges in 1884, *en route* from Cincinnati to Columbus; the other happened on 1 February 1896 as the

Lyceum was on its way to play in New Orleans. When it came to a creek at Bayou Pierre the train had to pick its way slowly over a flooded bridge, not knowing if it remained intact. The senior members of the party, whom Stoker termed 'Our little group', Irving, Ellen Terry and Loveday, took the experience calmly but others in the company were so panic-stricken that they confessed their sins, just as happens in *Snowbound*.

'A Deputy Waiter', the story of a gang of thieves who make the singing chambermaid sing the same song over and over to make it seem that she is practising, while they get away with the 'swag', ends with a toast being drunk to the unpopular tragedian, Wellesley Dovercourt: '". . . the glory of our Company, the pride of our Art" . . . The toast was drunk standing, and with a manifest respect on the part of all, which was a really effective tribute to his branch of his Art. Growl as they may, the companions of the Tragedian have always a secret respect, if not for the man, at least for the Artist.' This may have echoed the Lyceum Company's attitude towards Henry Irving, who was also a tragedian. Wellesley Dovercourt narrates another story, 'Work'us', in an elaborate fashion and with Irving's sardonic humour, even if one imagines that in real life the great actor would have been more aloof from the company. Towards the end of the story Stoker introduces Murphy: 'Being an Irishman, he was regarded by the Company as a humorist, and felt that he had to keep up that perilous reputation – just as he had to strain himself now and again to achieve a brogue.' This may derive from Stoker's experience as an Irishman in England. Murphy narrates 'A Corner in Dwarfs' about his experiences as a young man having to engage children illegally for a pantomime.

Although it appears towards the end of *Snowbound*, 'A Star Trap' was one of the earliest stories chronologically, having been published in slightly different form as 'Death in the Wings' in *Collier's Magazine* in November 1888. As Stoker recalled in *Personal Reminiscences of Henry Irving*, accidents were common in the theatre. He told of one in a New York theatre when a heavy gas cylinder fell on to the stage, missing Irving who was making a speech in front of the curtain but killing a limelight man underneath. 'A Star Trap' is the story of Mortimer, a beautiful young harlequin with whom all the women, including the married ones, are in love. One of these women is the young wife of Jack Haliday, the master machinist. The nub of the story is that Haliday doctors the trap which shoots the harlequin into the air so that it kills Mortimer. It is an effective horror story but is deflated at the end by the claim of the wardrobe mistress, who was there, that it is all a pack of lies, in much the same way that doubt is cast on the evidence underpinning the narrative at the end of *Dracula*.

PART FIVE

Under the Sunset

SIXTEEN

In the Valley of the Shadow

I shall try to do what I see lady journalists do, interviewing and writing
descriptions and trying to remember conversations.

(*Dracula*, Mina Murray to Lucy Westenra)

No more . . . duties at functions . . . no more of the bald, stale conven-
tionalities of an occupation which had lost its charm. He expected
every day to be now joyous with the realisation of ancient hopes. But
the expectation was not realised. The days seemed longer than ever,
and he actually yearned for something to fill up his time.[1]

When Lord Athlyne muses on his unhappiness at having nothing to do,
trying to persuade himself that this is freedom, he is mirroring the author's
predicament. Just before *Lady Athlyne* was published in 1908, Stoker had
written the story, 'In the Valley of the Shadow' (1907), in which the narrator
speaks of a 'blackness of despair' which grips him: 'This is the end of all
my little ambitions. This is, in truth, the bitterness of death.'[2] Other, friendly,
eyes observed Stoker's difficulty. Horace Wyndham, a visitor to Stoker's
home in these years, saw that:

Irving's untimely death must have been in many ways a great blow to
Bram Stoker. Apart from the sudden severance of a close friendship
between them that had existed for some forty years, it meant the abrupt
and entire cessation of his sole source of income. He had drawn a large
(but well-earned) salary from the Lyceum treasury, and had lived up to
every penny of it. Accordingly, on Irving's death, the problem of ways
and means began to press rather hardly. Still, despite the fact that he
was getting on in years, Stoker had plenty of grit, and thrust himself
into the rough-and-tumble anew, and with characteristic vigour. But he
met with many rebuffs, for the Lyceum tradition was not wanted in the
quarters where he offered his services. He even went after a five-pound-
a-week job at a Manchester Exhibition, and when the committee turned
him down, he did his best to get it for me instead.[3]

After the closure of the Lyceum and even before Irving's death, Stoker busied himself in a wide variety of activities. His situation now has been prefigured fictionally in *Dracula*, when Jonathan Harker declares: 'I did not know what to do, and so had only to keep on working in what had hitherto been the groove of my life. The groove ceased to avail me . . .' In 1902 he attended an exhibition at the Glasgow Fine Art Institute and a newspaper stated that 'Nothing . . . could have better exemplified the generous heart and kindly disposition of the big, genial Irishman' than his offer of a special gold medal for an imaginative study by the School of Art students. A Mr Newbery offered to make him Professor of Imagination to the art students when he grew tired of his present calling.[4]

But his changed situation was obvious both from the kind of work he attempted and the responses he elicited. Having turned down an offer by George Alexander of the job of business manager of the St James's Theatre in 1904 (as manager of St James's Theatre from 1891, Alexander had produced many major plays of the era, including Oscar Wilde's *Lady Windermere's Fan* and *The Importance of Being Earnest*), the level to which Stoker sank shortly afterwards is exemplified in an exchange of correspondence with William Gillette, an actor and playwright, in November 1905, just a month after Irving's death. Stoker wrote with a query: 'The Daily Telegraph – to which I am now attached – is interested in a question now being discussed in Paris. "Are Charities, benefited by actors' autographs – or can they be?" Would you let me have a line with your views . . .' Gillette's response was dismissive, with a note underneath: 'See here Stoker I answered as above before I deciphered your name. But bless my heart, my answer is the same now.' Stoker received a similar offhand response to the same query from Laurence Irving.[5] Overall, there is a pervasive sense of Stoker's diminished importance in his correspondence of the era. For example, we find Sir Lawrence Alma-Tadema, the artist who had been a friend of Stoker's for many years, asking him in 1901 to help find employment for a lady artist but regretting in 1907 that he cannot attend the dance performance of a Miss Hincks, whom Stoker was promoting, as he was too busy.[6] Florence's correspondence, too, suggests that she is sometimes working hard to make a social impression, without getting much encouragement.[7]

In October 1906, a number of newspapers announced that Madame Liza Lehmann, the talented song-writer, had completed a musical version of Goldsmith's *The Vicar of Wakefield* which had been arranged by the artist and writer, Laurence Housman, younger brother of the poet, A.E. Housman. Stoker was involved in the adaptation. Lehmann wrote to thank him for his suggestions and verses: 'I have embodied your idea in a short episode *very greatly* to the advantage of the piece . . .' She described it as idyllic, not grand, opera, 'delightfully melodious' and making considerable use of melodrama. Rehearsals started on 16 October with Isabel Jay as Olivia and David Bispham as the Vicar. Stoker was now acting as business manager to David Bispham, a well-known singer. They had long moved in the same theatrical circles with others such as Oscar Wilde and Henry Brodribb Irving, the great actor's son. Ironically, perhaps, when Isabel Jay and Bispham had written years previously to Henry Irving requesting the Lyceum version of *Olivia*, his letter of refusal was probably written by Stoker, whose familiarity with the stage version may well have had a bearing on his involvement with this musical. The Irish tenor, John McCormack, auditioned for the tenor role and impressed Stoker but McCormack ultimately rejected it. The production followed the usual procedure of touring the provinces – Newcastle, Manchester and Glasgow – before opening in London in November 1906. It ran at the Prince of Wales Theatre for several weeks but was not a success and this episode effectively ended Stoker's engagement with the theatre.

Stoker gained the company of his brother, Thomas, following Tom's retirement to London in 1899. Tom was the sibling whose education and career most closely paralleled his own. Born two years after Bram, on 20 August 1849, he too was educated at Trinity College Dublin and joined the Civil Service after graduation. Tom Stoker served in the Indian Civil Service from 1872 to 1899, holding the posts of Inspector-General of Registration and Commissioner of Excise and Stamps from 1891 to 1896 and was Chief Secretary to the Government of India from 1896 until his retirement in 1899. He married Enid, daughter of William Robert Bruce, Master of the King's Bench, Ireland, when he was almost forty-two. Florence called on the Tom Stokers just after their marriage and reported with exquisite condescension to her mother that her new sister-in-law was not pretty but had nice quiet manners.

A series of letters written by Tom to Enid in the 1890s paint a vivid picture of life in the Raj at that time.[8] The letters also provide some insights into Stoker family life. One contains a reference to Tom suffering from asthma, which raises the possibility that it may have run in the family and, if so, it could have had a bearing on the mysterious childhood illness that afflicted Stoker in his early years. Another mentions Charlotte Stoker sending seeds, showing how she remained involved with the lives of her children in their adult years. The inscription on the back of a photograph of Tom associated with this series of letters – 'no one is to bully me. Signed – Tom Stoker' – is indicative of the rough-and-tumble of his childhood among six siblings. Freudian interpretations of Stoker's childhood make much of supposed discordance among his siblings but all the extant evidence of their adult lives points to an exceptionally close-knit group. Tom stayed with his sister Matilda and her French husband, Charles, and reported that they were very happy; he expressed the hope that his own marriage would be equally so. He too stayed with his brother George in London and with Thornley in Dublin. And when Tom took up residence in London after his retirement, he lived at 42 Egerton Crescent, not very far from Bram and Florence in Chelsea. The two brothers were obviously close, as Tom features prominently in a profile of Stoker which appeared in the *Literary World* in 1905, to coincide with the publication of Stoker's novel, *The Man* and the information in the article bears all the hallmarks of having come from Stoker himself.[9] Tom too tried his hand at writing: his story, 'The Pundit', was published in the October 1900 issue of the *Pall Mall Magazine*. Tom had, in fact, had 'The Pundit' privately published in a collection of five short stories the previous year.[10] The story of an apparently deracinated Hindu who had become 'aggressively European' in dress and manners but who was actually operating an elaborate scam at the expense of his colonial masters, 'The Pundit' shares many of the preoccupations of Stoker's fiction: the nature of identity, cultural inter-action, between East and West especially, disguise, concealment and decep-tion, as well as displaying an ironic scepticism about the nature of the colonial enterprise in which Tom had spent his career. Tom was concerned and sympathetic when Sir Henry Irving died in 1905. He sent telegrams and followed up with a letter: putting the best gloss on it, he wrote that Irving was lucky to have died at the zenith of his powers, but he was keeping in touch with Florence who was worried – rightly, as it turned out – about the effect of Irving's death on Stoker.[11] Tom outlived Bram by many years but he remained friendly with his brother's widow and family.

Stoker's relationship with his sister Margaret and her husband, Sir William Thomson was less happy. Thomson succeeded Thornley as President of the Royal College of Surgeons in 1896 and, like him, was knighted. After serving with George Stoker in the Irish Hospital Corps during the Boer War, where they fell out, he returned to find himself showered with honours but with his practice gone and his income wretchedly small. He resorted to borrowing within the family. Margaret felt the humiliation of her circumstances keenly and bitterly resented the lack of support from her siblings, Thornley especi-ally. Part of Margaret's difficulty may have been political. She was dismis-sive of Thornley's Home Rule politics, which she attributed to the malign influence of his wife. However, she overlooked the fact that Bram shared these views and that they formed the basis of a political and personal alliance between the two brothers. Thomson died without recovering his situation and the newly widowed Margaret wrote to Tom Stoker in 1909 that she had 'always felt that you mistrusted the honorability of his conduct in the relations between himself and Dr. George Stoker . . .'[12]

Stoker was in no position to help the Thomsons in the first decade of the twentieth century. He was active on the lecture and after-dinner speaking circuit, putting his extrovert character and public speaking abilities to good use. Just how a good a speaker he was is clear from the accounts of contemporaries; one description, from 1905, while positive, alluded to a solitary streak in this most sociable of men:

> Needless to say, Mr. Bram Stoker is an Irishman through and through. A word from 'the man' or a glance from his big, burly figure, not to mention impetuous manner of talking and walking, leave no doubt as to his origin. With a keen sense of humour, and an almost inexhaustible repertoire of funny and characteristic stories, Bram Stoker is as fluent and witty a speaker as he is eloquent as a writer. Impulsive, quick-tempered, generous, and moody, like most complex personalities, he is liable to be misunderstood by the mere outsider, but to those who look below the surface and can sympathise with the artistic and literary temperament, Bram Stoker is as popular as he can be genial. A philosopher, and fond of his own society, preferring to spend most of his leisure amongst the characters of his creation, Bram Stoker has yet varied interests and his views are of a very broad-minded nature.

His friend, Hall Caine, also paid tribute to his abilities as a speaker: 'Some hint of this would occasionally reveal itself among the scarcely favourable conditions of a public dinner, when, as a speaker . . . he would strike, in the soft roll of his rich Irish tongue, a note of deep and almost startling emotion that would obliterate the facile witticisms of more important persons.'[13] In February 1907 he was warmly received when he travelled to Ireland to give a lecture to the Cork Literary and Scientific Society on 'The Organisation of a Theatre'. Around the same time, he presided over numerous debates and at banquets. He modelled for a portrait of 'William II building the Tower of London' for a panel in the Royal Exchange in London. He kept in touch with the theatre and his advice was still sought by some but his play, *Paul Ransome*, was rejected by the actor-manager of St James's Theatre in 1908, as clever and dramatic but ultimately unsuitable.

Stoker busied himself in the affairs of the Society of Authors, founded in 1884 to promote the interests of writers, and crossed swords with George Bernard Shaw, another of the society's activists. At a special general meeting convened to consider changing its constitution, Stoker found himself in opposition to the Fabian axis of Sidney Webb and Shaw and lost a series of votes on legalistic amendments. Their disagreements flared up in public view in 1907 when they differed on the issue of the Times Book Club. The club sold virtually new books to the public at heavily discounted prices and a dispute had arisen in 1906 between *The Times* and the Publishers' Association, which felt that the newspaper was in breach of the Net Book Agreement of 1901, whose purpose was to maintain a fixed retail price for books. In a letter to the *Daily Mail* in October 1906, Hall Caine opposed the NBA, which he felt was inimical to the interests of readers as well as authors. Shaw wrote to *The Times* in March 1907 defending his viewpoint in a row which had broken out in the Society of Authors over an attempt by publishers to organise a boycott of the Times Book Club. Shaw sided with *The Times* (as did Hall Caine) and Stoker with the publishers:

> Mr. Sidney Lee must have noticed that most of the authors who spoke against him were as mad as hatters on the subject. Take the case of Mr. Bram Stoker. His publisher has assured us that his 'Reminiscences of Sir Henry Irving' [*sic*] had not done any the worse for his refusal to sell it to *The Times* Book Club, a statement which no sane person could possibly have believed, though no doubt it was made with all the pathetic good faith of monomania on the warpath. Mr. Stoker gave away his publisher by avowing that he had suffered; but he declared with tears in his voice that he was proud of his martyrdom, and implied that he would willingly go to the stake with Mr. Heinemann in so good a cause as the destruction of *The Times* . . . All pretence that the publishers were acting in our interests was dropped . . . what carried the day was the passion for suffering like Mr. Stoker's . . .

The *Publisher and Bookseller* commented: 'We wish Mr. Shaw had tried to justify his doubt of Mr. Stoker's sanity with some shadow of proof. On the other side, there is no lack of evidence to show that both Mr. Stoker and his publisher acted on sound commercial principles.' Stoker had chosen the winning side, in that the Net Book Agreement survived until the 1990s. Notwithstanding these differences, there was some evidence of mutual influence in their writings. For example, the phrase 'The unexpected always happens' occurs both in *Dracula* and in *Man and Superman* (1903), where Shaw describes the relationship of the true artist to women as 'half-vivisector, half-vampire'.[14]

Stoker was involved in various other minor activities in the years leading up to his death. Both Irving and he had been members of a committee, set up in 1905, to build a Shakespeare memorial at the House of Lords and Stoker continued to be active in the project after Irving's death. Others involved included theatrical figures such as Sir Herbert Beerbohm Tree and Sir Johnston Forbes-Robertson, as well as Sir Aston Webb, architect of the Victoria and Albert Museum in London. Stoker was one of the signatories of a letter to the press on the subject in April 1908, which caused the *Yorkshire Post* to denounce the scheme the following month as 'absurd and impracticable' in the light of Stoker's negative attitude to the establishment of a national theatre.[15] Around the same time, Stoker acted as honorary secretary of a theatrical exhibition in Paris under the auspices of the French government.

In his Lyceum days, Stoker had enjoyed a healthy income. He had, however, suffered financial setbacks in the early 1890s, with his failed investments in Heinemann's continental publishing venture and Mark Twain's 1894 scheme. That he needed to borrow £600 from Hall Caine in 1896 shows that his finances had not recovered and presumably were still under strain at the time of the Lyceum's collapse in 1898. Following Irving's death, he was dependent for current income on what he could derive from publication. Opinions differ as to the seriousness of his financial situation; there are grounds for believing that he was living in virtual poverty (Stoker's own letters paint a fairly dismal picture and the offer of Anne, Lady Ritchie, the writer and literary editor who was the eldest daughter of the novelist, William Makepeace Thackeray, that Florence might read to her in the evenings for 3s. 6d. a time must have been humiliating) but he did leave a considerable estate on his death, the net value of which was £4,664, a substantial sum for the era (and to which Thornley's bequest of £1,000 would soon be added). Given the declining state of his health, Stoker may have been motivated to conserve his capital and limit current expenditure by a concern for how Florence would manage after his death: he had, after all, no pension and it would have seemed unlikely that his books would generate a reasonable income.

In February 1911, at the suggestion of his friend, Lady Ritchie, he set out his situation in applying to the Royal Literary Fund for a grant. As a result of 'another break-down' the previous year, he stated that he had been unable to do any work, with the exception of completing a book begun some time before, the preparatory study for which had already been largely done. This book was *Famous Impostors*, which had just been published, but Stoker did not anticipate receiving royalties from it for about a year. Even more to the point, he did not consider himself able to write other books: 'At present

I do not know whether I can in the future do much, or any, literary work, and I am emboldened to look to my fellow craftsmen in my difficulty.' He claimed to have no regular income except dividends from a small investment totalling £409 in capital. The previous year, 1910, he had received £166 for literary work, including advance royalties (Hall Caine had discreetly helped out with a loan in March of that year). While this may have been more than the average wage of the era, the Committee of the Royal Literary Fund, saw things differently and he was awarded £100 in March 1911; Stoker thanked the Fund for its 'most generous grant'.[16]

Most of Stoker's non-fiction work was published after the death of Irving and was no doubt part of an effort to keep himself afloat financially. There were a few exceptions. In August 1889, as Stoker and Henry Irving discussed stage art on their way to a holiday in the Isle of Wight, Stoker wrote down Irving's comments on the spot and some months later published a piece on 'Actor-Managers' in the *Nineteenth Century*, a predictable defence of the system of actor-managers of which Irving was the leading exponent. Stoker's 'Dramatic Criticism', published in the *North American Review* in 1894, in response to the assertion of the drama critic, William Archer, that the actor was a parasite upon the play, was altogether more combative. In the course of a savage attack on the alleged provincialism of certain dramatic critics, Stoker went so far as to allege that their ranks included criminals, lunatics, hospital cases, cranks and faddists. Whatever the reasoning behind it, his full frontal condemnation of the critics was an unusual tactic for a man whose media-handling skills were of the highest order and he drew hostile fire. The *Daily News* of 9 March 1894 contented itself with stating that Stoker had been very hard on provincial critics but the 'Spectator' column in the *Star* mocked Stoker's use of his academic qualifications: 'Mr. Bram Stoker . . . describes himself as M.A., but is, perhaps, even better known as a pleasant Irishman and acting manager of Mr. Henry Irving, LL.D.' Hinting at the incongruity of Stoker's attack on a medium he was adept at controlling: 'Mr. Stoker is a most amiable man . . . Everyone who knows him likes him,' the columnist intimated that he was most likely doing Irving's bidding: 'The voice, some hasty people may say, is the voice of Mr. Bram Stoker, M.A. (and a very pleasant Irish voice it is, too, with the sweetest little touch of the brogue), but the thoughts are the thoughts of Mr. Bram Stoker's chief.'[17] During Irving's lifetime, Stoker also wrote 'The Art of Ellen Terry', which appeared in the *Playgoer* in 1901, as did his poem, 'One Thing Needful', republished the following year.

In 1907 Stoker published two pieces on Ireland's major cities, Dublin and Belfast, in the *World's Work*. The journal devoted its May issue to Ireland in the belief that 1907 would be a special year for the country, with a royal visit in the offing, the prospect of Home Rule seemingly providing a solution to its political problems and a world's fair being held on the site of what is now Herbert Park in Dublin. In the words of its editorial, the purpose was to carry 'a message of hope from a new Ireland' whose salvation was to be accomplished by economic regeneration and cultural renaissance, symbolised by the success of the Gaelic League, which had 'sent a new thrill of life throughout the length and breadth of the Island'.[18] If Stoker did not write the editorial, its sentiments were close to his beliefs, as he made clear in his two articles. The subheading of the first, 'The Great White Fair in Dublin', said it all: 'How there has arisen on the site of the old Donnybrook Fair a great exhibition as typical of the new Ireland as the former festival was of the Ireland of the past' and Stoker hammered home his message of regeneration in the text, linking this late work with his early address as Auditor of the Trinity College Dublin Historical Society:

> The days of the Donnybrook Fair and all it meant, the days of the stage Irishman and the stagey Irish play, of Fenianism and landlordism are rapidly passing away, if they have not even now come to an end ... there has come in its place a strenuous, industrious spirit, spreading its revivifying influence so rapidly over the old country as to be worth more than even historical bitterness and sentimental joys.[19]

Stoker's second article, on the Harland and Wolff shipbuilding yard in Belfast, was a generally factual account, without political comment. Harland and Wolff later built the *Titanic* whose sinking would dominate news coverage at the time of Stoker's death.[20]

A few months after these articles appeared, on 28 July 1907, Stoker's interview with Arthur Conan Doyle appeared in the *World*, New York; a shorter version was published in the *Daily Chronicle* in London on 14 February 1908. Stoker's description of Doyle's house as almost a 'fairy pleasure house' recalled his own love of fairy tales and his use of them in his fiction. While Stoker made no reference to their shared experiences in the Irish Literary Society, he did attribute Doyle's love of literature to the influence of his mother, a wonderful storyteller of 'Anglo–Celtic stock'. Stoker focused on interests which he had in common with Doyle: criminology, a love of athletics and admiration of the United States.

Not all potential interviewees were as accommodating as Arthur Conan Doyle. Stoker called at Thomas Hardy's flat in the summer of 1907 in an attempt to interview him for the *New York World*. The name of the paper, however, brought back memories of its terrible review of *Jude the Obscure* in 1896 and Hardy wrote to Stoker a letter of polite but firm refusal, adding that if he were ever to agree to be interviewed, he would wish Stoker to do it.[21] Stoker generally had some connection with people he approached for an interview in these years. He was, in effect, trading on his old Lyceum network of contacts to generate some income. When he asked the scientist and antiquarian, Lord Avebury (whose family owned a bank), for his views about the present state of the financial world, to appear in the *New York World*, he did not know him personally but mentioned their mutual acquaintance, Canon Jack Robinson, a 'very dear friend' of his college days. Stressing that the circulation of the paper was enormous, Stoker set out the terms of the proposed interview: it would cover the man himself, his surroundings and a short chat. The typescript would be submitted for alterations and Stoker promised 'good faith'. He was as good as his word; he sent the draft text, which he had put into 'popular' form, for approval.[22]

Stoker again collected a favour from an old friend when he interviewed Sir W.S. Gilbert for the *New York World* later that year. While the piece contained little of intrinsic interest, Gilbert's public profile ensured that it was picked up by a number of other newspapers. Shortly after it had appeared in the *Daily Chronicle*, Stoker presided at the January 1908 dinner of the Vagabond Club at the Hotel Cecil in London and gave a eulogy of Gilbert, 'who had made a name for himself and done good work for the civilised world'. Around the same time, *Punch* carried a full-page spoof of the interview, under the heading, 'A Great Critic at Home'. This underlines the fact that Stoker still loomed sufficiently large in the Edwardian public consciousness to be the target of such satire.[23] A week after the Gilbert piece had appeared, the *Daily Chronicle* published Stoker's interview with Winston Churchill. Churchill agreed to see him because he had read *Dracula* – he was a fiction writer himself who had Poe among his books – and Stoker had been impressed by one of his short stories, the grim 'Man Overboard', about the last thoughts of a drowning man. Churchill was also influenced by the fact that Stoker had been a friend of his father, Randolph Churchill, who served as an unofficial secretary to his father, the seventh Duke of Marlborough, and Lord-Lieutenant of Ireland from 1876 to 1880. Stoker and Randolph Churchill moved in similar circles in Dublin prior to Stoker's departure in 1878: Churchill proposed a motion and spoke at the Trinity College Historical Society in 1877. The friendship continued after Stoker moved to London. Randolph Churchill came often to the Lyceum and was friendly with Irving; like so many of the late Victorian elite, he dined occasionally at the Lyceum's Beefsteak Room. In the late 1880s, Randolph had introduced the young Winston – then aged about thirteen – to Stoker, telling him that Winston would be 'a good 'un', promise which Stoker felt he had fulfilled by 1908. Stoker was impressed by Winston's physiognomy: 'The man with such a hand should go far.'[24] Winston Churchill maintained his connections with Stoker and the Lyceum network. He gave a dinner for Ellen Terry when he was Under-Secretary of State for the Colonies (1906–8) and Stoker was among those present. Florence gave a copy of *Personal Reminiscences of Henry Irving* as a wedding present when Churchill was married in 1908.

Stoker's advocacy of censorship has generated a good deal of interest in recent years, with critics seeing it as evidence of repressive tendencies, which relate to undercurrents in his fiction. It has even been argued that *Dracula* reflects a lifelong desire on Stoker's part to defend the arts from association with immorality.[25] As already noted, he did speak in favour of a motion that modern drama exhibited symptoms of degeneracy when he was an undergraduate at Trinity. As acting manager of the Lyceum, he was on good terms with George Redford, the examiner of plays at the Lord Chamberlain's Office, who declared himself always pleased to have a chat with Stoker, who could call on him at home or at his office.[26] It was, however, with the closure of the Lyceum that the defence of censorship became something of an *idée fixe* with Stoker. At a press dinner in 1903, he claimed that drama 'taught high-minded lessons of self-denial and patriotism, and it ought to have a worthy place in every disciplined state'. In October 1907, his address to a meeting of the White Friars Club, a London institution catering to those with an interest in the arts and science, was 'teeming with references to objectionable fiction', and his declaration that he was starting a crusade against the prurient novel 'created a sensation and provoked keen discussion'.

> 'This abomination – the fully-conceived [*sic*] novel,' cried Stoker, 'has great vogue both in Britain and America, and belongs to the category of pestilence that must be stamped out.
>
> 'We journalists and authors have the deepest responsibility in the matter. Our responsibility is equalled by that of the publishers.'
>
> At the close of the meeting, Stoker, whose Irish brogue gave a peculiar charm to the address, was surrounded by a throng of writers, who showered him with congratulation.

He returned to the subject the following month at a meeting of the Authors' Club when his call for an 'intellectual police', to keep immoral writers in order, generated wide publicity.[27] In an essay in the *Nineteenth Century and After* in 1908, Stoker argued that freedom must be buttressed by the self-restraint, which is, of course, practised by many of the virtuous characters in his fiction. Censorship of drama was based on the need to combat human weakness and was part of the war between God and the Devil. To prevent a downward spiral into decadence, censorship must be continuous and rigid and the powers of evil must be combated all along the line. Here we see a concept of evil as a welling phenomenon, which is about to burst the dam of virtue and engulf society, a danger previously manifest in a line of his fictional villains, including Dracula. In Stoker's mind, there was a sugges-tion of evil in all things, even in the imagination, but the fundamental problem was sexual: 'the only emotions which in the long-run harm are those arising from sex impulses'. The 'filthy and dangerous output' of writers on lewd subjects must be suppressed: 'if the plague-spot continues to enlarge, a censorship there must be'. Those who prostitute their talents to base ends might enjoy material rewards but could not expect 'the pleasures or the profits of the just – love and honour, troops of friends, and the esteem of good men'.[28]

Whether Stoker knew of his own likely syphilis at this time and was attempting to build societal structures that would prevent others suffering his fate is a moot point. However, it would be a mistake to see this piece as written by a syphilitic degenerate, as it is among Stoker's most lucid essays, whatever one thinks of its illiberal sentiments. He would also write clearly rational works after this and to connect it with the confusion evident in *The Lair of the White Worm* is to create a specious chain of logic. Stoker's interest in the concept of degeneration went back to his Trinity College auditorial address and derived from his upbringing and shaping by puritan influences. He returned to the issue with 'The Censorship of Stage Plays', published in the *Nineteenth Century and After* in the latter half of 1909. Stoker's piece was a negative examination of a report of a parliamentary commission on the censorship of stage plays. True to the old Lyceum values, he condemned literature dealing with the 'grim realities of life'. Stoker had, in fact, given evidence before the joint committee of both Houses of Parliament appointed to inquire into this subject in August 1909, together with George Bernard Shaw, G.K. Chesterton, J.M. Barrie and other distinguished literary and theatrical figures. He defended the system of censorship by the Lord Chamberlain and said it ought to be maintained as it had not hindered the growth of English drama. Stoker took exception to the Authors' Society being considered representative of authors as a body and asked that its evidence be regarded as representing only individual views. He had been a member of the society for over twenty years, but had left it because of its 'absolutely wrong ideas'.

Stoker claimed that West End theatre managers were satisfied with the present system of censorship. He certainly had some support for his views: a representative of the Theatrical Managers' Association expressed the strongest protest against abolition of censorship and a statement was read from Mrs D'Oyly Carte, the remarkable widow of Richard D'Oyly Carte who had founded the Savoy Theatre, in favour of the retention of the existing system. Some actors' organisations also supported the continuation of censorship: A.B. Walkley, drama critic of *The Times* and President of the Society of Dramatic Critics, believed censorship to be justified while W.S. Gilbert thought that audiences needed to be protected against 'outrages'. However quaint they may appear now, Stoker's ideas were representative of a powerful stream of thought in the theatrical business in which he had spent the majority of his working years. Also, he did not wholeheartedly embrace the thinking embodied in Max Nordau's *Degeneration* (1895), a vitriolic assault on much of nineteenth-century art as morally degraded. For example, while Nordau strongly attacked Gautier, along with his fellow nineteenth-century French writers, Baudelaire, Verlaine, Villiers de L'Isle-Adam and Huysmans as degenerate, Stoker found Gautier's *Mademoiselle de Maupin* a 'fascinating romance' and dealt sympathetically with the background of the real character in his *Famous Impostors*.[29]

Stoker's penultimate book, *Famous Impostors*, was published in London and New York in December 1910. He was asked to write it by the London publisher, Sidgwick & Jackson, an important fact to bear in mind for those who might see it solely as a natural outcome of Stoker's concern with secrecy and deception. He worked on the book throughout 1910. An unpublished preface, composed in August of that year, is well written and closely reasoned, demonstrating that he was not suffering from dementia (as has been claimed) less than two years before his death. Notes he made at this time reveal ambition to write further sections, which were not, however, realised.[30] The book was divided into chapters, such as 'Pretenders', 'Practitioners of Magic', 'The Wandering Jew', 'Witchcraft and Clairvoyance', 'Women as Men' and 'The Bisley Boy'. Many of the concerns embedded in Stoker's fiction are evident in his handling of this material: disguise, secrecy and deception;[31] the relationship between the sexes and ambiguity about gender; witchcraft and the occult; and the tension between credulity and science, a major element in his fiction, especially *Dracula*. For example, in the section dealing with 'Witchcraft and Clairvoyance' he notes that it 'is no easy task in these days, which are rationalistic, iconoclastic and enquiring, to understand how the commonality not only believed in witchcraft but acted on that belief' and records the shock of finding 'such a weird and impossible credulity [about witchcraft] actually rooted in the Statute Book of one's own country'.[32]

It was, however, the section on the 'Bisley Boy' which made the greatest impression. It investigated the claim that Queen Elizabeth I of England may have a man, the original female child having died in infancy and a male child substituted in her place. The inspiration came from a friend of Stoker's, Bertha Nicoll, who made him aware of the legend attached to Overcourt, a manor house in Bisley, part of the dowry of Queen Elizabeth I where the substitution allegedly took place. Although he was initially sceptical, preliminary investigation convinced Stoker that the theory could not altogether be put aside. He went over the ground with some friends at Bisley and, in his mind, possibility became probability. He pursued his research in the Public Record Office and the British Museum and its quality is evident in the impressive range of sources on Queen Elizabeth I used in the book. In its edition of 19 February 1911, under the heading 'Was Queen Elizabeth a Man?' the *Chicago Sunday Examiner* gave a three-page spread to the story, with many illustrations. While some American reviewers felt that Stoker had made a plausible case for the Bisley Boy theory, not everyone was convinced. One pointed out that the coffin at Bisley was six feet long and hewn of stone, making it unlikely to have been that of the female infant who was supposed to have died there. The *Saturday Review* described the Bisley Boy as the ingenious, if preposterous, gem of the tales in the book, most of which, it felt, could interest only unsophisticated readers or those sufficiently sophisticated 'to enjoy the humours of the writer's comically inflated style'.[33] The Bisley Boy story is nowadays accepted as having been the jocose invention of Thomas Kemble, Rector of Bisley from 1827, to fit the facts of the discovery of a child's skeleton in an old grave in the area.

SEVENTEEN

Bourgeois Fantasy

> And, too, it made me think of the wonderful power of money!
> What can it not do when it is properly applied . . .
>
> (*Dracula*, Mina Harker's Journal)

Stephen Arata's description of *Dracula* as 'a bourgeois fantasy of aristocratic power and privilege'[1] could be applied even more obviously to Stoker's *Lady Athlyne*. It was published eleven years after his Gothic masterpiece, in 1908, although he had been working on it since at least 1901. The irony was that the Irish 'Ascendancy', to which the Earl of Athlyne belongs, had been in decline from the 1870s, when they moved from an assured social position to increasingly being viewed as alien by themselves and by others, while both their property and influence diminished. The central male character of *Lady Athlyne* is an Anglo–Irish hybrid, the Earl of Athlyne, who is not only Irish, but also English, Welsh and Scottish, with corresponding lands and titles. Athlyne is no mere transplanted Briton in the Irish context; he is 'a Celt of Celts' and nationalistic rhetoric underlines his claims to true Irishness. Stoker probably derived the Athlyne name from the venerable Anglo–Irish Earldom of Athlone, which had been extinct since 1844. In contrast to Athlyne is the buxom, pleasant-faced Mrs O'Brien, who speaks in an Irish dialect. Counterpointing his aristocratic Irishness with a peasant, stage-Irish variety, she is fiercely loyal to the Edwardian social and political order. Athlyne's surname is FitzGerald, recalling that of Stoker's friend, Percy FitzGerald as well as that of the powerful Earls of Kildare who played a prominent role in Irish history. Indeed, the murder of John Alen, Archbishop of Dublin, in a rebellion by 'Silken Thomas' FitzGerald, the tenth Earl of Kildare, in Artane, where Stoker spent some years in his childhood, brought about the end of the family's hereditary viceroyalty and the pacification of Ireland by Henry VIII in the sixteenth century. If Athlyne reconciles Ireland and the rest of the British Isles politically, he is also a figure of social reconciliation at a time of divisive class tensions, having been born among his tenants and suckled by Mrs O'Brien.

Bored with an aristocratic life which consists of 'games in succession' and 'did not seem to lead anywhere' and disenchanted with a London social scene where a new breed of 'South African Millionaires', often a coded reference to Jews at this time, 'had set at defiance the old order of social caste, and largely changed the whole scheme of existing values', Athlyne decides to leave London. One senses in this Stoker's own feeling of being ill at ease in the new social currents of Edwardian England which had made anachronisms of both Irving and himself. In deciding to go to America incognito, to find a woman there who has been claiming to be his wife, Athlyne now mirrors his female protagonist in the theme of deception and disguise. He begins to feel 'an unmitigated fraud and a thorough scoundrel' on the basis that any form of dissimulation is obnoxious to a gentleman. At the same time, he delights in travel and in forming friendships with casual acquaintances, a reflection of Stoker's own experiences on the road with the Lyceum in the United States. He even dines at Delmonico's, a fashionable New York restaurant of the era frequented by Stoker and Irving on their American tours.

The person who has been playfully claiming to be Lady Athlyne is Miss Joy Ogilvie, a girl emerging into womanhood, daughter of Colonel Lucius Ogilvie, an upholder of the old chivalry of Kentucky. While in New York, Athlyne rescues Joy from a bolting horse but bribes the Irish policeman on the spot not to publicise his heroism. When Athlyne and Joy look into each other's eyes 'the whole world becomes crystal', this 'dawn of love' representing the coming together of the twin halves of a Platonic perfect soul. Stoker then outlines and validates Otto Weininger's (1880–1903) theory that the ideal man is entirely masculine and the ideal woman feminine; the attraction of each to the opposite sex depends on the proportion of masculinity/femininity in their character, with the most masculine man attracting the most feminine woman. Athlyne and Joy are, respectively, strongly masculine and feminine. Stoker reveals his adherence, not just to Weininger's theories, but also to a Darwinian view in which the principle of selection is one of Nature's laws, applying to the human as well as the animal worlds. Weininger, incidentally, a Jewish convert to Christianity, included in his *Geschlecht und Charakter* (Sex and Character, 1903) a chapter, 'Über das Judentum', which identified Judaism with the feminine and amoral as opposed to the masculine which related to Christianity. His work had a generally anti-Semitic influence, including on Hitler.

Stoker's concern with dreams and the unconscious as well as with fairy tales is expressed through the character of Joy. She dreams of being rescued repeatedly by a masterful Athlyne whose powers of command recall those of Dracula. Joy herself shares some of the Count's characteristics, including hypnotic eyes. When Athlyne goes to kiss Joy, her face changes and he sees a look of terror, which seems to turn her to stone. Joy's romantic dreams are counterpointed by Mrs Ogilvie's nightmares: 'constant wakings from vague apprehensions, horrible imaginings of unknown dangers; dread that she could not localise or specify'.[2]

By placing Athlyne and Joy in Ambleside, near where Wordsworth lived from 1813 until the end of his life, Stoker reasserts his adherence to the poet's pantheistic impulses. Joy expresses her relief at being in Ambleside, delighting in the change from the whirl of London to a place where nature seems to reign. She has quick sympathy with the forces and the moods of nature. Side by side with this celebration of rural purity, Stoker extolls the technological excitement of the motor car, the new sensation of the age. Athlyne invests in a powerful car which he realises can be an instrument of seduction. Joy is suitably impressed and both Athlyne and she are highly excited as they journey to Scotland in it. The role of the car in this novel may well have been inspired by the one owned by Stoker's friend, W.S. Gilbert, and may have reflected Stoker's unease, if he felt any, at Florence's excursions in it. However, it should also be noted that Shaw's *Man and Superman*, written in 1901–2, the time that Stoker was sketching out this novel, included a scene featuring a reverse chase in motor cars with a New Man chauffeur called Straker, which may well have been a pun on Stoker. Drawing on his own legal expertise and the researches on his behalf by Edward Dowden's brother, John, the Bishop of Edinburgh and a former acquaintance in the Trinity College Dublin Philosophical Society,[3] Stoker employed a provision of Scottish law, under which mutual consent constituted marriage, to have Athlyne and Joy lawfully married when they go north of the border. Hall Caine had availed of this provision to marry his young mistress, the mother of their two-year-old son, in Edinburgh in 1886, when he used the presence of the Lyceum in the city as cover. At the end of the novel, Athlyne and Joy have a proper English wedding in Westminster Abbey, where, of course, Henry Irving had been interred. On a note of suspension of what will clearly be explosive sexual relations, Stoker ended his last major romantic novel. David Glover has commented that the sexual substructure in *Athlyne* brings it close to 'the sexual epiphanies associated with the modern novel'.[4]

Stoker's next novel, *The Lady of the Shroud*, published by Heinemann in July 1909 and dedicated to Geneviève Ward, was also, like *Lady Athlyne*, sexually charged but was more overtly political, as well as ironically revisiting the vampire genre by having the Lady of the Shroud appear to be a vampire without actually being one.

Ernest Roger Halbard Melton's aunt, Patience, had married an Irishman, Captain Rupert St, or Sent, Leger, an army officer, who was reckless, gallant and profligate. Ernest's uncle, Roger, made his money trading with the East and bought an enormous estate in the Adriatic, in the Land of Blue Mountains. Roger Melton leaves his nephew one million pounds but stipulates that he must live in the castle of Vissarion in the Blue Mountains for six months and that he is not to change his British nationality. In the best tradition of Stoker's heroes, Rupert is a man of giant stature who has no fear of either material things or 'the world of mysteries in and beyond the grave'. The Land of Blue Mountains, a 'gallant little nation', which has maintained its independence for a thousand years and been governed by Voivodes wielding the influence of a Vladika (the title of the Prince-Bishop who ruled Montenegro), bears a close resemblance to Montenegro, the land of the black mountains, peopled by a race of fiercely independent mountaineers. In *Famous Impostors*, published two years after *The Lady of the Shroud*, Stoker wrote of Stefan Mali who passed himself off in Montenegro as the Tsar Peter III of Russia. Stoker had therefore clearly done some research on Montenegro, whose people he described as being so brave that cowardice was unknown amongst them. Turkey is the main threat to the Land of Blue Mountains, although its enemies seemed to include most of the major European powers, with the exception of Britain, cast as the defender of the cause of freedom. Rupert throws in his lot with the Land of Blue Mountains and decides that what it needs most is modern arms. The term, 'Gospodar', or prince, now used by the inhabitants of the Land of Blue Mountains to describe Rupert, was that applied to the real-life Danilo II, when he became ruler of Montenegro in 1851. Stoker's Balkan state is, however, to derive its constitutional framework from Britain and to function as a constitutional monarchy.

The title of the opening chapter, 'From "The Journal of Occultism"', demonstrates Stoker's continuing concern with the occult; Peter Caulfield, who is introduced early in the novel, has spent thirty years studying 'Spiritual Phenomena' and has seen a woman in a shroud standing up in a coffin-shaped ship. Her dark eyes seemed to gleam 'with a strange but enticing lustre' and she appears to be a vampire. Rupert and the Lady of the Shroud fall in love and finally marry in an underground crypt, after which they part, creating yet another temporarily non-consummated marriage in Stoker's fiction. She is, in fact, the Voivodin Teuta of Vissarian, heir to the throne of the Land of Blue Mountains, whom the Turkish Sultan plans to abduct and force into marriage, thereby claiming suzerainty over her kingdom. The Turks, needless to say, are defeated and Rupert becomes King, with Teuta, as Queen, retreating into domestic bliss.

The Land of Blue Mountains is to help secure British communications with its possessions in the East, while relying on Britain for defence against external aggression. Just like the Irish mountain in *The Snake's Pass*, the

Blue Mountains turn out to be full of minerals and Rupert plans to develop their wealth through the application of technology. Militarily too, the Land of Blue Mountains will be at the technological cutting edge through the construction of airfields which will enable it to command 'The Empire of the Air'. Henceforth, Stoker declares prophetically, 'no nation with an eye for either defence or attack can hope for success without the mastery of the air'. Stoker's accurate appreciation of the future importance of air power may have been inspired by H.G. Wells's *The War in the Air*, which had been published as a magazine serial and in book form in 1908. Like Wells's work too, Stoker's is a political novel, attempting to anticipate coming strategic trends and alliances. Rupert dreams – ultimately successfully – of a Balkan Federation. This will counter the aggression of the Dual Nation, Austria-Hungary, behind which lay a 'German lust for enlargement'. Russia too is seen as expansionist, a theme that had been preached for many years by his friend, the Hungarian traveller and strategic thinker, Arminius Vambery.

Stoker's engagement with the politics of the Balkans went deeper than reading contemporary fiction (he may have been influenced by Elinor Glyn's 1907 novel, *Three Weeks*, based on the 1903 murder of Queen Draga of Serbia, and by Anthony Hope's *The Prisoner of Zenda*). In 1908, he sought the advice of the traveller and writer, Archibald Ross Colquhoun, on books on the area. Colquhoun, claiming that recent books on the Balkans were all poor, not surprisingly recommended his own work, *The Whirlpool of Europe: Austria-Hungary and the Habsburgs*, the title of which may have been inspired by Stoker's own description of Transylvania in *Dracula* as 'the whirlpool of European races'. This book pointed out that a granddaughter of Queen Victoria was to be Queen of Romania and, while dismissing Pan-Slavism in general as impracticable, did allow that combinations among the southern Slavs were not impossible.[5] A contemporary notice in the *Bookman* wrote of Stoker's outline of a Balkan Federation as being essential to curbing Austria and Turkey; overall, the reviewer felt that *The Lady of the Shroud* was among Stoker's best work. An Australian reviewer, by contrast, felt that while the novel opened in the best manner of Radcliffe and Lewis, it degenerated into dreariness after it was made clear that the heroine was alive, and that it was overloaded with a mass of irrelevant detail.[6] Notwithstanding such criticism, *The Lady of the Shroud* was one of Stoker's more enduringly popular works, reaching its twentieth edition by 1934.

While opinions may have differed on the quality of *The Lady of the Shroud*, it did at least pursue a clear political path. Similarly, *Famous Impostors* was eminently rational. Stoker's final essay, on 'Irving and Stage Lighting', published in the January–June 1911 issue of the *Nineteenth Century and*

After, was also coherent. Nothing therefore illustrates the precipitate decline in Stoker's health in the final year or two of his life better than his last book, *The Lair of the White Worm*, written between March and June 1911. A bizarre and confusing novel, the story is full of incredible and fantastic sub-plots, with little overall coherence or consistency. Some parts have to be repeatedly re-read simply to try to make sense of them. Harry Ludlam has described Stoker struggling to write the *Lair* as illness increasingly took hold of him, sitting up in bed with a magnifying glass, trying to read what he had written. Ludlam has commented that the mystery of the book is the mystery of the mind of the man who wrote it. Daniel Farson has speculated that it could have been written under the influence of drugs being used to treat Stoker for Bright's disease.[7]

It begins with a classic Stokerian inheritance situation, where great-uncle Richard Salton tells young Adam Salton that he is to be his heir and gives him £200 to help him in the short term. Doom Tower is great-uncle Richard's family seat and he knows all the old prehistoric legends. Like Van Helsing, he uses ancient knowledge to guide the others in the struggle with evil. Stoker's concern with the political unity of the British state is again evident in this work: Richard Salton's property is in the heart of the old kingdom of Mercia, which contained traces of all the nationalities which would later merge and become Britain. Mercia was dominant in Anglo-Saxon England from the middle of the seventh century to the early ninth century; the Mercian King, Offa, laid the foundations of what became the English state in the eighth century. The most significant property in the area is Castra Regis, the family seat of the Caswall family. They are cold and dominant, with thick black hair indicative of vast strength and endurance and black, piercing eyes of hypnotic, mesmeric power. Local belief has it that the Caswalls have sold their souls to the Devil. Edgar Caswall, the present occupant of Castra Regis, had had a close association with Franz Anton Mesmer (the eighteenth-century physician whose system of therapeutics laid the basis for modern hypnotism) in Paris. Stoker's description of him – his 'brain was full of odd fancies; he was on the high road to mental disturbance' – may have reflected Stoker's own state of health at the time. Like Stoker (and Dracula), Caswall is amazingly strong; he seems to be 'acting rather in obedience to some unseen and unknown command than in accordance with any reasonable plan'.[8] That might also describe the plotting and characters of Stoker's novel. Caswall is hard, ruthless and dominant. By contrast, the face of Oolanga, his black lackey, 'was unreformed, unsoftened'. In Africa he had been a great man and practitioner of voodoo; now he is given to sickening cruelty. Probably the most bizarre character in a generally amazing cast is Lady Arabella March of

Diana's Grove who is surrounded by snakes. Adam Salton comes to the conclusion that she is, in fact, a snake.

When she was young, she had received a poisonous bite and developed a terrible craving for cruelty; Sir Nathaniel de Salis thinks that the White Worm, a monster of vast size and power, gained control of her as her soul was leaving her dying body. Stoker probably derived the concept of this vast, underground-dwelling worm from Wirt Sikes who wrote in *British Goblins: Welsh Folk-lore, Fairy Mythology, Legends and Traditions* of the legends of a dragon or demon, eagle or sleeping warrior which guarded underground treasure vaults in Wales. It was supposed to be a creature of vast size whose breath destroyed two districts, and it lay out of sight in a cave near a river. In Stoker's novel, 'savage Wales' – and danger – lies beyond the area in which it is set. Matthew Lewis's *Tales of Wonder* (1801) had featured 'The Laidley Worm of Spindlestone Heughs', the tale of a jealous queen and stepmother who turns a princess into a giant worm that also lives in a cave. The subject had a powerful attraction for Stoker's contemporaries, the Pre-Raphaelites especially. It inspired Swinburne, and the artist, Walter Crane, exhibited an oil painting of the Laidley Worm at the Grosvenor Gallery in 1881. *Punch* used the legend as the basis of a satire on slum landlords in 1890, which featured a full-page illustration of the London County Council as a knight, armed with the sword of sanitary reform, facing a huge worm or dragon, with bat-like wings, representing unwholesome landlordism, breathing disease and death.[9]

Caswall is plagued by a huge immigration of birds, which he decides to get rid of by constructing a vast kite, shaped like a hawk, which he controls from a tower. The confusion which now afflicted Stoker's mind is evident when he states, in successive paragraphs, firstly, that the kite seemed to give Edgar Caswall a new zest for life and, then, that he had grown morbid to a point where the neighbours thought he was going mad,[10] a fate that Stoker himself may have been suffering at the time. A theme of the book, as in *Dracula*, is the intrusion of a threatening past into the present; as Sir Nathaniel de Salis puts it: 'We are going back to the origin of superstition – to an age when dragons tore each other in their slime.' Like the Count, the White Worm has 'no soul and no morals', making it more dangerous than any the world has ever had to face, and it could take human shape. However, a major difference between this monster and Count Dracula is that the White Worm does not have supernatural powers; as in *The Lady of the Shroud*, Stoker follows the Radcliffean Gothic tradition of implying, then denying, such unearthly intervention in the plot. The men agree that the monster must be destroyed, while Sir Nathaniel cautions that 'we have to protect ourselves and others against feminine nature . . . she is a thing of the night'.[11] The men decide on the use of dynamite to destroy the White Worm. This is ultimately achieved when lightning runs down Caswall's giant kite and sets off the dynamite, which blows up the White Worm in its lair. Castra Regis and Diana's Grove are both destroyed. Stoker may have borrowed the concept of the use of electricity to destroy a castle from Jules Verne's *Carpathian Castle*.[12] As well at the defeat of evil, some other of Stoker's favourite themes intrude at the end: for example the clay of the area turns out to be valuable, giving scope for development.

Dedicated to Bertha Nicoll, who had inspired Stoker's interest in the Bisley Boy, *The Lair of the White Worm* was published in London in November 1911 with six coloured plates by Pamela Colman Smith, a writer and illustrator who was a member of the Golden Dawn and created the designs for the classic Rider-Waite deck of Tarot cards. She had travelled in the United States with the Lyceum Theatre on its 1899 tour and drew playful caricatures of some of the company, including Stoker as a sailor wearing an 'HMS Dracula' hat on board ship. An habitué of the Lyceum, the writer, Mrs William Kingdon (Lucy) Clifford, wife of a distinguished scientist and a regular correspondent who addressed him as 'My dear Uncle Stoker', asked him, in November 1911, how on earth a story as strange as the *Lair* came into his head. Describing it as 'very powerful', she felt that it ought to rival *Dracula* and 'especially in these days of the uncanny it ought to be a big success'.[13] She was right in terms of reviews as well as long-term popular favour: it was positively reviewed in the *Court Journal*, the *Daily Telegraph*, the *Referee* and the *Daily Mail*. The *Scotsman* commented that Stoker had demonstrated vivid imagination, subtle power of analysis and a supreme faculty for telling a bloodcurdling yarn. The *Times Literary Supplement* was a dissenting voice, stating that Stoker's work had 'degenerated into something very like nonsense' and describing the book as disjointed and 'very silly'.[14] For all its manic qualities, *The Lair of the White Worm* was a considerable success after Stoker's death. The first cheap edition was published in 1925 and sold well for years, being revived as a paperback in 1945 and 1961, as well as more recently. It was made into a movie (1988) by the English director, Ken Russell, with a cast that included Hugh Grant.

EIGHTEEN

The Dead Un-dead

Alas! I am unclean to His eyes, and shall be until He may deign to let me stand forth in His sight as one of those who have not incurred His wrath.

(*Dracula*, Mina Harker's Journal)

The bizarre nature of *The Lair of the White Worm* has fuelled the often lurid speculation surrounding the state of Stoker's health in his last years. What is clear is that he was a gravely ill man in his final six years, from 1906 until his death in 1912. His obviously poor condition was sufficiently bad for the *Westminster Gazette* to state in an obituary that, while his death had 'roused a feeling of keen regret amongst his many friends', this was 'modified, however, by the reflection that his life for some time past has been saddened by his physical condition'.[1] Stoker had had some health problems during his Lyceum years: he refused wine on board an American naval ship in 1894 as he was suffering from gout (in *Dracula*, the solicitor, Peter Hawkins, is afflicted with gout, which prevents him travelling to Transylvania to conduct business with the Count; he sends Jonathan Harker instead). However, his real health difficulties began in early 1906 when he had what he defined as a paralytic stroke: 'Fortunately that stroke was not a bad one and in a few months I resumed my work.' Noel Stoker attributed this 'slight stroke' to the worry and distress caused by Irving's death, describing his father afterwards as a broken man: 'The gout in my grandmother's ancestry in him took the form of Bright's Disease, & a long distressing course downhill. My mother tackled the difficulties most wonderfully.'[2]

However, the symptoms suffered by the narrator in the possibly autobiographical story, 'In the Valley of the Shadow', published in the *Grand Magazine* in 1907,[3] seem more psychiatric than the incapacity that one would associate with victims of a stroke. Indeed, some of these – delusions and violent rages for example – are consistent with late syphilis. When the narrator is brought to hospital by ambulance, his state of mind is established by his remark to the matron about faces he sees in the pattern of the curtain and he asks if any are her friends: 'Even when I got well I could sometimes see them in certain lights.' He has delusions of needing to save a man in danger, a reiteration of Stoker's familiar rescue theme, as well as imagining that his sister is having him spirited from house to house: 'Here began that absurd hatred and suspicion of her which only left me with the delirium.' The hint of violence becomes more explicit when the narrator declares to the doctor that he is a 'Mussulman and forbidden to drink spirits'. When the sister gives him a draught, he dashes it to the floor with the exclamation: 'Devil in human form, you tempt me to my destruction. Begone and let me die in the true faith.' He tries to escape from the hospital but is overpowered and brought back; when the staff complain that he is keeping them up, he responds: 'what is that to the loss of my soul?' After a series of interwoven fantasies of God and the Devil, of Satanic voices and divine reassurance, the narrator wakes from a peaceful sleep and finds that the crisis is past: 'I was as sane again as usual.' While the exact nature of the malady is not stated, it does seem to be a form of nervous breakdown or temporary insanity. If Stoker actually suffered an episode such as this – there is no evidence that he did so and any connection between the story and his real life must remain speculative – it may have happened after his 1906 stroke: a letter from a friend, the then immensely popular artist, Sir Lawrence Alma-Tadema, in 1907, referred to Stoker having been unwell. Another letter to Stoker, from Sir George Alexander, around this time, also referred to Stoker having been unwell but stated that what he had been through for some time past would have been enough to break even his 'iron reserve'.[4]

Stoker's health continued to deteriorate in the years after Irving's death. In a letter of condolence to Thornley Stoker about the loss of his wife, Florence wrote in 1910: 'Poor old Bram is no worse, this wet weather stiffens him up so, it makes it so hard for him to get about. He is an Angel of patience, & never complains, & it is so hard for him being so helpless.'[5] In a posthumous tribute, Hall Caine said of Florence's role at this time: 'Of the devotion of his wife during those last dark days, in which the whirlwind of his spirit had nothing left to it but the broken wreck of a strong man, I cannot trust myself to speak. That must always be a sacred memory to those who know what it was. If his was the genius of friendship, hers must have been the genius of love.'[6] For this obituary, which appeared in the *Daily Telegraph*, Caine used the heading, 'The Story of a Great Friendship', exactly the same as he had used for an obituary of Dante Gabriel Rossetti so many years previously. The great friendship was not, however, that between Stoker and himself, about which he was curiously reticent, but rather that between Stoker and Irving.

It was sadly appropriate, given their lifelong closeness, that Stoker and his brother, Thornley, should have declined towards death in parallel. In

November 1910, Thornley's wife, Emily, died. Gloom pervaded other branches of the extended Stoker family at this time. In January 1911 Stoker's sister Matilda wrote from Versailles, where she was living with her husband, Charles, a melancholy letter detailing an ageing family in declining health. Charles was not well; she wrote that he had had a relapse before Christmas. The news from Thornley was that he was getting better and settling into his new home. Matilda's idea that he might start 'collecting' once he was settled was, however, optimistic: his health continued to decline. Much the same was true of Stoker: Florence was keeping her in touch with the state of his health: he evidently was not well enough to write himself but she thought that the fine weather when it came might be of benefit to him. The letter reveals Matilda as a spirited, educated woman of fine perception: Stoker had just sent her a copy of *Famous Impostors* and she was indignant at what she saw as plagiarism of the 'Princess Olive' chapter in a magazine.[7] While he continued to live in London, Stoker may have taken up temporary residence by the sea at Fairlight Lawn, College Road, Deal, on the south coast of England, for health reasons in the last year of his life. He had been going to Deal for some time: in March 1904, he had written to Hall Caine from there when he was recovering from an illness which had kept him in bed for several weeks. Whatever literary inspiration he had previously derived from Cruden Bay, Stoker was a very sick man on his last visit there in 1911, when he stamped over the sands, waving his stick and shouting at the sea.[8] The stamping motion observed by the locals may be significant in that those afflicted with syphilis walk with an exaggerated downward motion (they are unsure of where the ground is, due to damage to the nervous system). To a casual observer, it would look very much like stamping.

Stoker died at his home at 26 St George's Square, close to the Thames, on Saturday evening, 20 April 1912, at the age of sixty-four. As the cause of death, his GP, James Browne, MD, wrote: 'Locomotor Ataxia 6 months, Granular Contracted Kidney. Exhaustion.'[9] The possible significance of this escaped Stoker's first biographer, Harry Ludlam, but not his second, Daniel Farson, who identified locomotor ataxia with syphilis (although he was mistaken in identifying it with the tertiary stage of the illness). He tied this in with Stoker allegedly being proud of his reputation as a womaniser; he was reputedly famous for his sexual exploits. Farson believed that Florence's alleged frigidity had driven him to other women, from whom he got syphilis, probably around the turn of the century, possibly from a prostitute in Paris. Stoker certainly did allude in fiction to the tolerant attitude of his contemporaries to private immorality: in 'The Secret of the Growing Gold', we are told that, as long as the character of Geoffrey Brent confined his dissipations to London or continental cities such as Paris and Vienna, anywhere in fact that was out of sight and sound of his home, it was tolerated by society (Stoker saw at first hand how the discreetly irregular private lives of Henry Irving and Ellen Terry escaped censure and, indeed, did not preclude their acceptance in the highest social circles). Farson's claims have been dismissed by one later biographer and regarded by another as 'unproven'. At the same time, critical theory has developed which relates Stoker's writing, especially *Dracula*, to an awareness of his syphilitic condition.[10] It is somewhat ironic that Dr Browne's honesty in including locomotor ataxia on the death certificate has given rise to so much controversy: in *Dracula* it was all so much easier when the two doctors, Van Helsing and Seward, agree to obscure the circumstances of Mrs Westenra's death on her death certificate to avoid an inquest and awkward questions being asked.

I have consulted eminent medical authorities to try to clarify an elusive and difficult subject: Dr Siobhan Murphy, Consultant Physician, Department of Genito-Urinary Medicine, The Patrick Clements Clinic, Central Middlesex Hospital Trust; J.D. Oriel, MD, formerly Consultant Physician in Genito-Urinary Medicine, University College, London; and Professor J.B. Lyons, MD, FRCPI, of the Royal College of Surgeons in Ireland, a distinguished author as well as physician.[11] Two issues are involved in trying to decide if Stoker was actually suffering from syphilis at the time of his death: did Dr Browne mean to imply that this was the case and, if so, how reliable was Browne?

Dr Siobhan Murphy feels it is unlikely that 'Locomotor Ataxia' was meant to refer to anything other than tabes dorsalis, one of the commonest diseases of the nervous system, almost inevitably connected with syphilis. It was described in the mid-nineteenth century as 'cause unknown', but, in the next few decades, the association between tabes and syphilis became generally understood and gradually the connection became irrefutable. The Wasserman test (1906) helped to clarify the connection. This authority has also commented that syphilis can give rise to strokes, so the fact that Stoker had a stroke six years before his death could be in keeping with a diagnosis of syphilis.[12] Dr Oriel points out that tabes dorsalis comes on fifteen to thirty-five years after infection and gives rise to many symptoms, including abnormal gait and optic atrophy leading to blindness; failing eyesight was a feature of Stoker's later years. The end result may be paralysis, blindness and incontinence, but the patient's intellect is not affected: it is not correct, therefore, to attribute the strangeness of *The Lair of the White Worm* to syphilis. Dr Oriel states that 'Granular Contracted Kidney' on the death certificate strongly suggests chronic nephritis, which causes scarring and loss of function of the kidneys. It is consistent with the previous diagnosis of Bright's disease. His conclusion is that Stoker died of uraemia from chronic nephritis; the balance of probability is that he was also suffering from syphilis but this was not the direct cause of death.[13]

The third authority consulted, Professor J.B. Lyons, reached a broadly similar conclusion: it was unlikely that Stoker had paresis, also known as general paralysis of the insane (GPI), due to widespread destruction of the brain in the tertiary stage of syphilis, but 'unless we are to impugn the competence of James Browne, MD, the diagnosis of "Locomotor Ataxia" resulting from syphilis must stand. Whether the underlying syphilis affected his artistry in any way whatever is highly speculative. The most likely effect of chronic ill-health is to diminish creativity.' Lyons also makes the point that, in those days, doctors often took it upon themselves to decide how much they told people; Browne may never have told Stoker that he had syphilis,[14] although his friend, Arthur Conan Doyle, who practised medicine until 1891, had a particular knowledge of the subject and locomotor ataxia is mentioned specifically in his book, *Round the Red Lamp* (1894); whether he would have enlightened Stoker had he guessed his condition is open to question. We do know that Browne was treating Stoker with arsenic (a classic treatment for syphilis at the time) in 1910, when Paul Ehrlich's arsenic-based anti-syphilis drug, Salvarsan, developed the previous year, became generally available. Alexander Fleming, who would later discover penicillin, was one of the few doctors in London at that time to administer Salvarsan by the then difficult method of intravenous injection. Whether Stoker was treated with Salvarsan, by Fleming or any other doctor, we simply do not know.

In relation to Browne's credibility, Professor Lyons notes that he took out the BCh. (Bachelor of Surgery) qualification ten years after he had graduated as a doctor, even though he was not required to do so, suggesting that he was a man of some quality. On the other hand, he was something of a wanderer, spending a number of years in general practice in various locations in the English provinces, before arriving in London about 1893. Browne's name disappears off the medical registers for two years, in the early 1890s. This could indicate misconduct, such as excessive drinking, but a medical practitioner could be taken off simply for not answering letters from the General Medical Council confirming his present address. Browne practised in Greenwich and West Bromwich before he settled in central London in 1903 and it is likely that he became Stoker's doctor around this time. He was a member of the Irish Literary Society (this may well have been the channel through which Stoker got to know and trust him) and a brother of Francis Browne, a celebrated Jesuit photographer of the era.

An account of Stoker's funeral appeared in *The Times* of 25 April 1912: it took place at Golders Green Crematorium, where the Reverend Herbert Trundle conducted a service in the chapel. Among those present were Laurence Irving, Hall Caine, Ford Madox Hueffer and Geneviève Ward. Wreaths were sent by Ellen Terry and Sir Arthur Pinero, among others. The attendance at the funeral by Hueffer, who later changed his name to Ford Madox Ford, is interesting, given that he does not appear to have otherwise featured in Stoker's life. He may have known Stoker through Violet Hunt, the writer and former lover of Oswald Crawfurd, whose *Black & White* magazine had published Stoker's short story, 'The Secret of the Growing Gold'; Stoker had first met Hunt in Whitby during the fateful summer of 1890. Ford's sympathy for Irish nationalism may also have been a point of contact between them.[15]

When Thornley died on 1 June 1912, within weeks of Bram's death, he left a personal estate valued at £10,315, a huge sum for the time. He bequeathed £1,000 to Bram and £200 to Bram's son, Noel. It has been claimed that there was resentment on the part of Florence about the other bequests in the will, which included £5,000 to his wife's nurse, Betty Webb, and £2,000 to Florence Dugdale. Ann Stoker, Stoker's granddaughter, has been quoted as saying that this 'infuriated the chronically hard-up Bram Stoker family, who referred to Florence Dugdale as "that woman who got the Stoker money"'. Stoker's family supposedly maintained that Florence Dugdale had been Thornley's mistress, under the cover of being a secretary, an allegation without any clear basis in fact.[16] As Ann Stoker was not born at this stage, she must have formed her impressions from family sources. However, as far as the record is concerned, the presence of Noel Stoker, who must have travelled over from London for the occasion, at Thornley's funeral is hardly indicative of a deep rift. Even more to the point, the relationship between Stoker's family and Betty Webb continued to be cordial and she appointed Noel as an executor of her will.

Following Stoker's death and burial, Florence moved rapidly to sort out her own life. Stoker's final will had been drawn up on 25 March 1912 and probate was granted on 15 May. She wrote without delay to the solicitors, pointing out that she was the sole legatee and all interests and powers formerly enjoyed by Stoker were now vested in her; she directed that all communication was to be with her and asked them to advise her about the exact nature and state of all existing arrangements. Noel Stoker witnessed the letter.[17] Stoker did not leave Florence as badly off as some have imagined; his estate had a net value of £4,664, almost half the amount left by his wealthy brother, Thornley.[18] This was a considerable sum and, apart from a continuing trickle of income from Stoker's writing, prior to the mass popular success of *Dracula*, the interest from it, assuming that it was invested, should have been a reasonable amount for a widow whose only child was well launched on his career as an accountant and who had, presumably, few outgoings.

On 7 July 1913 (Stoker would have appreciated that it took place on the seventh day of the seventh month!), Florence put Stoker's library up for sale at Sotheby's and it realised £400 12s. The more important items included works by George Meredith, Robert Louis Stevenson, James Whitcomb Riley, the American poet, and Walt Whitman. The death mask of Lincoln, by Augustus Saint-Gaudens, was sold for £10 10s., while the original manuscript of the dramatised version of Wilkie Collins's *The Woman in White* went for £20.[19] The manuscripts for *The Lady of the Shroud*, *Snowbound*, *Under the Sunset*, *The Lair of the White Worm* and the 'original notes and data' for *Dracula* were included in the sale. Florence was well pleased with the result. She wrote to a friend several years later, offering advice on literary sales technique:

> I think it is a mistake to turn back the leaves of the book of your past
> . . . The present is so interesting. I am meeting delightful people all
> the time, & out such a lot. You must have some wonderful autographs.
> I got nearly £100 for rubbish, I sold . . . at Sotheby's putting on a
> reserve. I should only put one or two of each writer's letters in the
> lot, reserving others for later sales. You'll get as much for a few as a
> lot of each man's autograph. I made over £400 on the 'Bram Stoker
> Library' & had no fine editions, so if you dispense your books, you
> should make quite a good sum. Where was Ed Dowden's Library sold?
> I believe in putting reserves on any good editions.[20]

She herself was advised by William Heinemann, and other of Stoker's friends, on how to make 'the best terms for his literary achievements'.[21] The men who were, however, of most use to her in this field were the long-suffering George Herbert Thring (1859–1941), Secretary of the Incorporated Society of Authors, London, and, later, Denys Kilham Roberts, also of the Society. She availed of their services to the utmost on a variety of matters to do with Stoker's literary estate, including translations into Irish, Polish, Spanish, Italian, German and Portuguese, mostly of *Dracula*. In 1929, Thring brokered an agreement between Florence and the Department of Education in Dublin for an Irish translation of *Dracula*. Florence's reaction was one of sour satisfaction: 'I am glad we shall get something out of the Irish Free State!'[22]

Florence agreed the publication of 'Dracula's Guest', in a volume of the same title, with other unpublished stories of Stoker's, with the publisher, Routledge, in December 1913. The book proved popular, going through three impressions in 1914 and a further ten in the next twenty years. Florence continued to display an impressive shrewdness. When Hamilton Deane's stage version of *Dracula* was being translated, she asked Thring where she stood in relation to translation rights. She was not keen on a request from a Plymouth drama group for permission to perform the play: 'I am not at all anxious for amateurs to handle "Dracula", is there a fee attached to such performances?'[23] It was, however, over the 'film piracy' of *Dracula* that she waged the bitterest battles. In May 1922 Florence became aware of the film, *Nosferatu*, by the German director F.W. Murnau. As the film's own programme claimed that it was taken from *Dracula*, Florence had a clear case for breach of copyright. She initiated legal action and obtained a first favourable judgment in May 1924 but appeals dragged on until July 1925. The German court ordered that all negatives and prints were to be destroyed, but a negative survived. An attempt to show it in London in 1925 was defeated but another attempt in 1928 was successful and it was screened in the United States in 1929. The film is now in general circulation.

A more successful route to bring *Dracula* to a mass audience was followed by Hamilton Deane, an Irish bank clerk turned actor, who applied in 1924 to Florence for the play rights; Noel remembered him telling the Stoker family that he had taken two copies of the book and cut out every piece of dialogue: 'On that basis, he most skilfully adapted the book for the stage, where it was produced at the Little Theatre.' He wisely decided to play the strong and sympathetic role of Van Helsing himself. After opening at a provincial English theatre in Derby in 1924 and a somewhat shaky start at the Little Theatre in London's West End in 1927 (attended by Florence), the play settled down to a long and successful run. In 1927 Horace Liveright acquired the American rights and John Balderston made a fresh adaptation. This version was also a great success.

In 1929 Florence received $40,000 for the film rights of *Dracula* and, with typical pragmatism, declared, after she had disposed of them, that she had 'no further interest in their future'.[24] Florence was being teased mercilessly about being 'Dracula's wife' at this time but she had the comfort of knowing that Stoker's posthumous legacy had left her a wealthy woman. Her granddaughter was under the impression that Florence invested the $40,000 in American stocks, then lost virtually all during the Depression, and had only enough left to create a downstairs lavatory at her home in Clareville Grove, which was named 'Drac' or 'room Dracula'! However, the estate duty form, drawn up after Florence's death at 4 Kinnerton Studios, Knightsbridge, on 25 May 1937, showed that the gross value of her estate came to over £20,000, a large sum indeed for the time.[25] In the years leading up to her death, she wrote chatty letters detailing her busy social life and delighted in reading popular fiction. She continued to keep an eagle eye on developments relating to the value of Stoker's literary estate, her sharp query to the Society of Authors in 1931 being fairly typical:

> I have been informed that Messrs Benn [Florence appears to have been mistaken about the name of the firm] have published a book entitled: 'Stories of Detection, Mystery & *Horror*' in which they have included a story of my husband's Bram Stoker. Will you please communicate with Messrs Benn, & find out who authorised them to use this story, as the copyright of all my husband's books are my exclusive property. I think I should get compensation if my information is correct. Sincerely Yours. A.F. Bram Stoker.[26]

Just as Stoker died two years before the First World War would sweep away the Victorian and Edwardian world he had inhabited, so Florence's death would come two years before the Second World War ushered in a new world which made it difficult even to comprehend the ideals that Stoker had defended so staunchly in his fiction. Yet, while Hollywood had begun to imprint the terror of the aristocratic Count Dracula on a global audience in the 1930s, it was only in the post-war period that Stoker's greatest creation came into its own, when, ironically, the values that had given rise to it were discarded by its egalitarian mass audience. Stoker's re-emergence from the shadow of his masterpiece was marked by the title of Francis Ford Coppola's 1992 film, *Bram Stoker's Dracula*. More than one hundred years after he first impacted on his suitably horrified Victorian readership, the hold of Stoker's imagination on our own is more secure than ever. *Dracula* is constantly resurrected and reinterpreted and inspires ever more imitations as time goes on. As a young man, Stoker was determined to achieve literary immortality but believed towards the end of his life that he had sacrificed his ambition to serve Henry Irving. Yet, while the great actor has receded to the confines of theatrical history, Stoker waxes stronger than ever through the medium of his fictional Count, one of the most enduring characters in world literature.

Abbreviations

Actor	Laurence Irving. *Henry Irving: The Actor and His World*, London: Columbus Books, 1951/1989
AS	Ann Stoker Collection (now at Trinity College Dublin)
BL	British Library
CS	Charlotte Stoker
Dalby	Richard Dalby. *Bram Stoker, A Bibliography of First Editions*, London: Dracula, 1983
DF	Daniel Farson/Daniel Farson. *The Man Who Wrote Dracula: A Biography of Bram Stoker*, London: Michael Joseph, 1975
ET	Ellen Terry
Fales	Fales Library, New York University
FB	Florence Stoker (née Balcombe)
Folger	The Folger Shakespeare Library, Washington D.C.
HI	Henry Irving
HL	Harry Ludlam/Harry Ludlam. *A Biography of Dracula. The Life Story of Bram Stoker*, London: Fireside Press, 1962
HPG	William Hughes and Andrew Smith (eds) *Bram Stoker: History, Psychoanalysis and the Gothic*, London: Macmillan, 1998
Leeds	Brotherton Collection, University of Leeds
Midnight	Peter Haining (ed.) *Midnight Tales*, London: Peter Owen, 1990
Morgan	The Pierpont Morgan Library
NS	Noel Stoker
NY	New York
NYPL	New York Public Library
OW	Oscar Wilde
Perrems	Bram Stoker. *Personal Reminiscences of Henry Irving*, 2 vols,

	London: William Heinemann, 1906
S	Bram Stoker
Senf	Carol A. Senf (ed.) *The Critical Response to Bram Stoker*, Westport, Conn. and London: Greenwood Press, 1993
Shades	Peter Haining (ed.) *Shades of Dracula, Bram Stoker's Uncollected Stories*, London: William Kimber, 1982
ST	Bram Stoker Collection, Shakespeare Centre Library, Stratford-upon-Avon
STP	press cuttings, Bram Stoker Collection, Shakespeare Centre Library, Stratford-upon-Avon
TCD MSS	Manuscript Collection, Library of Trinity College Dublin
Texas	Harry Ransom Humanities Research Center, University of Texas at Austin
TS	(Sir) Thornley Stoker
UPS	Undergraduate Philosophical Society [Trinity College Dublin] Minute Book
WW	Walt Whitman
WWC	Horace Traubel and Sculley Bradley (eds) *With Walt Whitman in Camden*, New York: Century Co., 1905; Philadelphia: University of Pennsylvania Press, 1953

Notes

I: Out of Ireland

1. Ancestral Ambition

1. Lever, *Charles O'Malley*, Vol. I, 29.
2. Noel Dobbs Collection, Richard Marlay Blake, Garaban, Ravensdale, Co. Louth to Lady Thomson, 10/3/1912.
3. Hayes, *The Last Invasion of Ireland*, 298; Pakenham, *The Year of Liberty*, 311.
4. *Freeman's Journal*, 18/9/1798.
5. AS, H. Stubbs, Ballyshannon, to Lady Thomson, 11/3/1912.
6. A contemporary described George Blake as a 'popish gentleman' – Myers and McKnight, *Sir Richard Musgrave's Memoirs*, 573 – and a modern historian of 1798 agrees that he was a Roman Catholic: Pakenham, *The Year of Liberty*, 308.
7. *Midnight*, 'The Spectre of Doom', 43.
8. Stoker, *Under the Sunset*, 6.
9. Proinsias Ó Drisceoil, 'The Famine as Instrument of Fate', review of Peter Gray, *Famine, Law and Politics* in the *Irish Times*, 23/3/1999.
10. *Midnight*, 'The Spectre of Doom', 40.
11. AS, copy of Charlotte Stoker's account of her experiences of the cholera in Ireland 1832, dated 6/5/1873, at Caen, France.
12. AS, typed notes [by t/L?] on CS.
13. AS, formal address to the Queen from the Queen's Institute for the Training and Employment of Educated Women, n.d.
14. Charlotte Stoker, *On the Necessity of a State Provision for the Education of the Deaf and Dumb of Ireland*, 3.
15. Ibid.
16. Charlotte Stoker, *On Female Emigration from Workhouses*, 9.
17. Stoker, *The Man*, 88; *Miss Betty*, 130–1; 'The Chain of Destiny', in *Shades*, 33.

18. Hopkins, 'Crowning the King, Mourning his Mother: *The Jewel of Seven Stars* and *The Lady of the Shroud*', in *HPG*, 145–7.

19. AS, W. Apinall [?] to TS, 8/4/1907.

20. AS, Copy of entry on TS under heading 'New Peers' from an unidentified publication.

21. AS, MS document in NS's writing, 'by WG Strickland 20 XI 1912'.

22. AS, MSS genealogical chart in NS's hand, incorporating census information on William Stoker.

23. *Index to the Act or Grant Books, and to the Original Wills, of the Dioceses of Dublin to the year 1800*, 132, Stoker, William and Frances Smyth, 1780 (Nature of Record = Marriage Licence Bond).

24. AS [Susan Stoker] to Noel [Stoker], Lake Cowichan, BC, Canada, 20/4/1924.

25. Leatherdale, *Dracula, the Novel and the Legend*, 224.

26. AS, documents in NS's handwriting, listing dates of letters in 1874 and giving a flavour of their contents; AS to S at 47 Kildare St, 7/12/1874; the letters themselves, including this one, were not in the AS collection when it was inspected by the author and must be considered lost.

27. *WWC* (Vol. IV), 184, S to WW, 18/2/1872; pointers to the intellectual climate in which Abraham raised his children include a childhood book retained by Thornley Stoker throughout his life, *Pierre and his Family; or, A Story of the Waldenses*, which set out to show that Waldenses were good people persecuted by the Roman Catholic Church of the time who had nonetheless managed to preserve and hand down the truths of the Bible: AS, *Pierre and his Family; or, A Story of the Waldenses*, By the Author of Lily Douglas, Edinburgh, 1824; Stamped Dublin Religious Library No. 239 49 Upper Sackville [Street, Dublin]. Another book which survived in the Stoker family collection was a prize presented to George Stoker for regular attendance and attention at St Mary's Sunday School in Dublin: AS, Mrs Sherwood, *The Little Woodman and his Dog Caesar[;] The Orphan Boy and The May Bee*, London, 1862; Inscribed: 'George Stoker A premium for regular attendance and attention at St Mary's Sunday School Easter 1864 Robt Tomlinson'.

28. AS, Alex Mcdonnell to Sir John Young, Education Office, Marlborough St [Dublin], 6/4/1853.

29. Senf, *Dracula between Tradition and Modernism*, 28, 100, 103.

30. R.F. Foster, 'A Speculative Stake in the Future' (review of Barbara Belford's biography of Bram Stoker), *Independent*, (London), 1 June 1996; Morash, '"Even under some unnatural condition": Bram Stoker

and the Colonial Fantastic', in Cosgrove (ed.), *Literature and the Supernatural*, 112; Glover, *Vampires, Mummies, and Liberals*, 9.

2. The Wondrous Child

1. Gerard, *Picturesque Dublin, Old and New*, 311.
2. Lewis, 'The Fatal Sisters', in *Tales of Wonder*, 337–51.
3. 'In Memoriam. Sir Thornley Stoker, M.D., Bart.; Fellow and Ex-President of the Royal College of Surgeons in Ireland', *Dublin Journal of Medical Science*, 134, 1912; copy kindly provided by Dr Denis Eustace, Medical Director, Highfield Hospital Group, Dublin.
4. Perrems, I, 31–2.
5. 'The Chain of Destiny', in *Shades*, 62–3.
6. Stoker, *The Mystery of the Sea*, 89.
7. Belford, *Bram Stoker*, 19.
8. Joseph S. Bierman, '*Dracula*: Prolonged Childhood Illness and the Oral Triad', *American Imago*, 29, 1972, 186–98, reprinted in Senf, 46–51.
9. Dr Denis Eustace, Consultant Psychiatrist, Highfield Hospital Group, Dublin (grandson of Marie Letitia Stoker), to the author, 22/4/1999.
10. William Stoker, *Pathological Observations, Part II*, 246–8.
11. William Stoker, *A Treatise on Fever*, 25–6.
12. William Stoker, *A Succinct Treatise on Medical Reform for Ireland*, 8, 20, 22, 29, 33–4.
13. Stoker, *The Shoulder of Shasta*, 30–4.
14. Stoker, *The Snake's Pass*, 11; *The Mystery of the Sea*, 30, 36–7.
15. Stoker, 'Dracula's Guest', in *Dracula's Guest*, 16; 'The Judge's House', ibid., 33; Stoker's bible is in the Noel Dobbs Collection.
16. O'Grady, *Standish O'Grady, The Man and the Writer*, 28–9.
17. *Literary World*, 15/11/1905.
18. 'Buried Treasures', *Shamrock*, Dublin, 13/3/1875.
19. 'The Crystal Cup' (1872), in *Shades*, 17.
20. McCarthy, *Irish Literature*, Vol. VIII, 3228.
21. Stoker, 'The Seer', in *Shades*, 128; *The Mystery of the Sea*, 8.

3. Master of Arts

1. Stoker, *The Man*, 77–9.
2. Jones, *Old Trinity*, 40.
3. Graves, *To Return to All That*, 121–2.
4. TCD MSS, Charles Barrington to [?] Glenstal, Newport, Limerick, 6/10/1920; Murphy, *Prodigal Father*, 33; Stoker, College Historical Society, 'Address Delivered . . . by the Auditor', Dublin, 1872; Jones, *Old Trinity*, 45; Graves, *To Return to All That*, 127.

5. Maunsell, *The Idler in College or, The Student's Guide*, 10–15.

6. Jones, *Old Trinity*, 41–2.

7. These paragraphs on Stoker at Trinity College Dublin are based on the college records, especially the following: TCD MSS Collection, College Records, MUN 29 2 & 3. Terms & Examinations: MUN V 30/24 Term and Examination Returns from Michaelmas 1864 to Michaelmas 1865; MUN V 30/25, 1865–6; V MUN 30 26 1866–7; V MUN 30 27, 1867–8; V MUN 30 28, 1868–9 and V MUN 30 29, 1869–70; V MUN 89 3, Students' Residence 1863–74; *A Catalogue of Graduates of the University of Dublin Vol. II* (2nd edition), Dublin and London, 1896, 235; *The Dublin University Calendar for the Year 1871*, Dublin, 1871, 123. Abraham Stoker is listed as Pensioner for Bachelor of Arts, 1 March 1870; 198.

8. *UPS, 1867–74*, Meeting of 8/5/1870.

9. *Saunder's Newsletter*, Saturday, 25/6/1870; *Daily Express*, Saturday, 25/6/1870; *Irish Times*, 27/6/1870.

10. Stoker, College Historical Society, 'The Necessity for Political Honesty', 'Address Delivered . . . by the Auditor', Dublin, 1872.

11. Dagg, *College Historical Society*, 229; TCD MSS, Minutes of the College Historical Society, meeting of 26/5/1869; Perrems, II, 31; Stoker, College Historical Society, 'Address Delivered . . . by the Auditor', Dublin, 1872; TCD MSS, Minutes of the College Historical Society, 2/3/1870 and 9/3/1870.

12. Stoker, College Historical Society, 'Address Delivered . . . by the Auditor', Dublin, 1872.

13. Lady Wilde, *Ancient Legends*, Vol. II, 335–8 and 353; Maume, 'In the Fenians' Wake'.

14. Schmitt, 'Mother Dracula', 25–43.

15. *Morning and Evening Mail, Freeman's Journal, Saunders Newsletter and Daily Advertiser, Irish Times, Evening Post, [Daily?] Mail*, [Dublin] *Evening Mail*, [Dublin] *Daily Express*, all 14/11/1872; *Newry Telegraph*, 16/11/1872.

16. Professor R.B. McDowell, 'Personalities in the Hist', Hist, 5/3/1970, in Budd and Hinds, *The Hist and Edmund Burke's Club*, 309.

17. Richardson, 'The Psychoanalysis of Ghost Stories', 428; Vrettos, *Somatic Fictions*, 163; Malchow, *Gothic Images of Race in Nineteenth-Century Britain*, 132–3.

18. Stoker, *Lady Athlyne*, 176; *The Mystery of the Sea*, 40; *The Man*, 3–4; Perrems, I, 31–2; TCD MSS, Minutes of the College Historical Society, 12/4/1871.

19. *Irish Times*, 2/9/1867; *Daily Express*, 2/9/1867.

20. *Daily Telegraph*, 1 [?] June 1868; 'Bell's Life in London', 6/6/1868; the report was dated 30/5/1868; *Morning Post*, 1/6/1868.

21. White, *Some Recollections of Trinity College, Dublin*, 7.

22. *Irish Times*, 24/5/1867.

23. STP [*Daily?*] *Express*, 6/5/1868; ST, unidentified press cutting, 7/6/1868 'University Athletic Sports'; Stoker, *The Essential Dracula*, 106.

24. *Saunder's Newsletter and Daily Advertiser*, 27/3/1871; *Daily Express*, 27/3/1871.

25. Stoker, *The Snake's Pass*, 170; Perrems, I, 122.

26. TCD MSS MUN/CLUB/RUGBY F./38/1/19, Charles Barrington to Dr [Watson], 9/2/1930; however, I can find no reference in the TCD MSS records to Stoker having been a member of the Trinity Boat Club; if the Barrington anecdote is true, he may not have been a regular oarsman; in TCD MS MUN BOAT CLUB 10.2, Dublin University Boat Club List of Members, Stoker is not listed although his period is covered; MUN BOAT CLUB 6.2, Dublin University Rowing Club was also consulted.

27. TCD MSS MUN/CLUB/RUGBY F./38/1/139, no author, n.d.

28. Ibid., F. 31, MS History of DUFC; *Irish Times* [?], 28/10/1867.

4. Petty Clerk

1. Stoker, *Miss Betty*, 82.

2. *WWC*, 181.

3. Quoted in McDowell, *The Irish Administration*, 24.

4. National Archives of Ireland, 'Files of Registrar of Petty Sessions Clerks', Report by Herbert Murray and Henry Robinson on the office of Registrar of Fines and Penalties, submitted to the Lord-Lieutenant on 18/1/1876. The Civil Service records tally with Stoker's entry in Parker, *The Green Room Book*, 355, which states that he was Inspector of Petty Sessions for two years before resigning from the Civil Service in 1878.

5. Stoker, *The Snake's Pass*, 191; 'The Burial of the Rats', in *Dracula's Guest*, 102.

6. Lady Wilde, *Ancient Legends*, Vol. II, 326; Aberdeen, 'The Sorrows of Ireland'; Antonio Ballesteros Ganzalez, 'Portraits, Rats and Other Dangerous Things: Bram Stoker's "The Judge's House"', in Stewart (ed.), *Other World*, Vol. II, 18–29.

7. Auberon, *The Nineteen Hundreds*, 126–30; Perrems, I, 31–2; HL, 109.

8. Morash, '"Even under some unnatural condition": Bram Stoker and the Colonial Fantastic', in Cosgrove (ed.), *Literature and the*

Supernatural, 95–119; see also Richards, *The Imperial Archive*, 5, with its claim that 'In *Dracula*, a monster is defeated by mastery of the means of information.'

9. Dowden, *Shakspere: A Critical Study of His Mind and Art*, 13.
10. Perrems, II, 98.
11. Perrems, I, 28.
12. 'The Castle of the King', in *Shades*, 76.
13. Parker, *The Green Room Book*; HL, 34.
14. White, *The Parents of Oscar Wilde*, 238; HL, 41.
15. Garrick Club, London, Percy FitzGerald scrapbooks, Vol. V, 158, 'Society in Dublin' column from unidentified newspaper, n.d.
16. *Irish Times*, 16/4/1938, 'Irishman's Diary'.
17. S to WW, Dublin, Ireland, Feb. 18, 1872, in WWC, 183.
18. AS, John J. Robinson [to S], 29 Leeson Park, Dublin, 1/1/[1880] and 7/1/[1881].
19. ST, R.F. Walsh to S, Yokohama, 13/3/1903.

5. Emerging Writer

1. *Dublin Evening Standard*, 14/2/1870; ST, *Irish Times*, ?/3/1870; *Saunder's Newsletter and Daily Advertiser*, 16/6/1870; *Era*, 16/4/1871.
2. Stoker, *The Shoulder of Shasta*, 138.
3. Stoker, 'Actor-Managers'; 'The Primrose Path'.
4. Stoker, 'John Lawrence Toole'.
5. Stoker, 'Americans as Actors', 243–52.
6. AS, Eliza Sarah Stoker, 1882, to Mr Billington, MS document in Noel Stoker's handwriting, listing the dates of letters written in 1874 from Abraham Stoker to Bram Stoker at 47 Kildare St., Dublin; these letters are no longer to be found in the AS collection, 18/5/1874.
7. Perrems, II, 167–9.
8. *Dublin Evening Mail*, 17/11, 18/11 and 21/11/1873.
9. Leeds, Geneviève Ward to S, Manchester, n.d.; Geneviève Ward to S, Paris, 1875; Lucy Ward to S, Leicester, 22/9/1875; Lucy Ward to S, London, 18/12/1875; four letters from Geneviève Ward to S, 1876–90; Geneviève Ward to S, London, 23/9/1876.
10. AS, MS document in Noel Stoker's handwriting, listing the dates of letters written in 1874 from Abraham Stoker to Bram Stoker at 47 Kildare St., Dublin; letter no longer in the AS collection.
11. AS, MS poem, unsigned but in Stoker's handwriting.
12. FitzGerald, *Memoirs of an Author*, Vol. I, 166; Graves, 'Memoir of Joseph Sheridan Le Fanu'.
13. Eglinton, *Irish Literary Portraits*, 65, 80–1.

14. S to WW, Dublin, 18/2/1872, *WWC*, 181–5; Perrems, II, 94–5; *UPS, 1867–74*, meeting of 4/5/1871.
15. Edward Dowden to WW, Cork, 23/7/1871, *WWC*, 133–5.
16. *WWC*, 398, 299; Perrems, II, 95–6.
17. *WWC*, 181–5; University of Virginia Library, WW to S, Camden, New Jersey, 6/3/1876.
18. Stoker, *The Snake's Pass*, 56.
19. AS, MS document in Noel Stoker's handwriting, listing the dates of letters written in 1874 from Abraham Stoker to Bram Stoker at 47 Kildare St., Dublin; letter no longer in the AS collection.
20. Stoker, 'The Crystal Cup'; ST [*Daily?*] *Mail*, 3/9/1872; *Shades*, 15: Haining observes that elements of the construction of this story would be used later in *Dracula*.
21. National Library of Scotland, S to the editor of *Blackwood's Magazine*, 6/10/1874 and 19/8/1875, 16 Harcourt St., Dublin.
22. AS, MS document in Noel Stoker's handwriting, listing the dates of letters written in 1874 from Abraham Stoker to Bram Stoker at 47 Kildare St., Dublin; letter no longer in the AS collection. This list is all that remains of this series of letters. This letter was dated 9/12/1874.

6. London in View!

1. Perrems, I, 14.
2. *Dublin Evening Mail*, 11/12/1876.
3. Perrems, I, 25–6.
4. Ibid., 28–33.
5. Terry, *The Story of My Life*, 178–9; Brereton, *The Life of Henry Irving*, 274; Fitzgerald, *Henry Irving, A Record of Twenty Years at the Lyceum*, Vol. I, 218; Scott, *From 'The Bells' to 'King Arthur'*, 30; *Actor*, 170–1; 278.
6. Perrems, I, 130, 305; Stoker, *The Watter's Mou'*, 143; Hughes, ' "It must be something mental": Victorian Medicine and Clinical Hysteria', in Stewart (ed.), *Other World*, Vol. II 56; see also Malchow, *Gothic Images of Race in Nineteenth-Century Britain*, 146; and Glover, *Vampires, Mummies, and Liberals*, 47 and 80.
7. *Dublin Evening Mail*, 19/6/1877.
8. Perrems, I, 42–4, 48–9, 53–4; *Actor*, 290–4.
9. Stoker, *The Essential Dracula*, 28; see also Macgillivray, 'Bram Stoker's Spoiled Masterpiece', in Senf, 61–8; George Bernard Shaw, 'The Exile', quoted in W. J. McCormack, 'Irish Gothic and After (1820–45)', in Deane, *The Field Day Anthology of Irish Writing*, 496; 'Mr Bram Stoker. A Chat with the Author of "Dracula", by Lorna', *British Weekly*, 1/7/1898, 185.

10. Perrems, I, 55–6; Roy Foster (*The Irish Story*, 98–9) quotes Charles Maturin, the author of *Melmoth the Wanderer*, on 'that terrible sensation, so common in the imagination of the Irish, of a being whom we believe not to be alive, yet know not to be dead, who holds a kind of hovering intermediate existence between both worlds and combines the passions of human existence with the power of a spirit'.

11. Perrems, I, 57–9.

12. Ibid., 60–1; interview with Ann Stoker, 5/4/1997.

13. Ellmann, *Oscar Wilde*, 99; Letter from the author to Merlin Holland, 23/9/1997, confirming an earlier conversation; OW to Reginald Harding [6/8/1876], in Wilde, *The Letters of Oscar Wilde*, 23–4, 54.

14. Stoker, *Miss Betty*, 48; *The Snake's Pass*, 150; *The Mystery of the Sea*, 215.

15. AS, MS will, 6/9/1894, by FB's mother, Philippa Anne Balcombe, living at Kew.

16. Shuttle and Redgrove, *The Wise Wound*, 252; Weldon, Introduction to *Bram Stoker's Dracula Omnibus*, viii.

17. DF, 213–15; Ann Stoker, interview with the author, 5/4/1997.

18. AS, FB to her mother, London, 21/7/1891.

19. AS, Eleanor Knott to Noel [Stoker], 27/6/1957.

20. *Era*, 6/2/1897.

21. Gladstone, *Mary Gladstone (Mrs Drew). Her Diaries and Letters*, 291.

22. J.B. Lyons, 'John Freeman Knott, 1853–1921'.

23. Ibid.

II: The Lyceum

7. An Uncommonly Useful Man

1. Perrems, I, 70–1; Stoker, *The Mystery of the Sea*, 166.

2. Hatton, *The Lyceum 'Faust'*, 32; Carr, *Mrs J. Comyns Carr's Reminiscences*, 214; Swears, 'Irving as Synorix', in *We Saw Him Act*, 195–6; Booth, *Palmy Days*, 53–66; Hatton, *Henry Irving's Impressions of America*, Vol. I, 35; Doyle, 'The Sign of Four', in *Complete Sherlock Holmes*, 185.

3. Perrems, II, 16; 23.

4. Caine, *My Story*, 349–51; Robertson, *Times Was: the Reminiscences of W. Graham Robertson*, 162.

5. Gladstone, *Mary Gladstone (Mrs Drew). Her Diaries and Letters*, 295.

6. Aria, *My Sentimental Self*, 87; Terry and Shaw, *Ellen Terry and Bernard Shaw: A Correspondence*, 166; Martin-Harvey, 'Irving as Lesurques and Dubosc', in Saintsbury and Palmer, *We Saw Him Act*, 126.

7. Perrems, II, 339; Stoker, *The Essential Dracula*, 356.
8. Carr, *Mrs J. Comyns Carr's Reminiscences*, 142–4; Terry, *The Story of My Life*, 174, 178.
9. Auberon, *The Nineteen Hundreds*, 126–30.
10. Surviving correspondence shows him dealing with the arrangements for Irving to sit for the sculpture by Onslow Ford (Leeds, HI to S, London, 12/1/1880); with Douglas Sladen, literary editor of *Queen*, about doing a feature on Irving and his son (Leeds, Douglas Sladen to S, 20/12/1897); a request from the *Review of Reviews* that Irving serve on an advisory committee (Leeds, W.T. Stead, editor, to HI, 21/12/1896); actors who wanted to discuss remuneration (Leeds, Robert Taber, actor, to S, London, 15/3/1899); personal issues such as the gunshot wound to Irving's son in 1891 (S to Mrs Robertson, 11/1/1891, replying to a letter to HI re his son's 'accident' with a gun (Daniel Farson Collection); Lyceum programme advertising (University of Reading Collection, Chatto & Windus to S, 30/12/[?] refusing offer of ad in Lycem programmes as being too expensive); authors such as A.W. Pinero who were writing plays for Irving (Texas, A.W. Pinero to S, 21/11/1895). Stoker was also a go-between for those like Eugene Field who wanted to communicate with Ellen Terry (Texas, Eugene Field to S, Illinois, 28/11/1893). He dealt with arrangements for critics to attend first nights (Texas, typed circular letter, dated Sept. 1889, to editors inviting dramatic critics to the first night of *The Dead Heart*); representing Irving at social and literary functions (Rare Book and Manuscript Collection, Columbia University, New York, S to Mr Scribner, NY, 14/12/1897; Irving could not be present at a dinner for Brander Matthews, so Stoker would attend instead); nasty correspondence with those aggrieved with Irving for some reason (ST, Prescott Warren to HI, 13/1/1894, on Harvard University headed paper, complaining of being called a 'damned scoundrel' and a 'rascally scoundrel' by HI and calling on him to apologise (ST S [in S's writing; draft reply for HI] to [Prescott Warren], Tremont Theatre [Boston, Mass.], 16/1/1894; S [in S's writing; draft reply for HI] to [Prescott Warren], Tremont Theatre, 15/7/1894); responding to earnest Christian pamphleteers (ST, W. Williams [to HI], 69 Drake St., Rochdale, 6 Nov. [no year], enclosing a pamphlet *May a Christian Go to the Theatre?* and S to W. Williams, 8/11/1894, in reply); dealing with importunate spongers (ST, C. Wilson to HI [as H. Brodribb Esq.], Hastings, n.d., asking for money for bills and press cuttings of Irving's productions to enable him to buy a small boat; C. Wilson to HI, Hastings, n.d., demanding more money; S to C. Wilson, 1/12/1892,

Lyceum headed paper, beginning 'Mr Irving is both amazed and disgusted at receiving such a letter . . .'); dealing with the licensing of the Lyceum productions (ST, G.W. Bedford, Examiner of all Theatrical Entertainment, to S, 17/7/1896, deals with licensing of *Madame Sans-Gene*); Irving's need for a coat of arms consequent on his knighthood (ST, Edward Bellasis, College of Arms, London, to S, 20/6/1895 and A.S. Scott-Gatty, College of Arms, London E.C., 26/6/1895); dealings with playwrights like Arthur Conan Doyle and their agents (ST, Conan Doyle to S, 15/3/1892 and 28/5/1895; Conan Doyle to S, Haslemere, n.d.; Addison Bright to S, London, 3/1/1898, enclosing a copy of Conan Doyle's play, *Sherlock Holmes*, part of a series of correspondence with Stoker); the arrangements surrounding Irving's lectures and public appearances (ST, James Drake Digby to S, London, 8/6/1898, deals with the printing of HI's Rede Lecture; also Patrick T. Doherty [?] to S, Mansion House, Dublin, 24/7/1895, deals with arrangements for HI's visit to Dublin); with the arrangements for Irving's readings outside London (ST, series of five letters from Dean F.W. Farrar to S, April/May [1897?], regarding Irving reading Tennyson's *Becket* at the chapter house of Canterbury Cathedral, as well as the publicity for these events; two letters J.M. LeSage (?) to S, *Daily Telegraph* headed paper, 4/5/1894 and 13/6/1898).

11. STP, *Globe*, 9/3/[?]: Stoker appeared in a court case involving the widow of Clement Scott and the Nielson Charity.
12. Stoker, *The Man*, 69.
13. Perrems, II, 102; Craig, *Henry Irving*, 162–4; Pemberton, *Ellen Terry and her Sisters*, 224–5; Terry, *The Story of My Life*, 165–6.
14. Jerome, *My Life and Times*, 145; Shaw, *Bernard Shaw: Collected Letters*, Vol. IV, 786–7.
15. *Stroud News*, 27/1/1911; Shaw, *Bernard Shaw: Collected Letters*, Vol. IV, 787.
16. Perrems, II, 172–4; Ward, *Both Sides of the Curtain*, 81.
17. Perrems, II, 175.
18. Leeds, Geneviève Ward to S, 1/4/1890; AS, Geneviève Ward to TS, 14/11/1910.
19. Leeds, C. V. Stanford to HI, London, 23/6/1896.
20. Perrems, I, 151–2.
21. George Pomeroy Goodale, STP, 'The Kaleidoscope', unidentified newspaper, n.d., review of Perrems; Stoker, *The Mystery of the Sea*, 166.
22. *Echo*, 27/3/1902.
23. 'Before Her Majesty, The Queen's Gifts to Mr. Irving and Miss Terry.

(By One Who Was There)', *Pall Mall Budget*, 2/5/1889, 551.

24. Edgar, *Martin Harvey: Some Pages of his Life*, 128–9.
25. Martin-Harvey, *The Autobiography of Sir John Martin-Harvey*, 63–4.
26. Ibid., 216–17, 221–3, 90–1, 178.
27. ST, ET to S, n.d.
28. Irving, *The Successors*, 106–8.
29. Malchow, *Gothic Images of Race in Nineteenth-Century Britain*, 132.
30. *Daily Telegraph*, 24/4/1912.
31. Perrems, I, 364.
32. Leeds, HI to S, Winchester, 11/10/1878; HI to S (in Dublin), Sheffield.
33. *Bookman*, Nov. 1906, 93.
34. Aria, *My Sentimental Self*, 110.
35. Stoker, 'Toole and Irving. 50 Years' Friendship'; Perrems, II, 177–89; STP, Stoker, 'John Lawrence Toole'.
36. Stoker, *The Essential Dracula*, 221; Perrems, II, 101, 206.
37. Perrems, II, 190–1; Leeds, two letters from Charles Kelly [Charles Wardell] to S, 10/3/1879 and [Dec.] 1878.
38. William Andrews Clark Memorial Library, University of California, Los Angeles, ET to S, 15/10/1880, Shelbourne Hotel, Dublin.
39. Stoker, 'Ellen Terry. An Appreciation'.
40. *Actor*, 395, 444, 448, 449; STP, *Sphere*, 13/7/[1905?].
41. *Actor*, 451–3.
42. Terry and Shaw, *Ellen Terry and Bernard Shaw: A Correspondence*, xxviii.
43. Chicago *Daily News*, 2/4/1888.
44. STP, New York *Commercial Advertiser*, 15/12/[189?]; *Blade*, Toledo, Ohio, 7/11[?]; Chicago *Daily News*, 2/4/1888.
45. Hatton, *Henry Irving's Impressions of America*, Vol. I, 11–12.
46. *Star*, 9/4/1896; Perrems, I, 301.
47. Perrems, I, 302.
48. Perrems, II, 290–1.

8. Gallant Conduct

1. Blunt, *An Illustrated Historical Handbook to the Parish of Chelsea*, 82.
2. The William Andrews Clark Memorial Library, University of California, Los Angeles, ET to S, 15/10/1880, Shelbourne Hotel, Dublin.
3. AS, 'Bram Stoker, by his Son, Noel Thornley Stoker', [8/11/1947]; AS, NS to Harry Ludlam, 20/1/1959.
4. AS, NS to Harry Ludlam, Feb. 1961.
5. Stoker, *The Man*, 18.
6. Stoker, 'Chin Music', in *Snowbound*, 135–6.

7. Stoker, 'The Dualitists', in *Midnight*, 45–6.

8. DF, 61.

9. STP, the '*Critic*'(?), 11/5/1889?

10. STP, *Midland Evening News*, 6/5/1890; see also STP, *Pall Mall Gazette*, 5/5/1890, which also reported on Bram being called to the Bar the previous week.

11. Senf, *Daughters of Lilith*, 205–6; see also Scott, *The Fabrication of the Late Victorian Femme Fatale*, 69 who makes the point that while Dracula is scrupulous about staying within the law, the good men of the novel frequently transgress it; Stoker, *The Mystery of the Sea*, 407.

9. Lyceum Literati

1. Noel Dobbs Collection, Margaret D. Thomson to Tom [Stoker]. Howth, Co Dublin, 20/7/[?].

2. Rare Book and Manuscripts Library, Columbia University, draft by S, 'Hallam, Lord Tennyson. Aldworth and Farringford Revisited'.

3. Perrems, I, 198, 200.

4. Levi, *Tennyson*, 290.

5. Stoker, *The Essential Dracula*, 301; Tennyson *Becket*; Perrems, II, 356.

6. Perrems, I, 216, 231.

7. Extract from Frank Harris, *My Life and Loves*, in Bram Stoker *et al.*, *Erotic* 83; ST, George Moore to S, 18/7/1895; see also Gerber, *George Moore in Transition*, 292–4.

8. Frazier, *George Moore*, 92, 135–6.

9. Pearson, *Bernard Shaw, A Biography*, 167; Shaw, *Bernard Shaw Collected Letters* Vol. I, 747–8, 782.

10. Archer, *The Theatrical World of 1894*, with an introduction by George Bernard Shaw, 73.

11. Holland, *Son of Oscar Wilde*, 42, 35.

12. Wilde, 'Olivia at the Lyceum', *Dramatic Review*, 30/5/1885, in *The Complete Works of Oscar Wilde*, 955–6.

13. OW to ET [3/1/1881], *The Letters of Oscar Wilde*, 74.

14. ST, OW to S, 16 Tite St., Chelsea, n.d. [1889].

15. OW to More Adey, Reading Prison, 8/3/1897, *The Letters of Oscar Wilde*, 422.

16. *Actor*, 579; Letter from the author to Merlin Holland, 23/9/1997, confirming an earlier conversation.

17. Author's recorded conversation with Ann Stoker, 5/4/1997.

18. Leeds, William Wilde to S, 146 Oakley St, London, 16/7/1895.

19. See, for example, Folger, S to 'My dear Willie' [Wilde], 31/12/1889.

20. *Midland Evening News*, Wolverhampton, 11/10/1901.

21. Piccadilly, 19/11/1891.
22. Moore, *A Journalist's Note-Book*, 279–85.
23. Ibid., 286.
24. Richmond on Thames Reference Library, Surrey, England, F. Frankfort Moore to Douglas Sladen, 13/10/1915.
25. Auberon *The Nineteen Hundreds*, 126–30.
26. 'Mr Bram Stoker. A Chat with the Author of "Dracula", by "Lorna", *British Weekly*, 1/7/1898, 185.
27. Quoted in Brown, *Ireland in Fiction*, 214; Moore, *A Journalist's Note-Book*, 316; F.F. Moore, *The Truth about Ulster*, 52–3, 55, 272.
28. Perrems, II, 126.
29. Caine, *Capt'n Davy's Honeymoon*.
30. University of Reading Library, Chatto & Windus to S, 10/7[?].
31. Fales, Hall Caine to S, 2/10/83.
32. Morgan, W.S. Gilbert to Mrs Stoker, London, 18/5/1887; W.S. Gilbert to Mrs Stoker, Grim's Dyke, Harrow Weald, 7/5/1897, 14/(?)/1899, 21/10/1900.
33. Morgan, W.S. Gilbert to Mrs Stoker, Grim's Dyke, Harrow Weald, 27/6/1901, 23/12/1902, 25/12/1902; W.S. Gilbert to Mrs Stoker, London, 8/1/1903; W.S. Gilbert to Mrs Stoker, Grim's Dyke, Harrow Weald, 16/5/1903, 17/5/1903, 22/7/1904.
34. Morgan, W.S. Gilbert to Mrs Stoker, London, 12/3/1911.
35. Doyle, 'The Adventures of the Sussex Vampire', in *Complete Sherlock Holmes*, 1360–71.
36. Yeats, *Autobiographies*, 47, 125.
37. Foster, *W.B. Yeats: A Life: 1*, 110.
38. Perrems, II, 100–1.
39. Ibid., 105.
40. Noel Dobbs Collection, Thomas Donaldson to S Phil[adelphia] Pa., 24/10/1889; ST, WW [to HI], Camden, New Jersey, 3/10/1889.
41. DF, 64–5; University of Reading Library, S to 'Mr Clemens' [Mark Twain], 16/3/1891; Twain to Mr Chatto, 29/3/91.
42. Texas, S.L. Clemens to S, 13/5/1908.
43. *Morning Advertiser*, 25/7/1892; *Freeman's Journal*, 19/10/1900.

10. Political Animal

1. Leeds, four letters from Rt. Hon. General Sir Dighton M. Probyn, VC, Keeper of Privy Purse to King Edward VII to S, 26/7/1883, 21/7/1902, 21/10/1906, 30/10/1906; General Sir Dighton Probyn [?], to S, Buckingham Palace, 14/10/1905; Philippa Sturt, The Royal Archives, to the author, 29/5/1997; ST, General Sir Dighton Probyn,

to S, Buckingham Palace, 25/7/1906; General Sir Dighton Probyn, to S, Sandringham Palace, 1/8/1906.

2. Leeds, Rt. Hon. W.E. Gladstone to S, 18/11/1890.

3. Perrems, I, 58–9, 343.

4. FitzGerald, *Memoirs of an Author*, Vol. I, 183.

5. AS, Baroness Burdett-Coutts to TS, 8/11/1879.

6. AS, Baroness Burdett-Coutts, to TS, 5/12/1879; BC to TS (fragment), n.d.

7. AS, Mr H.S. Braddyll to TS, 19/2/1881; W.L. Ashmead Bartlett to TS, 15/8/1880, 22/2/[?]; BC to TS, Shelbourne Hotel [Dublin], 30/8/[?]; TS to BC, 9/2/1880.

8. *Actor*, 332.

9. Perrems, II, 136; BL MSS, Lord Chamberlain's Office No. 245, *Robert Emmet, A Drama in Four Acts*, Dion Boucicault, Licence dated 1/11/1884, Theatre: Royal Greenwich; *The Times*, 14/8/1909.

10. Hall, *Random Records of a Reporter*, 129.

11. *Freeman's Journal*, 8/11/1910.

12. Cullen, *Life in Ireland*, 135; O'Grady, *Selected Essays and Passages*, 203–4.

13. Joyce, *Ulysses*, 444.

14. Hone, *The Life of George Moore*, 227–43.

15. Gogarty, *As I Was Going Down Sackville Street*, 291, 293.

16. Noel Dobbs Collection, Betty Webb to Mrs Bram Stoker, 25 Fitzwilliam Square, Dublin, 28/6/1933.

17. Perrems, I, 343–4.

18. Folger, S to [William] Winter, 14/9/1886.

19. Leeds, Justin McCarthy to S, n.d. ('Monday night').

20. Leeds, Justin McCarthy to S, Westminster Palace Hotel, 7/4/[?].

21. Leeds, Justin McCarthy to HI, Weimar, Germany, 6/9/1879.

22. STP, *Speaker*, 27/8/1892.

23. Perrems, II, 208–11.

24. Joyce, *Ulysses*, 144, 221, 354, 443, 710.

25. Stoker, *The Man*, 311; *Lady Athlyne*, 138.

11. Pre-Echoes of Dracula

1. *Saturday Review*, 26/11/1881, 677; *Daily Express* (Dublin), 12/11/1881, 6.

2. Leeds, William Fitzgerald to S, 7 Ely Place, Dublin, 30/6/1888; Leeds, Hallam Tennyson to S, 22/1 1882; STP, *Entr'acte*, [?]/1882.

3. Scott, *The Fabrication of the Late Victorian Femme Fatale*, 75, comments on the work of Lombroso and Ferrero alleging the inherent criminality

of all women and children: 'What terrific criminals would children be if they had strong passions, muscular strength and sufficient intelligence; and if moreover their evil tendencies were exasperated [*sic*] by a morbid psychical activity!'; 'The Dualitists' is a practical manifestation of this theory.

4. STP, *Star*, [?]/1891; Antonio Ballesteros Ganzalez, 'Portraits, Rats and Other Dangerous Things: Bram Stoker's "The Judge's House"' in Bruce Stewart (ed.) *That Other World*, Vol. II, 18–29; see also Milbank, '"Powers Old and New": Stoker's Alliances with Anglo-Irish Gothic' in William Hughes and Andrew Smith (eds) *Bram Stoker*, 12–27; Glover, *Vampires, Mummies, and Liberals*, 29.

5. Perrems, II, 154; Fitzgerald, *Henry Irving. A Record of Twenty Years at the Lyceum*, 218–28; Carr, *Mrs J. Comyns Carr's Reminiscences*, 149–56, 151; Carr, *Some Eminent Victorians*, 243, states that the trip to Nuremberg took place in the summer of 1886.

6. *Yorkshire Post*, 17/2/1894.

7. Leeds, William H. Ridenig, editor of *Youth's Companion*, Boston, Mass. to S, 21/9/1891; see also his letter of 17/11/1885 to S, on *Youth's Companion* notepaper, enclosing £2 for the poem, 'One Thing Needful'; 'One Thing Needful' was reprinted in *A Volunteer Haversack, containing Contributions of Certain Writers to the Queen's Rifle Volunteer Brigade: The Royal Scots*, Nov. 1902. Based on the story of Martha, Mary and Jesus, the one thing needful is Mary's loving heart (although Haining and Tremayne, p. 33 feel that the poem is a thinly disguised portrait of Walt Whitman.

8. Malchow, *Gothic Images of Race in Nineteenth-Century Britian*, 142–3.

9. Reprinted in *Midnight*, 120–36.

10. Stoker, *The Essential Dracula*, 97, 413.

11. Drummond, 'Bram Stoker's Cruden Bay', 23–8.

12. Manuscripts Department, University of Virginia Library, S to Mr [Samuel S.?] McClure [Doubleday & McClure?], 1/3/1893.

13. Lilly Library, Indiana University, S to 'My dear Waite', 31/1/1899.

14. *People*, 13/7/1890.

15. *Court Journal*, London, 28/9/1889.

16. STP, *Pelican*, 21/6/1890; *Bristol Times & Mirror*, [?]/1890; *Fashion and Sport*, 24/7/1890.

17. BL, Application from S to the Royal Literary Fund, 22/2/1911.

18. *Dublin Evening Mail*, 18/11/1873.

19. W. R. Wilde, *Irish Popular Superstitions*, 19, 98.

20. Lady Wilde, *Ancient Legends*, 14, Downey, *A House of Tears*.

21. Revelations 20:2; Isaiah 14:29.

22. Leeds, William O'Brien to S, 30/7/1890; and n.d.
23. Perrems, II, 133–4.
24. Leeds, William Fitzgerald to S, 30/9/1881.
25. Leeds, Michael Davitt to S, 17/11/1890; *Labour World*, 29/11/1890, 15.
26. Stoker, *The Watter's Mou'*, 29.
27. Stoker, *The Shoulder of Shasta*, 17.
28. Senf, 57–8; STP, *Daily [Mail?]*, n.d.; a long review describes it as a bright and breezy story, never dull or trivial and written in terse and crisp style.

III: Dracula

12. Dracula

1. Copy of a memorandum of agreement between Bram and Constable for the publication of *Dracula* (kindly provided by John Wyse Jackson).
2. Noel Dobbs Collection, Doubleday to FB, 1/4/1931.
3. Moretti, *Signs Taken for Wonders*, 107.
4. Stoker, *Dracula's Guest*, 12–21.
5. Ibid. Preface; HL, 114–16; Alison Milbank, in '"Powers Old and New": Stoker's Alliances with Anglo-Irish Gothic', in Hughes and Smith (eds) *Bram Stoker*, believes that 'Dracula's Guest' was an attempt to incorporate material from both Maturin and Le Fanu; AS, 'Bram Stoker, by his Son, Noel Thornley Stoker', [8/11/1947], *Shades*, 110; Haining and Tremain, *The Undead: The Legend of Bram Stoker and Dracula*, 19.
6. Eighteen-Bisang and Melton, *Dracula: A Century of Editions*, 15. Senf, *Dracula between Tradition and Modernism*, 51, credits Barbara Belford with this identification; it was, in fact, Clive Leatherdale's theory originally. Frayling, *Vampires: Lord Byron to Count Dracula*, 352; Leatherdale, *Bram Stoker's Dracula Unearthed*, 14–17; Leatherdale, *Dracula, the Novel and the Legend*, 222.
7. Eighteen-Bisang and Melton, *Dracula: A Century of Editions*, 15–16; see *Actor*, 460–1 regarding the probable influence of Bayreuth on Irving's Lyceum.
8. Bram Stoker material at the Rosenbach Museum and Library, Philadelphia, Pa.; I am deeply grateful to the Rosenbach for making copies of this material available to me.
9. 'Mr Bram Stoker. A Chat with the Author of "Dracula", by "Lorna"', *British Weekly*, 1/7/1898, 185; Jane Stoddart was the author of 'Lorna'; she wrote to Bram in June 1897 telling him that she had read *Dracula* with the greatest admiration and asking him for an interview for the

British Weekly; she also enquired if he would like to contribute 4,000 words to the *Woman at Home* magazine; Bram scribbled 'Lunch 28th 12.30' on her letter; Leeds, Jane Stoddart to S, 25/6/1897.

10. AS, NS to HL, 24/11/1957; NS [to HL], n.d.: fragment of MS, assumed to have been part of a letter or draft from NS to HL

11. The title is actually 'Transylvanian Superstitions'.

12. Bird, *Korea and Her Neighbours*, 303, 448. According to the listing in the British Library, this work was first published in 1898 but the modern reprint states that the publication date was 1897.

13. *Dublin Journal of Medical Science*, 134, 1912.

14. Gogarty, *As I Was Going Down Sackville Street*, 292.

15. Daniel Farson states that 7 East Crescent is where they are thought to have lodged (DF, 149); in Waters, *Whitby and the Dracula Connection*, it is claimed that Stoker stayed at 7 Royal Crescent Avenue, now 7 Crescent Avenue, where the landlady was Fanny Harker, hence Bram's use of that name; however, in Stamp, *Dracula Discovered*, it is stated that the Stokers' bedroom was on the third floor and their sitting room on the first or second floor of 6 Royal Crescent; it is also claimed that three ladies from Hertford, Isabel and Marjorie Smith and their friend Miss Stokes, became the prototypes for Lucy, Mina and Mrs Westenra respectively.

16. Perrems, I, 360–1.

17. Scott, *The Drama of Yesterday and Today*, Vol. II, 49–51, 83–4.

18. Leeds, W.G. Wills to S, n.d. [1882?]; W.G. Wills to S, 1884.

19. Moore, *Confessions of a Young Man*, 241.

20. Leeds, E[dward] Dowden to S, Dublin, 3/1/1879.

21. Dowden, *The Life of Percy Bysshe Shelley*, Vol. I, 40–51, 87; Vol. II, 1–43.

22. Dowden, *Puritan and Anglican*, 6–7; 23, 26–7, 35–68, 232–78.

23. Fermor, *Between the Woods and the Water*, 155–6.

24. Florescu and McNally, *Dracula: A Biography of Vlad the Impaler 1431–1476*, 142, 145; *Dracula, Prince of Many Faces*, 237, and *In Search of Dracula, The History of Dracula and Vampires*, 150. Reviewing their *Dracula: A Biography of Vlad the Impaler*, Maurice Richardson commented: 'It is maddening that, in spite of the mass of legend, no really coherent impression emerges.' *Observer*, 1/10/1974.

25. For the exact quotation, see Wilkinson, *An Account of the Principalities of Wallachia and Moldavia*, 19.

26. Wilkinson, *An Account of the Principalities of Wallachia and Moldavia*, 18; Stoker, *The Essential Dracula*, 41; this text has Dracula crossing the Danube at Voivode, which does not make sense, given that Voivode is a title, not a place; the Oxford University Press edition (p. 29) has 'as Voivode' which does make sense; 291, 360.

27. See Miller, *Dracula, Sense and Nonsense*, Chapter 5, 'Vlad the Impaler', for a detailed examination of the subject; Auerbach, *Our Vampires. Ourselves*, 134–5, regarding the tenuous nature of the relationship of Dracula to Vlad; Leatherdale, *Dracula, the Novel and the Legend*, 95, '. . . we cannot be over confident that Count Dracula is the resurrected Vlad the Impaler'; Senf, *Daughters of Lilith*, 201, notes that, unlike Vlad, Dracula is noble and vulnerable as well as demonic and threatening; for a different view, see Mulvey-Roberts, '*Dracula* and the Doctors: Bad Blood, Menstrual Taboo and the New Woman', in Hughes and Smith (eds) *Bram Stoker*, 78–95, which states that Dracula is modelled on Vlad the Impaler; and Elizabeth Bathory; Jonathan Barry, 'In Search of Dracula, A Personal Voyage', in Shepard and Power, *Dracula – Celebrating 100 Years*, 90–1, makes the case for Stoker having based his description of Dracula on contemporary documents; Treptow, *Dracula: Essays on the Life and Times of Vlad Tepes*, is a useful source for the historical Vlad.

28. Stoker, *The Essential Dracula*, 291–2.

29. Florescu and McNally, *In Search of Dracula*, 150; Peter Haining and Peter Tremayne, *The Undead*, 143.

30. Vambery, *Hungary in Ancient, Mediaeval, and Modern Times*, 306, 320.

31. Burton, *The Life of Captain Sir Richard Burton*, Vol. II, 43–4.

32. It has been claimed that the symptoms of 'furious' rabies closely resemble behaviour attributed to vampires. Bats, wolves and dogs, associated with rabies, transmit the disease to humans. There was a major epidemic of rabies in Hungary in 1721–8. Patients in the final stages of rabies have, incidentally, huge sexual potency. See Ward, 'Rabies May be the Root of Vampire Fears'; a connection between vampirism and porphyria, a rare hereditary disease, has been made by Dr Denis Eustace, Medical Director, Highfield Hospital Group, Dublin (letter to *Irish Times*, 12/11/1998).

33. Shelley, *Frankenstein*, 77.

34. Stenbock, 'A True Story of a Vampire', in Haining (ed.), *The Vampire Omnibus*, 158–69.

35. Verne, *Carpathian Castle*, 7, 22–3, 25.

36. Jones, *On the Nightmare*, 98–131; Joyce, *A Social History of Ancient Ireland*; Curran, 'Was Dracula an Irishman?'; O'Grady, *Selected Essays and Passages*, 31; Moretti, *Signs Taken for Wonders*, 105.

37. Foster, 'Protestant Magic: W.B. Yeats and the Spell of Irish History'; Glover, *Vampires, Mummies, and Liberals*, 25; Eagleton, *Heathcliff and the Great Hunger*, 154, 224, 187; Mc Cormack, 'Irish Gothic and After (1820–45)', in Deane (ed.), *The Field Day Anthology of Irish Writing*, 837–8.

38. Joyce, *A Portrait of the Artist as a Young Man*, 204.

39. Croly, *Salathiel the Immortal*, 1–2; Preface.

40. Murray, *A Fantastic Journey: The Life and Literature of Lafcadio Hearn*, 190; Lady Wilde, *Ancient Legends*, Vol. I, 12.

41. Lady Wilde, *Ancient Legends*, Vol. I, 15–16, 31–5, 52, 68–71, 74–6, 104, 117, 145–51, 205, 208, 169; Vol. II, 329; Lady Wilde, *Ancient Cures,* 66.

42. W. R. Wilde, *Austria*, 2, 9–10.

43. Lady Wilde, *Ancient Legends*, Vol. I, 193, 242; Vol. II, 294; Lady Wilde, *Ancient Cures*, 120.

44. Graves, *The Irish Fairy Book*, Preface.

45. *Punch*, 5/2/1881, 55; *Irish Times Magazine*, 18/11/2000, 16.

46. Lever, *Charles O'Malley*, Vol. II, 37.

47. Leeds, Lord Northcliffe to S, 27/5/97; James Knowles to S, 2/6/1897; Lord Glenerk (Sir Algernon Borthwich) to S, 4/6/1897; F.H. Field, editor of the *Literary World*, to S, 24/6/97; Sir Wemyss Thomas Reid, editor of the *Speaker*, to S, 26/6/97; Robert Leighton (on *Daily Mail* letterhead), to S, n.d.; Edgar Pemberton to S, 28/5/1897.

48. Leeds, Sir Henry Lucy to S, 14/7/97.

49. Opposite the title page of *The Mystery of the Sea*, William Rider, London, 1913; Senf, 61; Dalby.

50. *Athenaeum*, 26/6/1897, 835; *Daily Telegraph*, 3/6/1897.

51. STP, *Freeman's Journal*, 13/8/[?].

52. Noel Dobbs Collection, C.M.B. Stoker to S, 1/6/1897, 20/7/1897; Texas, Arthur Conan Doyle to S, 20/8/1897.

53. Leeds, John Sargent to S, 13/[?]/1897; the Revd Dr Lisdall to HI, 22 Herbert Place, Dublin, 13/7/189; W. Gladstone to S, 24/5/1897; Sir Melville Macnaughten, London Metropolitan Police, to S, 30/6/1897.

54. DF, 152; the Preface to the Icelandic edition is published in Leatherdale, *Bram Stoker's Dracula Unearthed*, 25–6.

55. *Commercial Advertiser*, NY, 1/11/1899; *Literary World*, 14/9/1900; *Echo*, 27/3/1902; *Washington Post*, 27/2/1904; *Literary World*, 15/11/1905; *Sketch*, 24/10/1906.

56. Leeds, Whitelaw Reid to S, 11/11/1899; Thomas Aldrich Bailey to S, 5/11/99.

57. *Free Press of Detroit*, Michigan, 18/11/1899.

58. *Home Journal* (NY), 15/11/1899; 'Book Ways and Worldly Ways', *Every Evening*, Washington, DC, 17/2/1899; *Chicago Daily News*, 15/12/1899.

59. Stoker, *The Essential Dracula*, 217, 295, 443; Arata, *Fictions of Loss in the Victorian Fin de Siècle*, 128–9; Clare A. Simmons, 'Fables of Continuity: Bram Stoker and Medievalism', in HPG, 34; Leatherdale,

Dracula, the Novel and the Legend, 237; Victor Sage, 'Exchanging Fantasies: Sex and the Serbian Crisis in *The Lady of the Shroud*', in HPG, 130.

60. Leeds, George Redford, Examiner of Plays, to S, 9/5/1897.
61. Leeds, Viscount Halifax, President of the Church Union, to S, 23/10/1897.
62. 'Another Dracula?', *Shades*, 134–5; Haining is quoting the account of Roger Sherman Hoar (1887–1963), later State Senator for Wisconsin and a science fiction writer under name Ralph Milne, who claimed that, as a seventeen-year-old Freshman at Harvard, he had a conversation with Stoker in which he articulated this ambition; Eighteen-Bisang and Melton, *Dracula: A Century of Editions*, 20. In 1902, for example, Bram staged a dramatisation of *The Mystery of the Sea* at the Lyceum (*Daily News*, 25/3/1902).

IV: Fading Splendour

13. The Lyceum Theatre Company

1. Shaw, *Bernard Shaw: Collected Letters*, Vol. IV, 207.
2. Perrems, II, 325, 300–2.
3. Ibid., 88, 326, 335–9.
4. Carr, *Mrs J. Comyns Carr's Reminiscences*, 221.
5. Gregory, *Lady Gregory's Diaries 1892–1902*, 304.
6. Perrems, II, 315–20.
7. Bancroft, *The Bancrofts: Recollections of Sixty Years*, 328.
8. Perrems, I, 272–5; see also Brereton, *The Life of Henry Irving*, 306–8, regarding the failure of *Dante*.
9. *Actor*, 453.
10. For example, Bram was rebuked by Irving for telling him that his part in *Olivia* was unworthy of him – and he queried Irving's expenditure on the sets for *Faust*; following the disastrous fire which destroyed much of the Lyceum scenery, Bram 'acted wisely and promptly' in letting the theatre for the coming season; when Irving embarked on his new career with the Lyceum Theatre Company he found that by the end of the season he had lost £4,000, less than the nominal salary 'upon which Stoker had so wisely insisted'; when Irving was invited to mount *Dante* at the Theatre Royal, Drury Lane in April 1903, Bram had misgivings and warned him that he could not afford the loss which failure of the play would entail (Irving had a stake of £12,000 in it) and *Dante* was indeed a disaster for Irving. *Actor*, 457, 468, 649–51, 622–3, 628.

11. *Actor*, 626.
12. HL, 129.
13. Hatton, *Henry Irving's Impressions of America*, 35; Fales, 'Homey Beg' [Hall Caine] to S, 11/10/97; Carr, *Mrs J. Comyns Carr's Reminiscences*, 152
14. Fales, Hall Caine to Major J.B. Pond, 1/10/1895; Hall Caine to S, from Greeba Castle, Isle of Man, 11/10/[18] 97.

14. 'Wholesome, Healthy, and Stirring Fiction'

1. Leeds, J.W. Arrowsmith to S, Bristol, 9/10/1894.
2. Leeds, Sir Henry Lucy to S, 2/3/1898; *Punch* 5/3/1898.
3. *Era*, 12/3/1898, 16; *Irish Times*, 26/2/1898.
4. *Bookman*, April 1898; *Daily Chronicle*; *Daily News* 2/3/1898; *Athenaeum*, 26/3/1898; *Graphic*, 26/3/1898; *Morning Post*, 4/3/1898; *Daily (?) Telegraph*, 2/3/1898; *Literary World*, 25/2/1898; *Sheffield Telegraph*, 16/2/1898; *Hull Daily Mail*, 23/2/1898; *Scotsman*, 18/2/1898; *Birmingham Gazette*, 23/2/1898; *Yorkshire Post*, 2/3/1898; *Gloucester Journal*, 26/2/1898; *Greenock Telegraph and Clyde Shipping Gazette*, 17/3/1898; *Northern Echo*, 14/1/1898; *Belfast News Letter*, 24/3/1898; *Catholic Times*, 23/3/1898; *Freemasons Journal*, 25/2/1898.
5. Adams, 'Bram Stoker'; Johnson is quoted in Delaney, *A Walk to the Western Isles*, 121.
6. Drummond, 'Dracula's Castle'.
7. Stoker, 'The Seer', in *Shades*, 128.
8. Stoker, *The Mystery of the Sea*, 36–7.
9. Dowden, *Shakspere: A Critical Study of His Mind and Art*, 16. The reviewer in the New York *Commercial Advertiser*, 5/4/1902, commenting that Stoker had something akin to genius in his line of fiction, linked it with Ann Radcliffe's *The Mysteries of Udolpho*; in 'Mother Dracula: Orientalism, Degeneration, and Anglo–Irish National Subjectivity at the Fin de Siècle', Cannon Schmitt argues that Stoker can be placed in the Anglo-Irish horror tradition of Le Fanu and Maturin whose *Melmoth the Wanderer*, 'an explicitly and relentlessly anti-Catholic work, marshals the Gothic's extensive machinery of paranoia for the purpose of demonizing the Irish followers of the Church of Rome as well as their Spanish allies'.
10. Stoker, *The Mystery of the Sea*, 272.
11. Leeds, J. Brodie Innes to S, Milton Brodie, Morres, Scotland, 20/7/1902; Stoker also sent him copies of his later books, of which Brodie-Innes generally professed a high opinion (Leeds, J. Brodie Innes

to S, 29/11/1903 re *The Jewel of Seven Stars*; 7/6/1908 re *Lady Athlyne*; 26/2/1909 re *The Lady of the Shroud*).

12. Leeds, Lord Glenerk, to S, 23/7/1902; Edgar Pemberton, to S, 23/7/1902; Sir Wemyss Thomas Reid to S, 17/8/1902; Crown Prince of Siam to S, 24/9/1902.

13. *Daily Mail*, 5/8/1902; *Daily Graphic*, 5/8/1902; *Era*, 9/8/1902; *Topical Times*, London, 16/8/1902; *Westminster Gazette*, 21/8/1902; *Northern Whig*, Belfast, 31/7/1902; *Liverpool Courier*, 12/8/1902; *Sunday Special*, 10/8/1902; New York *Sun*, 5/4/1902.

14. Stoker, *The Jewel of Seven Stars*, 119–20.

15. Ibid., 26; P.B. Shelley, 'Prometheus Unbound', in *English Romantic Poetry*, ed. Harold Bloom, Anchor Books, NY, 1963, 181; Stoker, *The Jewel of Seven Stars*, 132–3.

16. Stoker, *The Jewel of Seven Stars*, 136, 130, 134, 144; Christopher Frayling (*Vampires: Lord Byron to Count Dracula*, 70) has commented on how Stoker's knowledge of the occult interests of the Romantic poets featured in *Jewel*.

17. Glover, *Vampires, Mummies, and Liberals*, 92–3; Lisa Hopkins, 'Crowning the King, Mourning his Mother: *The Jewel of Seven Stars* and *The Lady of the Shroud*', in *HPG*, 134–50; Robert Edwards, 'The Alien and the Familiar in *The Jewel of Seven Stars* and *Dracula*', in *HPG*, 96–115; Robert Tracy, 'Loving You All Ways: Vamps, Vampires, Necrophiles and Necrofilles in Nineteenth-Century Fiction', in Barreca (ed.), *Sex and Death in Victorian Literature*, 32–59; Auerbach, *Woman and the Demon*, 24–5; Senf, 110–11.

18. Leeds, J. Brodie Innes to S, 29/11/1903.

19. *Sheffield Independent*, 2/12/1903; *Western Mail*, 20/8/1904; *New York Times*, 5/3/1904; *Philadelphia Press*, 5/3/1904; *Literary World* (Boston, Mass.), March 1904; *Books News* (Philadelphia), March 1904; *Aberdeen Daily Journal*, 30/11/1903; *Morning Post*, 1/12/1903; *Churchman*, New York City, 7/5/1904; *Press Post*, Columbus Ohio, 11/9/1904; *Journal* (Albany, NY), 21/2/1904.

20. New York *Herald*, 17/3/1904.

21. Stoker, *The Man*, 79–80.

22. Showalter, *Sexual Anarchy*, 38.

23. Stoker, *The Man*, 333–4.

24. Ibid., 380.

25. Ibid., 434.

26. *Daily Illustrated Mirror*, London, 13/9/1905; *Bystander*, 4/10/1905; *Literary World*, 15/11/1905.

27. *Outlook*, 23/9/1905, 406; *Saturday Review*, 14/10/1905; *Record Herald*

Chicago 3/9/1908, review of *The Gates of Life*; *Tasmanian Mail*, 17/3/1906; *Bristol Times*, 21/9/1905.

28. *Yorkshire Post*, 8/11/1905; *Vanity Fair*, 28/9/1905; *Speaker*, 19/9/1905; *Manchester Guardian*, 13/9/1905; *Birmingham Post*, 13/10/1905.

29. *Morning Post*, 19/9/1905; *Punch*, 27/9/1905; *Daily Telegraph*, 13/9/1905; *Daily Express*, 28/9/1905; *London Weekly News*, 17/9/1905; *Pall Mall Gazette*, 14/10/1905; *Bookman*, Oct. 1905; *Society Pictorial*, 28/10/1905; *Literary World*, 15/9/1905; *Staffordshire Sentinel* (Hanley) 9/10/1905; *Sheffield Independent*, 2/10/1905; *Bristol Western Daily Press*, 25/9/1905; *Leeds Mercury*, 18/9/1905; *Liverpool Courier*, 22/9/1905; *Onlooker*, 14/10/1905; *Glasgow Herald*, 14/9/1905; *Irish Times*, 22/9/1905.

30. David Glover (*Vampires, Mummies, and Liberals*, 14, 20–1) comments that *The Man* and *Lady Athlyne* are an attempt to formulate the truths of sexuality so as to ward off the threat of women's social and political rights and that in both novels there are 'angry ripostes to the growing movement for woman's suffrage'; Daniel Pick ('"Terrors of the Night": *Dracula* and "Degeneration" in the late Nineteenth Century') describes *The Man* as 'a kind of "positive eugenic" homily, the saga of the struggle to get good stock together', and states that the women in *The Man* are in trouble from themselves: 'The dangers are all internal, there are no monsters.'

V: *Under the Sunset*

15. The Final Curtain

1. Perrems, II, 337–8.
2. Ibid., 341–4.
3. STP, 'The Kaleidoscope' by George Pomeroy Goodale, unidentified newspaper, n.d.
4. ST, ET to S, n.d.
5. Shaw, *Bernard Shaw: Collected Letters*, Vol. III, 39, 383; Holroyd, *Bernard Shaw*, Vol. I, 351–61, 365.
6. *Times Literary Supplement*, 19/10/1906, 353.
7. Perrems, I, 129.
8. Ibid., 298–9; Perrems II, 2–5, 203–5; review of *Personal Reminiscences of Henry Irving* in the *Book Lover*, 1/12/1906: in a generally unfavourable review, the writer wondered if the truth would ever be known about Ellen Terry's connection with Irving and the cause of its disruption.
9. Perrems, II, 364–6.

10. *The Times*, 22/4/1912; *Evening News*, 22/4/1912.

11. *Sketch*, 24/10/1906, 52; STP, unidentified newspaper, n.d., review of the literature of 1906 by Edward Hawke; *Bazaar*, 2/1/1907; *Tatler*, 13/12/1906; ST, New York *Life*(?), 17/1/1907; *Book Lover*, 1/12/1906; *Bookman*, Nov. 1906; STP, 'Printer's Pie' column, *Tribune*, 14/8/1908.

12. STP, *Sheffield Free* (?) *Press*, 21/3/[1907?].

13. STP, 'The Kaleidoscope' by George Pomeroy Goodale, unidentified newspaper, n.d.

14. Hatton, *Henry Irving's Impressions of America*, Vol. II, 29–38; FitzGerald, *Henry Irving. A Record of Twenty Years at the Lyceum*, Preface, vi–vii; Brereton, *The Life of Henry Irving*, 59–60.

15. Information provided by Dr Jeanne Keyes Youngson, founder of the Count Dracula Fan Club, now the Vampire Empire, and the Bram Stoker Memorial Association.

16. Graves, *To Return to All That*, 134 and *Irish Literary and Musical Studies*, 63; Le Fanu, *Seventy Years of Irish Life*, 122–7, provides useful background on the poem.

16. In the Valley of the Shadow

1. Stoker, *Lady Athlyne*, 54–5.

2. 'In the Valley of the Shadow', in *Shades*, 199.

3. Auberon, *The Nineteen Hundreds*, 129–30.

4. STP, Bailie (?), Glasgow, 14/11/1902.

5. Leeds, S to William Gillette, 2/11/1905; William Gillette to S, 3/11/[1905]; Laurence Irving to S, n.d.

6. Leeds, Liza Lehmann Bedford (Mrs Herbert Bedford) to S, 1906; Alma-Tadema to S, 1/5/1901 and 13/12/1907.

7. See, for example, Leeds, FB to Madame Pauline Donalda-Seuilliac, opera singer, 21/12/1907.

8. Series of letters from Tom Stoker to Enid Bruce; some were written from 54 St Stephen's Green and some from India; lent to the author by Dan Farson.

9. *Literary World*, 15/11/1905.

10. *The Pundit and Other Stories*, by T. Stoker, CSI [1899] (five stories in all), Noel Dobbs Collection.

11. ST, Tom Stoker to S, 42 Egerton Crescent, SW [London], 14/10/1905.

12. AS, Margaret D. Thomson to Tom [Stoker], 54 St Stephen's Green, East, Dublin, 15/11/[1909].

13. STP, *MAP* [?], 7/10/[1905]; *Daily Telegraph*, 24/4/1912, 'Bram Stoker. The Story of a Great Friendship. By Hall Caine'.

14. *The Times*, 25/3/1907; *Publisher and Bookseller*, 20/3/1907; Stoker, *The*

Essential Dracula, 142; Shaw, *Man and Superman* (1905) Library of the Future CD-ROM, 3rd edition, World Library, Irving, Calif., 1995.

15. *British Architect*, 3/4/1907; *Birmingham Post*, 24/4/1908, letter to the editor of the *Daily Post* from the Executive Committee of the Shakespeare Memorial, including Stoker; STP, *Yorkshire Post*, 2/5/1908(?).

16. BL, printed form from the Royal Literary Fund; S received £100 on 9/3/1911; BL, S to Llewellyn Roberts, Royal Literary Fund, 9/3/1911.

17. *Daily News*, 9/3/1894; *Star*, 10/3/1894.

18. 'Ireland in 1907, an Editorial Appreciation', *World's Work*, 9 (54), London, May 1907.

19. Stoker, 'The Great White Fair in Dublin', 570–6; see also the *Dublin Evening Mail 1823–1923 Centenary Number*, 63, 'Donnybrook Fair' for an account of the violence and drunkenness at the fair in its former incarnation; William, Hughes, 'Introducing Patrick to his New Self: Bram Stoker and the 1907 Dublin Exhibition', 9–14, for an analysis of Stoker's article; and Lever, *Charles O'Malley*, Vol. II, 177, for a reference to Donnybrook Fair in a ballad.

20. Stoker, 'The World's Greatest Shipbuilding Yard'.

21. Special Collections, Miller Library, Colby College, Waterville, Maine, Thomas Hardy to S, 1/7/1907.

22. BL, S to the Rt. Hon. Lord Avebury, 21/11/1907; S to 'Dear My Lord [Avebury]', 25/11/1907, enclosing a typescript of conversation for approval/amendment.

23. 'A Great Critic at Home', *Punch*, 8/1/1908.

24. Stoker, 'Mr Winston Churchill Talks of his Hopes, his Work, and his Ideals to Bram Stoker'.

25. Maggie Kilgour, 'Vampiric Arts: Bram Stoker's Defence of Poetry', in *HPG*, 47–8.

26. Leeds, George Redford to S, 1/3/97.

27. *Morning Advertiser*, 30/3/1903; *Los Angeles Sunday Times*, 20/10/1907; *The Times*, 19/11/1907.

28. Stoker, 'The Censorship of Fiction'.

29. Nordau, *Degeneration*, 296–301; Stoker, *Famous Impostors*, 235–41.

30. Manuscript Room, Trinity College, Dublin, Unpublished preface to *Famous Impostors*; the titles, 'Fulfilled Ambitions' and 'The Game Begins' were written on blank pages in his notes.

31. Glover (*Vampires, Mummies, and Liberals*, 75), states that, in *Famous Impostors*, 'Stoker reveals a fascination with deception and disguise while also denying its efficacy in some of its commonest forms.'

32. Stoker, *Famous Impostors*, 149.

33. STP, *Columbus Journal* [?], 25/12/1910; *Stroud News*, 27/1/1911; *Saturday Review*, 1/4/1911; *Chicago Sunday Examiner*, 19/2/1911; *Bookman*, Jan. 1911, 456–7; *Evening Transcript* (Boston), 24/12/1910; STP, *Banner* (USA), n.d.; *Punch*, 22/2/1911. Senf, 165–72 quotes from further reviews, including in the *Independent, Spectator, Dial, Athenaeum* and *Literary Digest*.

17. Bourgeois Fantasy

1. Arata, *Fictions of Loss in the Victorian Fin de Siècle*, 114.
2. Stoker, *Lady Athlyne*, 88.
3. Leeds, Rt. Revd John Dowden, Bishop of Edinburgh, to S, 20/1/1901; see also the Revd William M. Sinclair, Archdeacon of London and Canon of St Paul's, to S, 13/3/1901 and 20/5/1901.
4. Glover, *Vampires, Mummies, and Liberals*, 131.
5. Leeds, Archibold Ross Colquhoun, postcard to S, 11/6/1908; Colquhoun, *The Whirlpool of Europe*, 326, 268, 288.
6. Senf, 155–6; *Sydney Morning Herald*, 8/8/1909.
7. HL, 148–9; Phyllis A. Roth, *Bram Stoker*, 80–1, makes a similar comment, that the only real mystery is that of motive for the characters' actions; DF, 217.
8. Stoker, *The Lair of the White Worm*, 69–70.
9. Sikes, *British Goblins*, 392–3; Lewis, *Tales of Wonder*, 434–42; *Punch*, 15/11/1890.
10. Stoker, *The Lair of the White Worm*, 64.
11. Ibid., 113; Rebecca Scott (*The Fabrication of the Late Victorian Femme Fatale*, 77) comments that Sir Nathaniel's warning that playing the masculine against the feminine is the only hope of progress; otherwise atavistic women will drag men back to the primal abyss, to sexuality, and to irresponsible bestiality; H.L. Malchow (*Gothic Images of Race in Nineteenth-Century Britain*, 142) states that the danger of Lady Arabella lies in masculinity rather than femininity: she has been transformed into a serpent, an image of the male member; Robert Tracy ('Loving You All Ways: Vamps, Vampires, Necrophiles and Necrofilles in Nineteenth-Century Fiction', in Barreca (ed.), *Sex and Death in Victorian Literature*, 53) sees the central sexual anxieties of the *Lair* as the fear of sexually aggressive women, especially women who also represent a sexual threat to other women: 'This may record Stoker's final revulsion against women as the proximate source of the disease which he knew was killing him.'
12. Verne, *Carpathian Castle*, 166; David Seed ('Eruptions of the Primitive into the Present: *The Jewel of Seven Stars* and *The Lair of the White*

Worm', in *HPG*, 202) comments that the cataclysms at the end of the novel are ushering in a new order; Stoker draws on the apocalyptic paradigm for the three phases of the final denouement: the revelation of the monster; the ultimate battle which seems to include Nature itself; and the ushering in of a new order, in this case with a new era of prosperity for the estate under Adam's benign ownership.

13. Leeds, Mrs William Kingdon (Lucy) Clifford to S, 15/11/1911.
14. Quoted in Dalby 65; HL, 149; Senf, 173.

18. *The Dead Un-dead*

1. The *Daily Sketch* 23/4/1912 obituary of Stoker states that his death came 'after six years' illness'; *Westminster Gazette*, 23/4/1912.
2. BL, S to the Committee of the Royal Literary Fund, 25/2/1911; AS, NS to HL, n.d., fragment of a MS, assumed to be part of a letter; AS, typescript, 'Bram Stoker, by his Son, Noel Thornley Stoker' [8/11/1947].
3. Republished in *Shades*, 198–204.
4. Leeds, Sir Lawrence Alma-Tadema to S, 4/11/1907; Sir George Alexander to S, n.d.
5. AS, FB to TS, 4 Durham Place, 7/12/[1910].
6. *Daily Telegraph*, 24/4/1912; Hall Caine, 'Bram Stoker. The Story of a Great Friendship'.
7. ST, M[atilda] Petitjean to S, Versailles, 21/1/1911.
8. Forrest, 'Castle Dracula', 6–7.
9. AS, Copy of Stoker's death certificate.
10. DF, 212, 233–5; Belford, *Bram Stoker*, 122; Haining and Tremayne, *The Undead*, 182.
11. (1) Dr Siobhan Murphy, Consultant Physician, Department of Genito-Urinary Medicine, the Patrick Clements Clinic, Central Middlesex Hospital Trust, wrote a paper for the author on the subject, dated 12/13 May 1997 – I am indebted to my friend and colleague, Mr Philip McDonagh, and his wife, Dr Ana Greville, for putting me in touch with Dr Murphy. (2) J.D. Oriel, MD, formerly Consultant Physician in Genito–Urinary Medicine, University College, London also wrote an extensive paper for the author on the subject of Stoker's health – I am indebted to Dr Murphy for putting me in touch with Dr Oriel. (3) Professor J.B. Lyons, MD, FRCPI, of the Royal College of Surgeons in Ireland, a distinguished author as well as physician, prepared a paper and discussed the issues involved in Stoker's health at length with the author in taped conversations on 9 July 1998 and 21 August 1998; needless to say, I owe a debt of gratitude to all the above for their great

kindness in taking such trouble over this issue.

12. Paper by Dr Siobhan Murphy, 12/13 May 1997.

13. Paper by J.D. Oriel, 1997.

14. Paper by Professor J.B. Lyons, 9/7/1998; Professor J.B. Lyons, taped conversations with the author, 9 July 1998.

15. *The Times*, 25/4/1912; see Judd, *Ford Madox Ford*, 274 re Irish nationalism and p. 474 (index) re Violet Hunt.

16. Gittings and Manton, *The Second Mrs Hardy*, 66, quoting 'Personal information, Bram Stoker's grand-daughter'.

17. Lilly Library, Indiana University, FB to Messrs D. Appleton & Co., May 1912.

18. *The Times*, 18/5/1912.

19. Ibid., 8/7/1913; see also *The Times*, 20/6/1913.

20. TCD MSS, Florence Stoker to Phil [?], 31/1/1921; ref: 7117/1/1.

21. University of Newcastle, FB to Mr Bang, n.d.

22. BL MSS Department, correspondence between Florence Stoker and the Society of Authors; and Dept of Education, Dublin to G. Herbert Thring, Secretary, Incorporated Society of Authors, London, 20/11/1929.

23. BL MSS Department, Florence Stoker to Mr Thring, 30/11/1929; Florence Stoker to Kilham Roberts, Society of Authors, 26/8/1931.

24. BL MSS Department, Florence Stoker to Kilham Roberts, 1/10/1931.

25. AS, newspaper cutting, *Daily Mail*, 13/8/1979, interview with Ann Stoker by Charles Catchpole; AS, *Sunday Post*, 11/11/1979, in which she repeats the claim that Florence lost all the film money in the American depression; AS, copy of estate duty form following Florence's death.

26. BL MSS Department, Florence Stoker to Kilham Roberts, Society of Authors, 1/3/1931.

Bibliography

WORKS BY BRAM STOKER

Novels/Extended Fiction

Under the Sunset, London: Sampson Low, Marston, Searle & Rivington, 1882 [1881] (collection of short stories)

The Snake's Pass, London: Sampson Low & Co., 1891 [1890]; Brandon, Dingle, Ireland, 1990

The Fate of Fenella, London: Hutchinson & Co., 1892, 3 vols. Stoker contributed a chapter, 'Lord Castleton Explains', to this multi-authored work

The Watter's Mou', New York: L. DeVinne & Co., 1894; London: The Acme Library, 1894; London: A. Constable and Co., 1895

The Shoulder of Shasta, London: Archibald Constable & Co., 1895. Reprinted with annotation and introduction by Alan Johnson (Clive Leatherdale, series ed.) Westcliff-on-Sea, Essex, UK: Desert Island Dracula Library, 2000

Dracula, London: Archibald Constable & Co., 1897

The Essential Dracula, ed. Leonard Wolf, New York and London: Plume, 1975/1993 is the version used by the author

Dracula: or The Un-Dead, a Play in Prologue and Five Acts, ed. Sylvia Starshine, Nottingham, UK: Pumpkin Books, 1997

Miss Betty, London: C. Arthur Pearson, 1898; London: New English Library, 1974

The Mystery of the Sea, London: William Heinemann, 1902; London: William Rider, 1913

The Jewel of Seven Stars, London: William Heinemann, 1903; New York: Harper Bros, 1904. Reprinted with annotation and editing by Clive Leatherdale, Westcliff-on-Sea, Essex, UK: Desert Island Dracula Library, 1996

The Man, London: William Heinemann, 1905; published as *The Gates of Life*, New York: Cupples & Leon Co., 1908 (abridged by the author); London: Robert Hayes, n.d. [c. 1920] (abridged)

Lady Athlyne, London: William Heinemann, 1908

Snowbound: The record of a theatrical touring party, London: Collier & Co., 1908. Reprinted annotated and edited by Bruce Wightman, Westcliff-on-Sea, Essex, UK: Desert Island Dracula Library, 2000 (collection of short stories)

The Lady of the Shroud, London: William Heinemann, 1909; Gloucestershire: Alan Sutton, 1994

The Lair of the White Worm, London: William Rider, 1911

Dracula's Guest, and Other Weird Stories, London: George Routledge & Sons 1914; reprinted Dingle, Ireland: Brandon, 1990 (collection of Stoker's short stories)

Shades of Dracula, Bram Stoker's Uncollected Stories, ed. Peter Haining, London: William Kimber, 1982 (collection of Stoker's short stories)

Midnight Tales, ed. Peter Haining, London: Peter Owen, 1990 (collection of Stoker's short stories)

Non-Fiction

'The Necessity for Political Honesty', University of Dublin, College Historical Society, 'Address Delivered . . . November 13, 1872, by the Auditor', Abraham Stoker, A.B., Dublin: John Charles & Son, 1872

The Duties of Clerks of Petty Sessions in Ireland, Dublin: John Falconer, 1879

A Glimpse of America. A Lecture given at London Institute, 28/12/1885, London: Sampson Low & Co., 1886

Personal Reminiscences of Henry Irving, London: William Heinemann, 1906

Famous Impostors, London: Sidgwick & Jackson, 1910

Short Stories/Poems

The stories listed below are those not included in the two collections of short stories published in Stoker's lifetime or shortly afterwards, *Under the Sunset* and *Dracula's Guest*, or were first published under a different title.

'The Crystal Cup', *London Society*, 22 (129), pp. 228–35, Sept. 1872

'The Primrose Path. A Serial in Ten Chapters', *The Shamrock*, 12 [Dublin] pp. 289–93; 312–17, 6 Feb. – 6 March 1875; 330–4; 345–9; 360–5. Reprinted with an introduction by Richard Dalby, Westcliff-on-Sea, Essex, UK: Desert Island Dracula Library, 1999

'Buried Treasures. A Serial in Four Chapters', *The Shamrock*, 12 [Dublin] pp. 13–25 March 1875

'Our New House', London: *The Theatre Annual*, 1886

'The Dualitists or the Death Doom of the Double Born', London: *The Theatre Annual*, ed. Clement Scott, 1887

'Death in the Wings', *Collier's*, Nov. 1888

'The Man from Shorrox',' *Pall Mall Magazine*, Feb. 1894, pp. 656–69. Illustrated by W. Thomas Smith

'Lord Castleton Explains', [Chapter X of *The Fate of Fenetta* (a collaborative novel)], *The Gentlewoman*, 4, 1892

'The Red Stockade', *Cosmopolitian Magazine*, Sept. 1894

'Crooken Sands', *Illustrated Sporting and Dramatic News*, 1 Dec. 1894

'A Baby Passenger', *Lloyd's Weekly Newspaper*, 19 Feb. 1899

'A Young Widow', *Lloyd's Weekly Newspaper*, 26 March 1899

'A Yellow Duster', *Lloyd's Weekly Newspaper*, 7 May 1899

'The Seer, *The London Magazine*, Nov. 1901

'One Thing Needful,' a poem by Stoker, published in *A Volunteer Haversack*, containing contributions of certain writers to the *Queen's Rifle Volunteer Brigade: The Royal Scots*, Nov 1902. It was reprinted in *The Queen's Carol: An Anthology of Poems, Stories, Essays, Drawings and Music by British Authors, Artists and Composers*, London: *Daily Mail*, 1905

'In the Valley of the Shadow', *The Grand Magazine*, July 1907

"Eroes of the Thames, The Story of a Frustrated Advertisement', *The Royal Magazine*, Oct. 1908, pp. 566–70

'The Way of Peace', *Everybody's Story Magazine*, Dec. 1909, pp. 204–9; reprinted in the *Bram Stoker Society Journal* 1 [Dublin] pp. 34–41, 1989

'Greater Love', *The London Magazine*, 33, pp. 161–8, 1914

Articles

'Actor-Managers', *The Nineteenth Century*, 27 [London], pp. 1040–51, Jan.–June 1890

'Recollections of the Late W.G. Wills', *The Graphic*, 19 Dec. 1891

'Dramatic Criticism', *The North American Review*, 158 [New York] pp. 325–31, 1894

'The Art of Ellen Terry', *The Playgoer*, [London], Oct. 1901, pp. 39–48

'Ellen Terry. An Appreciation', *The Northern Echo*, 27 April 1906

'Toole and Irving. 50 Years' Friendship', *Daily Telegraph*, [London], 1 Aug. 1906

'John Lawrence Toole', *Morning Leader*, 1 Aug. 1906

'The Great White Fair in Dublin', *The World's Work*, 9 (54), pp. 570–6 [London], May 1907

'The World's Greatest Shipbuilding Yard', *The World's Work*, 9 (54), pp. 647–50 [London], May 1907

'The Tendency of the Modern Stage. A Talk with Sir W.S. Gilbert on Things Theatrical', *The Daily Chronicle*, 2 Jan. 1908

'The Question of a National Theatre', *The Nineteenth Century and After*, [London], 63 (371) Jan. 1908

'Mr Winston Churchill Talks of his Hopes, his Work, and his Ideals to Bram Stoker', *The Daily Chronicle*, 15 Jan. 1908

'Sir Arthur Conan Doyle Tells of his Career and Work, his Sentiments towards America, and his Approaching Marriage', *The World* [New York], 28 July 1907. Shorter version in *The Daily Chronicle*, 14 Feb. 1908

'How Mr Pinero Writes Plays, Told in an Interview by Bram Stoker', *The Daily Chronicle*, 15 Feb. 1908

'The Work of William De Morgan, an Artist, Manufacturer, and Inventor who Began Writing Novels at the Age of Sixty-four', *The World's Work*, [London], 12, pp. 160–4, July 1908

'The Censorship of Fiction', *The Nineteenth Century and After*, [London], 64, pp. 479–87, July–Dec. 1908

'Americans as Actors', *The Fortnightly Review*, [London], 85, new series, Jan.–June 1909

'The Censorship of Stage Plays', *The Nineteenth Century and After*, [London], 66, pp. 974–89, July–Dec. 1909

'Dead-Heads', *The Fortnightly Review*, [London], 86, new series, July–Dec. 1909

'The American Tramp Question and the Old English Vagrancy Laws', *The North American Review*, [New York], 190, pp. 605–14, 1909

'Irving and Stage Lighting', *The Nineteenth Century and After*, [London], 69, Jan.–June 1911

Other Works

Aberdeen, Ishbel, Countess of. 'The Sorrows of Ireland', *Yale Review*, Oct. 1916

Acheson, Alan R. *A True and Lively Faith: Evangelical Revival in the Church of Ireland*, Church of Ireland Christian Fellowship, 1992

Adams, Norman. 'Bram Stoker', *The Leopard Magazine*, June 1976

Allen, Dennis W. N. *Sexuality in Victorian Fiction*, London: University of Oklahoma Press, 1993

Allen, Vivien. *Hall Caine: Portrait of a Victorian Romancer*, Sheffield: Sheffield Academic Press, 1997

An Alphabetical List of the 50, 20, *and* 10 *Freeholders and Leaseholders as Registered in the County of Dublin . . . up to 1st July 1837*, Dublin: Dillon McNamara, 1835 and 1837

Arata, Stephen. *Fictions of Loss in the Victorian Fin de Siècle*, Cambridge: Cambridge University Press, 1996

Archer, William. *The Theatrical World of 1894*, with an introduction by George Bernard Shaw, London: Walter Scott, 1895

Aria, Mrs Eliza. *My Sentimental Self*, London: Chapman & Hall, 1922

Auberon, Reginald [Horace Wyndham]. *The Nineteen Hundreds*, London: G. Allen & Unwin [1922]

Auerbach, Nina. *Woman and the Demon: The Life of a Victorian Myth*, Cambridge, Mass.: Harvard University Press, 1982

Auerbach, Nina. *Ellen Terry: Player in her Time*, London: Phoenix House, 1987

Auerbach, Nina. *Private Theatricals: The Lives of the Victorians*, Cambridge, Mass.: Harvard University Press, 1990

Auerbach, Nina. *Our Vampires, Ourselves*, Chicago: University of Chicago Press, 1995

Ausubel, Herman. *John Bright, Victorian Reformer*, New York: Wiley, 1966

Bancroft, Squire and Bancroft, Marie Effie. *Mr and Mrs Bancroft on and off the Stage*, London: R. Bentley & Son, 1888

Bancroft, Sir Squire and Bancroft, Marie Effie. *The Bancrofts: Recollections of Sixty Years*, John Murray, 1909

Bardsley, C.W. *A Dictionary of English and Welsh Surnames*, London: Henry Frowde, 1901

Baring-Gould, Sabine. *The Book of Werewolves* [1865], London: Senate, 1995

Barreca, Regina (ed.). *Sex and Death in Victorian Literature*, Basingstoke and London: Macmillan, 1990

Bazett, L. Margery. *Telepathy and Spirit-Communication*, with a foreword by Sir Frank Benson, London: Rider, 1928

Belford, Barbara. *Violet. The Story of the Irrepressible Violet Hunt*, New York: Simon & Schuster, c. 1990

Belford, Barbara. *Bram Stoker. A Biography of the Author of Dracula*, London: Weidenfeld & Nicolson, 1996

Benson, Sir Frank. *My Memoirs*, London: Ernest Benn, 1930

Benson, Mary. 'Discovering Irish Ancestors', research paper, copy supplied by the late Sean Ronan

Bingham, Madeleine. *Henry Irving and the Victorian Theatre*, London: Allen and Unwin, 1978

Bird, Isabella, *Golden Chersonese*, London: John Murray, 1883

Blair, Robert. *Robert Blair's The Grave*, ed. R.N. Essick and M.D. Paley, London: Scholar Press, 1982

Blake, Martin. *Blake Family Records 1300–1700*, London: Elliott Stock, 1902/5

Blunt, Reginald. *An Illustrated Historical Handbook to the Parish of Chelsea*, London: Lamley, 1900

Boas, Guy. *The Garrick Club, 1831–1964*, London: Garrick Club, 1964

Boner, Charles. *Transylvania: Its Products and People*, London: Longmans & Co., 1865

Booth, J.B. *Palmy Days*, London: Richards Press, 1957

Boxwell, William and Purser, F.C. *An Introduction to the Practice of Medicine*, Dublin: Talbot Press, 1924

Bremont, Anna, comtesse de. *Oscar Wilde and His Mother*, London: Everett, 1911

Brereton, Austin. *The Life of Henry Irving*, London: Longmans, 1908

Brodie-Innes, J.W. *The Astrology of the Golden Dawn*, ed. Darcy Küntz, Washington: Holmes Publishing Group, 1996

Brontë, Emily. *Wuthering Heights* [1847], London: Penguin, 1994

Brown, Stephen. *Ireland in Fiction*, Dublin and London: Maunsel, 1919

Brown, Terence. 'Edward Dowden: Irish Victorian', in *Ireland's Literature*, Mullingar: 1988

Browne, Sir Thomas. *Works of Thomas Browne*, 6 vols, London: Geoffrey Keynes, 1928–31

Budge, Sir Ernest Aldred Wallis. *The Egyptian Book of the Dead* [1895], New York: Dover Publications, 1967

Budge, Sir Ernest Aldred Wallis. *The Egyptian Magic* [1899], London: Arkana, 1988

Bunyan, John. *The Pilgrim's Progress* [1678 and 1684], London: Penguin 1965 and 1987

Burke, Sir Bernard and Burke, Ashworth. *A Genealogical and Heraldic History of the Peerage and Baronetage, etc.*, London: Harrison & Sons, 1912

Burke, Edmund. *A Philosophical Enquiry into the Origins of Our Ideas of the Sublime and Beautiful*, (1757), Oxford: Oxford University Press, 1990

Burtchaell, George Dames and Sadleir, Thomas Ulick (eds). *Alumni Dublinensis: A Register of the Students, Graduates, Professors and Provosts of Trinity College in the University of Dublin (1583–1860)*, Dublin: Thom, 1935

Burton, Sir Richard F. *Wanderings in West Africa from Liverpool to Fernando Po*, London: Tinsley Bros, 1863

Burton, Richard F. *Vikram and the Vampire or, Tales of Hindu Devilry*, London: Longmans, Green, 1870

Burton, Sir Richard F. *The Kasidah of Haji Abdu El Yezdi*, London: Bernard Quaritch, 1880

Burton, Isabel. *The Life of Captain Sir Richard Burton*, London: Chapman and Hall, 1893

Byrne, Patrick F. *Witchcraft in Ireland*, Cork: Mercier, 1967

Caine, Hall. *Capt'n Davy's Honeymoon (including The Last Confession & The Blind Mother)*, London: Heinemann, 1893

Caine, Hall. *My Story*, London: Heinemann, 1908

Caine, Hall. *King Edward: A Prince and a Great Man: A Pen Portrait*, London: Collier & Co., 1910

Caine, Hall. *King Albert's Book: A Tribute to the Belgian King and People from Representative Men and Women throughout the World*, ed. Hall Caine, London: *Daily Telegraph*, 1914

Calmet, Augustin. *The Phantom World*, ed. Revd Henry Christmas, London: Richard Bentley, 1850

Campbell, John Gregorson. *Superstitions and Witchcraft and Second Sight in the Highlands and Islands of Scotland*, Glasgow: J. MacLehose & Sons, 1900

Campbell, John Gregorson. *Witchcraft and Second Sight in the Highlands and Islands of Scotland*, Glasgow: J. MacLehose & Sons, 1902; reprinted Wakefield: EP Publishing, 1974

Carr, J. Comyns. *Some Eminent Victorians: Personal Recollections in the World of Art and Letters*, London: Duckworth & Co., 1908

Carr, Mrs J. Comyns. *Mrs J. Comyns Carr's Reminiscences*, ed. Eve Adam London: Hutchinson & Co., 1925

Catalogue of Graduates who have proceeded to degrees in the University of Dublin, Dublin, 1869; Vol. II (second edition), Dublin: Hodges, Smith and Foster and London: Longmans, Green, 1896

Catalogue of Valuable Printed Books, Autograph Letters, and Illuminated and Other Manuscripts including the Library of the late Bram Stoker Esq., London: Sotheby, Wilkinson & Hodge, 7 July 1913

City of Dublin Election March 1857: List of Voters and for whom they Voted, Dublin: Browne & Nolan, 1857

City of Dublin Election May 1859: List of Electors for the Year 1859, Distinguishing the Names of those who Exercised their Franchise at the above Election, and Showing for whom they Voted, Dublin: Shannon & M'Dermott, 1859

Coakley, D. *The Irish School of Medicine: Outstanding Practitioners of the 19th Century*, Dublin: Town House, 1988

Colles, Ramsay. *In Castle and Court House, Being Reminiscences of 30 Years in Ireland*, London: T. Werner Laurie, 1911

Collins, Wilkie. *The Woman in White* [1860], London: Penguin, 1974

Colquhoun, Archibald R. and Colquhoun, Ethel. *The Whirlpool of Europe: Austria-Hungary and the Habsburgs*, London: Harper, 1907

Connolly, S.J. (ed.). *The Oxford Companion to Irish History*, Oxford: Oxford University Press, 1998

Cosgrove, Brian (ed.). *Literature and the Supernatural*, Dublin: Columba Press, 1995

Craft, Christopher. *Another Kind of Love: Male Homosexual Desire in English*

Discourse 1850–1920, Berkeley and Los Angeles: University of California Press, 1994

Craig, Edith and St John, Christopher. *Ellen Terry's Memoirs*, London: Gollancz, 1933

Craig, Edward Gordon. *Henry Irving*, London: J.M. Dent & Sons., 1930

Crane, David. *Lord Byron's Jackal: A Life of Edward John Trelawny*, London: HarperCollins, 1998

Craven A. and Lentaigne, J. *A List of Registered Voters of County Dublin*, Dublin: Browne & Nolan, 1852

Croly, Revd G. *Popery and the Popish Question, Being an Exposition of the Political and Doctrinal Opinions of Messrs. O'Connell, Keogh, Dromgole, Gandolph, &. &.*, London: Whittaker, 1825

Croly, Revd G. *Protestantism the Polar Star of England*, London: Wakefield, [1828]

Croly, Revd G. *England the Fortress of Christianity*, London: Walbrook, [1837]

Croly, Revd G. *Salathiel the Immortal*, revised edn, London: Routledge, Warne & Routledge, 1859

Crosse, Andrew F. (Fellow of the Chemical Society) *Round the Carpathians*, Edinburgh & London: Blackwood, 1878

Cuellar, Francisco de, and Stapleton, Jim. *The Spanish Armada 1588. The Journey of Francisco De Cúellar*, Ireland: De Cúellar Project Committee, 2001

Cullen, L.M. *Life in Ireland*, London: Batsford, 1968

Curran, Bob. 'Was Dracula an Irishman?', *History Ireland*, Vol 8. No 2, Summer 2000

Dagg, T.S.C. *College Historical Society, A History (1770–1920)*, Cork: C. N. Dagg, *c*. 1969–70

Dalby, Richard. *Bram Stoker, A Bibliography of First Editions*, London: Dracula, 1983

Daly, Nicholas. 'Irish Roots: The Romance of History in Bram Stoker's *The Snake's Pass*', *Literature and History*, 4 (2), 3rd series, Autumn 1995

Daly, Frederick [pseudonym of L.F. Austin]. *Henry Irving in England and America 1883–84*, London: T. Fisher Unwin, 1884

Deane, Seamus (ed.). *The Field Day Anthology of Irish Writing*, Derry: Field Day, 1991

Deane, Seamus. *Strange Country: Modernity and Nationhood in Irish Writing since 1790*, Oxford: Clarendum Press, 1997

Delaney, Frank. *A Walk to the Western Isles after Boswell and Johnson*, London: HarperCollins, 1993

Denny, Norman (ed). *The Yellow Book: A Selection*, London: Bodley Head, 1949

Dingley, R.J. 'Count Dracula and the Martians', in *The Victorian Fantasists*, ed. Kath Filmer, London: St Martin's Press, 1991

Disher, M.L. *The Last Romantic. The Authorised Biography of Sir John Martin-Harvey*, London: Hutchinson & Co., 1948

Dodge, W.P. *The Real Sir Richard Burton*, London: T. Fisher Unwin, 1907

Donaldson, Thomas. *Walt Whitman the Man*, London: Gay & Bird, 1897

Dowden, Edward. *Shakespere: A Critical Study of His Mind and Art*, London: Kegan Paul & Co., 1875

Dowden, Edward. *The Life of Percy Bysshe Shelley*, London: Kegan Paul & Co., 1886

Dowden, Edward. *Puritan and Anglican: Studies in Literature*, London: Kegan Paul & Co., 1900

Dowden, Edward. *Essays Modern and Elizabethan*, London: J.M. Dent & Sons, New York: 1910

Dowden, Edward. *Fragments from Old Letters: E.D. to E.D.W., 1869–1892*, London: J.M. Dent & Sons, 1914

Dowden, Edward. *Poems*, London: J.M. Dent & Sons, 1914

Downey, Edmund. *A House of Tears*, London: Ward and Downey, 1886.

Doyle, Sir Arthur Conan. *Round the Red Lamp*, London: Methuen, 1894

Doyle, Sir Arthur Conan. *The Case for Spirit Photography*, London: Hutchinson & Co., 1922

Doyle, Sir Arthur Conan. *The Spiritualists' Reader. A Collection of Spirit Messages from Many Sources . . .*, Manchester: Two Worlds Publishing Co., 1924

Doyle, Sir Arthur Conan. *Pheneas Speaks. Direct Spirit Communications . . . reported by A.C. Doyle*, London: Psychic Press, 1927

Doyle, Sir Arthur Conan. *Complete Sherlock Holmes & Other Detective Stories*, Glasgow: HarperCollins, 1994

Drummond, James. 'Bram Stoker's Cruden Bay', *The Scots Magazine*, April 1976

Drummond, James. 'Dracula's Castle', *The Weekend Scotsman*, 26 June 1976

The Dublin Almanac, Dublin: Pettigrew & Oulton, 1837

Dublin University Football Club 1866–1972, Dublin: Dublin University Football Club, 1973

Du Maurier, George. *Trilby* [1894], London: J.H. Dent, 1992

Eagleton, Terry. *Heathcliff and the Great Hunger: Studies in Irish Culture*, London: Verso, 1995

Edgar, George. *Martin Harvey: Some Pages of his Life*, London: Grant Richards, 1912

Eglinton, John. *Irish Literary Portraits*, London: Macmillan & Co., 1935

Eighteen-Bisang, Robert and Melton, J. Gordon. *Dracula: A Century of Editions, Adaptations and Translations*, Santa Barbara, California: Transylvanian Society of Dracula, 1998

Ellmann, Richard. *Oscar Wilde*, London: Hamish Hamilton, 1987

Ellmann, Richard. *James Joyce*, London: Oxford University Press, 1959; pb. 1966

Erkmann, Emile and Chatrian, Pierre Alexandre. *The Bells or, The Polish Jew*, New York: De Witt, 1872

Farson, Daniel. *The Man Who Wrote Dracula: A Biography of Bram Stoker*, London: Michael Joseph, 1975

Farson, Negley. *The Way of a Transgressor*, London: Gollancz, 1935

Fermor, Patrick Leigh. *Between the Woods and the Water, On Foot from Constantinople from the Hook of Holland: The Middle Danube to the Iron Gates*, London: Murray, 1986

Fisher, Henry W. *Abroad with Mark Twain and Eugene Field*, New York: Nicholas L. Brown, 1922

FitzGerald, Percy, *Henry Irving. A Record of Twenty Years at the Lyceum*, London: Chapman & Hall, 1893

FitzGerald, Percy. *Percy FitzGerald Scrapbooks*, Garrick Club, London (unpublished)

FitzGerald, Percy. *An Apology for the Life of the Rt. Hon. W.E. Gladstone; or, The New Politics*, London: Ward & Downey, 1885

FitzGerald, Percy. *Memoirs of an Author*, London: R. Dentley & Sons, 1894

FitzGerald, Percy. *Chronicles of the Bow Street Police-Office, with an Account of the Magistrates, 'Runners', and Police; and a Selection of the Most Interesting Cases*, London: Chapman & Hall, 1888

Fleetwood, John. *History of Medicine in Ireland*, Dublin: Browne & Nolan, 1951

Florescu, Radu R. and McNally, Raymond T. *Dracula: A Biography of Vlad the Impaler 1431–1476*, London: Hale, 1974

Florescu, Radu R. and McNally, Raymond T. *Dracula, Prince of Many Faces: His Life and Times*, Boston: Little, Brown & Co., 1989

Florescu, Radu R. and McNally, Raymond T. *In Search of Dracula: The History of Dracula and Vampires*, London: Robson Books, 1995

Ford, T.W. *Henry Brougham and his World*, Chichester: Barry Rose, 1995

Forrest, Vivienne. 'Castle Dracula', *The Leopard Magazine*, Sept. 1991

Foster, R.F. 'Protestant Magic: W.B. Yeats and the Spell of Irish History', Chatterton Lecture on Poetry, *Proceedings of the British Academy*, 75, pp. 243–66, 1989

Foster, R.F. 'A Speculative Stake in the Future' (Review of Barbara Belford's biography of Bram Stoker), *The Independent* (London), 1 June 1996

Foster, R.F. *W.B. Yeats: A Life: 1. The Apprentice Mage 1865–1914*, Oxford and New York: Oxford University Press, 1997

Foster, R.F. *The Irish Story: Telling Tales and Making It Up in Ireland*, London: Allen Lane, The Penguin Press, 2001

Frayling, Christopher. *Vampires: Lord Byron to Count Dracula*, London: Faber & Faber, 1991

Frazier, Adrian. *George Moore, 1852–1933*, New Haven and London: Yale University Press, 2000

Freud, Sigmund. 'The Uncanny', in *The Complete Psychological Works of Sigmund Freud*, Vol. XVII, trans. James Strachey, London: Hogarth Press and Institute of Psycho-Analysis, 1962

Gal, Stephen. *Hungary and the Anglo-Saxon World*, Budapest: Officina Printing and Publishing Co., 1947

Gauld, Alan. *A History of Hypnotism*, Cambridge: Cambridge University Press, 1992

Gerard, Emily de Laszowska. 'Transylvanian Superstitions', *The Nineteenth Century*, 18, pp. 130–50, July–Dec. 1885

Gerard, Emily de Laszowska. *The Land beyond the Forest: Facts, Figures, and Fancies from Transylvania*, 2 vols, Edinburgh and London: William Blackwood & Sons, 1888

Gerard, Frances. *Picturesque Dublin, Old and New*, London: Hutchinson & Co., 1898

Gerber, Helmut E. *George Moore in Transition*, Detroit: Wayne University Press, 1968

Gibson, John and Green, Richard. *My Evening with Sherlock Holmes*, London: Ferret, 1981

Gittings, Robert and Manton, Jo. *The Second Mrs Hardy*, London and Seattle: Heinemann, 1979

Gladstone, Mary. *Mary Gladstone (Mrs Drew). Her Diaries and Letters*, ed. Lucy Masterman, London: Methuen & Co., 1930

Glover, David. *Vampires, Mummies, and Liberals: Bram Stoker and the Politics of Popular Fiction*, Durham, NC & London: Duke University Press, 1996

Goethe, J.W. von. *Faust as Faustus: A Dramatic Mystery, The Bride of Corinth; The First Walpurgis Night*, trans. John Martin Anster (of Trinity College Dublin), Barrister at law, London: Longman, 1835

Gogarty, Oliver St John. *As I Was Going Down Sackville Street*, London: Rich & Cowan, 1937

Gordon, John Campbell, Marquess of Aberdeen and Temair. *Tell Me Another*, London: E. Arnold, 1925

Gordon, John Campbell and Gordon, Ishbel Maria; Marquess and

Marchioness of Aberdeen and Temair. *More Cracks with 'We Twa'*, London: Methuen, 1929

Graves, Alfred Perceval. 'Memoir of Joseph Sheridan Le Fanu', in J.S. LeFanu, *The Purcell Papers*, Vol. I, London: Bentley & Son, 1880

Graves, Alfred Perceval and Stanford, Sir Charles V. *Irish Songs and Ballads*, London: Novello, 1893

Graves, Alfred Perceval. *Irish Literary and Musical Studies*, London: Elkin Matthews, 1913

Graves, Alfred Perceval. *To Return to All That*, Dublin and London: Talbot Press/Jonathan Cape, 1930

Graves, Alfred Perceval. *The Irish Fairy Book* [1909], London: T. Fisher Unwin, 1997

Gray, Peter. *Famine, Law and Politics: British Government and Irish Society, 1843–1850*, Dublin: Irish Academic Press, 1999

Gray, Bishop Robert. *The Theory of Dreams*, London: F.C. & J. Rivington, 1808

Greenslade, William. *Degeneration, Culture and the Novel, 1880–1940*, Cambridge: Cambridge University Press, 1994

Gregory, Lady Isabella Augusta. *Lady Gregory's Diaries, 1892–1902*, ed. James Pethica, Gerrards Cross, Bucks: Colin Smythe, 1996

Gwynn, Stephen. *Dublin Old and New*, London and Dublin: Browne & Nolan, 1938

Haining, Peter. *The Dracula Scrapbook*, London: New English Library, 1976

Haining, Peter (ed.). *The Vampire Omnibus*, London: Orion, 1995

Haining, Peter and Tremayne, Peter. *The Undead: The Legend of Bram Stoker and Dracula*, London: Constable, 1997

Hall, J.B. *Random Records of a Reporter*, London: Simpkin, Marshall; Dublin: Fodhla Printing Co., 1928

Hamill, John and Gilbert, Robert (eds.). *Freemasonry*, London: Mackenzie, 1992

Handbook on Irish Genealogy, Dublin: Heraldic Artists [Royal Irish Academy], 1973

Hardy, Emma and Hardy, Florence. *Letters of Emma and Florence Hardy*, ed. Michael Millgate, Oxford: Clarendon, 1996

Hardy, Thomas. *The Letters of Thomas Hardy*, ed. Carl J. Weber, Waterville, Maine: Colby College Press, 1954

Harris, Frank. *My Life and Loves* an excerpt from Bram Stoker *et al.*, *Erotic Tales of the Victorian Age*, New York: Prometheus Books, 1995

Hatton, Joseph. *Henry Irving's Impressions of America*, 2 vols. London: S. Low, Marston, Searle & Rivington, 1884

Hatton, Joseph. *The Lyceum 'Faust,'* London: Virtue & Co., 1886

Hawthorne, Julian. *Shapes That Pass: Memories of Old Days*, London: John Murray, [1928]

Hay, Victor. *Ferelith*, London: Hutchinson & Co., 1903

Hayes, Richard. *The Last Invasion of Ireland*, Dublin: Gill, 1937

Higgins, Michael D. 'The Gombeenman in Fact and Fiction', *Etudes irlandaises*, 10, nouvelle série, Université de Lille, Dec. 1985

Hill, Jacqueline. *From Patriots to Unionists*, Oxford: Oxford University Press, 1997

Hodges, Patrick Hanks and Flavia Hodges. *A Dictionary of Surnames*, Oxford: Oxford University Press, 1988

Hoffman, Andrew, *Inventing Mark Twain. The Lives of Samuel Clemens*, London: Weidenfeld & Nicolson, 1997

Holland, Merlin. *The Wilde Album*, London: Fourth Estate, 1997

Holland, Vyvyan. *Son of Oscar Wilde*, London: Penguin, 1954/1957

Holroyd, Michael. *Bernard Shaw*, 4 vols, London: Chatto & Windus, 1988–92

Hone, Joseph. *The Life of George Moore*, New York: Macmillan, 1936

Hough, Richard. *The Ace of Clubs: A History of the Garrick*, London: André Deutsch, 1986

Howe, Ellic. *The Magicians of the Golden Dawn: A Documentary History of a Magical Order, 1887–1923*, London: Routledge & Kegan Paul, 1972

Huch, Ronald K. *Henry, Lord Brougham, The Later Years, 1830–67*, Dyfed, Wales: E. Mellen Press, 1993

Hughes, William. *Bram Stoker. A Bibliography*, Queensland: University of Queensland Press, 1997

Hughes, William, 'Introducing Patrick to his New Self: Bram Stoker and the 1907 Dublin Exhibition', *Irish Studies Review*, 19, Summer 1997

Hughes, William and Smith, Andrew (eds). *Bram Stoker: History, Psychoanalysis and the Gothic*, London: Macmillan, 1998

Igoe, Vivien. *A Literary Guide to Dublin*, London: Methuen, 1994

Index to the Act or Grant Books, and to the Original Wills, of the Dioceses of Dublin to the Year 1800; 1800 to 1853, Dublin: HMSO Alexander Thom & Co, 1895

Inglis, Brian. *The Freedom of the Press in Ireland 1784–1841*, London: Faber & Faber, 1954

Irving, Laurence. *Henry Irving: The Actor and His World*, London: Faber 1951; rpr. pb. London: Columbus Books, 1989

Irving, Laurence. *The Successors*, London: Rupert Hart-Davis, 1967

Jerome, Jerome K. *My Life and Times*, London: Murray, 1926

Jerome, Jerome K. *Stage-land*, London: Chatto & Windus, 1889

John, St John. *William Heinemann: A Century of Publishing*, London: Heinemann, 1990

Johnson, Major E.C. *On the Track of the Crescent: Erratic Notes from Piraeus to Pesth*, M.A.I. F.R. Hist.S., etc., Illustrated from Sketches by the Author, London: Hurst & Blackett, 1855

Jones, Ernest. *On the Nightmare*, London: Hogarth Press, 1931

Jones, Thomas Mason. *Old Trinity*, London: Dentley, 1867

Joyce, James. *Dubliners* [1914], London: Penguin 1956

Joyce, James. *A Portrait of the Artist as a Young Man* [1916], London: Penguin, 1960

Joyce, James. *Ulysses* [1922], London: John Lane/the Bodley Head, 1937

Joyce, Patrick Weston. *A Social History of Ancient Ireland*, London: Longmans & Co., 1903

Judd, Alan. *Ford Madox Ford*, London: HarperCollins, 1990

Kane, Robert. *The Industrial Resources of Ireland*, Dublin: Hodges and Smith, 1845

Kayman, Martin A. *From Bow Street to Baker Street: Mystery, Detection and Narrative*, London: Macmillan, 1992

Keating, P.J. *The Haunted Study: A Social History of the English Novel 1875–1914*, London: Secker & Warburg, 1989

Kenyon, Charles Frederick. *Hall Caine: The Man and the Novelist*, 1901

Kiberd, Declan. *Inventing Ireland*, London: Vintage, 1995–6

Kiberd, Declan. *Irish Classics*, London: Granta, 2000

King, Stephen. *Danse Macabre*, London: MacDonald, 1981

Kipling, Rudyard. *The Man Who Would be King and Other Stories*, Ware, Herts: Wordsworth Editions, 1994

Klein, Viola. *The Feminine Character*, London: Routledge & Kegan Paul, 1971

Lambert, Eric. *Mad with Much Heart: A Life of the Parents of Oscar Wilde*, London: Muller, 1967

Le Fanu, W.R. *Seventy Years of Irish Life*, London: Edward Arnold, 1893

Le Fanu, J. Sheridan. *The Watcher and other Weird Stories*, London: Downey & Co., 1894

Leather, R.K. and Le Gallienne, R. *The Student and the Body-Snatcher*, London: E. Matthews, 1890

Leatherdale, Clive. *Dracula, the Novel and the Legend*, Wellingborough: Aquarium, 1985; rev. edn. Brighton: Desert Island Books, 1993

Leatherdale, Clive. *The Origins of Dracula*, Westcliff-on-Sea, Essex: Desert Island Books, 1995

Leatherdale, Clive. *Bram Stoker's Dracula Unearthed*, Westcliff-on-Sea, Essex: Desert Island Dracula Library, 1998

Lecky, William Hartpole. *History of the Rise and Influence of the Spirit of Rationalism in Europe*, London: 1865

Ledger, Sally. *The New Woman: Fiction and Feminism at the Fin de Siècle*, Manchester: Manchester University Press, 1997

Legge, Edward. *King Edward in his True Colours, With Appreciations of Edward VII by Comte d'Haussonville and Arminius Vambery*, London: Eveleigh Nash, 1912

Lever, Charles. *Charles O'Malley, the Irish Dragoon*, Dublin: William Curry, 1842

Levi, Peter. *Tennyson*, London: Macmillan, 1993

Lewis, Matthew. *Tales of Wonder*, London and Dublin: P. Wogan, 1801

Lewis, Samuel. *A Topographical Dictionary of Ireland*, New York and London: Kennikat, Press, 1970. Facsimile of 1837 edition

Library of the Future. CD-ROM, 3rd edition, Irving, California: World Library, 1995

Lovecraft, H. P. *Supernatural in Literature*, New York: Dover, 1973

Lucas, E.V. 'The Creator of *Trilby*: A Note on George du Maurier: Days from a Diary', *The Times*, pp. 15–16, 6 March 1934

Luce, J.V. *Trinity College Dublin, The First 400 Years*, Dublin: TCD Press, 1992

Ludlam, Harry. *A Biography of Dracula: The Life Story of Bram Stoker*, London: Fireside Press, 1962

Ludlam, Harry. *My Quest for Bram Stoker*, New York: Dracula Press, 2000

Lyons, F.S.L. *John Dillon*, London: Routledge & Kegan Paul, 1968

Lyons, John B. *Brief Lives of Irish Doctors*, Dublin: Blackwater, 1978

Lyons, John B. 'John Freeman Knott, 1853–1921', *Long Room, Bulletin of the friends of the Library, TCD*, 34, pp. 31–46, 1989

Lytton, The Rt. Hon. Lord (Edward Bulwer-Lytton). *Eugene Aram*, London, Ward Lock & Co., 1883

MacLysaght, Edward. *Irish Families: Names, Arms & Origins*, Dublin: Helicon, 1957

MacLysaght, Edward. *More Irish Families*, Galway, O'Gorman, 1960

MacLysaght, Edward. *A Guide to Irish Surnames*, Dublin: Helicon, 1964

MacLysaght, Edward. *Supplement to Irish Families*, Dublin: Helicon, 1964

Malchow, H.L. *Gothic Images of Race in Nineteenth-Century Britain*, Stanford: Stanford University Press, 1996

Malcolm, Elizabeth. *Swift's Hospital, A History of St Patrick's Hospital, Dublin, 1946–1989*, Dublin: Gill & Macmillan, 1989

Mansoor, M. 'Oriental Studies in Ireland. From Times of St Patrick to the Rise of Islam', *Hermathena*, 1 (12), pp. 40–60, Nov. 1943, Dublin

Marigny, Jean. *Vampires: The World of the Undead*, London: Gallimard/ Thames & Hudson, 1993

Marshall, Richard. *Witchcraft, The History and Mythology*, Leicester: Magna, 1995

Marston, E. M. *Frank's Ranche or, My Holiday in the Rockies*, London: Sampson Low & Co., 1886

Martin-Harvey, Sir John. *The Autobiography of Sir John Martin-Harvey*, London: Sampson Low, Marston & Co. [1933]

Marx, Karl. *Capital*, Vol. I [1867], Harmondsworth: Penguin, 1976

Masters, Anthony. *The Natural History of the Vampire*, London: Hart-Davis, 1972

Maume, Patrick. 'In the Fenians' Wake: Ireland's Nineteenth-Century Crises and their Representation in the Sentimental Rhetoric of William O'Brien MP and Canon Sheehan', *Bullán, An Irish Studies Journal*, 4, Autumn 1998

Maunsell, William Pryce. *The Idler in College or, The Student's Guide*, Dublin: 1850

Maxwell, Constantia. *Dublin under the Georges 1714–1830*, London: Faber & Faber, 1937

Maxwell, Constantia. *History of Trinity College Dublin 1591–1892*, Dublin: University Press, 1946

[Mazuchelli, Elizabeth Sarah]. *'Magyarland'; being the Narrative of our Travels through the Highlands and Lowlands of Hungary*, By a Fellow of the Carpathian Society, London: Samson Low, Marston, Searle & Rivington, 1881

McCarthy, Justin. *Ireland since the Union*, London: Chatto & Windus, 1887

McCarthy Justin. *Reminiscences*, London: Chatto & Windus, 1899

McCarthy, Justin (ed.). *Irish Literature*, 10 vols, Philadelphia: John D. Morris & Co., 1904

McCarthy, Justin. *The Story of an Irishman*, London: Chatto & Windus, 1904

McCarthy, Justin. *In Spacious Times*, New York: John Lane, 1916

Mc Cormack. W.J. *Sheridan Le Fanu and Victorian Ireland*, Oxford: Clarendon Press, 1980

McDowell, R.B. *Public Opinion and Government Policy in Ireland, 1801–1846*, London: Faber & Faber, 1952

McDowell, R.B. (ed.). *Social Life in Ireland 1800–45*, Dublin: CRC/Three Candles, 1957

McDowell, R.B. *The Irish Administration*, London: Routledge & Kegan Paul, 1964

McDowell, R.B. 'Personalities in the Hist', Dissertation on past members of the Hist, 5 March in 1970. In Declan Budd and Ross Hinds (eds). *The Hist and Edmund Burke's Club*, Dublin: Lilliput Press, 1997

McDowell, R.B. and Webb, D.A. *Trinity College Dublin 1592–1952*, Cambridge: Cambridge University Press, 1982

McNally, Raymond T. *Dracula Was a Woman: In Search of the Blood Countess of Transylvania*, London: Hale, 1984

Medical Register, The, London: 1889–1912

Meinhold, William. *Sidonia the Sorceress*, trans. Lady Jane Wilde, London: Parlour Library, 1847; London: Ernest Benn (Julian Edition), 1926

Melton, J. Gordon. *The Vampire Book: The Encyclopedia of the Undead*, Detroit: Visible Ink, 1994

Melville, Joy. *Mother of Oscar: The Life of Jane Francesca Wilde*, London: Allison & Busby, 1999

Meredith, Owen. *Poems of Owen Meredith (The Earl of Lytton)*, [Edward Bulwer-Lytton], London: Walther Scott, 1890

Miller, Elizabeth. *Dracula, Sense and Nonsense*, Westcliff-on-Sea, Essex: Desert Island Books, 2000

Millet, F.D. *The Danube, from the Black Forest to the Black Sea*, London: Osgood & McIlvaine, 1892

Moore, Frank Frankfort. *A Journalist's Note-Book*, London: Hutchinson, 1894

Moore, Frank Frankfort. *The Truth about Ulster*, London: Eveleigh Nash, 1914

Moore, George. *Confessions of a Young Man*, London: Swan-Sonnenschein, Lowrey & Co., 1888

Moore, George. *Conversations in Ebury Street*, London: Heinemann, 1936

Moretti, Franco. *Signs Taken for Wonders: Essays in the Sociology of Literary Form*, London: Verso, 1983

Müller, Max. *The Life and Letters of the Rt Hon Max Müller*, edited by his wife, London: Longmans, Green & Co., 1902

Mulvey-Roberts, Marie (ed.). *The Handbook of Gothic Literature*, Basingstoke and London: Macmillan, 1998

Murphy, William M. *Prodigal Father: The Life of John Butler Yeats (1839–1922)*, Ithaca, NY and London: Cornell University Press, 1978

Murray, Ian. 'Some Alternatives to the Bar', draft article by the former Archivist, the Honourable Society of the Inner Temple, London, attached to a letter from Dr C.M. Rider, Archivist, the Honourable Society of the Inner Temple, London, to the author, 19 Feb. 1997

Murray, Paul. *A Fantastic Journey: The Life and Literature of Lafcadio Hearn*, Folkestone, UK: The Japan Library, 1993; Michigan: University of Michigan Press, 1997

Murray, Paul. 'W.B. Yeats and Bram Stoker', *The Yeats Journal of Korea*, 12, 1999

Myers, S.W. and McKnight, D.F. (eds). *Sir Richard Musgrave's Memoirs of the Irish Rebellion of 1798*, Fort Wayne, Indiana: Round Tower, 1995

Nordau, Max. *Degeneration*, New York: D. Appleton, 1895

Norris, Samuel. *Two Men of Manxland*, Douglas: Norris Modern Press, 1947

O Cuiv, Brian (ed.). *Seven Centuries of Irish Learning, 1000–1700*, Thomas Davis Lectures, Dublin: Stationery Office, 1961

O hOgain, Daithi. *Myth, Legend & Romance: An Encyclopaedia of the Irish Folk Tradition*, London: Ryan, 1990

O'Donnell, E.E., SJ. *Father Browne's Ireland*, Dublin: Wolfhound Press, 1989

O'Donnell, E.E., SJ. *A Life in Pictures*, Dublin: Wolfhound Press, 1994

O'Grady, Hugh Art. *Standish O'Grady, The Man and the Writer*, with a foreword by Alfred Perceval Graves, Dublin: Talbot Press, 1929

O'Grady, Standish. *Selected Essays and Passages*, Dublin: Talbot Press, [1918]

Oram, Hugh. *The Newspaper Book: A History of Newspapers in Ireland*, Dublin: MO Books, 1983

O'Rorke, Terence. *The History of Sligo: Town and County*, Dublin: J. Duffy and Co., [1890]

Osborne, Charles C. (ed.). *Letters of Charles Dickens to the Baroness Burdett-Coutts*, London: Murray, 1931

Pakenham, Thomas. *The Year of Liberty*, London: Hodder & Stoughton, 1969

Parker, Christopher (ed.). *Gender Roles and Sexuality in Victorian Literature*, Aldershot: Scolar Press, 1995

Parker, John (ed). *The Green Room Book*, London: 1908

Pearson, Hesketh. *Bernard Shaw: A Biography*, London: MacDonald and Jane's, 1975

Pemberton, T. Edgar. *Ellen Terry and her Sisters*, London: C. Arthur Pemberton, 1902

Perrault, Charles. *Perrault's Popular Tales* [1697], edited from the original editions, with introduction &c., by Andrew Lang, trans. Oxford: Clarendon Press, 1888

Perrault, Charles. *The Fairy Tales of Charles Perrault* [1697], trans. Guy Miège, rev. J.E. Mansion, London: George Harrap, 1922

Pethica, James (ed.). *Lady Gregory's Diaries 1892–1902*, Gerrards Cross, Bucks: 1996

Petrie, W.M. Flinders. *Egyptian Tales*, London: Methuen & Co., 1895

Pick, Daniel. '"Terrors of the Night": Dracula and "Degeneration" in the Late Nineteenth Century', *Critical Quarterly*, 30, Winter 1988

Polidori, John William. *The Vampire and Ernestus Berchtold; or, The Modern*

Oedipus: Collected Fiction of John William Polidori, ed. D.L. Macdonald and Kathleen Scherf, Toronto: University of Toronto Press, 1994

The Post Office Directory and Calendar for 1836 . . . containing an alphabetical list of the nobility, gentry, merchants and others in Dublin and vicinity, Kingstown, &c., with a variety of useful information, Dublin: General Post Office, 1835

Praeger, Robert Lloyd. *The Way That I Went: An Irishman in Ireland*, Dublin: Figgis, 1937

Reaney, Percy H. *A Dictionary of British Surnames*, London: Routledge & Kegan Paul, 1976

Reid, Hilda. *One Hundred Years in a Chelsea Parish*, Chelsea: J.B. Shears & Sons [1939]

Richards, Jeffrey. *Sir Henry Irving: Theatre, Culture and Society*, Keele, Staffordshire: Ryburn, 1994

Richards, Thomas. *The Imperial Archive: Knowledge and the Fantasy of Empire*, London: Verso, 1993

Richardson, John. *The Annals of London*, London, Cassell, 2000

Richardson, Maurice. 'The Psychoanalysis of Ghost Stories', *The Twentieth Century*, 166 (994), Dec. 1959

Robert, Stewart. *Henry Brougham 1778–1868: His Public Career*, London: Bodley Head, 1986

Robertson, W. Graham. *Time Was: The Reminiscences of W. Graham Robertson*, London: Hamish Hamilton, 1931

Robinson, F.K. *A Glossary of Words Used in the Neighbourhood of Whitby*, English Dialect Society, London: Trübner & Co., 1855

Rossmore, Lord. *Things I Could Tell*, London: Eveleigh Nash, 1912

Roth, Phyllis A. *Bram Stoker*, Boston: Twayne, 1982

Row, Arthur. *The Royal Lyceum Theatre*, Dawlish: Channing Press, 1938

Rudwin, Maximilian. *The Devil in Legend and Literature* [1931], La Salle, Illinois: Open Court Publishing, 1959

Ryan, Alan (ed.). *The Penguin Book of Vampire Stories*, London: Bloomsbury, 1987

Ryan, Philip B. *The Lost Theatres of Dublin (Ireland)*, Westbury: Badger, 1998

Rymer, James Malcolm, or Prest, Thomas Pecket. *Varney the Vampire or, The Feast of Blood*, London: E. Lloyd, 1847; New York: Dover, 1973

Saintsbury, H.A. and Palmer, Cecil. *We Saw Him Act: A Symposium on the Art of Sir Henry Irving*, London: Hurst & Blackett, 1939

Schmitt, Cannon. 'Mother Dracula: Orientalism, Degeneration, and Anglo-Irish National Subjectivity at the Fin de Siècle', in *Bucknell Review: Irishness and (Post)Modernism*, ed. John S. Rickard, Lewisberg: Bucknell University Press, 1994

Schneider, Kirk J. *Horror and the Holy*, Chicago: Open Court, 1993

Scott, Clement. *From 'The Bells' to 'King Arthur': A Critical Record of the First Night Productions at the Lyceum Theatre*, London: John MacQueen, 1896

Scott, Clement. *The Drama of Yesterday and Today*, London: Macmillan & Co., 1899

Scott, R.H. *Fishery Barometer Manuel*, London: HMSO, 1887

Senf, Carol. *Daughters of Lilith: An Analysis of the Vampire Motif in Nineteenth-Century English Literature*, Ann Arbor: State University of New York at Buffalo, 1979

Senf, Carol A. (ed.). *The Critical Response to Bram Stoker*, Westport, Conn. and London: Greenwood Press, 1993

Senf, Carol A. *Dracula between Tradition and Modernism*, New York: Prentice Hall International, 1998

Seymour, St John D. *Irish Witchcraft and Demonology*, New York: Dorset, 1992

Seymour-Smith, Martin. *Robert Graves*, London: Hutchinson, 1982

Shaw, George Bernard. *Bernard Shaw: Collected Letters, Vol. I–Vol. IV*, ed. Dan H. Laurence, London, Max Reinhart, 1965–88

Shaw, George Bernard. *Shaw: An Autobiography 1898–1950. The Playwright Years*, ed. Stanley Weintraub, London: Reinhardt, 1971

Shaw, George Bernard. *Man and Superman* [1905], Library of the Future CD-ROM, 3rd edition, Irving, California: World Library, 1995

Sheehy, Jeanne. *Walter Osborne*, Ballycotton, Co. Cork: Gifford & Craven, 1974

Sheehy, Jeanne. *Walter Osborne*, Dublin: National Gallery of Ireland, 1983

Shelley, Mary. *Frankenstein* [1818], Oxford: Oxford University Press, 1980

Shepard, Leslie. *Bram Stoker: Irish Theatre Manager and Author*, Dublin: Impact Publications, 1994

Shepard, Leslie and Power, Albert. *Dracula – Celebrating 100 Years*, Dublin: Mentor Press, 1997

Showalter, Elaine. *Sexual Anarchy: Gender and Culture at the Fin de Siècle*, London: Bloomsbury, 1991

Shuster, Seymour. 'Dracula and Surgically Induced Trauma in Children', *British Journal of Medical Psychology*, 46, London: British Psychological Society, pp. 259–70, 1973

Shuttle, Penelope and Redgrove, Peter. *The Wise Wound: Menstruation and Everywoman* [1978], London: Paladin, 1986

Sikes, Wirt. *British Goblins: Welsh Folk-lore, Fairy Mythology, Legends and Traditions*, London: Sampson Low, Marston, Searle & Rivington, 1880

Silver, Alain and Ursini, James. *The Vampire Film: From Nosferatu to Bram Stoker's Dracula*, New York: Limelight Editions, 1994

Smith, Andrew. 'Bram Stoker's *The Mystery of the Sea*: Ireland and the Spanish–Cuban–American War', *Irish Studies Review*, 6 (2) pp., 1998

Smyly, J.G. *Index of Contributors to Hermathena 1873–1943*, Dublin: Hodges Figgis, 1944

Southey, Robert. *Thalaba the Destroyer*, London: Longman, Hurst, Rees and Orne, 1809

Stamp, Cordelia. *Dracula Discovered*, 2nd edition, Whitby: Abbey Press, 1988

Stedman, Jane W. *W.S. Gilbert: A Classic Victorian & His Theatre*, Oxford: Oxford University Press, 1996

Steen, Marguerite. *A Pride of Terrys: Family Saga*, London: Longmans, 1962

Stewart, Bruce (ed.). *That Other World: The Supernatural and the Fantastic in Irish Literature and its Contexts*, Vol. II, Gerrards Cross, Bucks: Colin Smythe, 1988

Stewart, Bruce. 'Bram Stoker's Dracula: Possessed by the Spirit of the Nation?' *Irish University Reviews*, 29 (2), Autumn/Winter 1999

Stoddart, Jane. 'Mr Bram Stoker. A Chat with the Author of "Dracula", by "Lorna"', *The British Weekly*, p.185, 1 July 1898

Stoicescu, Nicolae. *Vlad Tepes Prince of Wallachia*, Bibliotheca Historica Romaniae Monographs XXI, Editura Adademiei Republicii Socialiste Romania, Bucharest, 1978

Stoker, Bram *et al. Erotic Tales of the Victorian Age*, New York: Prometheus Books, 1995

Stoker, Charlotte M.B. *On the Necessity of a State Provision for the Education of the Deaf and Dumb of Ireland*, Dublin: Alexander Thom, 1863

Stoker, Charlotte M.B. *On Female Emigration from Workhouses*, Dublin: Alexander Thom, 1864

Stoker, George. *With 'the Unspeakables'; or, Two Years' Campaigning in European and Asiatic Turkey*, London: Chapman & Hall, 1878

Stoker, George. *Songs of the Red Cross and Other Verses*, London: George Pullman & Sons, 1907

Stoker, Matilda. 'Sheridan and Miss Linley', *London Illustrated Magazine*, April 1887

Stoker, William, MD. *A Treatise on Fever with Observations on the Practice Adopted for its Cure in the Fever Hospital and House of Recovery, in Dublin Illustrated by Cases, One of the Physicians of that Institution, and Licentiate of the King and Queen's College of Physicians, in Ireland*, London: Longman, Hurst, Orme & Brown, 1815

Stoker, William, MD. *Pathological Observations, Part II, On Continued Fever,*

Ague, Tic Doloreux, Measles, Small-pox, and Dropsy, etc., Dublin, London [Longman] and Edinburgh, 1829

Stoker, William, Esq., MD. *A Succinct Treatise on Medical Reform for Ireland, etc.*, Dublin: Milliken & Son, 1836

Stokes, William, *William Stokes, His Life and Work (1804–1878)*, London: Fisher Unwin, 1898

Stott, Rebecca, *The Fabrication of the Late Victorian Femme Fatale, The Kiss of Death*, London: Macmillan, 1992

Strickland, Walter G. *Dictionary of Irish Artists*, Dublin and London: Maunsel, 1913

Stubbs, John William. *The History of the University of Dublin*, Dublin: Dublin University Press, 1889

Sturgis, James L. *John Bright and the Empire*, London: Athlone Press, 1969

Summers, Montague. *The History of Witchcraft*, London: Senate 1994

Summers, Montague. *The Vampire* [1928], London: Senate, 1995

Tennyson, Alfred, Lord. *Becket, A Tragedy in a Prologue and Four Acts, As Arranged for the Stage by Henry Irving and Presented at the Lyceum Theatre on 6th February 1893*, London: Macmillan, 1893

Tennyson Alfred, Lord. *Demeter and Other Poems*, London: Macmillan, 1893

Tennyson Alfred, Lord. *The Works of Alfred Lord Tennyson Poet Laureate*, London: Macmillan, 1894

Terry Ellen. *The Story of My Life*, London: Hutchinson, 1908

Terry, Ellen. *Ellen Terry's Memoirs*, with preface, notes and additional biographical chapters by Edith Craig and Christopher St John, London: Victor Gollancz, 1933

Terry, Ellen and Shaw, George Bernard. *Ellen Terry and Bernard Shaw: A Correspondence*, ed. Christopher St John, New York: Fountain Press and London: Constable & Co., 1931

Thom's Irish Almanac and Official Directory, Dublin, various years

Thompson, Slason. *The Life of Eugene Field*, New York and London: D. Appleton & Co., 1927

Thornley, David. *Isaac Butt and Home Rule*, London: Macgibbon & Kee, 1964

Todhunter, John. *The Banshee & Other Poems*, London: Kegan, Paul, Trench, 1888

Todhunter, John. *The poison-flower, a Phantasy, in 3 Scenes*, London: Nassau Steam Press, 1891.

Todhunter, John. *Essays*, with a foreword by Standish O'Grady. London: Elkin Matthews, 1920

Todhunter, John. *Goethe's Faust*, Oxford: Basil Blackwell, 1924

Tracy, Robert. *The Unappeasable Host: Studies in Irish Identities*, Dublin: University College Dublin Press, 1998

Traubel, Horace and Bradley, Sculley (eds). *With Walt Whitman in Camden*, Philadelphia: University of Pennsylvania Press, 1953

Trelawny, Edward John. *Recollections of the Last Days of Shelley and Byron*, Introduction by Edward Dowden, London: Henry Frowde, 1906

Treptow, Kurt W. *Dracula: Essays on the Life and Times of Vlad Tepes*, New York: Columbia University Press, 1991

Tropp, Martin. *Images of Fear: How Horror Stories Helped Shape Modern Culture (1818–1918)*, Jefferson, N.C. and London: McFarland & Co., 1990

Tyrrell, R.Y. and Sullivan, Sir E. (eds). *Echoes from Kottabos*, London: Grant Richards, 1906

Vambery, Arminius. *Arminius Vambery His Life and Adventures, Written by Himself*, London: T. Fisher Unwin, 1884

Vambery, Arminius. *Hungary in Ancient, Mediaeval, and Modern Times*, With the collaboration of Louis Heilprin, 2nd edition, London: T. Fisher Unwin, 1887

Vambery, Arminius. *The Story of My Struggles. The Memoirs of Arminius Vambery*, London: T. Unwin Fisher, 1904

Van Esbeck, Edmund. *One Hundred Years of Irish Rugby*, Dublin: Gill and Macmillan, 1974

Verne, Jules. *Carpathian Castle [Le Château des Carpathes]* [1893], London: Arco, 1963

Vicars, Sir Arthur (ed.). *Index to the Prerogative Wills of Ireland 1536–1810*, Dublin: Ponsonby, 1897

Vrettos, Athena. *Somatic Fictions: Imagining Illness in Victorian Culture*, Stanford: Stanford University Press, 1995

Ward, Geneviève and Whiteing, Richard. *Both Sides of the Curtain*, London and New York: Cassell & Co., 1918

Ward, Margaret. 'Rabies May Be the Root of Vampire Fears', *The Irish Times*, 26 Oct. 1998

Warwick-Haller, Sally. *William O'Brien and the Irish Land War*, Dublin: Irish Academic Press, 1990

Waters, Colin. *Whitby and the Dracula Connection*, Whitby: Whitby Press, n.d.

Watson's Almanack, Dublin, 1831

Weintraub, Stanley. *Whistler: A Biography*, London: Collins, 1974; New York: The Capo Press, 2001

Weldon, Fay. Introduction to *Bram Stoker's Dracula Omnibus*, London: Orion, 1992

Wells, H.G. *The War in the Air*, London: George Bell & Sons, 1908

Welch, Robert (ed.). *The Oxford Companion to Irish Literature*, Oxford: Oxford University Press, 1996

West, Trevor. *The Bold Collegians: The Development of Sport in Trinity College, Dublin*, Dublin: Lilliput, 1991

White, H.O. *Edward Dowden, 1843–1913*, Dublin: Dublin University Press, 1943

White, Newport John Davis, DD. *Some Recollections of Trinity College, Dublin*, Dublin: Hodges Figgis, 1935

White, Terence De Vere. *The Parents of Oscar Wilde*, London: Hodder & Stoughton, 1967

White, Walter. *A Month in Yorkshire*, London: Chapman and Hall, 1858

Whitman, Walt. *Walt Whitman: The Correspondence*, Vol. III, *1876–1885*, ed. E. H. Miller, New York: New York University Press, 1964

Whyte, Frederic. *William Heinemann*, London: Jonathan Cape, 1928

Wilde, Lady Jane Francesca ('Speranza'). *Poems*, Dublin: James Duffy, 1864

Wilde, Lady Jane F.S. ('Speranza'). *Ancient Legends, Mystic Charms, and Superstitions of Ireland, with Sketches of the Irish Past*, London: Ward & Downey, 1887

Wilde, Lady Jane Francesca ('Speranza'). *Poems*, Dublin: James Duffy, 1864

Wilde, Lady Jane F.S. ('Speranza'). *Ancient Legends, Mystic Charms, and Superstitions of Ireland, with Sketches of the Irish Past*, London: Ward & Downey, 1887

Wilde, Lady Jane F.S. ('Speranza') *Ancient Cures, Charms, and Usages of Ireland: Contributions to Irish Lore*, London: Ward & Downey, 1890

Wilde, Oscar. *The Letters of Oscar Wilde*, ed. Rupert Hart-Davis, London: John Murray, 1962

Wilde, Oscar. *More Letters of Oscar Wilde*, ed. Rupert Hart-Davis, London: John Murray, 1985

Wilde, Oscar. *The Complete Works of Oscar Wilde*, Glasgow: HarperCollins, 1994

Wilde, William R. *Austria, its Literature, Scientific & Medical Institutions*, Dublin: 1843

Wilde, William R. *Irish Popular Superstitions*, Dublin: James McGlashan, 1852

Wilkinson, William. *An Account of the Principalities of Wallachia and Moldavia with Various Political Observations relating to them*, Late British Consul resident at Bukorest, London: Longman, Hurst, Rees, Orme & Brown, 1820

Wills, Freeman. *W.G. Wills, Dramatist and Painter*, London: Longman, 1898

Wills, W.G. *Faust, in a Prologue and Five Acts, Adapted and Arranged for the Lyceum Theatre from the First Part of Goethe's Tragedy*, 1886

Winter, William. *The Shadows of the Stage*, London: Macmillan, 1892

Wolf, Leonard. *Horror, A Connoisseur's Guide to Literature and Film*, New York: Facts on File, 1989

Yeats, W.B. *Autobiographies*, London: Macmillan & Co., 1955

Yeats, W.B. 'Swedenborg, Mediums, and the Desolate Places', in *Explorations*, London: Macmillan, 1962

Yeats, W.B. *Writings on Irish Folklore, Legend and Myth*, London: Penguin, 1993

Zanger, Michael. *Mt. Shasta, History, Legend & Lore*, Berkeley, California: Celestial Arts, 1992

Index